THE DECLINE
AND FALL
OF THE ATHENS
OF WEST AFRICA

THE DECLINE AND FALL OF THE ATHENS OF WEST AFRICA

AKIBO ROBINSON

Library of Congress Control Number:		2023908778
ISBN:	Hardcover	978-1-6698-7696-0
	Softcover	978-1-6698-7695-3
	eBook	978-1-6698-7694-6

Print information available on the last page.

Rev. date: 07/17/2023

To order additional copies of this book, contact:
Xlibris
844-714-8691
www.Xlibris.com
Orders@Xlibris.com
853186

CONTENTS

FOREWARD

Originally, the book I wanted to write bore nothing in common with the "Decline and Fall of the Athens of West Africa"; the book I ended up writing. My aim was to write a sequel to my first book, 'One Stone Revolution", published by Lulu Publishers in 2015. Indeed, I started work on the sequel to the "One Stone Revolution", when one evening the thought occurred to me, why not write a book on the "Rise and Fall of the Athens of West Africa"? In fact, the decline of the value systems in Sierra Leone was being extensively discussed or voiced in national fora: fall in educational standards, widespread indiscipline in the society, rampant corruption, etc. It then occurred to me that, that was a topic worth researching, especially why Sierra Leone was known then, as the "Athens of West Africa".

The book took long in writing. Work on the manuscript started during the Ebola Virus Disease that invaded the Manor River Basin Countries of Guinea, Sierra Leone and Liberia; I had to leave the shores of Sierra Leone together with my spouse for a while and stayed in the United States of America. It was during this time that I started my research on the topic, while at the same time I started writing. Reading and writing went on reasonably smoothly because of the conducive environment; accessibility to literature materials was smooth and easy; accessing the internet for research materials, whether downloading books as articles was fast. Otherwise, books could easily be purchased from Amazon, Barnes and Noble etc. But then our stay in the United States was not permanent, and we had to return to Sierra Leone. Once we returned, the ball game changed completely as work on the manuscript slowed down. Perhaps it was all for the better as that provided me with the opportunity to include more current information in the manuscript as the time period became longer. It allowed the author to have relative perspective of the governance systems of not only the APC, but also the SLPP, including the four years that the Bio-led SLPP had been in governance.

The title of the manuscript metamorphosed from, the "Rise and Fall of the Athens of West Africa" to the "Decline and Fall of the Athens of West Africa". I cannot consciously state when this change took place, but as I carried on my research and narrating the story of the "Athens of West Africa" I came to realise that our country had not gone through any golden age, not when Sierra Leone was under the Colonial yoke of Britain, nor when we gained our independence. The Imperial Masters exploited the country's natural wealth for their own benefit, stripping the country's assets, while subsequent Prime Ministers and Presidents plundered the country's resources to satisfy their selfish propensities while ignoring the plight of the suffering masses.

Finally, I did not set out to write a history book, but to tell a story about the "Athens of West Africa," especially, why it became known as such. Of course, tradition informs us that the Greek City States as they existed then were known for and by their strengths. While Sparta was known for its might, Athens was known for its learning, thus by inference, Sierra Leone was termed as such because of its learning. These days, when the term "Athens of West Africa" is mentioned, it is in the past tense. Whenever mentioned, it is usually referred to as "that used to be the Athens of West Africa". The glory days are gone. Will Sierra Leone attain that status ever? One thing that can be said, other countries in the sub-region are not at a standstill, they are all making progress. Educationally, Sierra Leone is languishing at the bottom of the ladder.

Akibo E Robinson
August 2022

REVIEW

Many books have been written about the territory which the Portuguese explorer Pedro da Cintra reportedly discovered in 1462 and named Lion Mountains because of its spectacular range of mountains visible from the sea. In my view, however, none is as enlightening, informative, and entertaining as Akibo Robinson's ***The Decline and Fall of the Athens of West Africa.***

This is the second book from the pen of an author whose first book ***One Stone Revolution*** featuring the crisis- laden reign of military juntas in Sierra Leone and the brutal civil war made waves among the population young and old in Sierra Leone and beyond. Now Robinson makes a wide sweep of historical events spanning the founding in 1787 of what was called *the province of freedom* and the precipitous occurrences draping the landscape of a country which has hobbled over the years, to its present state. This book will no doubt generate a lively debate among readers with its distinctly assertive, but not opinionated, outlook and interpretation of events.

The title of the book is very fascinating: ***The Decline and Fall of Athens of West Africa.*** The reference to Athens, the ancient citadel of civilization and learning, will not be lost on the reader. Ancient Athens is regarded as a symbol of freedom, art, and democracy by the civilized world. References to Athens conjure up an image of an intellectually superior state with very strong, stable political institutions and populated by a race reputed for their unimpeachable integrity. This implicit comparison with the ancient citadel of stability and conscience prompts some dubiety which anyone attempting to critique the book will have to confront. At the heart of these ruminations will be the disturbing question: ***Was Sierra Leone ever the Athens of West Africa?*** Was Sierra Leone in all its turbulent history with the insipid and unwelcome intervention and interference of the colonialists, the British, and the incessant conflicts between the dissonant factions ever a stable enough state to be compared either implicitly or explicitly with ancient Athens?

Admittedly, Freetown which later became the capital city of Sierra Leone has been historically regarded as the Athens of West Africa. Indeed, the late Professor Eldred Durosimi Jones has argued that the designation is best attributed to Fourah Bay College in Freetown, which was at one time the foremost tertiary institution of learning in Africa south of the Sahara, rather than even to Freetown, much less to the country Sierra Leone. The author of the book is quite appropriately using the appellation which has come to be accepted by many, but the reader will have to decide whether in fact this appellation could be justifiably applied to Sierra Leone, the country. Or can we read some irony into the author's use of the expression? Our author is full of wit and irony laced with some droppings of cynicism, so this might be a possibility. From the outset the reader must be warned not to take what the author says at face value. Metaphorical meanings with a healthy dose of irony abound in the narrative.

This book takes a panoramic view of what many, rightly or wrongly, regard as the days of prosperity, ethics and integrity of the country now called Sierra Leone. However, in his broad sweep of historical events, the author zooms in on the factors which led to what he calls, a 'decline' and with the eyes of an eagle graphically dissects the intrigues, machinations and scheming which served to 'glue' the demographically disparate elements into what the colonialists saw as a cohesive and geographically sustainable state which they named Sierra Leone.

Many historians have attempted an interpretation of the checkered history of the territory. These include the Scottish historian Christopher Fyfe (1920 – 2008). Indigenous pioneers of the territory's history include Professor Akintola Wyse, Professor Cecil Magbaily Fyle (both deceased) and Professor J.A.D. Alie, and Dr. Joseph Bangura who are still actively researching the subject. These historians have attempted a recording of the history of the country from distinctly different perspectives. Robinson is not a historian himself. Nor is he a student of politics. He studied Economics in the university. But he is brave enough to attempt an analysis of such a colossal subject *as he sees it.*

One of the strongest points of this book is the author's ability to prevent the book from descending into merely a historical treatise or a partisan political work. He achieves this by inserting intuitive, insightful, and incisive comments which impose some order on the material he is presenting. The authorial voice is never allowed to be subsumed into the breathtaking narration of events. It might be argued that in some instances the authorial voice is so pronounced that it intrudes into the subject of discussion. But this really would be a matter of opinion. Can it be argued that this is history blended with insight and interpretation? The author claims in his Preface to the book that it is not a historical analysis. This is for the reader to decide.

What is certain nonetheless is that the book cannot be confined merely to the shelves and desks of history professors and their students. It will not only be of immense interest to political scientists, and students of politics. but also, to ordinary observers like me interested in understanding the sequence of events that led the country to its present state, and why these events occurred. The reader's interest is sustained throughout by the author's sometimes spontaneous comments on events which are clearly close to his heart. He is not an outsider looking in. He lived through some of the events himself and bemoans the current state of affairs in the country. Interestingly though, he does not merely bemoan the course of events. He goes further to articulately attribute responsibility for the current state of affairs. His comments are unsparing, and one can imagine that readers will trip over one another to react either positively or negatively to the perspectives expressed in the book. The controversies which the book is envisaged to generate in fact make the book well worth reading.

The first four chapters are interesting enough. They trace in great detail the history of the colony of Freetown and the yoking together of the different peoples which formed the demographic population of what became known later as Sierra Leone. This period stretches from the early days of the arrival of the various settler groups to the signs of potential conflicts which were to later break to the surface.

Interesting perspectives are offered on the historically controversial Hut Tax War. Many historians state what they regard as the bare facts and even in a few instances blame the conflict on the intransigence of the leader of the natives Bai Bureh. Robinson's perspective is completely different. He as it were, turns the story bandied around on its head. For Robinson the tax levied was manifestly unjust and bore with it the potential for violent conflict. These early chapters set the tone for what is to become a very spirited discussion of the genesis of the current situation in Sierra Leone and the reader will follow, thoroughly fascinated, as brick by brick Robinson builds up the story which has culminated in the present state of Sierra Leone. An interesting aspect of the author's description in these chapters is his focus on the bigotry which informed most of the decisions which the British made on behalf of the people of the colony and the protectorate and the lack of sincerity of the so-called "masters".

The reader's interest is sustained all the way throughout the first four chapters by the writer's gentle sarcasm and insightful comments, and controversial interpretation of the events in the early history of Sierra Leone. But the story really comes to life in Chapter 5 titled **Tactical Battlelines: Politrics, Who Won?** This chapter's title is fascinating and calls for some discussion. The word *'politrics'* is used on a metaphorical level; the genealogy of this word yields a captivating scenario of use. The word 'polly' is the Krio equivalent of the parrot, a bird quite common in the tropics. Krio is the de facto (maybe not the de jure) lingua franca of Sierra Leone and is widely spoken all over the country. The reference here is to the African grey parrot (Psittacus) notable for its advanced mental activity and its ability to talk. But it is reputed for mimicking speech rather than generating speech of its own. Herein lies the irony of the author's use of the expression. He veers away from the parrot's acute mental ability to its reputation as a talkative spewing out sometimes meaningless phrases – like the politician. On this level the use of the word has an ironic twist. Politicians, most especially African politicians, have built up a reputation for loquacity. And in Africa most of this is regarded as talk, talk and talk.

But this is not all. Even more interesting is the use of the suffix -trics (tricks). The focus swings from the garbled phrases of the politician to his insincerity, intrigues, and deceit. The use of the pronoun 'his' here is deliberate. During almost the entire period on which this book focuses, men have been in the forefront of politics in Sierra Leone. Even now as I write, women are still jostling for space on the political platform of Sierra Leone.

Chapter 5 throws the spotlight on this aspect of politics in Sierra Leone in its formative years. The author attempts to unravel the triggers for the intrigues which were characteristic of the period of the 1920s. The narrative of the 1920s and the years that followed was to say the least rather convoluted and had many layers to it. Robinson carefully picks his way through this, looking at the different levels of conflict: that between the provincial people and the British, that between the provincial people and the inhabitants of the colony, that between both the provincial and colony people on the one hand, and the British on the other. What immediately becomes obvious in Robinson' interpretation of the events is the dysfunction of the administration. Each faction was selfishly pushing its own agenda without due consideration of the wishes and interests of the others. There was nothing even remotely related to a consensus. It is during this period that in Robinson's assessment that the 'battle lines' were drawn, setting the stage for the turbulent period to follow,

The events that follow - from Chapter 6 to the end of the book - build up on the argument that the chaos of the formative years of the country – colony and protectorate – sounded a death knell for the amalgamated territory. Doom as it would appear according to Robinson. was portended right from the forced amalgamation of the colony and the protectorate.

Chapter 7 is a narration of the path to the attainment of independence. This narration is laced with the author's incisive comments. It is the commentary which actually keeps the reader fully interested. The events themselves might have appeared dull and dour but the author's comments rescue them from becoming uninteresting and boring. The author's almost conversational tone serves to take the reader into his confidence, as if he were speaking directly to the reader. His narration therefore achieves an immediacy of experience which many other books of this nature lack. Sometimes the reader has the impression that this is an internal monologue with the narrative seeping out of the author's stream of consciousness. The impression is almost created that the reader is eavesdropping on the ruminations cavorting through the narrator's lively mind. This elevates the book from the level of a mere historical or political treatise to that of a classic.

The author's rendition of contemporary events effectively starts in Chapter 12 Brief Interlude. He traces the events which occurred from the military coup in 1998 to the change of power from President Kabbah's SLPP Government to Ernest Bai Koroma's APC Government and back to the SLPP Government in 2018 under the present Head of State Retired Brigadier Julius Maada Bio. It is best to allow the reader to make a judgement on the comments and opinions expressed on this period since events are still unfolding as I write. Like everything else in life, politics is dynamic and fluid situations work themselves out as the years advance. As he peers into the crystal ball the reader can only wonder whether his prognostications will be realized in the coming years. If you will excuse the cliché here, posterity will judge. Suffice it to say though, that his analysis is coherent and meets the requirements of a book which merits the reader's attention. The book is of medium length and could be read in one or two sittings principally because of the interest which it generates.

The controversies which the book might generate have been hinted at earlier. The book is well-researched, and Robinson provides evidence for most of the thoughts expressed. But any book making an interpretation of political events especially contemporary events is bound to elicit divergent views in readers. This is not unexpected. In this book history merges with politics to make an explosive blend. When one adds the conversational tone and almost casual and random thoughts that run through the book, it is fair to say that all sectors of society will have something in it to either glorify or criticize. Other writers will no doubt be gearing up to provide a rejoinder either supporting or debunking Robinson's interpretation of the events. Either way, the book would have made a mark on the literary canvas of Sierra Leone.

KENNETH OSHO.

AUTHOR OF *FOUNDATION ENGLISH FOR SENIOR SECONDARY SCOOLS & THE UNIVERSITY.*

JANUARY 2023.

GLOSSARY

APC   -   All People's Congress
SLPP   -   Sierra Leone People's Party
COPP   -   Consortium of Political Parties
UPP   -   United People's Party
WAYL   -   West Africa Youth League
NEC   -   National Electoral Commission
ECSL   -   Electoral Commission, Sierra Leone
SSL   -   Statistics Sierra Leone
MDA   -   Ministries, Departments, Agencies
IMF   -   International Monetary Fund
WB   -   World Bank
Af.DB   -   African Development Bank
TRC   -   Truth and Reconciliation Commission
FBC   -   Fourah Bay College
SLGS   -   Sierra Leone Grammar School
AWMS   -   Annie Walsh Memorial School
MBHS   -   Methodist Boys High School
MGHS   -   Methodist Girls High School
BSL   -   Central Bank of Sierra Leone
NPRC   -   National Provisional Ruling Council
AFRC   -   Armed Forces Revolutionary Council
U.N.   -   The United Nations

E.U.	-	The European Union
R.U.F	-	Revolutionary United Front
NCWA	-	National Congress of West Africa
CEA	-	Committee of Educated Africans
SLNC	-	Sierra Leone National Congress
SLYL	-	Sierra Leone Youth League
CFAO	-	Compagnie Francaise de L'Afrique Occidental
SCOA	-	Société Compagnie Occidental Afrique
INEC	-	Independent National Electoral Commission
ULIMO	-	United Liberation Movement

ACKNOWLEDGEMENTS

My first duty is to acknowledge the divine hand of the Almighty on my life; my profound gratitude is tendered for giving me another lease of life. The major portion of this work was accomplished under severe stress caused by a life-threatening condition. My sincere gratitude goes to my spouse Janette, who put up with all my idiosyncrasies during the entire exercise. She also typed the entire manuscript.

My thanks go to Dr Adjai Robinson and Mr Leslie Scott who proof-read the first draft. I would also like to take the opportunity to recognise the critical review of the manuscript by Dr Cecil Blake and the tireless effort of Mr Kenneth Osho (retired Head of the English Department, Fourah Bay College), who reviewed and edited the entire work.

I would be remiss in my duty if I did not acknowledge the input of Mrs Julia Williams in designing the cover page, and the photographic skills of Mr Akilano Akiwumi who provided the cover-page photo-graphs

The author takes the responsibility of any deficiencies and errors in the manuscript.

Chapter One

EARLY (KNOWN) HISTORY

As kids attending primary school, we were taught that Sierra Leone was discovered in 1462 by Pedro da Cintra, a Portuguese explorer. In present day Sierra Leone, ask the man in the street, he would parrot that same belief. But, our history dates far back into the past. Archaeological remains showed that Sierra Leone had been inhabited for at least 2,500 years, populated by successive movements of peoples from other parts of Africa[1] European contacts with Sierra Leone were among the first in West Africa. In 1462, Portuguese explorer Pedro da Cintra on sighting the famous Cotton tree from the sea knew he was near a landmass of a part of Africa. And since there was at the time a severe thunderstorm raging, over this mountainous landmass, hearing the noise, and being in Africa, he thought it was caused by lions roaring and lo and behold, the name Sierra Leone became etched in history, and the land came to be called lion mountains which is the meaning of the Portuguese nomenclature. However, it should be stated that quite recently, this claim that Pedro da Cintra was the first European to set foot in Sierra Leone, has been debunked putting the date much earlier in the same century, by a Portuguese priest[2]. Whatever the case, what is not in dispute is the fact that the

---

[1]   The Encyclopaedia Britannica

[2]   Dr Cecil Magbaily Fyle

country had existed long before Europeans set foot in it. Before the beginning of its European history, it was peopled by numerous politically independent native groups with their own languages and customs. What is true and should be expected, Sierra Leone as it is now was not what it used to be. Before the Europeans, there were chiefs and kings, hence we read about King Jimmy and others. It was not one cohesive society, nor a homogenous country. Life in those days before the "Age of Reason" was fraught with internal wars for territory and authority. European civilisation brought stability and Western values into our society, that cannot be gainsaid but at the same time, it also brought along certain unsavoury situations. Slavery at the time was part of the African society. When the Europeans came, they put a new, if rather disastrous and demeaning face to it.

Not that the Africans were not much interested in acquiring slaves, the Portuguese, the Dutch, the French and the English who arrived later were certainly more interested in buying Africans, transport them in horrendous conditions in ships across the Atlantic to the plantations in North America and the West Indies. Initially, the methods of the slavers were raiding and kidnapping when the opportunity arose. However, this strategy after a while was not lucrative enough so they engaged the services of local inhabitants to aid them in their inhuman acts. Some chiefs were willing to part with a few of the less desirable members of their tribes for a price; others went into the war business- inhabitants were captured and sold for a fortune in articles of rum, cloths, beads, copper and muskets.[3] In this unholy trade, they exchanged cheap European manufactures for slaves. When the market became depressed, more often than not, the British fuelled conflict among communities by supplying the chiefs with guns; these guns were then used offensively to capture prisoners who were then sold as slaves to the traffickers[4] Those who were not sold, their conditions were much better than those sold into

---

[3]   The Encyclopaedia Britannica "Sierra Leone History"

[4]   A Nationalist History of Sierra Leone. Dr Cecil Fyle

slavery in the Americas, the West Indies and Brazil. Question: would these Europeans have succeeded had they not been aided by fellow Africans? We will never know. However, Africa has not changed. Our countrymen are still aiding citizens of richer nations to plunder our resources. History records that over six million Africans perished just crossing the Atlantic. Not only were they transported in unhygienic and degrading conditions, yoked and chained to each other, but when they arrived and were sold to their apparent slave masters, they were treated as chattels and without any human rights. In those days how could they talk about human rights when they were treated as sub-humans? Imagine, being removed from your natural habitat, where you had not only your freedom, but you had your dignity and identity. Once sold into slavery, not only did our forefathers lose their freedom and dignity, but they also even lost their identity, their culture, their family and their religion. The African American lost all of these! Before casting blame, we should always remember that. Yes, some have made it, rather the exception to the rule. Taking into account all of our sufferings at the hands of our slave and colonial masters, the question of reparation is taboo. It has been broached in many fora, but it has been like kicking against the pricks!

Just imagine! The debate on reparations is extant but acceptance of their sins and making atonement is taboo. Those who committed these atrocities do not want to accept or even apologise for the sins of their forefathers, committed against the black race. How can they? Yet they talk about charity to developing countries when they agonise over aid, which in most cases probably benefit the donor more than the recipient. Just think! "Europeans slaked their need for labour in the colonies-in the mines and on plantations-not only enslaving indigenous Americans but also by shipping slaves across the Atlantic from Africa. Up to 15 million of them. In the North American colonies alone, Europeans extracted an estimated two hundred and twenty-two million, five hundred and five thousand and forty-nine (222,505,049) hours of forced labour from African slaves between 1619 and 1865. Valued at the US minimum wage, with a modest rate of interest, that's worth $97 trillion-more than the entire global GDP". They will not pay for reparations but considering the worthlessness of the black man/woman, "when Britain abolished slavery in 1834, it compensated the slave owners to the tune of 20 million pounds, the equivalent of 200 million pounds today.[5]

In the 17th century when Portuguese influence waned in Sierra Leone, the most significant European group to engage in the slave trade was the British. Around 1628, they had a "factory" in the vicinity of Sherbro Island, where they conducted all their business, mainly trade with Africans. In 1663, Charles II (the reigning King of England during that period) granted a charter to a company, the Royal Adventurers of England to conduct trade in Africa. To conduct their business, this company built a fort in the Sherbro and Tasso Islands in the Freetown estuary. As this fort was repeatedly plundered by the Dutch and French and pirates, the Tasso Island fort was moved to nearby Bunce Island, which later became a centre for receiving and transporting slaves across the Atlantic. In 1652, the first slaves in North America were brought from Sierra Leone to the Sea Islands off the coast of the Southern United States. By the 18th century, slavery was a thriving business for the Europeans; slaves were taken from Sierra Leone to the plantations of South Carolina and Georgia where their rice-farming skills made them quite valuable. Britain and British seafarers played a major role in the transatlantic trade in captured Africans between 1530 and 1810. Over 15 million Africans (some writers put this figure close to 20 million), were captured and shipped to the Caribbean Islands and the Americas. Many more died during the raids, on the long marches to the coast and on the infamous middle passage due to the inhuman conditions on and off the slave ships.

Britain outlawed the slave trade in 1807 and the British Navy operating from Freetown took active measures to stop the Atlantic slave trade.

---

[5] Enough of aid – let's talk reparations. Jason Hickel. Culled from the Guardian,27/11/2015

The Colony of Freetown was established between 1787 and 1792 for the resettlement of African American slaves who fought for and sought refuge from the British during the American Revolutionary war and had been relocated to England and Nova Scotia. The coastal peninsula region that had been occupied by the Temnes was the site selected by British philanthropists and abolitionists for the establishment of this colony. Between 1800 and 1855, the population was further augmented by the resettlement of Caribbean ex-slaves and freedmen, disbanded African soldiers, and Africans liberated on the high seas by the British Naval Squadron following the abolition of the slave trade.[6] The area, said to have previously been a slave market, was purchased from the local Koya Temne sub-chief, King Tom and regent Naimbana, a purchase the Europeans understood, ceded the land to the new "settlers" for ever. However, disputes arose and King Tom's successor, King Jimmy burnt the settlement to the ground in 1789.

The colonial history of Freetown started in 1791 with Thomas Peters, an African-American who had served in the Black pioneers and settled in Nova Scotia as part of the Black Loyalist migration. Peters travelled to England in 1791 to report grievances of the Black Loyalists who were treated badly and discriminated against. Following on this and other occurrences, Lieutenant John Clarkson was sent over to Nova Scotia to register immigrants willing to go to Sierra Leone. A total of 1,196 former American slaves from free African communities around Nova Scotia were recruited. They were put in ships and set sail for Freetown early in the year of 1792 and arrived in St George Bay between February 26 and March 9, 1792, but alas! Not all of them made it to Sierra Leone; sixty-four perished[7]. A paltry number, compared to the millions of souls that were lost on the original crossing, due to the inhumane and cruel behaviour of the slavers and their cohorts. Clarkson and the settlers built Freetown on the former

---

[6]   The Journal of Sierra Leone Studies Vol 3 Edition 1, (2014)

[7]   A New History of Sierra Leone. Joe A.D. Alie

site of the first Granville town which was sacked by King Jimmy in 1789 and had remained a jungle before the rebuilding of the colony.

And indeed, Clarkson and the settlers toiled under difficult and singularly hostile conditions to sustain the new settlement and in this they succeeded. Contemporary articles tend to accord derogatory descriptions to the first settlers that were transported to the Colony of Freetown, such terms as "Black Poor", "Slaves" etc were and are still used. However, what these writers have not acknowledged is the fact that against all odds, hostile climatic conditions, hostile communities all around, a view echoed in the All Peoples' Congress' "The Rising Sun, A History of Building for the Future",[8] not only did they survive, but they were also able to establish an excellent city! And what has also not been acknowledged is the fact that when these settlers arrived, a considerable number could read and write the English language.[9] Perhaps recognising the effort put in against all odds by Clarkson and his immigrants, that is why in times of calamity, especially those that are man-made, Sierra Leoneans still appeal to" Governor's Clarkson's prayer for his struggling colony". According to this prayer, there is a portion that states "should any person have a wicked thought in his heart or do anything to disturb the peace and comfort of our colony, let him be rooted out Oh God, from off the face of the earth; but have mercy upon him hereafter". Call it superstition or what you will, whenever the country goes through a period of calamity, like the civil war and the Ebola Virus Disease (EVD), and when there is a feeling that those in governance had not dealt fairly and with probity, this prayer becomes a mantra against those trampling our rights. Has it worked; who can say? However, many of our leaders, deemed to be the culprits have not escaped unscathed; from the likes of the first President, Siaka Stevens, Saidu Momoh

---

[8] "These settlers sent through a mixture of philanthropy and embarrassment ... arrived during the rainy season to encounter scant shelter, disease and open hostility from the indigenous population"

[9] The Journal of the Sierra Leone Society. Edited by Michael Crowder. New Series No 23, July 1968

who followed in his footsteps, to Foday Sankoh who brought untold suffering upon our countrymen and Valentine Strasser, one cannot say fortune smiled on them. Even going back to the days of Albert Margai, the second prime Minister of our nation, he who wanted to make Sierra Leone a one-party state, his end was not dignified. Yet, we humans, never learn from past mistakes. Subsequent leaders and those in the corridors of power continue to plunder state resources, enriching themselves while the masses live in abject poverty!

In considering this prayer, there is another portion never given much thought. That is the portion that states "let not a few wicked men among us draw down Thy vengeance upon the colony". Now considering the wealth of our resources, we are languishing in poverty. We have had a civil war just when we thought the country was getting ready for the take off into sustained growth. The war ended, we started building our fledgling democracy, and bang! The Ebola Virus Disease struck, being perhaps more devastating than the eleven-year civil war. And again, another disaster has struck this small but potentially wealthy country where most of the people live in abject poverty. On the morning of the 14th of August, the nation woke up to the sounds of a catastrophic mudslide in one of the mountain ranges in the Freetown Peninsular. Over 500 souls perished; in fact, considering the nature of our cultural practices, one cannot put an exact figure to the number of people killed. We are hearing that over a thousand souls perished, but one cannot be certain. One thing though, given the nature of our service and recovery facilities, many bodies are still buried under the rubble that will never be retrieved. The foot of Mount Sugar Loaf will be the final resting place of those men, women and children who perished and whose mortal remains could not be primed out of the makeshift or mass graves! Is Sierra Leone under a curse? This is a question many have uttered and not been able to come to terms with. One thing though, we never seem to learn lessons that would change our behaviour. We go through difficult periods and vehemently call on the Almighty to remove whatever was plaguing us; as soon as we enjoy a respite, we forget all about the difficult times we had gone through and return to our old bad ways; in times of calamity we proclaim our religiosity and belief on the Almighty, calling upon his name vehemently and making all kinds of promises, even calling for and having national days of prayer. As soon as remission comes, we retrogress. Alas, that is our human attitude.

In the 1800s, Sierra Leone was still a small colony consisting of the peninsula area only, not yet what we know as Sierra Leone today; that was to come later, through trade, mainly in slaves, and diplomacy by the British. The Colony apart, the bulk of the territory of the country was inhabited by indigenous people like, the Mendes, the Temnes, the Limbas, the Susus, who themselves migrated from other parts of Africa, and the Lokos, among others. During the period of the 19th century, that was to change basically through trade and diplomacy in the form of treaty making and military adventurism by the British. The treaties that were concluded with local chiefs dealt primarily with commerce, keeping roads open to allow the British to collect duties and adjudicating disputes between neighbouring chiefs. For this, they were paid a stipend. Later on in the century, when the scramble for Africa by European nations, such as Britain, France, Germany, Spain, Belgium, that led to the partition of Africa in a treaty signed in Germany, the British, facing intense competition from the French into their area of influence in Sierra Leone, tried to forestall the French from making incursions into Sierra Leone. To finalise the country's boundary, the British Government in 1890, instructed Governor Hay in Sierra Leone to get from chiefs in the area, friendship treaties containing a clause forbidding them to trade with another European power without British consent.[10] On a passing note, just like slavery, the Scramble for Africa brought immense wealth to Europe. Take Belgium for example, her lust for ivory and rubber killed some 10 million Congolese – yes 10 million innocent Africans – roughly half that country's population. The wealth gleaned from that plunder was syphoned back to Belgium to fund beautiful stately architecture

---

[10]   History of Sierra Leone. Christopher Fyfe P. 486

and impressive public works, including arches, parks, and railway stations – all the markers of development that adorn Brussels today, the bejewelled headquarters of the European Union.[11]

In January 1895, a boundary agreement was signed in Paris, roughly fixing the line between French Guinea and Sierra Leone. Unfortunately, Africa was partitioned on geographical lines, rivers, watersheds, parallels, not political. More generally, the arbitrary lumping together of disparate peoples into geographical entities decided only by the colonial powers has been a source of continuing conflict and strife throughout Africa, Sierra Leone not excepted. In this day and age, tribalism plagues all aspect of life, mostly to the detriment of progress. But should it always be like this? Should not tribalism enhance growth and transformation into a modern homogenous society? This author believes it can, if we look towards the higher values of our commonalities rather than focus on the baser traits of tribalism as we are doing today – regionalism, ethnicity, loyalties, blind and unquestioned support, to name a few. After over sixty years of independence, we are still grappling with these ills. Successive political leaders, starting with Albert Margai, have used it to the detriment of the country's development and entrenching themselves in the corridors of power.

Whether we take either 1787 when the black poor from Britain was settled in Granville Town, or 1792 when the first group of settlers from Nova Scotia arrived in Freetown, Sierra Leone was under colonial rule for over 170 years. Gaining her independence in 1961, means that Sierra Leone has shed the yoke of the colonial power for over 60 years. The environment created in West Africa by the Scramble for Africa, was quite interesting geographically. From the North of Senegal, right down to the West of Nigeria, each Anglophone country was neighbour to a Francophone country. Innocuous as it may seem, what it did was to prevent common communication

---

[11]   King Leopold's Ghost. Adam Hochschild

and natural bonding between neighbours especially as in the Anglophone countries English became the official language and in the Francophone countries, French became the official language. The consequence then was enormous. Fancy, a West African national say in Ghana being able to communicate comfortably with a British national over three thousand miles removed but cannot communicate freely with his neighbour in Ivory Coast. This is now changing due to globalisation and the treaties of cooperation that have been concluded among these countries. Imagine a time when it was easier travelling to east Africa from West Africa, going via Europe than travelling through Africa. Even at this day and age, compare travelling from Senegal to another West African country, let us say Sierra Leone, with travelling from any West African country to any European city. Yes, we have had independence but what have we done with it? We now have the ECOWAS and other Eastern and Southern blocs, but they are focused on the political rather than the economic. We are still beholden to these colonial powers. In colonial days, we were exploited, and we continue to be exploited, all in the name of poverty, lack of development capital and foreign direct investment, not forgetting that canker worm corruption which to a large extent is responsible for African poverty: greedy, selfish and corrupt leaders and officials. We have our independence, but do we have our freedom?

Colonial structures still linger. Travelling from one West African country to another is still a challenge, but most of these countries had railways or used to have railways, constructed by the colonial powers for trade and resource exploitation. Hence, our railway system was from north to south, from the interior to the coast, never from east to west, or vice versa, crossing national borders. This is the situation many African countries found themselves in during their colonial history. Has it changed? Well perhaps but not much, especially in West Africa.

In those days, Sierra Leone had a preeminent position in what was known then as British West Africa, The Gambia, Sierra Leone, Ghana (the Gold Coast as it was known then), and Nigeria. In the early days, Freetown served as the residence of the British governor who also ruled the Gold Coast (now Ghana) and the Gambia. According to a European who visited Sierra Leone in the early 20th century, "Around you are many European steamers, coaling, watering, victualling loading or discharging cargo. The sight is superb. But only after you have sighted other ports along the coast do you realise why more ships call at Sierra Leone than at any other West African port. Accessibility to the shore, facilities for coaling, and the possession of an excellent water supply give it this pre-eminence".[12] In the same story, a lady traveller in 1911 described Freetown as "the most beautiful spot on the West Coast".[13] As another writer, writing before this era put it, "Sierra Leone was tranquil and the inhabitants were satisfied because the Negroes considered it a good country rich in everything; therefore men who went to Guinea were not highly thought of if they had not been there in the same way as we [in Portugal] think poorly of anyone who has not been to France or Italy".

In those bygone days when one would consider the world to be technologically less advanced, systems, however primitive or basic were established, society was well ordered there was discipline and also respect in all facets of the society. Lines of authority were clearly defined and adhered to. As illustration, responsibility of markets was shifted from the colonial government to the Freetown Municipality by the Freetown Municipality Act of 1863, by which the Vegetable market in Water Street (the Big Market), the Meat Market in Garrison Street (the Grain Market), the City Market (Kroo Town Road), the King Jimmy Market (King Jimmy Wharf), and the Fish Market (Rock Street), came under the authority of the Freetown Municipality. By this Act, the Freetown Municipality was also responsible for providing streetlights. Believe it or not, before the First World War, there were 332 lamp-pillars with street lamps, necessitating the employment of

---

[12]   Sierra Leone, Its Peoples, Products and Secret Societies.by H Osman Newland

[13]   Ibid

thirty lamp-lighters responsible for lighting these lamps.[14] The author can recollect in his younger days, and not too long after the colonial period, certain street lights, especially those at main junctions, were still under the responsibility of the Freetown City Council; usually, those lights were switched off by midnight. What progress have we made? Even in the 19th century, our streets were lit by streetlights. By 1894, there were 60 streetlamps in Freetown. What can we say now; the streets of Freetown, the capital city in the 21st century, are mirrored in darkness because lighting is now a luxury and not a necessity! How can we progress without energy? Explaining our backwardness does not need any rocket science.

Let us for a moment turn our attention to education. One of the first universities in sub-Saharan Africa was established by the missionaries in Sierra Leone. Fourah Bay College was established in 1827, and until 1969 was affiliated to the University of Durham in the United Kingdom. At establishment, it soon became a magnet, attracting students from other English speaking West African countries. Students came from Nigeria, the Gambia, Ghana, even from eastern and southern Africa in those halcyon days. For more than a century, it was the only Western-style University in western sub-Saharan Africa, training teachers and even doctors. Church Mission Schools (CMS) were also established in the 19h century; schools like the CMS Grammar School established in 1845 the Annie Walsh Memorial School so renamed in 1849; the Methodist Boys High school and the Methodist Girls High school, established in 1874 and 1880 respectively. Church missions also established primary schools all over the country. The greatest contribution of the CMS in those days was in education. By 1841, they had 21 elementary schools, apart from the two secondary schools they had already established[15]. The Government also established the Bo school originally for the sons of

---

[14]   Ibid

[15]   Topics in West African History. Adu Boahen with Ade Ajayi and Michael Tidy

chiefs, in Bo in 1904 and a Girls' school in Moyamba the Harford School. The Albert Academy School for boys was established in Freetown in 1904. In 1906, Sierra Leoneans, led by the European wife of the Reverend Osora founded the Freetown Secondary School for Girls.[16] The Catholics not to be left behind, founded the St Edwards Primary School for boys in 1865 and followed up with a secondary school for boys in 1922.

The name "Athens of West Africa" came to be attached to Sierra Leone in those days because of her educational standing in West Africa, more so the establishment of Fourah Bay College in 1827, and its affiliation to Durham University in 1876. Like the Athens of old, it became a centre of learning. Small as the territory was and still is, consider, by the census of 1860 the percentage of the population under education was 22, whereas in Prussia the percentage was 16, and in England 13! And the effect was manifested in the intellectual, moral, and religious improvements in the country.[17] Fast forward to the 21st century, that eminence of Sierra Leone has disappeared. In the ranking of universities in Africa, none of the colleges in Sierra Leone is ranked among the first two hundred. How are the mighty fallen.

According to some historians, the second half of the 19th century witnessed the rise of Sierra Leoneans (Krios) in various spheres in the societies along the West African Coast. Many became merchants, lawyers, doctors, teachers, journalists, and clergy men. They were to be found not only in what was then the hinterland of Sierra Leone, but even along the West Coast of Africa plying their trade and professions. They became pioneers of Western education and Christianity in West Africa.[18]

---

[16]   The Krio of Sierra Leone. An Interpretative History. Akintola Wyse

[17]   Sierra Leone Inheritance. Christopher Fyfe

[18]   A New History of Sierra Leone. Joe A.D. Alie

Also, Sierra Leone small as it was, was credited with a series of firsts in West Africa and also in Sub-Saharan Africa.

- In 1792 the first democratic election conducted in Freetown by the Krios was the first time in history that women cast their votes
- In 1808 the Post Office was introduced in Freetown and was the first in West Africa
- In 1843, the Gambia and the Gold Coast (Ghana)were administered from Sierra Leone
- In 1866 Lagos, in Nigeria came under the administration of Sierra Leone
- In 1867 the Supreme Court of Sierra Leone became the final Court of Appeal for civil and criminal justice for the Gold Coast (Ghana), the Gambia and Nigeria
- In 1927 Kissy Asylum Mental Home was built and became the first mental hospital in Sub-Saharan Africa
- In 1927 Freetown was the first City in West Africa to have electric lights
- Also, in 1927 Freetown became the first city in West Africa to be linked by air via the Gambia to the United Kingdom
- In 1927 the Sierra Leone Broadcasting Service (S.L.B.S.) was the first Radio Station in Sub-Saharan Africa to be linked to the outside world by the British Broadcasting Service (BBC).

Moreover, Sierra Leoneans excelled in the fields of education, law, medicine, journalism to name a few. Accordingly, when writing about the brilliance of Sierra Leoneans in the early colonial period, and the contributing factors for this tiny enclave to be termed the Athens of West Africa, a few names of importance come to mind. Mention should be made of J.C. Taylor, Adjai Crowther, C. Paul and P.J. Williams, for their pioneering work in Linguistics. A.B.C. Sibthorpe was a botanist, Geographer, Exhibitor, painter, and artist; he was the author of The History of Sierra Leone (1868); Claude George, a Durham graduate was the author of The Rise of

British West Africa (1903). Samuel Coleridge Taylor composed the opera Hiawatha. Sponsored by the British, William B. Davies and James Africanus Horton qualified as medical doctors from Scottish Universities. To wit, they were the first Africans to qualify as doctors from a British University. After its affiliation to Durham in 1876, the college produced its first Durham graduates: Nathaniel Davies, Isaac Oluwale, Obadiah Johnson and A.E. Metzger in 1879. Sierra Leoneans also excelled in British Universities. Christian Cole, and George Gurney Nicol were the first Africans from a British colony to graduate from Oxford (1876) and Cambridge (1879) respectively.[19]

In the sphere of journalism which is now a very important tool of public opinion and the democratic process, Sierra Leone had carved a space in what was then known as British West Africa. It was in Sierra Leone in 1801 that the earliest effort at real journalism was made, followed by Ghana in 1822. Nigeria and the Gambia saw this development much later, in 1863 and 1883 respectively.[20]

In 1801, the Sierra Leone Gazette a government paper, was published, and sent to the Sierra Leone Company directors in London. The gazette was continued in 1808 when the British Crown took over the reins of government from the Sierra Leone Company. Unlike the present-day Sierra Leone, though an official government paper, it did not always echo the views of the government. In such instances, some effort was made to muzzle the press by the governor who was the British Government representative in the Colony. Unlike now, these efforts did not succeed. Journalism was not limited to the government press. For a time, the responsibility of newspapers' publications was undertaken by religious organisations, such as the Wesleyan Missionary Society and the American Missionary Society. Private individuals also carried their own newspapers and from time

---

[19]   Ibid

[20]   The Journal of Sierra Leone Studies. Ed by A.P. Kup, New Series, No 12. Dec 1959

to time, there were many of these. In 1855, the first Sierra Leone newspaper owned by a private individual appeared, "the New Era" a weekly published by William Drape.[21] This newspaper was deemed to be a thorn in the flesh of the Colonial Government so much so that the Governor sought to ban it. The publisher maintained that he was seeking after the truth and taking this information to the people. It alluded to what it called "the responsibilities of journalism which embraced: an exposure of falsehood, regardless of the high places upon which it may be throned (sic); and a vigorous enunciation of truth, regardless of the calumnies and suspicions to which such advocacy... may expose [the journalist]".[22] Some of the notable newspapers published were: The Sierra Leone Watchman; The Sierra Leone Weekly Times and West African Record; the Sierra Leone Observer and Commercial Advocate; The Negro; and the Independent. "Including ephemeral publications, well over thirty different newspapers were published in Sierra Leone during the 19th century".[23] Believe it or not, Bonthe in those days had a newspaper, "The Early Dawn" which first appeared in the early 1860s under the auspices of the American Missionary Association.[24]

Before independence, the entire running of the country was based on the Westminster style of government, the judiciary, the legislature, and the executive. Before Sierra Leone became a republic, the Queen was the ceremonial head like all other Commonwealth countries, while we still had a Prime Minister as the constitutional head of state. Even the jurisprudence was based on English law. In those days, the Privy Council was the highest court. If one felt aggrieved by the

---

[21] The Journal of the Sierra Leone Society. Edited by A.P. Kup, New Series No 8 June 1957

[22] The Journal of the African Society. Edited by Michael Crowder, New Series No 23. July 1968

[23] The Journal of the Sierra Leone Society. Edited by A.P. Kup, New Series No 8 June 1957

[24] Ibid

decision taken in the Court of Appeal, there was leave to appeal to the Privy Council. Just extrapolating, it would have been interesting to see how the constitutional saga would have played out between the President and the Vice President who was removed from office by the President on a constitutional technicality that had to be resolved in the courts. Unfortunately, our constitution is written unlike the British Constitution which is largely unwritten and governed by tradition. There is no reason to revert to the courts for interpretation as is done under the American Constitution. A distinction here is in place. Apparently, the separation of powers is observed and practised in the United States; once a Supreme Court decision is reached, everybody abides by it. Not so in Africa, Sierra Leone included. There is a perception that there is no separation of powers among the legislature, the executive and the judiciary. Consequently, a recourse to the courts for interpretation of the constitution does not lay the issue to rest. Because of this perception, especially when the courts find for the Establishment, there is always a cry of interference by the executive! This was never the case in the heyday of the "Athens of West Africa".

This is not to say the colonial system was all glee and joy for all, especially Sierra Leoneans. Indeed, this writer must hasten to say, as evidenced by the colonial system in other colonies, in India, in the Caribbean and elsewhere, the locals or nationals were treated in some cases if not all like second class citizens. In the administration, locals could not aspire to certain positions in the Civil Service; there were certain social and sport's clubs that were the preserve of the colonial classes, the golf club in the capital, Freetown comes to mind. Even the houses that they constructed, were removed from the "hoi polloi", the Patricians, they lived in exclusive areas that were looked upon as "Reservations" in those days.

In spite of the fact that there were educated Sierra Leoneans in the professions, lawyers, doctors, teachers, administrators, when it came to employment, they were discriminated against and treated with the utmost disdain and prejudice. Notwithstanding our colonial ties and predilection for things British and Western values, the governed were always treated as inferiors, no matter the level of education attained; many derogatory terms were used to describe the Sierra Leonean. This contempt was summarised up in Akintola Wyse's book, the Krio of Sierra Leone in a pronouncement by Ormsby-Gore as follows: "The Englishman has naturally an instinctive dislike of assimilation. We like to keep our life distinct from that of other races whether European or not. The more another people acquire our culture, outlook and our social habits, very often the wider becomes the gulf between us. . . We frequently get on better with people different from us and we appreciate the differences more than the points we have in common. . . ." With this kind of mind set, could the Sierra Leonean boss the Colonial or even be at par in positions of employment? Resoundingly no as circumstances proved. Many professionals, in the law, medicine, teaching and administration were prevented from holding executive positions even when they were better qualified than their British counterparts. In 1917, W. Awunor Renner a barrister was refused a placement as an Assistant District Commissioner because there was no place for an African in that category. On the other hand, a war veteran in the person of Colonel Hart was appointed as District Commissioner, his qualification, he belonged to the military. Dr E.H. Taylor-Cummings, the first Sierra Leonean to hold a Public Health qualification was passed over for the position of Medical Officer of Health; instead, the position was given to a European who was unqualified for the post, but later on sent for training. To all intent and purposes, one can say, the European treated the African with disdain, all because of colour and this is with us today; it has not gone away, neither in Europe, nor in America, nor in Australia, not even in South Africa, even with the breaking down of Apartheid. Racism continues to rear its ugly head.

In the area of politics in those days, it was a tussle between the Sierra Leonean and the Colonial administration.

Notwithstanding these aberrations, the country was orderly, and the institutions of government functioned as they should, the judiciary, the police, the Civil Service as we used to know it including the colonial administration, the schools and colleges, few in number as they were in those days. All operated under the prescribed law and the system was compromised for nobody, not even for the governor in those days, who will be the equivalent of our president of today.

Chapter 2

SNAPSHOT OF THE EARLY DAYS OF COLONIALISM

The scramble for and partitioning of Africa by the European powers were undertaken for philanthropic reasons. That would be emphatically an incorrect statement; also it was not for civilising the people of a continent that for a long time was regarded as "dark". The real reason for Europeans coming to and colonising the continent of Africa was a demand for raw materials felt by the imperial powers, France, Britain, Germany, Belgium, Portugal, Spain and Holland, and providing markets for their manufactured goods. For Sierra Leone, the colonial power happened to be Britain, which also had the remit over the Gambia, the Gold Coast now Ghana, and Nigeria. These were the four countries in West Africa that formed British West Africa. The French had their own counterpart, French West Africa, comprising Senegal, Mali, French Guinea, Ivory Coast, Togo (part German), Dahomey now Benin and Cameroon.

No matter what people say, whether from the side of the imperial power or from that of the colonised people, the colonial yoke was not easy to carry. The British saw themselves as superior to the African natives and the relationship with the colony of Freetown was not an easy one. In general, the settlers, so-called, from Nova Scotia, the Maroons from the West Indies who were repatriated to Sierra Leone, were educated to a certain degree, at least they were literate in the English language and also had numeracy skills. Nonetheless, the imperialists refused to recognise this fact and initially did not utilise the abilities of the Africans to the fullest. Rather, they would employ their European counterparts who were less qualified. To quote from Christopher Fyfe's Book on Sierra Leone's Inheritance "Is it not a sad matter, then, that English Rulers, of all Rulers in West Africa should initiate a policy of repression among Natives when they could find no cogent – no sufficient, no reasonable reason for this policy, except, perhaps, this utterly unworthy one namely – that they alone, as being masters, might enjoy these good things of the country which they never created."[25] During this time, apart from a few acting positions, in the Judicial Department, Africans were not placed in the positions warranted by their qualifications and experience. Due to these policies, the white man came to be seen in the eyes of the natives a usurper of their land and the right to responsible administrative positions, Vis – a – Vis their status in the society. They believed, if unjustly, that the development of the land was for the well-being of the white man, and the utter suppression of the natives of the place.[26]

However, this did not happen. When growing up, I used to hear the popular saying that Sierra Leone was the white man's grave. A popular belief then was that but for the mosquitoes, the white man would not have left Sierra Leone. Yes, it was true that many of them perished during the early colonial period, but so did the settlers. More importantly, the mortality rate in Sierra Leone, was not higher than in colonies in the West Indies or in India where the British had taken a foothold, for that matter. Be this as it was, this gave rise to the Imperialists, disengaging themselves from the heart of the city and setting abode on higher ground, in what now is known as Hill Station,

---

[25]   Sierra Leone Inheritance. Christopher Fyfe

[26]   Ibid

as a means of minimising the incidence of malaria. Thus, they built an exclusively European reservation up at Hill Station which in those days, was inaccessible to the Natives.

Notwithstanding this reaction of the European to the climate and ecology of the land, it was maintained that active horsemen, bustling merchants, gay (as in cheerful) officials moved on all sides with cheerfulness.[27]

If anyone wondered how the railway to Hill Station came into existence, here lies the explanation. It was not constructed for trade, nor for public transportation but for the exclusive use of the Colonialists who were living at Hill Station but had to travel to the centre of the city to work. By that time, there was a railway from Cline Town to Songo, facilitating transportation of produce from the Provinces to the Port and also transporting passengers to and fro. As one would expect, the natives were only entitled to travel third class even when travelling on government business. Not so the imperialists. They were entitled to first class. When the mode of transportation got difficult, and hazardous they were carried on hammocks by the natives. These were early days yet.

Yes, the Imperialists thought of the natives as imbeciles, although they would not voice this in the open, this mind-set did not impede the African from parading his skills all along the West African coasts. They could be found not just in Sierra Leone but also all along the British West Africa and Togo Land, and even in the Congo Free State working as government officials, magistrates, teachers and missionaries. In some cases, some were able to raise the capital to purchase ships and started a prosperous trade all along the West African coast. A group of "Liberated Africans" went back to Nigeria to found their own communities. Sierra Leoneans were known along the West Coast for their enterprise and administrative acumen. Not surprisingly, because of those excursions, Sierra Leoneans have strong

[27] ibid

ties with these other West African countries, most notably Nigeria. In the same order, one would find Sierra Leonean communities settled in many of these countries; up to the decade of the eighties, Sierra Leoneans were revered and respected all along the West Coast. Not so now!

The layout of Freetown itself was quite orderly. It was described on April 9th, 1841, as "more beautiful and magnificent than it was yesterday. From the front windows, Freetown looks as if marked upon a map on a gigantic scale; and although there is sameness and formality in the long straight streets, crossing each other at equal distances, yet the irregularity of the different buildings embowered as they all are in trees – the ships constantly in the harbour – the Bullom Shore with its shining sandy beach and perpetual verdure – the broad blue sea stretching out till bounded by the horizon – form a relief to what might otherwise be considered tame and wanting in variety."[28] This same writer maintained that "Indeed from Cape Sierra Leone upwards, the coast is beautifully diversified by little promontories, shady bays, and the lake-looking creeks…; but the most remarkable feature of all this is the mixture of cultivation and wildness".[29] There were European farms arranged in neat rows with their nicely-cut lime hedges, vineyards, gardens and pleasure grounds; while close to these bright, clean, and oasis-looking spots, on one side rise the great lone hills and to the other lie wide bleak plains called "grass fields".

The writer can attest to the fact that up to the decade of the seventies, the layout of Freetown was quite orderly and sometimes serene. What we now call the business district was a business district indeed. Central Freetown was not a residential area but populated by shops, and offices. As such after business hours usually by 5 pm in the evening, the area was completely deserted and calm reigned from what is Joaque Bridge in the West end to the Eastern Police Station

---

[28]   ibid

[29]   ibid

in the East. One seldom saw people crowding in those areas, let alone street vendors hawking their goods; nor people crowding at Garrison Street fighting to board taxis and Poda Podas to exit the city. Almost all the streets in central Freetown were lined with trees on both sides. Then it was a pleasant thoroughfare strolling down Bathurst Street, or Gloucester Street, or Wellington Street or even Garrison Street in those days. Walking down those thoroughfares one could not help but be orderly and disciplined, not because indiscipline and disorder were abhorrent to our culture, but because the atmosphere was so serene, disorder or indiscipline would create a discordant note and completely out of step with the behavioural pattern of the day. Then, hawkers were not tolerated on the streets. Traders sold their wares in stores and shops and marketplaces. But then there were other modes of gainful employment than hawking; the City Council did not collect dues from hawkers in the streets but sellers in the marketplaces.

Although the society was not as advanced then as it is today, with all the modern-day conveniences and social media advancement, life was more orderly and day-to-day living was not as chaotic as it is today. Established institutions functioned as they should function and people undertook their responsibility seriously and diligently. Nothing extra was demanded from an official to carry out his job, from those in the classrooms the teachers, to those in the administration the civil servants, including the security forces the military and the police, to those in the health sector, the doctors, nurses, porters etc, and those in the business sector the traders, etc. Whatever profession or trade one was engaged in, there was dignity in labour and one's self-esteem was not out of the window; any misstep would bring shame upon the perpetrator. Yes, in those days, self-esteem was a commodity that was highly regarded; no amount of money could purchase it.

Before the British took full control of the entire country of Sierra Leone, the administered territory was limited to the colony of Freetown; however, their interest in the surrounding areas, then known as the hinterland was limited to trade. They were not interested in its administration as this would necessitate incurring costs. Even in the Colony, they were reluctant to assume responsibility for administration for the same reason. In taking over from the Freetown Company which had administered the Colony since 1792, the raison d'etre was that the Colony should pay for its own existence. But, when the French threatened to infiltrate into the so-called "Hinterland," they changed their tune and extended their sphere of influence.

In the early days of the Colony, it was not smooth sailing for the Africans, especially as they already had British education and were familiar with their customs and traditions. The system of government established in the colony was different from all the other colonies. The British governed through a representative Governor and an Executive Council; this body made all the administrative and political decisions. In 1863, it was expanded to become a Legislative Council comprising four advisers and three or four unofficial members nominated by the Governor.[30] Those nominated by the Governor naturally were those who toed the government's line. The Africans felt aggrieved, given their emancipation, not participating in their own government; they were not given the opportunity to elect their own representatives. As one would expect, being educated and intelligent, the natives constantly agitated for representation in the conduct of their affairs. During these controversial confrontations, issues that required difficult decisions were usually referred to the Secretary of State for the Colonies for adjudication and there were many of these. Again, as was to be expected, the Colonial Office more often than not sided with the Governor. Before 1896, interaction with what was then named the hinterland was restricted to trade and keeping the peace that ultimately provided a conducive environment for this trade. Administration of the Protectorate evolved over time, given Britain's reluctance to be involved with the running of the territory. Nonetheless, this situation changed in the late 19th century through the adventurism of the French into the territories north of Sierra

---

[30]   The Krio of Sierra Leone. An Interpretive History. Akintola Wyse

Leone. The scramble for Africa galvanised the British into taking action in protecting their interests in the hinterland as they realised that a deeper hinterland was essential if the valuable port of Freetown was to remain viable. There was a danger of encirclement by the French, busily extending their colony of Guinea to the east.

The first step towards establishing a protectorate in the hinterland of Sierra Leone started in 1889 with the establishment of a Frontier Police force, comprising of European officers and both inhabitants from the Colony and the hinterland. This force was tasked with assisting the chiefs to keep order and prevent wars breaking out among neighbouring communities. They were specifically instructed not to meddle in the domestic affairs of these people. To all intent and purposes, this force did not perform these tasks efficiently and dispassionately; there were frequent complaints from the chiefs of the abuse of power and trust by this force. As a result of the poor execution of their duties recommendations were made to gradually reduce the force and appoint political agents or district commissioners to oversee the affairs of the territory. This recommendation was accepted by the Colonial Office with the stipulation that the Protectorate should be administered by Europeans only.[31] In 1896, Britain declared a protectorate over the entire region within these frontiers. This was achieved through negotiation and coercion where the situation warranted as the chiefs did not take kindly the imposition of British rule over their sovereignty. This resulted in some of them forfeiting their rights and privileges, also their absolute authority over their people.

The protectorate was administered from, but not by the Colony of Freetown, through a Native Affairs' Division. In fact, before the arrival of the British, the people of the Protectorate had their own way of administering their affairs. They had a system of Kings and Chiefs which was abolished by the British. The Protectorate Ordinances

---

[31]   The Sierra Leone Inheritance. Christopher Fyfe

of 1896 and 1897 abolished the title of King and replaced it with Paramount Chief; chiefs and kings had been formerly selected by leading members of the community, by these ordinances, they could be deposed or installed at the will of the Governor. Most of their judicial powers were removed and given to courts presided over by British District Commissioners. Disputes that did not involve the loss of liberty or life were investigated and settled by the headman, but with the right of appealing the decision to the paramount chief. Graver crimes like witchcraft, adultery, murder, and abuse of a superior, which were punishable by slavery or death were invariably referred to the paramount chief.[32]

Much has been made of and said about the resentment of the protectorate in paying taxes to the British, most notably the House tax. There are other aspects of this relationship that are not discussed in common fora. There were Europeans and people from the Colony of Freetown domiciled in various parts of the Protectorate, engaged mainly in trade and commerce. As recorded by Dr M.C.F. Easmon in the Journal of Sierra Leone Society, New Series No. 8, there was the case of a Mr John Macormack, an Irishman who spent 51 years in West Africa, engaged in Commerce. He was a successful merchant who participated in the development of the community, holding the position of a senior government official, member of the Council; several times he was the Governor's direct representative in the Protectorate for the purpose of signing treaties etc. In one way or the other, he met with the Temne chief Bai Kur Kamali Furay of Mabang and took his son, the young Yarreh under his wings. He arranged for him to be educated and even had him sent to England for education and training in the early 1860s.[33] Religious institutions, like the Church Missionary Society, the Wesleyan Methodist and

---

[32] The Journal of the Sierra Leone Society Edited by Michael Crowder. New Series No. 22 January 1968

[33] The Journal of the Sierra Leone Society. Edited by A.P. Kup; New Series No. 8, June 1957

some American Churches, were not only evangelising, but were also establishing schools in various parts of the Protectorate.[34]

During those early days, communal life revolved around trade and commerce, yet the inhabitants engaged in farming and fishing. Factories were established along water ways to process and export products from the Protectorate. For instance, at Yonnibana, Messrs Lever Brothers had erected a large factory to process oil palm. To carry out this operation, Lever Brothers were given a monopoly of twenty-one years for the extracting of palm oil and the cracking of palm kernels by machinery; an event of ground-breaking consequences: the establishment of machine power to add value to the raw materials produced in the country. As Osman Newland put it "the establishment of a great factory by Messrs Levers Brothers Ltd, completely equipped with the most modern machinery for extracting palm oil and cracking palm kernels, will however release from these two kinds of work, tens of thousands of human beings and enable them to be usefully and profitably employed in increasing progressively, the area of land under palm, kola, cacao and maize etc, and thereby swell the volume of the supply of these articles and add enormously to the wealth resources of Sierra Leone. This was in the 19th century, yet in the 21st century, we are still allowing multinationals to rape and pillage our natural resources and grappling with a policy of value-addition to create jobs and increase wealth! It is not uncommon these days to lease land to foreign exploiters for 99 years and only a pittance (a tiny fraction of the rentable value of the land), is paid to the community people while most of the proceeds of the rent find their way into the pockets of private individuals, usually elders of the community.

One of the tasks of the Paramount chiefs then was to construct and maintain what was then called "improved roads" (probably what we now call feeder roads) for which they were paid a stipend. For this they

---

[34] (To be described later), many authors have recorded this ...

used the local labour of young men in the community. It is recorded that Madam Humonyaha, who was a progressive chief engaged no fewer than 400 labourers to make up her roads for about 8 miles in the Konnoh boundary.[35] "A bridge was being built over a running stream in one town, but as much inconvenience was being experienced in getting labourers, to attend the mechanics, I enquired the reason and was told that the labourers had not been paid for their services and no allowance was given them for food. The Government considered that as the making of roads and bridges in this district in particular was for the improvement of the town, and as the chief and people were to benefit most, the chief should provide men free of cost for the Roads and Works Department[36]. Even in those days, local labour was used to construct and maintain public infrastructure. Today, there is a lot of youth unemployment, and we are still struggling to maintain our public infrastructure. We shamefully contract large foreign firms who even bring their own labour to work on our public infrastructure. While the authorities may contend that the funds used are foreign aid and loans, there are some roads that attract domestic revenues. Not casting blame on the government authorities only; there is a good supply of locally well-trained civil engineers, but they would rather sit behind a desk than forming engineering firms that can compete with these foreign firms. Their complaint? They did not have the necessary equipment to engage in this type of work. What a shame they could not begin to think out of the box about ways for mobilising resources to establish their own domestic firms.

---

[35] Sierra Leone. Its People, Products and Secret Societies. H. Osman Newland

[36] Ibid

Chapter 3

PEACEFUL CO-EXISTENCE/ TROUBLED TIMES?

In 1895, by an Order-in-council, issued by the British government, the Colony was empowered to legislate for the territories around it; and in 1896, the Colony proclaimed this territory to be a British Protectorate governed from the Colony. Put together, the Colony and the Protectorate closely correspond to what is now present-day Sierra Leone.[37]

Even before the marriage of the Protectorate and Colony, the political development of Sierra Leone had not been a smooth ride. There is evidence that the British administration deliberately fostered divisions between ethnic groups, between Colony and Protectorate.[38] The indigenous peoples did not accept easily, the imposition of British rule over their affairs. They were viewed as foreigners who had scant respect for their culture and traditions. Many of these were abolished and "foreign systems" imposed on them. As a consequence, there were many incendiary events some resulting in brutal conflicts between the British and the local people. The most famous/notorious

---

[37]   For a detailed history refer, Christopher Fyfe, A history of Sierra Leone; M. Kilson, Political change in a West African State et al

[38]   Refer "Sierra Leone. A Political History. David Harris

(depending on where you are standing) being the Hut Tax War in 1898. The then Governor declared a house tax of between 5s and 10s was to be collected annually from every household in the Protectorate. Not only was this an infringement on the authority of the chiefs but some considered it absurd that a foreign power not invited should impose a tax on property not belonging to them; a tax to be paid to the interloper by the natural owners. This was considered anathema. Did they have the right? In today's global village, these very same powers who plundered African and other nations' resources to build their empire are complaining about the influx of immigrants and refugees, whose plights are probably caused by the mess they left behind and are still plundering these countries through their technology! Many of our countries gained our independence a long time ago, but how independent are we? We are still going begging for aid, cap in hand because we have not managed our resources to benefit our nationals; we continue to collude with foreigners to plunder our economies. On the other hand, multi-nationals of these countries continue to exploit and plunder our raw materials and given investment incentives in the form of non-payment of tax, duty waivers to do so! A recently concluded research by Action Aid estimated that Africa lost over 12 billion dollars of tax revenue to these companies!

Before 1896, the territory that is now called Sierra Leone was comprised of the Colony of Freetown located on parts of the Western Area peninsula and assorted islands off the coast of south of the peninsula.[39] In 1896, the British annexed what was then known as the "hinterland" which now became the "Protectorate" and together with the Colony which came under British influence in 1787, the nation state of Sierra Leone became nascent. This marriage between the colonialist, the colony and the protectorate if it could be so described could be viewed as one of convenience more than anything else. The British established two different systems of administration. The Colony was governed by a Legislative Council that was not representative

---

[39]   Sierra Leone, A Political History. David Harris

of the governed; the head was the Governor who reported directly to the Colonial Secretary in London. The Protectorate already had their traditional system of governance, through traditional chiefs this system was used by the British to govern the Protectorate, a type of indirect rule as was used in Nigeria, but originally piloted in Sierra Leone. From the outset or from its origins, Sierra Leone was not a homogenous state, nor was it federal or unitary. Yet the Imperialists administered it as one. In the Protectorate, the traditional leaders still ruled their fiefdoms but were strictly supervised by their Colonial Masters. In the Colony, the inhabitants were governed by the imperialists who did not deem it proper that their voice should be heard, or their presence felt in the Legislative Council. In the Protectorate while the Chiefs had some control over their subjects, the Colony could not make the same claim as the Colonial rulers were aliens. The enactment of laws was not uniform; separate and different laws were enacted for the Protectorate and the Colony, for a nation considered to be united. So from the outset of the establishment of Sierra Leone as a nation state, the fundamentals of discontent had been set or prescribed. Trying to integrate the Protectorate and the Colony was a daunting task and on reflection on the path the country has followed along regional, tribal and ethnic lines if we were honest with ourselves, we cannot write about this integration as a success story. After over a hundred and twenty years of governance we the inhabitants are still perplexed in putting, region, tribe, clan first instead of the nation of Sierra Leone. Not that subsequent leaders, moreover those home-grown did not have the opportunity to put this right, instead this fragmentation, if one should term it as such, was used to further their nefarious and selfish ends.

Back to 1896, this was the nation that the Imperialists forged, a mix of disparate peoples if one should call it that. Since that time, and even before, the state of Sierra Leone was fraught with tensions among its inhabitants. In the early period, it was war between chiefdoms, vying not for territory but for slaves and riches. After nationhood, this tension manifested itself in the form of regionalism, tribalism but fortunately not religion. Somehow religion has never been a source of conflict in Sierra Leone as it is in many other countries. Muslims and Christians have co-existed peacefully. When it comes to religious co-existence, Sierra Leone is a model country, and this aspect of its development should never be down played.

Annexation of the protectorate did not stop the wars that the treaties made by the British to secure peace and access to trade routes, but merely shifted the conflict to another level. All through the years, taxes were not levied on the inhabitants to maintain an administration. Suddenly, when the British took charge, a tax, known as the hut tax was levied on the Protectorate, according to the Governors, to undertake the administration of the territory. Let it be known here that a land tax was levied on the Colony, and it was met with stiff resistance; the tax was later discontinued. Of significance here, as this action of resistance had a devastating effect on some so-called parties to the war. Like their counterpart in the Colony, the Protectorate stubbornly refused to pay this tax for property they owned especially as the British were seen as interlopers. This refusal resulted in what has now been known as the "Hut Tax War". This war was fought on two fronts, in the South where no focused leadership emerged and, in the North led by a famous chief going by the name of Bai Bureh. Crushing this rebellion was more difficult in the North than in the South; while resistance was planned in the Northern front by the resistors, the same cannot be said of the South. However, the resistance was crushed by the imperialists and the leaders in the North banished. The Krios who originally made contact with the Protectorate through trade and who also refused to pay the land tax were seen as collaborators with the British by the Protectorate and as instigators by the British since they resisted paying the land tax.

This was the kind of environment that the nation of Sierra Leone was conceived. From the start, it would appear that there was mistrust in every quarter and the British did nothing to build trust among a diversified people. If anything, the British administration deliberately fostered divisions between ethnic groups and between the Colony and the Protectorate.[40]

The society then was not as complex as it is in modern day Sierra Leone. The main economic livelihoods centred on agriculture and commerce, and this was exploited to the full by the imperial power. Evidence of this could be found in the way and manner the country's transport system developed. Now that the rulers had legal access to the interior, physical access was still lacking. To remove this constraint, a railway was built, linking the port of Freetown, the capital city to the provinces, mainly the agriculturally productive areas. Thus, the first railway in British West Africa was constructed between 1895 and 1908, beginning from Freetown, passing through Bo and Kenema and reaching its eastern terminus in Pendembu in 1908, then through to its Northern terminus at Makeni in 1914.[41] Its main function was to transport agricultural produce to Freetown for onward shipment to Europe. Passenger travel was definitely not the primary aim for constructing the railway: neither towns, nor cities were linked by rail. The trains were slow (narrow gauge) and the fares beyond the means of the local inhabitants.

During these early days of nationhood, the main concern was consolidation of power and influence on the one hand and agitation for authority over one's affairs on the other. In the case of the British, their interest was in a more orderly and peaceful society in which they can open and develop new sources of raw materials and markets for manufactured goods. The Chiefs would like to maintain authority over their subjects, while the inhabitants of the Colony were agitating for self- representation in the Legislative Council.

There was the Protectorate, largely rural and communal; one could even say rustic, but not in a pejorative way. The Paramount chief the

---

[40]   Sierra Leone. A Political History. David Harris

[41]   Ibid

traditional ruler was virtually in control of everything. The land, vast tracts of it, was held in trust for the people. On the other side was the Colony which was relatively more modern with a different land tenure system. On this side, contact with the outside world was greater, there were more schools and other institutions. According to data for 1888, out of a total population of 75,000 in the Colony, some 12,700 were occupied as merchants, traders and hawkers, and 12,317 were classified as farm labourers. Since the population density was high in the Colony, other occupations emerged to serve the specialised needs and demands attendant upon urbanisation. By the 1920s, the number of Africans employed in modern enterprises had increased. An official population census in 1921 showed that out of a total African population of 85,163, some 40,750 persons were occupied in the money economy.[42] Nonetheless, these two significantly different entities had been joined together to form a unitary state. Even the land tenure system was different. In the protectorate there was no free hold as individuals could not own land. In the Colony, land was free hold and was not communally held. This might seem insignificant. Of a total land area of 71,000 square kilometres, the Western area on which the Colony is situated is only about 500 square kilometres. Economic history has demonstrated that without reforming the land tenure system, development would scarcely occur. In Europe, Japan and elsewhere it was after the reformation of a feudal system that development was kick-started in these various countries.

The imposition of colonial rule over the protectorate was supposed to bring stability to a region that was fraught with tribal and inter-tribal wars, mainly to gain territory and collect war booty in the form of slaves that could be sold as a means of wealth creation. Treaties were concluded with the warring chiefs by the British to put an end to these wars, stop the selling of slaves, since the slave trade had already been abolished, and prepare the enabling environment for the exploitation and subsequent export to European lands of the country's

---

[42]   Political Change in a West African State. Martin Kilson

primary commodities. Over one hundred years later, the situation has not changed. Sierra Leone is still rich in natural resources, but they scarcely benefit the majority of the inhabitants. The powers that be continuing to make inimical agreements with sometimes companies of doubtful provenance to strip Sierra Leone of its assets.

In the Sierra Leone of those days, the newly constructed railway inefficient as it was then, opened up thriving market towns along the rail track, from Bauya unto Pendembu. As much as providing and improving market accessibility to productive areas, the construction and operation of the railway provided wage employment for between 2,000 and 3000 persons; since these workers were paid wages, it meant that the monetised economy was being expanded, slowly facilitating ease of transactions.

In pursuance of their mandate, if we could call it that, the imperialists established institutions and laws that would govern the behaviour of the Protectorate primarily to keep the peace between and among the different tribes and groups. They started with a so-called Frontiers' police responsible to maintain law and order but they were not to interfere in the local affairs of the inhabitants. This did not work as the authority given to the Frontier Police Force was grossly abused. This force was supervised by Europeans and comprised of Colony inhabitants. As far as the European was concerned, Power and responsibility became the prerogative of the Europeans who ruled the Colony and the Protectorate as they thought best, with little direct reference to the inhabitants' interests.

Considering the traditional structure already in existence where power (if not absolute over the people) was vested on the chiefs, initially, they benefited from the indirect rule imposed by the British and became the moneyed men in a mainly rural society; they converted these new opportunities into economic gains, while claiming as many customary privileges as possible. They claimed greater shares of state authority and transformed it into private commercial advantage.[43] For chiefs, British rule with its conditions of greater stability and the opportunity that accompanied official recognition replaced war as a means of attaining wealth status.[44]

The discovery of iron ore in the North and diamonds in the South East in the 1930s made Sierra Leone more attractive to the Colonialists. Aforetime, the British Government was reluctant to take the reins of rulership from the British Company that was running the Colony. From their view point, the territory was of little economic importance. The thinking was, Sierra Leone did not have the capacity to pay for its administration which was not only unfair but was far from the truth. One could say that this view developed out of ignorance. Strangely, at the time, other colonial territories in the West Indies and the sub-continent of Asia, were not paying for their administration; administrative costs were borne by the British Government.

Once these valuable minerals were discovered, they became game changers. In 1931, the Sierra Leone Development Company (DELCO), was formed to exploit the Marampa iron ore mines in Port Loko in the North. As a consequence of this discovery, a 52-mile railway was constructed to take the ore to Pepel, for shipping out of the country. Interestingly, the gauge of this railway was wider and assumedly more efficient in transporting rolling stock than the railway transporting agricultural produce from the South East.

In the South and East, alluvial diamonds were discovered in 1930, leading to changes in the socio-economic profile of the country. As usual, with haste, the imperialists proceeded to conclude long-term country-wide deals with a De Beers subsidiary, Sierra Leone Selection Trust (SLST). Since the diamonds could literally be plucked from the

---

[43]   Corruption and State Politics in Sierra Leone. William Reno

[44]   Ibid

ground (alluvial), both the company and the Colonial Government had a hard time in controlling the mining of these precious stones.

The discovery of diamonds changed the consciousness of the country's inhabitants once its value was known. As the deposits were alluvial, it did not take much to harvest the gem, so it was like a free for all; and many who would have remained in poverty, if they were lucky enough discovered instant wealth. On the other hand, those not so fortunate toiled and toiled, sometimes for a lifetime without finding a single carat of diamond. Another part of the downside was that each parcel of land in the diamondiferous area was subject to rampant and uncontrolled excavation in search of this "forever diamond" resulting in environmental degradation.

As the land tenure system predominating in these areas vested ownership in the hands of the chiefs for the use of the inhabitants of those areas, the British sought their assistance to control this rampant land degradation. Apart from legislating on the exploitation and marketing of this precious gem, they increased the incentives given to the chiefs to administer their chiefdoms. In an unsuccessful attempt to bring these chiefs to their way of thinking, their official incomes were increased from 500 pounds sterling per annum to 10,000 pounds sterling per annum, a twenty-fold increase![45] However this enticement did not succeed in reducing illicit mining of diamonds.

Suddenly, a territory that posed fiscal challenges to the British in its administration became an extremely viable prospect. These fiscal gains brought about by the discovery and mining of diamonds brought along other challenges, especially to the authority of the imperial power over the traditional rulers, more especially the Kono chiefs. According to traditional laws some of which were acceptable to the British, these minerals were the property of the chief and the people. Considering the wealth and power reposed in these gems, the authorities would not tolerate that countervailing power to exist

---

[45]   Sierra Leone. A Political History. David Harris

alongside. In response to this phenomenon, the Colonial government embarked on a series of reforms to contain the authority of the traditional rulers and also appropriate ownership of the country's mineral wealth.

Earlier in the century, the Syrians had succeeded in infiltrating the trade sector of the country, selling consumable wares like beads etc. The author could remember in those halcyon days, the terminology "coral", the name given to those Syrians engaging in the trading of beads, clothing etc. At the discovery of diamonds, they widened their area of influence into the diamond trade.

While the foreigners were benefiting from this windfall, it was doubtful how much the country in general and Kono in particular benefitted. To prevent Sierra Leonean from engaging in the diamond business, the Colonial Government signed a 99 year lease agreement with SLST giving them exclusive mineral rights over the entire country. At that time, they were required to pay a 26% tax on net profits. Presently mining companies are required to pay a 3% tax on profits to the people of Sierra Leone for exploiting her mineral wealth. Can we really say the nation is benefiting from her wealth? Looking at the parlous state of our economic and social life, it is beyond imagination that Sierra Leoneans are still wallowing in the depth of poverty.

Chiefs' economic power and control were further strengthened by the Colonial Government as chiefs' customary modernisation proceeded. The Sierra Leone Protectorate Nature Law ordinance of 1905 sanctioned chiefs' rights to customary tribute but upheld as mandatory chiefs' rights to forced labour. Would this be amazing or perplexing? Consider the British who were at the vanguard of the slavery abolition movement, condoning the custom of forced labour in a territory they governed. In fact, it was embarrassing to say the least that although slavery and the slave trade had been abolished, they still condoned the trade in slaves among chiefdoms in Sierra

Leone. Fancy, Sierra Leone in those days was used as naval base by the British to attack African Slave ships on the African Coast to liberate those Africans who were being shipped to be sold as slaves in America!

In any case, the maintenance of some of these customary rights by colonial rulers enhanced chiefs initial advantage over other segments of the population under the money or exchange economy. Chiefs' customary rights to tribute and labour were readily convertible from wealth in kind to money and capital.

Still on the modernisation of Sierra Leone Society, on the educational sphere, whether by chance or design, the colonial government tended to favour the so-called pagan south and east against the Islamised north. In consequence, educational institutions proliferated more in the south than in the north, as both the government and to a large extent the missionaries concentrated their effort in the areas of education evangelism. Slowly, the protectorate was being transformed from a communal society into a modern one. Contact with the outside world, through education, trade and the development of the mining sector, all helped to create a modern society. Notwithstanding this movement, present day Sierra Leone especially in the provincial areas, remains largely rural and undeveloped.

In the colony, the tension between the imperial power and the inhabitants was intense. From the onset, there was no fraternisation between them. In fact, it could be contended that the British administration deliberately fostered divisions between ethnic groups and between the colony and the protectorate. Strengthening "tribal patriotism" was indeed an aim; attempts were made to portray the Krio, as 'degenerate' and an interloper in the protectorate. [46] At the time, many Krios perceived the Colonial Government as widening the gap between the Protectorate and the colony. In the Protectorate, the native was instructed that the land was his, and that his "brother"

---

[46] *Sierra Leone. A Political History. David Harris*

THE DECLINE AND FALL OF THE ATHENS OF WEST AFRICA

the Krio was a degenerate creature, a man whose pretensions had no foundations and an interloper.[47] Then as now, some Sierra Leoneans considered the Krios as descendants of the Black Poor and slaves, this term being used pejoratively. Unfortunately, these views still pervade our society, but we tend not to accept or confront it. Even some policy documents, the Krios are referred to as "non-natives" and the felt view is that the Krios do not have the right of primacy in the land they have settled for so long ago. Those of us who agitate as such should return to our history books to research who were the original inhabitants of Sierra Leone. They would be surprised! What they failed to realise was that one cannot run away or hide from one's past, at the same time the past should not hold back one's development and enlightenment as time progresses. Notwithstanding their ancestry, even in the early days of the settlement of the Colony, the Krios were a force to be reckoned with, not in spite of, but despite their ancestry. In all probability the White man cannot conceive that a people that they treated as slaves for centuries could match their intelligence and become proficient in many of their skills and professions. There was the rub and perhaps the origin of racism. It is the writer's view that those who discriminate do it not out of superiority but out of fear, trying to protect some aspects of their territory.

The relationship between the imperial power and the governed in the Colony was more accommodating than friendly, both sides had to work together to achieve their respective ends, divergent as they were. While the British was pushing for mercantilism, the Krios wanted to develop a nation and take responsibility for their governance.

Given this situation, as educated and experienced in Western values as the Krios were, they faced an uphill task in securing jobs that were commensurate with their skills and training. Even when they were professionally qualified, sometimes better qualified than their Colonisers, they were refused employment in the colonial

---

[47]   Sierra Leone Inheritance. Christopher Fyfe OUP 1964

41

administration; when employed it was on a level lower than what they deserved. Whether in the medical field, the legal system or even in governance, their skills were unrecognised, and a less qualified Colonial was given the job over the heads of the Africans. The Colonial to salve his conscience always hid under the imagined (by them) incompetence of the African.[48]

Discouraging as the situation was, it dampened neither the spirit nor the enthusiasm of the Krios to blaze their trail abroad and within. In response to or as a reaction to the treatment meted out by the Colonials, they spread their tentacles far and wide in West Africa and beyond.

In those days, the question of good governance did not arise; the imperial power was imperious in every sense, and nobody dared question their authority. Decisions were taken without consulting the local populace, they were only responsible to the Government in England which was omniscient and omnipotent. Being the imperial power with all their might and resources at their disposal, they were the lords who must be obeyed. Consequently, to vent their feelings and bring to the attention of the governors that they had mental faculties and feelings, the local inhabitants resorted to 'pressure groups to champion their causes. They might not have succeeded given the imperious nature of the colonial government, or succeeded only partially, but they were laying the foundation for what today is known as "civil society". Various groups emerged between the mid-19th century and the First World War, to question the assumption of colonial rule and to press for participation in their own governance.[49] An interest group known as the Sierra Leone Mercantile Association was founded in 1851, aiming to play a constitutional role in electing the first African to sit in the Legislative Council. It did not succeed

---

[48] See Akintola Wyse's "The Krio of Sierra Leone. An interpretive History for a detailed analysis

[49] ibid

entirely but, it metamorphosed into the Sierra Leone Chamber of Commerce which still exists today.[50] The Sierra Leone Bar Association, an outspoken critic of the colonial government was formed in 1899 with the aim of looking after the interests of its members, and to strengthen the legal profession in discharging its functions responsibly and effectively. The African Civil Servants Association came into existence in 1908 to protect the interests of its members.

To facilitate the administration of this nascent state, the colonial administration had to pass laws to safeguard the security of the state and its people. From the onset, the colonial power treated the Colony and the Protectorate as distinct entities, no matter what our perceptions were and are. The writer is of the belief that the Colonials for their own benefit/advantage, pitted one entity against the other. It has been over 160 years now and we are still at each other's throat. The British used regionalism to advance their cause, whatever that was, now at this present time, our politicians employ tribalism to gain political and economic mileage. Shall we ever get a leader and president like the late Julius Nyerere of Tanzania that can effect this transformation from tribal to national onwards to patriotism? Should we as Sierra Leoneans be honest with ourselves, it is a doubtful prospect, but this may be a pessimistic view. In those early days, the Colony had its Legislative Council while the Protectorate had its Council of Chiefs; the Colony had an executive arm, while the Protectorate had its native administration; the Colony had its Judiciary, while the Protectorate hade its Native Courts. From the onset, we had the belief that Sierra Leone was a unitary state because the British treated it as such, or wanted us to believe that it was so, while in reality, the country was administered like a federal entity.

---

[50] Ibid

Chapter 4

TROUBLED TIMES

With the foregoing can we say then that with the stroke of a pen people with different backgrounds, from different origins, with different cultures, were brought together as a nation? According to the author(s) of "The Rising Sun", since the arrival of the first black settlers, Sierra Leone's history has been distinguished by two predominant features: the need to integrate and peacefully unite an ethnically diverse population, and a desire to control and monitor oppression by external forces. For over 200 years, the checking of these destructive tendencies was not possible. The vice-like grip of the colonial masters and the ravaging effects of tribalism and prejudice acted against the emergence of Sierra Leone as a truly free and independent nation[51] In a similar vein, Solomon Pratt in his book, "Jolliboy", an autobiography did state that "the British system of colonial administration had failed to engender homogeneity of nationhood among these different groups after the attainment of independence.[52] An order made on the 24th August 1895 under the Foreign Jurisdiction Act gave the Legislature of the Colony the authority to make laws for the Protectorate people. Between 1896

---

[51]   The Rising Sun. Researched and written under the direction of the APC Secretariat

[52]   Jolliboy. A Most Un-Ordinary African Boy. Solomon A.J. Pratt

and 1897, a series of ordinances passed by the Legislative Council established British jurisdiction over the Protectorate and also made the necessary provisions for its administration. So what do we have here? A Colony that had been under British rule for over one hundred years and a Protectorate that was just coming under British jurisdiction governed like a unitary and harmonious entity; this, as we know now, was far from the truth. The body or institution governing this entity was neither representative of the people of the Protectorate, nor those of the Colony. On the other hand, through a system of indirect rule, the Protectorate was ruled by their chiefs and they had some authority over certain customary laws. The Colony was governed directly through the Colonial Legislative council imposed by the British and governed by British laws and jurisprudence. This difference in administration and laws exposed colonial prerogatives and deficiencies. Although fully imbibed with democratic tenets and principles, the Colony had nothing to do with chieftaincy. On the other hand, administration in the Protectorate was left to a great extent, in the hands of the chiefs. The Legislative Council could make laws for the Protectorate but in a display of expediency, the chiefs were allowed to legislate for their subjects. A confusing twin track legal system with many regional perturbations were created.[53] Due to this twin track approach, one is left with a dualistic land tenure system: free-hold in the Western area, and in the Provinces where ownership is more or less communal, in a system where land cannot be bought or sold. Today, we are experiencing some of the consequences such as, overcrowding in Freetown coupled with environmental degradation, while many land areas in the outlying provincial villages are virtually deserted. In 1901, the Colonial government enacted the Protectorate Ordinance, in 1903, they passed the Protectorate Courts Jurisdiction Ordinance and the Protectorate Law Ordinance in 1905; these laws were made exclusively for the governance of the Protectorate. This state of affairs definitely was a recipe for confusion, distrust and disillusionment, especially among the people of the Colony.

---

[53]   Sierra Leone. A Political History. David Harris

If the broad aims of the Colonialist were philanthropic, then they would have made a considerable effort to unite the peoples of the Colony and the Protectorate. But no! They had other motives; the repercussions of which are still being felt in our society; fermenting discord and exploiting the outcome to their own advantage. At the time, taking into account the local conditions, it is the writer's viewpoint that their main concern should have focused primarily on reconciling the differences of both entities so that an atmosphere of trust and togetherness would have been the hallmark of our society; that would have laid a solid foundation for the development and progress of our country, Sierra Leone. Perhaps, the violence and indiscipline that permeate our communities today would not have occurred. The aim could have been union between the classes and the masses, union between the high and the low, between the rich and the poor, and mark well, between the people of the Colony and the Protectorate.[54] Nevertheless, this is the system of government our Colonial masters imposed upon our country Sierra Leone, and after a long period of colonial rule, and over 60 years of being an independent and Republican state, Sierra Leone is still fragmented should we be honest with ourselves! What more evidence do we need, rather than the ethnical divide and violence that permeated our recent presidential and Parliamentary elections! Politics is a continuous activity in Africa as even when the dusts had settled, the governors and the governed continue with politics instead of focusing on governance. To hear phrases like "dis nar we turn" (this is our own time), "dis nar wi government" meaning the government of the party and not the government for the country, is very common. In the same vein, the incumbent government, instead of focusing on governance and the task at hand, would spend time on vilifying the actions of the ousted government as if the voters were not already cognisant of their failings! Why else did they vote them out of office?

---

[54]   H. C. Bankole Bright and Politics in Colonial Sierra Leone, 1919 – 1958. Akintola J. G. Wyse

Neither the people of the Protectorate, nor the inhabitants of the Colony were satisfied with this type of arrangement, thus, this resistance or abhorrence to alien rule gave rise to the formation of local, national and cross-country groupings. One such group was the National Congress of West Africa (NCWA) seeking to bring together, Africans from the four British Colonies of the Gambia, The Gold Coast (Ghana), Nigeria and Sierra Leone, to advance their cause in the British Empire, agitating for better treatment and equal status for all British subjects. The idea of this Congress was first mooted in 1914, but the beginning of the First World War in 1914 interrupted its solidification. In 1920, this became a reality. As far as the founding fathers of the Sierra Leone chapter were concerned, membership was drawn, primarily from the Krios, leading to questioning the representation of this group as a mouthpiece for the inhabitants of the entire country. It was also the opinion of many that it was an elitist society as its composition was drawn mainly from the professional classes and religious bodies. In its defence, members maintained that they tried reaching out to the people of the Protectorate but were constrained by accessibility and the weather.

In a similar vein, the Committee of Educated Africans (CEA), was formed by the People from the Protectorate to bring their needs to the attention of the Colonial administration. Initially, the CEA formulated "its declaration of aims, drawn up as an address to welcome the Governor, Sir Alexander Ransford Slater in his familiarisation tour of meeting the people. In the terms of the Colony-Protectorate division, they wanted representation in the Legislature and development for their people. In welcoming the Governor in 1922, they averred that among other things, without the consent of the 200 ruling houses no elective franchise should be granted to a handful of Colonial (Colony) Africans on behalf of Protectorate Aborigines. Moreover, when requesting that educated persons who were not chiefs should be chosen as Protectorate representatives, the CEA had in mind previously those who were related to traditional rulers. They also observed that Educated Aborigines were few and far between in the Protectorate, but in the Southern Province (Mende Country), competent candidates could even be obtained to directly represent the still unrepresented 1,350,000 Aborigines in the Protectorate. To keep the Legislature continuously supplied with qualified aboriginal members, the sons and nominees of Protectorate chiefs, at that time, attending the Bo School should be trained for it before finishing their course.

In his response, Governor Slater cast blame on the Krios, saying that they were responsible for their plight and not the Colonial government. In this, the governor was being disingenuous or economical with the truth. Of course the Krios were not in government and neither were they the legislators nor the policy makers. That there was no foundation for this response was attested by the fact that the Krios themselves were complaining about the disparaging behaviour of the British towards them, and giving a deaf ear to their situation.

Illustrating the dis-ingenuity of the British, while acceding to the demands of the C.E.A., two years previously, the Krios requested elected representation but were told that those who made the request were unrepresentative of the people. The Colonial authorities retorted that they were self-appointed and not chosen by the people so could not act on behalf of the people. On the face of it, this was quite proper especially in the confines of democracy and good governance. But where the double standards manifested was when Governor Slater accepted the demands of the C.E.A. They were not chosen by the people and not representative of the Protectorate.[55]

Given this prevailing state of affairs, the seeds for suspicion and distrust were already being sown before the amalgamation of the Colony and the Protectorate. While some in the Colony deemed it unfitting for the Legislature to have representation from people who at the time were deemed not to be British subjects, there were

---

[55] Bankole Bright and Colonial Politics in Sierra Leone 1919 – 1958. Akintola J.G. Wyse

48

those in the C.E.A. who were of the opinion that the people in the Colony should not legislate for them. They had always felt that their interests were not being looked into by the Krios who seemed to be enjoying all the benefits from the wealth of the country, two-thirds of which were produced by the Protectorate, the deprived and greater part of the country. So what they demanded as of right was direct representation for the people of the Protectorate. They wanted representation in the Legislative Council and more development for their people.

These were legitimate claims one cannot gainsay, but the British in their duplicity, painted the Krios as being responsible for the plight of the people in the Protectorate, which was very far from the truth. From the onset, the Colonial power had sought to drive a wedge between the two constituent parts of the country, a scenario that would allow them free access to exploiting and plundering the country's resources. Harris asserted that there was evidence the British administration deliberately fostered divisions between Colony and Protectorate.[56] Under their dual system of administration, for example, the protectorate elements in the Colony who satisfied the voting criteria could vote for Colony representatives; not so in the Protectorate! Krio inhabitants in the Protectorate were disallowed from exercising their democratic right. At best, their legal status was nebulous. The Krios it should be noted had every reason to ally themselves with the Protectorate leadership. After all, they had innumerable economic interests in the Protectorate and had long sought to protect those interests. Thus it would make sound sense not to antagonise the protectorate leaders. Unfortunately, these interests were a major cause for the Protectorate leaders' opposition to the Sierra Leone National Congress, especially the Chiefs who frequently played havoc with the political impotence of Krio businessmen in the

---

[56] Sierra Leone: A Political History. David Harris

Protectorate, exploiting them at will[57]. Of course these Protectorate leaders would contend that they were protecting the interests of their people. Considering the fact that these two entities were brought together, did the Colonial government engage in breeching this divide in the interest of nationalism, no. Instead they used it to set the Protectorate against the Colony, all in the name of imperialism. Under this prevailing mindset, any move by either side to foster rapprochement and togetherness was viewed with suspicion.

Although it may seem to readers of history that the two groups that is, the C.E.A. and the S.L.N.C. were only concerned with parochial interests, there were those on both sides of the divide that recognised the advantages of coming together as a unit to fight the common enemy, the Colonial power. Few overtures were made to bring these two entities together but whatever successes achieved were short lived. One such occasion was the invitation by A.E. Tuboku-Metzger, a Vice-President of the S.L.N.C. to the leaders of the C.E.A. to join forces and support each others' claims on the Colonial government. This invitation was not honoured, but another grouping, the Sierra Leone Aborigines Society emerged, comprising of Protectorate and Colony leaders. This society was committed to establishing intercourse among all classes of Aborigines to further their interests, be it political, educational or social, and to promote their welfare.[58] Unfortunately, this was not an homogeneous group thus, when ever a constitutional conflict or political differences arose between the Africans and the Colonial authority, regional, tribal or ethnic considerations would overshadow issues between the governors and the governed. And uppermost in the minds of the Protectorate group was the disparity between the Colony and the protectorate. Consequently, redressing this disparity was made a condition for supporting actions put forward by the Krios against the Colonial

---

[57] Bankole Bright and Colonial Politics in Sierra Leone 1919 – 1958. Akintol J.G. Wyse

[58] Ibid

government. On the other hand, the Krios resisted the inclusion of chiefs in the Legislative Council as they were considered the puppets of the Colonial power.

At this time, the idea of trade-off was of no consequence as each group stuck to its position, thus furthering the distrust between both parties. Upon this mindset, the constitutional provisions of 1924 were made.

In this context, the 1924 Constitution sought to address apparently, the problems posed by the Colony and the Protectorate; did it?

On representation, the Legislative Council was expanded to 12 official and 10 un-official members. Until 1924, the Legislature was comprised of only 6 official members including, the Governor and 4 nominated un-official members, 3 of whom were Africans, and the other European. In the new expanded Legislative Council of 1924, of the 10 un-official members, 2 were to represent commercial banking and general European interests; the remaining 8 were distributed as follows: 3, elected Africans and 2 nominated Africans representing the Colony; 3 nominated Paramount chiefs from the South, East and the North, representing the protectorate. Of note is the fact that as early as 1924, democratic principles were being introduced to Sierra Leone. Of course, there was no universal adult suffrage yet as voting was restricted only to the Colony, and even at that, not every adult was given the franchise to vote. This franchise was given to elite Africans only on the criteria of being literate, the owner or occupier of any house, warehouse, counting house, shop, store or any building in the electoral district of which the annual value is not less than ten pounds in the urban electoral district, and six pounds in the rural electoral district. On the other hand, an adult with an annual income of one hundred pounds in the urban electoral district or sixty pounds in the rural electoral district was qualified to vote.

This revised constitution provided a platform for both the Protectorate and Colony representatives to formally debate topical issues, especially those of more relevance to their own welfare; indeed there was no shortage of these as to be expected, individuals from different backgrounds and with different agendas. The real power though resided in the hands of the Colonialists. Decision making rested with the Executive Council and no Sierra Leonean was a member of that Council then, it was the monopoly of the Europeans.

Topical issues ranged from the exorbitant salaries paid to European Civil servants, who were deemed by the Krios in the Colony to be less qualified and less experienced, to the discriminatory and disrespectful behaviour of the District Commissioners to the Chiefs.[59] There was also the issue of unfair trade practices meted out to Krio Businesses. While European firms received subsidies and other incentives from the Colonial government, a deaf ear was given to local businesses for these same incentives. As a result, the domestic enterprise could not survive in this atmosphere of unfair competition. In modern day parlance, they were not provided with a level playing field. Many local enterprises were engaged in printing, manufacturing of agriculture products such as sugar, tobacco, coffee, soap and even brandy and rum, yes that's correct brandy and rum! No trade incentives were given to these businesses to support and sustain their production. If anything, they were discouraged from running their enterprises. A case in point. A Sierra Leonean ventured into the business of chocolate manufacturing, selling cheaply in the domestic market. Noticing the demand for this product in the domestic market, the Colonial government invited the British firm, Cadbury to export chocolate to Sierra Leone, which they did at a considerably lower price than the price of the local producer. Of course, there was only one outcome, the local product was kicked out of the market.[60]

---

[59] An exhaustive narrative can be found in Kitson's Political Change in a West African State.

[60] Ibid

Not surprisingly, the Protectorate Representatives used their position in the Legislative Council to advance their own interests. They agitated for more posts in the Civil Service, more schools, roads, health and medical services. They themselves experienced the discrimination and disrespect by the District Commissioners. In this light, they agitated for limited self-government. Just like their counterparts in the Colony, they wanted a free hand in the running of their affairs.

The representatives of the Colony and the Protectorate did not present a united front in their approach to agitating with the Colonial authority. Each group protected its tuff which sometimes gave the impression that they were antagonists. This state of play was of course not lost on the British. If anything, it was the perception of the Krios that the government was widening rather than seeking to bridge the gap between the inhabitants of the Colony and the Protectorate. It was their belief that the inhabitants of the Protectorate were instructed that the land was theirs and that the inhabitants of the Colony that is the Krios were a degenerate people whose pretensions had no foundation and who were interlopers. When differences occurred between the two groups of people, the Krios were seen to be the aggressors; the Colonial government used every opportunity to portray the Krios as strangers in the Protectorate.[61]

Two years after the enactment of the new constitution that sought to give more representation to the inhabitants of the country, a strike occurred in the Railway in 1926. The core reason for the strike was the discriminatory practices of management. African workers were treated quite differently from their European counterparts.[62] For example, before an African was promoted, he was subjected to a test; not so for the European, never mind the qualification and experience. The Freetown community was solidly for the strikers which angered

---

[61] Sierra Leone Inheritance. Christopher Fyfe. OUP 1964

[62] Exhaustively narrated in Joe A.D. Allie's "A New History of Sierra Leone

the Colonial government. The Governor Sir A.R. Slater felt that it was a widespread defiance of discipline and revolt against authority.[63] How was this aberration dealt with?

The Colonial Secretary to the Governor, proposed that as a mark of their displeasure with the unworthy behaviour of the entire Krio community, the Colonial government should suspend for an indefinite period, that part of the constitution which provided for an elected element in the Legislative Council.[64] Although the Governor thought it harsh, thus not giving sway to that advice, a harsh punishment was meted upon the strikers, so as to get at the Krio community. Pensionable employees who had participated in the strike were sacked and the salaries of many other workers reduced. There was a Railway Workers' Union. This was also banned.[65] Also, the Freetown City Council which had been in existence since 1893, was dissolved because the governor felt council workers lacked the requisite experience. Apparently, the Freetown City Council was the victim of a colonial government that concentrated authority in the hands of the white and resented the survival of a municipality run by Africans. Successive governors regularly presented it as a scapegoat along with the whole Krio community for disturbances in Freetown, notably the 1919 anti-Syrian riots and the 1926 railway strike. In 1925, financial malpractices in the council were disclosed and some officials were prosecuted. The following year the Mayor, editor of the leading newspaper in Sierra Leone, Weekly News and a highly respected public figure was charged with conspiracy to defraud, along with the Town Clerk; and the City treasurer was given a nine month prison sentence. Then on the recommendation of a

---

[63] Political Change in a West African State. Martin Kilson

[64] ibid

[65] A New History of Sierra Leone. Joe A.D. Alie

Commission of Inquiry, the City Council was dissolved and replaced by a Municipal Board.[66]

Indeed, the Colonial administration toyed with idea of trade unionism for a brief while, but when the activities of the originator, the leading agitator for workers' right did not go down well with colonial policy, the movement suffered a natural death when the leaders were incarcerated.

In 1938, I.T.A. Wallace Johnson returned to Sierra Leone from his travels abroad to form the Sierra Leone Youth League (SLYL), a branch of the larger body, the West African Youth League (WAYL), aiming to champion the cause of workers' rights. The Sierra Leone chapter i.e. the SLYL, focused its energy on mobilising urban labour, ensuring equitable distribution of the country's wealth and also unite the people of the Colony and the Protectorate. Imagine, while a European expatriate fresh from school was paid a salary of four hundred pounds per annum, excluding perks, an African with 30 years or more experience was paid not more than three hundred and seventy-two pounds annually, as chief clerk.[67] Working conditions were poor and abysmal and the treatment of African workers by their European counterparts disrespectful, to say the least. The Sierra Leone Youth League took an exception to these conditions and behaviour consequently, they mobilised the workers to form trade unions in order to agitate for better conditions of service and humane treatment of African employees. Indeed, the call to "arms" gave rise to the emergence of a few trade unions, such as, the Public Workers Union, the All Seamen's Union and the Diamond Workers' Union. True to form, the Colonial administration did not recognise these unions, nevertheless, the unions undertook the task of collective bargaining with the employers. Unfortunately, not much

---

[66] Article by Dr. Akintola Wyse. Published in Africa. Journal of the International African Institute. Cambridge University Press. 2011

[67] Ibid

was achieved as was to be expected, the employers and government were of the same ilk, they were cut from the same cloth. A series of labour unrest followed. Given this unstable scenario, coupled with the radical stance taken by the movement's founder, I.T.A. Wallace Johnson was imprisoned together with other founding members of the SLYL at the onset of the Second World War. In truth, their cause and effort put into trade unionism was not lost, as in 1942, the British Government sent a trade unionist to Sierra Leone to organise the Labour Movement.[68]

It was not only Wallace Johnson and his Youth League who opposed the unpopular policies of the Colonial administration. The African members of the Legislative Council pursued vigorously, the cause of the Africans, respect of their dignity, fair and equitable treatment of African workers and rationalisation of their condition and service in the administration. At this point in time, representation was not according to political parties, but more probably according to the regional divide, i.e., the Colony versus the Protectorate. Nevertheless, the constructive opposition mounted up by the African representatives in the Legislative Council resulted in some constitutional concessions acceded to by the Government. In November 1938, a Standing Finance Committee consisting of more African members than European members was established to monitor the supplementary expenditure of the government after the budget had been approved. Then in 1943, the Executive Council, which was only comprised of European members admitted two Africans into their ranks.

Admittedly, the decision by the Colonial powers to integrate the Colony and the Protectorate was not only fraught with great challenges, but the process changed the political landscape of the country. It is widely held that the process followed undermined the dominance of the Krios in the political and business space of the nation-state. This has been a topical issue since. What we cannot

---

[68]   Ibid

escape from is the fact that given that modernisation was coming into the country through democratisation, it was only a question of time but the landscape of the country would have changed anyway. As we say in this part of the World, politics is numbers. In a democracy it is not that ability goes out through the window, but the driving force is popularity and not ability.

Chapter Five

TACTICAL BATTLE LINES – POLITRICS, WHO WON?

Dare I say the 1924 Constitutional amendment pitted the pro and antagonists at each other's throat? If so, who was the enemy? It beats the imagination that the common enemy was not the imperialist power that logic demanded, but the representative factions of the Colony and the Protectorate. From the onset the battle lines were drawn, each faction guarding its own "territory". On the Colony side, there were strong personalities like Dr Bankole Bright, Beoku Betts, J.C.O. Crowther etc, while on the Protectorate bench, there were men like Dr Milton Margai, Chief Caulker, Chief Kamanda Bongay etc.

Imagine a legislature where the representatives instead of working for the building of a coherent, homogeneous nation were watching the interests of their tribe or region. Granted, at this point in time, one would doubt whether the Legislature, especially the African representatives had the authority to effectively legislate for the country. The impression given was that the representatives were deeply divided on regional/tribal lines which unfortunately played into the hands of the Imperialists. According to Siaka Stevens in his book, "What Life Has Taught Me", the neglected majority of Sierra Leoneans in the hinterland were beginning to kick, not just against the

British mastery, but also against the relatively over-privileged status of the coastal Colony. Continuing, he stated that "tribal antagonism was always just below the surface and sometimes it broke through to make fissures in Protectorate unity. He however stated that "the crucial issues among Sierra Leoneans were between Colony and Protectorate".

The Protectorate bench felt the representatives of the Colony had no interests in their development, only concerned with activities that had a colony flavour. On the other hand the Colony bench was not comfortable with the representatives of the Protectorate, citing all kinds of differences, ranging from literacy, not being British subjects and such like. Current at the time, while the people in the Colony were more literate, they were fewer in number. Contrarily, the people in the Protectorate though less educated had greater numbers. And as we have come to realise, democracy is numbers, and not ability or education, at least in this part of Africa. At that time the phrase was not yet coined, but that was what the representatives were pushing. Together with the British, they were of the opinion that the natural wealth of the country was concentrated in the Provinces, logically, a greater portion of the cake was demanded. They were also of the opinion that the Colony as a state was not viable. On hindsight, we know that that premise would not hold. States like Singapore, other small Pacific island states have survived on fewer resources!

The slogan "democracy is numbers" did not originate in modern day politics. As far back as the 1920s that was realised by the Protectorate representatives in the Legislature. They stoutly refused to buckle under the arguments of the Colony representatives parroting the mantra "we have the numbers and the resources. The feeble challenge by the Colony on the basis of literacy did noy sit well with the Colonialist power.

Given this scenario, the Protectorate representatives pushed for regional development, the construction of schools, health facilities and good roads etc, all legitimate claims as the Protectorate was so far behind the Colony as far as development was concerned. Fast forward almost a century, given that Sierra Leone has enjoyed over sixty years of independence from the colonial yoke, how much has that scenario changed? Of course it has changed. The regions are still playing catch-up with the Western area, with urbanisation becoming a severe constraint on the amenities of Freetown. In spite of the census data, the population in the Capital has topped a million, with the city being overcrowded, idle youths plying their trade of diplomatic harassment "poppay you borbor day yah", waiting for some largesse to drop into their hands. At the other end, villages in the regions remain sparsely populated and relatively backward. It is even possible that the plight of those people then were better than the plight of the current inhabitants.

Consider, given these legitimate claims by the Protectorate, had both sides sat down to reach a consensus of all the issues and challenges that the country was facing and presented a united front before the Colonialists, what trajectory Sierra Leone would have taken? But no each group was pushing their own agenda at the expense of a consensus. Quite an ideal environment for the Colonial government's strategy of "divide and rule".

Immediately after the First World War, prices of commodities shot up and the condition of the wage-earner deteriorated. This resulted in another strike by railway workers and rioting against the Syrian traders who were thought to be the main culprits of the price hike; notably, they hoarded rice, creating an artificial scarcity of the country's staple and selling at exorbitant prices. There was a lot of looting and destruction of their businesses. It was also felt, rightly or wrongly that the Syrians were displacing Krio businessmen in the market place. Interesting really. Fast forward a century and a half, our economy is now in the hands of foreigners, be they Chinese, Indians, Lebanese claiming to be citizens, but seldom participate in civic activities, they are content to sit back and exploit our resources and our people. It is the writer's belief that when Sierra Leoneans take charge of their economy, poverty will be reduced, the national cake will be shared fairly, corruption will be minimised and Sierra Leone will take its rightful place in the global village. Then and only then we will refrain from going cap in hand begging for hand-outs from the developed nations many of which are not as resource-endowed as Sierra Leone. Then also we will seize the initiative of determining what we want Sierra Leone to be like, from the World Bank, the IMF, the European Union and of course, the Chinese who are now our god-father, mercilessly exploiting our resources, willy nilly!

To continue our story, the strike was called off and the rioters quelled, at a cost. The Colonial government in 'their wisdom' accused the Krios as the instigators of the strike, meting out severe punishment to some of them. The Freetown City Council was fined five thousand pounds and believe it or not, some of the Syrian traders were compensated.[69]

Similarly, the new constitution was tested no sooner it was passed by a series of actions that occurred in the Colony. To quote from Joe A.D. Alie's book, A New History of Sierra Leone, "barely a year after the introduction of the 1924 Constitution, serious political problems erupted between the Krio and the Colonial administration. Note the narrative given, not Sierra Leoneans or the people, but a segment of the population. The point being made here is, since the beginning of our colonial history our mind set was not national but regional and tribal. At the time, the Protectorate Assembly was not yet in existence, but the Legislative Council consisted of both Colony and Protectorate members. The reference made here was to the Railway strike of 1926. All be it the railway was a national asset; by 1926, the railway had reached its terminus at Pendembu in the East passing through Moyamba and Bo in the South, and also the terminus of Makeni in the North. The author is also convinced that the workers then did not come from only one tribe, the Krios.

---

[69] Adequately treated by Joe A.D. Alie in "A New History of Sierra Leone".

We have made a lot of noise and are still making a lot of noise about democracy and good governance. These are terms or facets that are rammed down our throats by the West. More importantly, aid from their governments are linked to democratic good governance when it suits them. Most of the oil rich countries, especially in the Middle East are not aid dependent like us in Africa, but when it comes to doing business, democratic good governance never features in the negotiations. In this case, "what is good for the gander is not good for the goose". The thinking is, Africa is no more of strategic interest to the West!

Coming back to our colonial experience, can we say democracy was practised during the colonial era in Sierra Leone? According to the dynamics of British rule, this beats our imagination. In the Legislative Council, the unofficial members usually the Sierra Leonean citizens, did not have any say in framing policies and laws, only the official members who were all Europeans had that responsibility. Real power lay with the Executive Council and the Governor. Until 1951, Sierra Leoneans were not members of this power-broking body. Notwithstanding they clamoured for authority to be given to the unofficial members, but to no avail.

In an atmosphere of unrelenting racism and discrimination, the concerns of the Krios remained unresolved and articulate citizens started speaking against the short-comings of nominated representation. Cries of no representation no taxation began to be heard.[70] These utterances and arbitrariness of imperial rule culminated in the formation of associations, committees etc. as a kind of platform to mount an effective opposition to Colonial rule. Of pre-eminence was the National Congress of British West Africa (NCBA), a pan-African movement committed to "redress the wrongs and iniquities of the Colonial system, to secure a role for the African

---

[70] The Krio of Sierra Leone. An Interpretative History. Akintola Wyse

in the Establishment and to participate in the governance of their less articulate comrades[71]

This organisation should have served as an effective platform for African opposition against the ills of imperialism. Unfortunately, the Sierra Leone Chapter, i.e. the National Youth League, was criticised for its elitism, and non-representation of the inhabitants of the Protectorate. The view conveyed was that its membership consisted of mainly the Krios, there were no members from the Protectorate. Nevertheless, in spite of this perception, the Youth League stood for national as against regional or tribal issues. During its deliberations, in meetings and conferences, it presented papers on, health and medical matters, labour and employment of Africans in government service, agriculture, education and judicial reforms.

From the other side, the Protectorate collectively advanced regional issues, seemingly acting as a counter measure against Colony groupings. In this regard, mention can be made of the Committee of Educated Africans (CEA), formed in 1922, happened to be the first modern political movement formed in the Protectorate; its composition was limited to Protectorate members only. Their main thrust was to bring to the attention of the Colonial government, the backwardness of their condition. They believed that their interests, whether erroneously, were not being properly addressed by the Krios, who seemingly were enjoying all the benefits from the country's resources. Primarily, they were agitating for more development for their people and direct participation in governance.

It will not be an exaggeration to say that Colony and Protectorate relations were fraught with suspicions from both sides and had always been a highly topical issue. Nowadays, the contest if one should put it so, is not between the Protectorate and the Colony, but between the tribes and regions. Just as in colonial days the British used this divide to advance their own ends, so it is that now, the Politicians as leaders,

71   Ibid

use tribalism and regionalism for political advantage especially in garnering votes during elections, and plugging top positions in the government and other public services. Considering, it would not be far-fetched to say that much has not changed. The pattern and stage set by the British so long ago, are still being practised by our political leaders. On this wise perhaps, the blame for our political imbroglios can be laid squarely on the doorsteps of our colonial leaders. Would this be fair? In some other African countries with the same colonial past, their conditions have changed; Tanzania under the great Mwalimu Nyerere is a country that comes to mind.

Indeed, the colonial government responded to constitutional change through the conflict between the Colony and the Protectorate. There was a presumption by the colonial government that given the intra-African conflict, basic constitutional concessions would more likely than not keep the African community divided. Indeed, this was correct as was evidenced by the reaction of the Colony and the Protectorate to the 1924 Constitution.[72]

Also, this intra-African feud benefited the chiefs, the least politically assertive of the African groups. By virtue of their strategic role in local colonial administration, they paradoxically benefitted from being opposed by the Colony elite, inasmuch as the colonial government reacted by granting them a key position in the new constitutional order. This romance between the chiefs and the colonial government enabled the chiefs to expand the sources of their influence and power, while simultaneously buttressing as best they could, their traditional authority. In this way, the chiefs gained a favourable vantage point which in the post-war era facilitated their claim for a permanent status in the constitutional structure of Sierra Leone.

Indeed, the economy then was not as complex as it is now; politics was in its infancy and democracy whatever there was, was very loose, no affiliation with political parties, let alone political ideologies.

---

[72]   Political Changes in a West African State. Martin Kilson

A situation or scenario the unofficial representatives of both the Colony and the Protectorate should have used to their advantage to gain political and economic mileage from the colonial government. Inadvertently, just as there were no political parties during this period, we can also proffer the absence of career politicians in the Legislature. These representatives apart from the chiefs, were men with full-time professional jobs, for whom politics was an important side-line. They combined their professional businesses with their representation in the Legislative Council. For the Protectorate one can reference Dr Milton Margai and Dr John Karefa-Smart, both medical doctors, for the Colony, there were, H. C. Bankole-Bright, also a medical doctor, and A.E. Tuboku-Metzgar whose company owned a fleet of buses.

These representatives at the time were not paid for their services, but they served the nation dutifully. Consider present day politicians. Indeed, how times have changed. At present, Parliamentarians earn relatively a good wage, and are even pensionable, receiving different types of allowances. Days gone by, the author does not even believe that those representatives of halcyon days, were given sitting fees!

To be fair, one cannot compare the complexities of present-day society to the society of the early to mid 20th century. Before the discovery of iron ore and diamonds, the imperial power was having second thoughts on the viability of continued support to the nascent Colony, ridden with the anopheles mosquito, a land which, to coin a phrase, became known as "White Man's grave". But for the French who were moving Southwards through what was then known as French Guinea acquiring territory by conquest, the British might have given up the territory under their administration. However, they stayed and exploited the newly discovered wealth of the country, not only the minerals but also our agricultural resources and hospitable tropical climate. In fact, just recently (quite recently), while listening to the BBC's Focus on Africa programme, the author came to learn that a rare type of coffee, indigenous to Sierra Leone, mostly grown in the South Eastern Province, known as Stenophilia was exported in the 19th century. Presently, research is being conducted to trace this rare crop and try revitalising its cultivation.

What obtained in the early days of the Country's ascent, control was in the hands of the Colonial government, whose Headquarters or domicile was far removed from the colonised territory. Also, the socio-economic structure in those days was very dissimilar to what it is today. In today's Sierra Leone, players and participants are operating in a more complex society. A modern economic system probably started evolving with the discovery of iron ore and diamonds, together with the construction of the railway and a road infrastructure system. Migratory patterns changed as young men and even foreigners congregated into the mining areas, apart from the railway which was public sector, a wag- earning class developed in the private sector leading to changes in the individual's purchasing power. People's taste and aspiration might even have been affected.

It has been mentioned that control in all forms was vested in the hands of the colonial authority. One would ask, who were the main beneficiaries of this wealth? At a time when there were no indigenous banks, let alone a Central bank, neither was there control over its money supply, who had the final say in the utilisation of the proceeds of the sale of our diamonds and iron ore? Not the indigenes but of course those who had control of the country. Sierra Leone benefitted from taxes levied on foreign companies, primarily from Britain that were exploiting our wealth. To compound the situation who levied the taxes? The Colonial administration. Sadly, even today, we are still asking these same questions, what has changed, we are supposed to be independent, which we have been for over half a century, but are we in control? It is no longer the Colonial power, but the IMF and the World Bank and possibly the Chinese. And to think some other minerals have been discovered.

Chapter Six

CHANGING FORTUNES

With all the bickering among the protagonists, i.e., the Colonialists, the inhabitants of the Colony and those of the Protectorate, one would be forgiven for thinking that life in Sierra Leone centred around political and constitutional profit and loss.

Before the discovery of diamonds, iron ore and its agricultural potential. The British Government thought it was a drain on her budget to support or take over the reins of government from the Sierra Leone Company. Nonetheless, the counter-veiling circumstances of the time forestalled their dithering over taking over the colony and Sierra Leone became a Crown Colony in 1808.

Before the discovery of minerals, economic activity was mainly centred on agriculture, and true to its mercantilist philosophy, the colonial government saw the agricultural potential as the production and export of raw materials for the home industries and creating an ever-expanding market for British manufacturers. The development of the country as far as the Colonial government was concerned, was ancillary. Unfortunately this philosophy has determined the pace and pattern of our economic growth. Over 60 years since the British Colonial government departed our shores, we are still grappling with economic diversification and value-addition. With all the political propaganda by past and current governments, ranging from the green revolution, rice self-sufficiency, agenda for change and prosperity, coupled with all the anomalies in the economic system, it is the author's belief that Sierra Leone is far from the "take off" into self-sustained growth. During the colonial era, we did not go cap in hand begging, but at the present with all our resources and being in charge of our own destiny, the only way our leaders believe to bring development into the country is to be traipsing all over the globe seeking for aid and investors. We have failed and are still failing to see the potential that resides in the country.

Until the exploitation of diamonds and iron ore in the early 1930s, agriculture was the backbone of the economy, both in employment and output, a role it continues to play in the 20th and 21st centuries. In those days, the country was noted for the exportation of piassava, palm kernels, coffee, cocoa beans, all in their unprocessed form. Over a century and a half after, piassava has disappeared, to be replaced by cheaper synthetics. Sierra Leone has still not been able to add value to its coffee and cocoa products. We are still exporting the beans, amid the noise of value addition made by successive governments. Nowadays, there has been some effort in the processing of palm kernels.

Circumscribing all this development was the colonial government's policy of conservation and improvement of the land and forests for generations. Self-sufficiency in foodstuff that was being produced in the country, and aid rapid expansion of agricultural exports. The institution charged with this responsibility was the Department of Agriculture established in 1911. On hindsight, it is difficult to see how the actions of the colonial regime fit the policies they were advancing. At the time, the infrastructure to implement such policies was non-existent. When they started construction of the transport infrastructure, they built a railway linking the fertile agricultural areas and the port in Freetown, feeder roads were also not in existence and farms were not connected to markets. In a similar vein, no factories were established then to process our agricultural produce. Factories that existed then were those established by Krio entrepreneurs, who supplied the domestic market. Krio traders collected the agricultural products from the hinterland, palm oil, palm kernel, rubber, kola nuts, for export to the world markets[73]. They also stimulated the systematic cultivation of cash crops by the indigenous tribes[74].

It would be safe to assume that life in those days was more sedate for the inhabitants with less complex economy than we are witnessing and experiencing at present? Governors and laws were respected, there was discipline, order and organisation. The laws were there not to be feared but respected. Justice was more or less equitably dispensed. There was no adverse pressure on the land area in the colony as we are now experiencing, and therefore even without the existence of an institution of urban and town planning, not only the Provinces conformed to orderliness, city bye-laws were in existence and these laws were complied with. Contrast that with the present when even with institutions charged with the responsibility of town planning and environmental protection, there is rampant land misappropriation and environmental degradation.

As the modernisation of the economy progressed, especially after the colonial period so the political will to tackle these challenges to a proper, healthy and comfortable way of life deteriorated to a point where we can say it is non-existent.

Following the 1927 discovery of diamonds, the colonial government signed a concessionary agreement with the Sierra Leone Selection Trust (SLST) in 1932. This agreement gave the SLST a ninety-nine year monopoly on exploration and mining in return for a 27.5 per cent tax on net profits[75]. It should be noted that this agreement was

---

[73]   Political Change in a West African State. Martin Kilson

[74]   Ibid

[75]   Corruption and State Politics in Sierra Leone. William Reno

concluded at a time of the Great Depression of the early 1930s, which was a global phenomenon. Alas! what a bonus for the imperial power. The Governor at the time, Governor Pollett realised that the key to underwriting growing state capacity, especially the Great Depression, lay in first achieving fiscal security with the aid of foreign direct investment. On the policy front, dare we say this is sound economic policy that would benefit the investor and the colonial government.

Compare with today policy makers, mining tax is a paltry 3.5%. How ridiculous, especially considering that mining companies of the present day enjoy all kinds of incentives, from duty waivers to tax holiday, all in the name of attracting foreign direct investment.

Nevertheless, with this discovery the whole dynamics changed and a new paradigm was entered into by the country.

Sierra Leone operated a bifurcated land tenure system, free-hold in the Western Area and communal ownership in the Protectorate. This system unfortunately has not changed, our leaders (political) have determinedly maintained that system while disadvantaging a group of people (the Krios) who cannot purchase land in the Provinces, but also stifling development in the Provinces. Economic history informs that only when the land tenure system was liberalised, that the other factors of production were energised into development activity.

Fancy, it was in this kind of environment that the discovery of minerals was made and in the area of communal ownership of land and not in the area where land ownership was free-hold. This agreement went further in 1933. Perhaps out of greed or eagerness, considering the fact that this event occurred during the time of the Great Depression, the colonial government unilaterally extended SLST's lease area to include the entire country[76].

---

[76]   Ibid

Diamond mining in those days and up to the late 20th century was alluvial. In fact there was talk that one could virtually pluck diamond from off the ground. Thus, how can this discovery be monopolised as the colonial government was trying to do? Of course this did not work as many people took to mining and according to the government, they were declared illegal miners. In the same vein, many aliens flocked to the diamond mining areas, as it became a free for all. As one of the writer's teacher used to say in his class when he thought his students were not applying their minds intellectually, "come one, come all, seats free, no collection."

On the socio-economic side, this meant business was not going to be conducted as usual. For one thing the system of exchange i.e., the barter system had to change, considering the exchange value of commodity being dealt with. This also created a class of wage earners, from the labourers, the speculator, the diamond buyers who became primarily Lebanese, an independent class of private sector individuals, not depending on the public sector for employment. Also, the Krios who in earlier days were the entrepreneurs by the time of the diamond explosion had been pushed back in that role by the Syrians and the Lebanese. Even the agricultural sector, the Syrians and the Lebanese became the middlemen between the farmers and the buyers, the Produce Marketing Board in this case.

Other beneficiaries indirectly, were the Chiefs, but not the common people for whom the land was held in trust. In fact it was reported that in certain chiefdoms where diamonds were mined, chiefs allocated plots to strangers rather than to local residents. Why? Because strangers paid a "consideration" for use of the plot. Thus a share of diamond sales went directly into the Chiefs' pockets. [77] Indeed the indigenous people were right in their thinking that they were being unjustly treated by the colonial government and the chiefs in not allowing them to mine in their own land.

---

[77]   Ibid

Around the same time, iron ore (a heavy metal) was discovered in Marampa in the Port Loko District. Because of its chemical make-up it cannot be smuggled as was common in the diamond trade. According to economic orthodoxy, industries can be located at the source of its raw materials usually heavy industries, near the market usually light industries, and those that were footloose i.e., anywhere, at the source of its raw materials or at its market precincts. Because of the weight of iron ore, the logic was to locate the processing plant at the source of the raw material, which would have been of extensive value to Sierra Leone's export. That was not to be. The excuse, the smelting of iron ore required extensive power that the country did not have, and the skills necessary to work the plant. Over 70 years of development, with the 3rd / 4th largest deposit of iron ore, over 11 billion tons, Sierra Leone still exports iron ore. The cause, the required power is not available, and the skills are not available. Nothing has changed. Expatriates are brought in at the present time and paid very fat salaries. But of cause the management of these companies will tell you that they are creating employment for the locals, and successive governments swallow this hook, line and sinker. It never occurred to our policy makers to compare the total wage bill of the companies' few expatriate staff with the total wage bill of the many local staff. Their attention is fixed rather on the volume (quantity) than the value. And if these expatriate salaries are tax exempt, it was a great loss of government revenue, while the paltry wages of the local workers are taxed. Where is the equity?

Nevertheless, mining and other productive activities especially in agriculture expanded employment in the formal sector. Mindful of previous actions of workers to voice their protests in strike actions, the Colonial government created an environment for the resolution of workers discontent. The wage-labourers for example, by the late 1930s had registered some advance in trade union organisation. By 1940 there were seven registered trade unions in Sierra Leone and eleven by 1942. A series of labour laws marked the colonial government's response to this development. These laws included the

Trade Union Ordinance No. 31 of 1939 that established machinery for the registration of unions; the Trade Disputes (Arbitration and Enquiry Ordinance, No. 14 of 1939) that provided for arbitration of strikes and disputes; and the Workmen's Compensation Ordinance, No. 35 of 1939 that established conditions for payment of compensation to injured workers.[78]

Nevertheless mining did have a significant impact on the economy of Sierra Leone. Apart from creating a labour force of wage earners, especially in the Marampa mines, diamond mining in the South East even if illegal enriched some people overnight. In the decades of the seventies, when many African countries were going through foreign exchange crises caused by a hostile international market – adverse terms of trade, amid huge debt repayment – Sierra Leone could still boast of having a six-month import cover. The author still remembers in those days, people from Ghana used to travel to Sierra Leone to purchase consumable items, we all took it as fun, little did we know that through mismanagement by our political leaders and bad economic policies we would experience the same situation. A situation that occurred after Sierra Leone hosted the Organisation of African Union Heads of State Conference in 1980! Alas, the Middle Eastern countries have utilised their God-given natural resource, oil, to develop their respective countries, turning deserts into modern metropolis. Botswana in Southern Africa has transformed her economy, with her abundance of diamonds. Sierra Leone with all her wealth cannot begin to transform her economy! Our leaders do not hesitate to go cap in hand begging for aid from countries that cannot compare for natural wealth. To some of us, this is shameful.

While our minerals have contributed to economic growth, especially in the decades of the seventies, there had been periods of dis-equilibrium in other sectors and population demographics. Because

---

[78] Sierra Leone Labour Report, 1939-1940, in Political Change in a West African State. A study of the Modernisation Process in Sierra Leone

of the relative ease that alluvial diamonds could be mined, and the comparatively high returns for relatively less arduous labour, agricultural workers migrated to the mining areas, at the expense of the development of the agricultural sector. The country which was exporting rice to the sub-region and beyond before then suddenly lost that capacity and it has never been regained. On a similar vein, the discovery of diamonds impacted on the migratory patterns not only of the youth who gravitated to the mining areas but also foreigners from nearby countries.

On the other hand, inhabitants from the Protectorate were moving to the colony in search of greener pastures and to enjoy or experience better facilities and amenities that did not exist in the Protectorate. Also some very limited urbanisation outside Freetown and the Western Area had occurred by the 1920s – at least 8 urban localities in the provinces having population of 1,000 or more people existed in 1922. After World War 2 new roads and transportation facilities made it easier to reach district and provincial administrative centres where developing health and social facilities, amenities, and opportunities for wage employment acted to attract both seasonal and permanent migrants from the surrounding rural populations. The rapid expansion of diamond mining in the 1950s stimulated the rise of new urban centres that drew not only local people but also many from the sub-region.[79] Similarly there were Krios who went and settled in the Protectorate, to establish trading, commercial and factory businesses. Nevertheless, Freetown has always been a centre of attraction. Unfortunately, these amenities, and facilities have not expanded to cope with the influx of migrants from other areas.

Slowly but surely, the nascent state of Sierra Leone was moving from rural communities to being a modern state and Freetown the capital city was becoming cosmopolitan. Apart from indigenous businesses, European firms like the United Africa Company (UAC), an arm of

---

[79]   Area Handbook of Sierra Leone By Irving Kaplan

Unilever, G. B. Ollivant, the Kingsway Store, the Cold Storage; stores that in modern day, would be termed departmental stores, started doing business in what we now call the Central Business District (CBD) of Freetown. There was also the Patterson – Zochonis (PZ) partly Greek and partly British, together with French enterprises like the CFAO and SCOA.[80]

Sierra Leoneans, or more precisely, the Krios, especially the liberated Africans who settled in the Colony, were renowned for their commercial skills. Apart from establishing trading links with the Protectorate they also ventured into other West African territories, stretching from Nigeria to the Gambia. Alas, the coming of European merchants aided by the policies of the colonial government put the Krio traders out of commission. Nevertheless, Sierra Leone and other West African countries began to attract European firms, looking for new markets for their manufactured products, and raw materials to supply the factories in the European countries. In Sierra Leone British and French firms took advantage of this situation.

In 1879, two friends set up a trading post in Freetown at Wilberforce Street called Paterson Zochonis. This company was incorporated in England and traded mainly in palm oil produce, groundnuts, coffee and timber. By the time it went out of business in Sierra Leone it was operating like a department store where durable consumer items, consumer goods were being traded.

The United African Company Ltd. Was a merchant company originally trading in the West African colonies of the British Empire. In March 1929, the Niger Company merged with its rival the African and Eastern Trade Corporation Ltd, to form United African Company (UAC). Its trade regime consisted of palm oil, groundnuts, and cocoa; it also traded in manufactured goods such as textiles, metal goods such as pots, cutlery and tools; and provisions. From the 1930s, and especially after the second World War, this trade changed in response

---

[80]   Ibid

to African economic development needs. Emphasis shifted to the sale of more sophisticated consumer goods and the equipment needed for industrial development.

A grand colonial business of the French was the French West African Company – Compagnie Francaise de l'Afrique Occidental (CFAO). It was the successor to the small French trader in Western Africa established by Charles-Auguste Verninck in 1845 with branches in Senegal, Sierra Leone, Liberia, the Cote d'Ivoire and Nigeria. The CFAO bought tropical commodities from African farmers, particularly, groundnuts, palm oil and palm nuts and rounded up its cargo with items such as bird-feathers and leather. However, the CFAO's main interest was in selling. It became a general store for both Europeans and Africans, dealing in ammunition, furniture, metal-wares and textiles and other household products.

The Freetown Cold Storage was established by two Swiss pioneers, Schumacher and Straumann in the early 1900s. Their dealings were mainly in processed foods including meat products and drinks; but they diversified and built the first air-conditioned cinema, the Odeon, in West Africa.

The SCOA (Société Compagnie Occidental Afrique) was established by two Swiss traders who set up some factories in Sierra Leone in 1898. The SCOA sold European manufactures consumed by not only the colonialists but also the African population. On the other side of the coin, it exported raw materials like palm oil, groundnuts, skins of beef, sheep and goats, rubber, gum and other products necessary for industry and commerce.

Establishing trading links with Europe could be said to have evolved from the slave trade. The Rokel estuary was an important source of fresh water for the sea traders and explorers who opened a bay for trading goods such as swords, kitchen and other household utensils in exchange for beeswax and fine ivory works. By the mid 1550s slaves replaced these items as the major commodity. By 1650s, English, French, Dutch and Danish interests in West Africa had grown; during the years, 1662 – 1759, some 106,800 slaves were exported on ships of the British Empire.[81] So even before the founding of the Colony of Sierra Leone, trade links had existed between West Africa and Europe.

Put into perspective, our colonial history is sometimes either glorified or denigrated. Frequently we harangue that although we are politically independent our navel strings are still attached financially and economically to our colonial masters. Still, we go cap in hand requesting for financial and technical assistance from the industrialised countries when in reality, Africa as a continent has far more natural wealth than these very same countries. Perhaps, just perhaps, our present day behaviour can be traced back to our colonial past, a past that we have not made a conscious effort to break away from. It is the author's view that our tastes have been conditioned on the material goods manufactured by the industrialised countries; commodities we can produce ourselves if our leaders especially set their minds to it. We have to break away from this dependency syndrome, even the aid that we think we are getting from them.

Let us for a moment consider a statement attributed to Lord Macaulay purportedly addressing the British Parliament in 1835. (It has been debunked that he made that speech as at the time he was stationed in India). Quoting "I have travelled across the length and breadth of Africa and I have not seen one person who is a beggar, who is a thief; such wealth I have seen in this country, such high moral values, people of such calibre, that I do not think we would ever conquer this country, unless we break the very backbone of this nation, which is her spiritual and cultural heritage. And therefore I propose that we replace her old and ancient education system, her culture, for if the Africans think that all that is foreign and English is good and greater

---

[81]   History of Merchant Shipping and Ancient Commerce. W. S. Lindsay

than their own, they will lose their self-esteem, their native culture and they will become what we want them, a truly dominated nation". Indeed this is what colonialism has done to us. We have felt inferior to the European race and even today, our leaders do not stand up to them. How else can the President of the United States of America publicly abuse our countries as I quote "shit hole"? Give the devil his due the late Robert Mugabe carved his own space among them; he brooked no nonsense.

Once the Province of Freetown was established, trade moved from slaves to passengers and goods. The Elder Dempster Lines, one of UK's, largest shipping companies then, established a passenger and freight service to British West Africa, before the second World War. It was served by three mail vessels; MV Aureol, MV Apapa and MV Accra.

This was before the advent of air travel. Considering that travelling by road to Europe was an impossibility, apart from the absence of road links the thought of which is unthinkable, sea transportation was all that existed in those days. Then transportation of colonial officials and their families, tourists, students and freight was the pre-eminence of the Elder Dempster Lines. However, by the mid 1960s, faced with competition from air transport the fall in passengers as the colonial service was virtually over in West Africa, the passenger service was becoming less and less profitable. Of the three ships serving the West African trade, two, the MV Apapa and MV Accra were sold in 1968. The MV Aureol, the last purchased in 1951, carried on service but becoming unprofitable, it was taken out of service in 1972. On 16th March 1972, the MV Aureol made its last West African sailing out of Liverpool. Thus ended one of the iconic service in the colonial history of West Africa.

Of course developmental strides were made in other sectors of the economy; in transport and infrastructure, the road network was expanded, villages and towns were being connected, all in the interest of the colonial government, for the exploitation and exportation of our raw materials to the parent country and importation of manufactured products to the colonial state. Schools were being built mainly by religious missionary societies primarily in the South and East, but not in the North, probably because there was a strong Muslim influence there where there were koranic schools already.

Notwithstanding these developments, Sierra Leone developed unevenly during the colonial days because of the development and control strategy of the colonial government.[82] Take the case of Education for which Sierra Leone became known as the "Athens of West Africa." By 1900, 7,000 students were enrolled in primary schools out of an estimated 14,000 children of school age (Sumner 1963). On the other hand, less than 900 children were enrolled out of an estimated population of 1,500,000 in the Provinces (Corby 1990). There were even inter-regional disparities as the 1931 Census showed. The percentage of children attending school in the North was 0.97%, while it was 4.75% in the South (Sumner, 1963).

---

[82] Young People, Education and the New Wars: The Case of Sierra Leone. Mitsuko Matsumoto. Unpublished D. Phil Thesis.

Chapter Seven

THE ROAD TO INDEPENDENCE

When the second world war ended, there was a paradigm shift in the politics of Colonialism; there was a change in the global international relations and that changed the international power politics as the world dominance of Britain was on the wane, while the United States of America and the Soviet Union became influential players on the international scene. These two countries had scant experience in Colonialism. The war also gave rise to the League of Nations comprising of a few countries, especially those involved in the Second World War, that later was enlarged later to become the United Nations. In his first peacetime address to the House of Commons in 1946, the secretary of State for the colonies commented "it is our policy to develop the colonies and all their resources so as to enable their peoples speedily and substantially improve their economic and social conditions, and as soon as may be practicable, to attain responsible self-government. The idea of one people dominating or exploring another is always repugnant. It is not domination in anyway to abandon peoples who have come to depend on us for their defence, security, development and welfare. To us the colonies are a great trust, ad their progress to self-government is a goal towards which His Majesty's Government will assist them with all the means in their power. They shall go as fast as they show themselves capable of going."[83] A "wind of change" was moving across Africa, although it was only during the Prime Ministership of Harold Macmillan that this view was given utterance.

Interestingly, history informs us that the founding fathers or architects of the Colony Settlement in 1792, intended that the returnees from Nova Scotia, to Sierra Leone were to be responsible for their own governance[84], Granville Sharpe intended the free settlers of the Province of Freedom should elect their own government and rule themselves. Perhaps this was as a result of the war of American independence in which these settlers fought for the colonial power Britain, who at the end had to cede power to the American colonies. They might not have had the stomach for another war.

Also it may have been they were of the opinion these settlers had the ability to govern themselves. Some countries in the British Empire like Kenya and India had to struggle to unchain their colonial yoke. Sierra Leone, on the other hand had a smoother road to independence. Whatever opposition existed, came from within, as there were those who thought Sierra Leone was not ready. The State of Sierra Leone was dichotomous, in all its forms of governance, the legal systems were not harmonised, neither was there social integration or any attempt at social integration between the Colony and the Protectorate. In all aspects of development, this dichotomy cut across, health, education etc. While the leaders in the Protectorate were clamouring for development, the leaders in the Colony were agitating for more say in the administration of their own affairs. Indeed this had been the primary challenges since the amalgamation of the Protectorate in 1896. The Provinces are much more developed now, but the general

---

[83]   Sierra Leone Inheritance. Christopher Fyle.

[84]   Political Change in a West African State. A Study of the Modernisation Process in Sierra Leone. Martin Kilson

trend continues. Our rural areas are still relatively underdeveloped, and social amenities in these areas are virtually non-existent.

On the realisation that the British Empire was crumbling the colonial government in Sierra Leone embarked on establishing the structures that would sustain the march towards self-government. Indeed the Protectorate by now was also clamouring for independence. At the 1943 – 44 session of the Legislature, Paramount Chief Caulker declared "we want the government to give us a free hand in our own affairs. If we are not fit for self-government, let the government give us a trial.[85]

No matter what we might say, the British were sticklers of systems. In this regard, even though the Protectorate, and also the Colony were agitating for self-government they considered the establishment of certain prerequisites before this road could be followed.

To this end, they tried to bring the Protectorate up to speed by undertaking some reforms, which saw the establishment of the District Councils and the Protectorate Assembly in 1946. The formation of the District Councils allegedly was to serve as local authorities to help develop themselves and offer some participation in government to people outside the chiefly class.

The Protectorate Assembly a deliberative body comprising the Paramount Chiefs and Native Authorities and a few members of the educated elite, charged with discussing issues affecting the Protectorate. Interestingly enough, more than half of the Protectorate 42 Assembly seats were reserved for paramount chiefs (26 in all) indirectly elected to the Assembly by the Native Administrations and District Councils. The remaining seats in the Assembly were held by officials of government departments (11 seats), one representative of European and one Krio business interests, one missionary representative, and 2 educated Protectorate Africans.

---

[85]   Ibid.

Unfortunately this move gave the appearance of consolidating chiefly power and influence; the Protectorate people had moved from where they were in 1896. They can now boast of an educated elite, no matter how thin a group, not belonging to the chiefly class. As was to be expected, they raised their voice against this composition. They desired a more direct and independent role in the Political Affairs of the Protectorate. In spite of the patronage of the Paramount Chiefs this new elite formed the Sierra Leone Organised Society (SOS) in July 1946 in order to express their views on post-war development.[86] The SOS criticised the influence of chiefs in the Protectorate Assembly, the post-war local government system, and the Central Legislature.[87] The SOS was concerned about the representation of the common people in the Protectorate Assembly, and also the fact that the electoral franchise was not extended to the common people.

One year after the establishment of these institutions the governor expressed satisfaction with their performance and determined that it was time to take the first step towards constitutional progress. To this end, a new constitution was promulgated in 1947. The new constitution provided for an un-official majority in the Legislative Council, in itself a liberal move away from the usual control of the Legislative Council by the colonial government. However, the more radical move under this new constitution was what J. A. D. Alie in his book "A New History of Sierra Leone" called the "transfer of power". There was transfer of power in the sense that the new constitution provided for an elected unofficial membership: ten (10) of the unofficial members were to be elected from the Protectorate (Nine by the Protectorate Assembly, and one nominated by the Governor from among the members of the Protectorate Assembly), and four (4) elected from the colony. Radically, power shifted from

---

[86] Political Change in a West African State. A Study of the Modernisation Process in Sierra Leone. Martin Kilson

[87] Ibid.

the colony, as represented by the Krios to the representatives of the Protectorate.

As was to be expected, the Krio representatives strongly resented this move by the Colonial Government and looked for ways and means to forestalled this loss of power on their own part. And indeed, one was found in the nature of the educational status of the Protectorate representatives, and that happened to be their literacy. The chiefs' influence was still predominant in the Protectorate and because the electoral franchise was indirect (elected by the District Councils) and not direct, almost all of the Protectorate representations were chiefs, a system that even small Protectorate elite was averse to. At the beginning of the debate, they sided with the colony to make literacy one of the criteria for election into the Legislative Council. This of course, would have disqualified many of the chiefs, logically putting members of the Protectorate elite in a prime position to speak for their people in the council. However, as the debate over this issue of literacy turned acrimonious, the protectorate elite closed ranks with the chiefs, who welcomed the constitutional provisions, for they saw in these provisions a whole range of new opportunities for the social political advancement of the Protectorate.

On the part of the British, before exiting the stage, they wanted to design a good exit strategy that was sustainable. Britain practised democracy, after evolving from a monarchical, and brief dictatorial state (Cromwell's Puritonic System). And as is now being ramped down our throats, democracy is numbers; and indeed, the population of the colony was about one-tenth the total of the entire country; also, the bulk of the resources, minerals, agricultural lands, were to be found in the Protectorate. Going back to the history, the beginning of democracy can be credited to the Greeks of the 6th Century B.C., and it meant then the rule for the people by the people.

The Greek system of government was perhaps closer to true democracy or rule by the people than any other in history. They

84

viewed dictatorship as the worst possible form of government, so their government evolved as the exact opposite. Their civilisation was broken down into small city states, and all men voted on all issues of government. There were no representatives in the Greek system of government, instead, they ruled themselves directly; each man was a life-long member of the decision making body. Theirs was almost a total democracy except for the fact that women and slaves were not considered citizens, therefore, they were not allowed to vote. The form of democracy that is now being practised the world over, is what is now termed representative democracy, whereby citizens are given the franchise, based on certain criteria, usually age, to vote for who will represent them in the legislative assembly. This was the governing principle on which the colonial government based the new constitution. Looking at the behaviour or response to the 1947 constitutional changes by the Krios, the tendency is to focus on their obfuscation because of their loss of importance in the constitutional progress of the country. The literacy criterium aside, they had some legitimate concerns and of paramount importance was the inequitable land tenure system. While the protectorate inhabitants had and still have access to land in the colony, the Krios, being non-natives were not accorded the same access to land in the Protectorate. To this day, that situation has remained the same. After independence, successive governments for political reasons have not had the will to change it.

In any group, gathering, institution and the like, there are different shades of opinion as well as moderate and extremist individuals. During the debate for the implementation of the Stevenson Constitution There were N. A. Cox-George and Thomas Decker who appealed for a balance that would, as far as possible, satisfy both the colony and protectorate groups. For instance, Cox-George proposed a declaration of a single Sierra Leonean citizenship, and also a bicameral legislature which would allow the more educated elite to be the real legislature. There were also other Krios like Harry Sawyerr, Dr. S. M. O. Broderick, H. E. John, Lettie Stuart, Rev. N.

Jones (Laminah Sankoh) with moderate views who sided with the protectorate for the sake of peace and unity.

The decade of the 1950s witnessed a watershed in the political history of Sierra Leone. The realisation that the colonial government was slowly relinquishing power, brought a flurry of activities among the representatives of the colony and the protectorate. Previously the battle lines had been between the colony and the protectorate. Suddenly, alliances began to be formed around issues, although the protectorate-colony divide was always at the background.

In 1954 another colony party emerged, the United Progressive Party led by an eminent lawyer C. B. Rogers-Wright, who was joined by another firebrand radical, I. T. A. Wallace-Johnson. Accordingly, political parties were formed to advance the interests of the colony and protectorate aspirations. Following upon the failure of the colony groups to alter significantly the provisions in the 1947 constitutional proposals, the National Council of Sierra Leone, a purely colony (Krio) party was formed in August 1950; its leader was the veteran H. C. Bankole Bright, a medical doctor by training. Since its formation in 1951, the NCSL began campaigning for independence to the colony, especially as the Krios were losing their dominance of the Legislative Council, in which they were now outnumbered by the protectorate representatives, given the demography of the country. As to be expected this proposal was rejected by the colonial government.

Not to be outdone, the Sierra Leone Peoples Party was founded in April 1951, some eight months after the NCSL was established. Like the NCSL, it chose as leader, a medical doctor, Dr. M. A. S. Margai. The SLPP was comprised of the Sierra Leone Organisation Society and the Protectorate Education Progressive Union (PEPU). Also, the Peoples Party under a Krio, A. N. Jones, who later changed his name to Laminah Sankoh, merged with the SLPP. The SLPP was formed in response to the post-war constitutional reforms. It was almost exclusively a protectorate affair. The bulk of the founding members wanted to call it "The Protectorate People's Party" but a few wise heads including its leader Milton Margai prevailed otherwise. Nonetheless, the substance of the SLPP's programme was mainly centred on Protectorate interests. Primarily, it sought to end the Krio dominance in the central colonial government. As is the case at present it is not uncommon for one to hear that the SLPP was the mother of party politics in Sierra Leone. This is true as long as it is the oldest party existing in Sierra Leone at present; however it should be noted that it was not the first political party that was formed in the country.

Another party that come into existence in the early 1950s was the Kono Progressive Movement (KPM) led by a druggist T. S. Briwa, himself a son of Kono. Its aim was very specific. For all the wealth/resources that Kono contributed to the National Product through the proceeds from diamond mining, the District was neglected and undeveloped. In this regard, the aim of the party was to ensure that the Kono people receive the benefits they should deserve in terms of economic development for diamond exploitation.

Not to be outdone, another colony party emerged in 1956 with the name, the Sierra Leone Independence Movement (SLIM), whose leader was an outspoken lecturer at Fourah Bay College. It appealed to young Krio intellectuals because of its uncompromising stance against colonialism. As its nomenclature implied, theirs was a movement to march against the yoke of colonialism. Perhaps because its thrust was specific, strangely, it found some common grounds with the Kono Progressive Movement and the two parties formed a merger to become the Sierra Leone Progressive Independence Movement (SLPIM). For a time, this was what the emerging political landscape looked like in Sierra Leone.

Initially and interestingly, some of these parties cut across tribal lines. The Sierra Leone People's Party, which is currently seen as a South-Eastern (Mende) party was comprised of Temnes, Krios and

Mendes. Lamina Sankoh, a founding member, was a Krio, and so was Constance Cummings John, who was the first female Mayor of the municipality of Freetown. This characteristic is self-evident in the Sierra Leone Progressive Independence Movement and even the United Progressive Party principally Krio reached out to inhabitants of the protectorate. Was this then a subjugation of tribal affiliations to the national good? Unfortunately, this was only a marriage of convenience which did not last as is borne out by the incidents mainly political marginalisation and violence that are occurring in our present day society. Perhaps the founding fathers' motto of the SLPP, "One country, one people" was and is an illusion as in 1951 at its formation, its aim was to advance the claims of the Protectorate peoples.[88] Its establishment came in direct response to the activities of the NCSL. Its intention was to represent, defend and advance Protectorate interests. [89]

It is but sad that at the onset or even before the onset of political consciousness in Sierra Leone, political activity was intensely but detrimentally partisan. Unfortunately we have not moved away from partisan politics. During this period the main protagonists were the Sierra Leone Peoples Party (SLPP), led by Milton Margai and the Sierra Leone National Congress (SLNC) led by Dr. Bankole Bright. Interestingly, both were medical doctors. Discussing politics in those days, what comes to mind was the apparent or seeming gulf between these two leaders, usually epitomised by this exchange during the implementation of the Steveson's new constitution specifically for official members of the Legislative Council to choose those who should be invited to join the government. After disagreeing about the representation the NCSL leader asserted that the peoples of the colony and the protectorate were like two hills standing opposite each other and can never meet. From his own side, the leader of the SLPP did respond that if the Krios remained intransigent to the

---

[88]   The Krios of Sierra Leone. An Interpretive History. Akintola Wyse

[89]   A New History of Sierra Leone. J. A. D. Alie

implementation of the constitution, then he would have no alternative than to remove these foreigners (Krios) from our land!

Notwithstanding the tension between all parties brought about by the changes that the Stevenson Constitution would make, the colonial government, set about their task with equanimity. In September 1951, the provisions of this constitution came into force. By November of the same year, according to the provisions in the constitutions, elections were conducted on a very (interesting) franchise. Elections in the Freetown and the Sherbro Urban District were conducted on a limited franchise, but all the existing parties were eligible to contest the elections. Voting in the protectorate was indirect, through the twelve District Councils. The participation of the parties in the colony was restricted, they were not part of the District Councils. Nevertheless any argument against the democratic basis of the conduct of these elections would be theoretical. Even if they had contested, they would not have won a single seat.[90] The 1951 elections returned three NCSL, two SLPP and two Independent candidates in the colony. Of the fourteen emerging from the Protectorate, four were card carrying SLPP members but all including the Paramount Chiefs subsequently declared for the SLPP.

According to democratic principles, the new Governor, Beresford-Stooke appointed the leader of the SLPP, Dr. Milton Margai, Chief Minister becoming the leader of Government Affairs. Usually, in the political history of Sierra Leone, people are apt to state that the SLPP governance in Sierra Leone began in 1961 when the country achieved self-government. Strictly speaking, that is not a true representation of the facts. Political partisanship was in its infancy in the 1950s, but from the time African majority occurred in the Legislative Council, the SLPP was the lead in government business and all other parties were in opposition. In this case, the NCSL became the opposition.

---

[90] The Krio of Sierra Leone. An Interpretative History. Akintola Wyse

Oppositional politics established itself in the Legislative Council. The opposition party, the NCSL opposed many governing party (SLPP) measures, almost all of which were subsequently enacted; on the other side, the NCSL made their own proposals and these were mostly defeated. Debates were rancorous and often revolved around Krio and hinterland identities rather than policy. As a result of this identity crisis, progress was scarcely made in harmonising the colony and the protectorate. As such, the distinction between the colony and the protectorate was not really removed by the time of the 1951 elections.

This situation suited the colonial authority well; a situation they were cognisant of, even if not created by them. The least they could have done was to heal this breach, but they did not.

In their march towards decolonisation, on the basis of democratic principles, the Governor, Sir George Beresford Stooke chose only the SLPP members, having more seats in the Legislature, for his African nominations to the Executive Council. In terms of present day governance structure, this represented part of the Executive branch of the government. Subsequently, the Governor declared that in accordance with the discretion vested in him by Her Majesty's Royal Instruction, charged the following Ministers with responsibility as follows:-

Dr. M. A. S. Margai	- Health, Agriculture, Animal Husbandry and Forest
Mr. A. M. Margai	- Education, Local Government and Social Welfare
Mr. M. S. Mustapha	- Public Works, Railway and Road Transport, Port and Marine, Civil Aviation, Meteorology
Mr. A. G. Randle	- Commerce and Industry, Cooperation, Post and Telegraph and Fisheries

Mr. S. P. Stevens   - Surveys and Land, Mines, Labour and Geological Survey

Chief Bai Farima Tass II   - Minister without Portfolio

In the words of Siaka Stevens "I knew, at a level of conviction deeper than reason, that it was an important step for Sierra Leone to have black ministers in power, for native Africans to exercise responsibility for policy in our own country for the first time in 150 years."[91] Although power was not completely vested in the hands of the black Africans it is noteworthy that there were only six ministers to run the entire administration. Again to quote Siaka Stevens when he was first made a minister in the Executive Council in 1954 "An impartial and efficient civil service is essential for the successful performance of one's ministerial duties. A good Civil Servant, whatever his own political views may be, must prepare himself to serve loyally a Minister of any party, whether he be a true blue conservative or a red hot communist."[92]

In a similar vein, the leader of the NCSL made a very strong statement when these Ministers were selected. The thinking was that he was being obstructionist and felt very strongly as power was being transferred from the colony to the protectorate. The leader of NCSL, H. C. Bankole Bright averred "It is whimsical to think of the type of men in the executive council who are being called upon to control the present Heads of Departments. But apart from this intellectuality, there are other qualities necessary for the post of Ministers. You have to consider that you have to put in the position men of integrity: men who are inspired, men who should take an interest in treating cautiously the people they have got to deal with." However insulting at the time, what a profound statement, especially the last part about integrity, caution and care in serving the people. Unfortunately, looking down the line, Sierra Leone has never produced visionary

---

[91]   What Life Has Taught Me. Dr. Siaka Stevens.

[92]   Ibid

and inspired leaders. Nor can we even say that our political leaders have been men of integrity. All of them seem to have some baggage or the other, resulting in the looting of government coffers, trampling on citizens' right and trying to perpetuate their hold on power. Siaka Stevens' newly acquired status brought with it a sudden surge of popularity from the most unexpected quarters. "The crowds of my own people who haunted me night and day, I understood for I was now the butt of their complaints and the dispenser of their remedies".[93] He also talked about gifts to those in power. He averred "Many of those who came to see me bore gifts. The giving of gifts to those in power such as our chiefs is not new to Africa. Nor deplorable as it may be, is bribery, traditionally known as "shake hand" because a person who seeks a favour has something to conceal in his right hand which he passes to the one from whom he hopes to obtain favour….." Indeed, a profound and telling statement. Although Siaka Stevens did mention that neither the gift offered freely, nor the amount involved in the shake hand was of much value (at the time) our modern day politics after independence has been plagued with corruption at the highest level. It is no longer favour for something done, but a demand for something to be done, an act that seems to have been at the cost of progress and development. The term "ten per cent (10%)" has attracted so much importance in the running of government business, nowadays.

Unfortunately for the newly appointed Ministers, it was not an auspicious time to be assuming the reins of power. Following the cessation of hostilities in the second world war, reconstruction activities in the theatres of conflict were still on-going and war was looming between Korea and the United States. The diamond rush of 1954, which caused labour to migrate from the agricultural sector, to the mining sector, coupled with a series of bad harvests led to a dramatic rise in food prices. As wage levels remained the same, workers agitated for wage increases to compensate for the rise in food

---

[93]   What Life has Taught Me. Dr. Siaka Stevens

prices. The employers and the employees failed to agree an increase in wages that was acceptable to all parties. Consequently, a general strike was called on the 9th February which turned out to be violent as there was considerable looting of shops, and vandalisation of public property and utilities.[94]

Sadly for these new Ministers, a first in Sierra Leone politics they were thrust at the deep end of things, through no fault of theirs. The houses of Siaka Stevens, Albert Margai and M. S. Mustapha were vandalised. The reason? The rioters felt the Ministers were not sympathetic to their cause. In the same year, another wave of protest was sparked off this time in the Protectorate caused by the dissatisfaction of the people, with the way and manner the chiefs were administering their chiefdoms: imposing inequitable taxes, living ostentatiously and abusing the human rights of their subjects. The people revolted, from Kambia in the North to Ribbi in the South. Considerable damage was done to the chiefs' properties and some of them had to flee into temporary exile.[95]

After all this, necessary steps were taken to investigate the causes and proffer solutions to stem these types of riots. A commission was set up by the colonial government, which met and made recommendations, apportioning blame where necessary and proffered solutions.[96] The commission decided that local government bodies were largely to blame for the riots in the Protectorate, five chiefs were deposed and five chiefs resigned.

Unlike present day politicking it is noteworthy that in all of this there was no mention of culprits being affiliated to anyone party. The causes were economic and social, and there was no need to cast

---

[94] The Strike is widely discussed in "What Life has Taught Me." Dr. Siaka Stevens

[95] What Life Has Taught Me. Dr. Siaka Stevens

[96] For details of the Report, refer to "What Life Has Taught Me." Dr. Siaka Stevens

blame on any one party to gain political mileage, a facet that is now common in our modern-day politics. Whenever there is violence the culprits are usually members of the opposition even though those involved in these violent acts may not even be card holders of any one party.

Another important aspect to all of this was people's right to exercise protest against the establishment for things they deemed to be wrong. The strike in Freetown turned violent as people were expressing their frustration at the intransigence of their employers. Lives were lost, properties destroyed. However the law took its course and justice was dispensed equitably. Those rioters who were arrested were brought before the law and they were judged accordingly. The author can testify to that. Then a boy in primary school he witnessed the complete vandalisation of a public stand pipe and violent assault of his elder cousin by the leader of the gang of rioters. About six months after this incident, the author was able to identify the perpetrator of the said assault who was visiting a neighbour. A report was lodged at the Police Station and the alleged culprit apprehended. After a series of adjournments the case was brought before the Supreme Court at which a "small boy" had to testify which he did. The culprit was sentenced to a term of three years imprisonment.

To continue with its march towards decolonisation, it was time to have another election after the Legislature by 1957 had served for a term of five (5) years. Previous elections were held on limited suffrage. In 1957 all this was changed and universal adult suffrage was practised for the first time in Sierra Leone. Party politics was also in full swing and this election was contested by the SLPP, the NCSL, the United Progressive Party (UPP), and the Sierra Leone Independent Progressive Party. Proper political campaigning had not yet developed neither did we have political rallies then. Also there was no violence as yet, but the influence of the chiefs was very strong, In spite of the weak political relationships of the party members, the results were a foregone conclusion. The SLPP emerged from the elections with 23 seats including 9 of the 14 in the colony and the UPP had 5 seats and Independents took 11 of the seats. Of the 11 Independents, and all the paramount chiefs sided with the SLPP.[97] Not surprisingly, the NCSL, the oldest party was obliterated, its leader, Bankole Bright lost his deposit. Its appeal was too elitist and its ideology very narrow, amply put, "preventing the protectorate people holding the reins of power."

After the 1957 elections many political shenanigan started, illustrating how fragmented and loose our political parties were. The SLPP was the main force to reckon with, but it started showing cracks among its leadership, when some of the radical, younger men of the party thought the leader, Milton Margai was too conservative, moving too slowly on a march to independence and most times kow-towing to the dictates of the colonial government. So Albert Margai challenged his older brother Milton Margai for the leadership of the SLPP which he won by the slimmest of majority (one), a majority nevertheless. Nonetheless being Margai the younger, he was prevailed upon to step aside and allow seniority not popularity in this case to prevail. After this imbroglio, Albert took a more passive role and became a back-bencher in the House of representatives as it was now called.

Of course all those who were involved in this challenge were put out to pasture: stripped of their Ministerial positions.

After a year as a back-bencher, Albert Margai decided to server ties with the SLPP. In 1958, he formed the People National Party (PNP), together with Siaka Stevens, one of his staunch supporters; he himself became a casualty of the failed leadership position as he was stripped of his Ministerial portfolio. Many of the younger radical members of the SLPP joined Albert Margai in this exodus, also many of the professional and educated young men flocked to the PNP as they were becoming disillusioned with the policies of Milton Margai.

[97] Sierra Leone. A Political History. David Harris

He was deemed to be too cautious and not in tune with the common man, but leaned more towards the chiefs.

Most of the PNP's popularity was in Freetown, but this unfortunately was not reflected in the local elections. Instead of a general election before independence which some members were agitating for, the government decided to call local elections in 1959. Unfortunately for the nascent PNP, their popularity was not reflected in the results of the election, their performance was disastrous. In the District Council elections, the PNP could only manage 29 out of the 309 contested seats. The result in the capital city, i.e. in the Freetown City Council election the party did not win any seat.

The PNP's foray into politics was a short one, there was no determination, perhaps no plans to last the distance. There was a school of thought with the view that Albert Margai formed the PNP as a political manoeuvre designed to wrest concessions from Milton Margai. Given the situation at the time, although the PNP's performance in the 1959 local elections was disastrous, the party was an obstacle in the path of the SLPP.

In 1960, providence came into the SLPP/PNP divide in the guise of a visit to Freetown by Mr Alan Lennox Boyd who was until October 1959 secretary of state in the United Kingdom. Sir Milton Margai (knighted in 1959) called a meeting of all political leaders to discuss constitutional proposals for independence. Using his diplomatic skills, Sir Milton got all the political party leaders to agree to a united front, to push for independence. Thus came into existence the National United Front with Sir Milton as its leader, all the other parties having been dissolved. This indeed was a diplomatic coup by Sir Milton. Dissolving all the parties and coming together under the banner of a united front, served to silence the strident opposition voices calling for elections before independence. Also this move turned attention now to the composition of the delegation that would negotiate for independence, and also those who would be in his cabinet after independence. As a reward for shelving elections before independence the opposition members were promised ministerial portfolios after independence.

This call for election before independence came as a result of what happened in other colonies before they gained independence from Britain. In Ghana a country in the sub-region with close ties to Sierra Leone, which gained her independence in March 1957, there was election before independence. This was one of the reasons for the election before independence call, added to the fact that as far as the opposition was concerned, the mandate of the people should be sought. For Milton Margai and the SLPP, this was a no brainer. Given the circumstances at the time, the fractious nature of the party, Sir Milton did not want anything to upset his applecart as no matter what cost, he was determined to bequeath the legacy of independence to Sierra Leoneans.

Come May 1960, it was decided that the governor should no longer take the chair at the Executive Council, that chair should now be occupied by the Premier, whose title should be changed to that of Prime Minister. It was also agreed that Sierra Leone should become independent on 27th April, 1961. Interestingly, before his death in 1958 Bankole Bright who was the thorn in the flesh of the colonial government had declared that Sierra Leone should become independent by 1961.

A delegation comprising of members of the United Front, but dominated by the SLPP was assembled by the Prime Minister, and negotiations for independence were held in London at the Lancaster House from 29th April to 4th May 1960. At a pre-conference meeting the delegates had chosen to speak with one voice. However, at the negotiations there was one dissenting voice, that of Siaka Stevens, who with Albert Margai had left the SLPP to form the PNP. According to him, he was not comfortable with the defence arrangements. Notwithstanding his dissent, the other members of the delegation signed the document granting independence to Sierra Leone in April 1961.

However before the epic event arrived so much happened in the political landscape of Sierra Leone. On their return from the negotiations, true to his word Sir Milton Margai rewarded those of the other camp who supported him. Albert Margai was appointed Minister of Natural Resources, later on becoming Minister of Finance. Cyril Rogers-Wright former leader of the UPP was made Minister of Housing and Country Planning, eventually becoming the Minister of External Affairs. The only voice of dissent, Siaka Stevens on his return (he returned home before the other members of the delegation) continued where he left off by forming the elections before independence Movement (EBIM). He was unsuccessful in pushing this call forward. Attracting people like Wallace Johnson who was not comfortable with allying with the SLPP, and some of the grass-root people who were dissatisfied with the SLPP, in September 1960, formed the All People's Congress (APC) political party to provide an alternative platform to the SLPP. And indeed it did provide an alternative platform to the SLPP. Two months after its formation, the APC shocked the establishment by winning the elections to the Freetown City Council.

After the conference, the United Front apparently had served its purpose and by the time of independence all the member parties of the United National Front agreed a dissolution of their formal structure and merged into the SLPP. Thus by the time of independence in the strict term of the word, Sierra Leone was practising a two-party system, the SLPP. the governing party and the APC, the official opposition.

Following on the protestations of the APC, calling for general strike against the government, thinking that the APC wanted to derail the independence process and destabilise the country, Sir Milton panicked, declared a state of emergency and arrested forty-three

APC members including Siaka Stevens and Wallace Johnson. A week before the event, they were incarcerated for a month while the independence celebrations took place. At the dawn of the 27th April 1961, the green, white and blue flag was unfurled to the crowds at the Recreation Grounds, Brookfields, and the Union Jack ceased to be the emblem of the newly independent country.

The transition from a colonial state into an independent state was relatively peaceful, when compared to some other countries. The anti-colonial disturbances of the Gold Coast (Ghana) and Guinea, where strikes and boycotts had contributed to the removal of the British in March 1957 in Ghana and where French had left taking with them everything portable - even light bulbs, it was reported – after a "no" vote in the 1958 French Community referendum in Guinea, were not features of Sierra Leone's removing the colonial yoke. The violence of Cameroon or Nyasaland (later Malawi) and the outright war footing in the colonies of Kenya and Rhodesia (Zimbabwe), and the Portuguese territories of Angola, Mozambique and Guinea Bissau were unthinkable in Sierra Leone. Another important feature in the transfer of power in Sierra Leone, some structures of self-rule had been in place in the colony for a decade and the civil service was staffed by a cadre of educated and experienced Sierra Leoneans, albeit mostly the Krios.[98]

A question always making the rounds even now was, "Was colonialism a good thing for Sierra Leone?" Much as it is a question making the rounds the author believes there is no simple answer; in most cases it would also depend on what side of the fence one was standing. It cannot be an outright success or failure, there were some good facets and some bad. There is also another question to answer. However, there are countries in Africa, Liberia and Ethiopia that were not colonised, and they have not been left behind in the global village. Two hundred years for some is a long time, like in politics in which

---

98

even a week is a long time. In the history of the nations though, relatively, it is not considered to be. Colonisation in Sierra Leone lasted for about two hundred years.

Indeed, when the British came, the Protectorate was embroiled in local wars a facet of life in those days. The British stabilised the situation by entering into peace treaties with the chiefs, the main reason being to protect the trade routes and keep them open. The main beneficiaries were British as keeping the trade routes open allowed them to exploit the resources in those areas. Not forgetting that the British at some point aided chiefs in their conflicts with their opponents in the taking of slaves who were later shipped to America and the West Indies.

It is a widely held view that the British rule in Sierra Leone was divisive and highly centralised. They succeeded in divide and rule. Unfortunately, our leaders did not recognise that, for what it was. In spite of the differences between these two entities, the colony and the Protectorate were never integrated nor harmonised by the British; they operated different systems of government. In the Protectorate through the chiefs, a system generally considered traditional and by direct rule in the colony which was a modern form of government. This cleavage has had a devastating effect on the Politico-socio-economic development of Sierra Leone. Now when a political party wins an election, it is not a government for the people, but a government of and for the party. The colonial period was not all doom and gloom, far from it. It brought along with it, modernisation of a traditional society and institutionalised many systems that were loosely operated in the society. A school of thought argues that colonialism weakened our traditional system of chieftaincy and destroyed indigenous systems of government.[99] Nonetheless could these traditional systems have projected the country to modern day development? Many of the developed nations today had feudal systems also. Only when these

---

[99]   A New History of Sierra Leone. Joe A. D. Alie

nations decided to discard these feudal systems were they able to progress into a fast pace of development. For instance, in Britain, there was the demesne system where the feudal lords owned all the land and the serfs were expected to work these lands at no wages at all. Just like the chieftaincy system in Sierra Leone which is still in operation in the 21st century. It was only when the land tenure system was liberalised that development began to occur in Britain. Japan also went through this very same cycle.

Indeed, the British brought western education to Sierra Leone, we cannot gainsay, that fact, especially the effort and work put forth by the church missionary societies. As was stated earlier, it was because of education that Sierra Leone became known as the "Athens of West Africa". However, this education was characterised by inequality in provision and somehow elitist in nature. Note the founding of the Bo School to educate only the sons of the paramount chiefs who would later be part of the British administration indirect rule in the Provinces. However, the level of educational enrolment was high in the colony. By 1900 7,000 students were enrolled in primary schools out of an estimated 14,000 children of primary school age. On the other hand, less than 900 children were enrolled out of a population of 1.5 million in the protectorate.[100] Also within the protectorate there was a great disparity between religions. According to the 1931 census, the percentage of children attending school was 0.97% in the North while it was 4.75% in the South. These disparities in education were partially explained by the fact that education was largely developed by the Church Missionary Society from the early colonial days. Compared to the North, which had a strong Muslim influence, the missionary endeavours were more successful and took hold in the South. Although the missionaries opened more schools in the South, the North it should be pointed out had Islamic Schools too. They in a manner of speaking education was being taken to the North. The difference? It was not western education.

---

[100]

Similarly, during the colonial period, Sierra Leone's development was characterised by disparities. The pattern of development that the colonial government envisaged was to extract unprocessed row materials, such as agricultural products and other natural resources from Sierra Leone to Britain. Consequently, the British made the urban areas centres for trade and administration, where raw materials went out and manufactured goods came in. Activities were particularly centred around Freetown which had one of the largest natural harbours in the world. A railway was established from Freetown penetrating through to the South-eastern corner of the country, to transport the rich agricultural products from that region. On the other hand the North – where the railway only reached up to Makeni because of relatively less productive lands beyond – was neglected apparently, in the development agenda of the colonial government. In any case there is a school of thought that contends that the rail network directed and promoted the modernisation of the country, through to the provision of social services, including education, and the development of banking and cooperate organisations. There is some truth in this as testified by the impact the closure of the railways in the early 1970s, had on the socio-economic activity of Sierra Leone.

Under the colonial regime, Sierra Leone was opened for trade, mainly with Britain. As far as industrialisation was concerned, nothing was done on that front. Agricultural and mining products were extracted and shipped to Britain without any attempt made at value addition which would have benefited the exporting country more. This came to haunt the country in the decades of the 80s and 90s when the prices of primary products took a down turn and many developing countries began experiencing adverse terms of trade. Yes, the British opened up and stabilised the country, but to whose benefit? Were their actions philanthropic or exploitative. Perhaps philanthropy was an anecdote instead of the primary cause. The road network was poor and this became quite evident when the railway was shut-down in the early 1970s. Thriving towns along the railway route were hard hit, activities stagnated and suddenly all these towns like Bauya, Yonibana, Kangahun, lost their importance. Also importantly, prices of foodstuff suddenly shot up. Sierra Leone has not recovered since.

Even in the field of education where the country got the name of "Athens of West Africa", when the British left educational services were grossly inadequate, the number of schools both primary and secondary did not match up with the school going age population. After over 150 years of colonisation, the literacy rate was below 20%, quite distressing! What held true for education also held true for health; hospitals were few as were the medical practitioners. In present day parlance we talk about exit strategy. The focus of the colonial regime was more political (constitution) than otherwise. As such when the British left, they left a huge gap in some areas of capacity building in the country, which had to be filled by expatriates. With a good exit strategy, challenges could have been addressed in the training of more professionals in various fields such as medicine, engineering, mining especially taking into consideration the mineral wealth of the country.

Chapter Eight

THE DAWN OF A NEW ERA

Dawn of a new era indeed, or more of the same, or even worse than it used to be? Only time will tell. The independence was greeted with Euphoria by most if not all dancing, jubilating and what you will. This event has been described at length in various literatures. It would have been interesting at the time to take a survey to determine what independence meant to individuals, archive the results and then from time to time repeat the same survey and compare the results. The author is certain that people's views would range from the radical, to the liberal, to the conservative, such as complete severance from the past, continue map a middle of the way progression, or continue with the same as usual, not upsetting the applecart.

The Conference was over, independence was here now we have Sierra Leoneans running their own state of affairs, or should we say, apparently running their own state of affairs. At the helm of all of this was Sir Milton Margai, one of the architects of our independence. As the leader of the SLPP, the party that ultimately won the last election, held in 1957, he became the first Prime Minister of independent Sierra Leone. Unfortunately, Sir Milton's reign as Prime Minister of independent Sierra Leone was short lived as he died in 1964, three years after leading Sierra Leone to independence.

However, before his death, Sir Milton presided over a peaceful transition of power. Although he was seen to be conservative and removed from the people as he did not believe in the mass' populism, but rather working through the chiefs, he appeared considerate and sensitive to regional sentiments. His cabinet was regionally balanced. His government was based seemingly on the rule of law and the notion of separation of powers. His approach to governance was more conciliatory than confrontational. This is not to say that his three years as the head of government were smooth sailing all the way.

All the while during the colonial rule decisions on governance development, social life, finance, the economy were made and implemented by the colonial regime, the governor and his executive council. With independence, the new government had to deal with the international community and domestic economy especially the challenges of creating the enabling environment building proper infrastructure, physical, economic and social, for Sierra Leone to take its place in the world community. At independence, it became a member of the British Commonwealth, but there was also the world financial order, the Bretton Woods institutions, the World Bank and the IMF. This was no easy task, however as the saying goes, a journey of a thousand miles begins with the first step.

The independence constitution made for the separation of powers between the executive, the legislature and the judiciary, very important tenets of democracy and the practice of good governance. In the halcyon days of Sir Milton's leadership this principle of separation of powers was maintained and he never tried tampering with either the legislature or the judiciary. If there was executive order then, he never used it, practising proper parliamentary democracy as the system was then. If there was any blight in his stewardship it was the incarceration of some APC politicians, Siaka Stevens included, during the independence celebrations for fear of them either rightly or wrongly destabilising the process. Similarly, He tried to curb the activities of the APC and limiting the damage that party could cause to the SLPP in the forth-coming 1962 elections, the first general elections after independence.

Chiefs were not involved in politics usually; they were supposed to be above politics and impartial in their decision making. However, because of the close links Sir Milton had with the chiefs, he used this influence to get the chiefs to harass APC politicians and in most cases prevent them from campaigning in their chiefdoms. The first post-independence elections were held in 1962, under Sir Milton's watch. This was also the first election that was conducted under universal adult suffrage; now there was no Protectorate nor colony franchise, the independence constitution abolished all of that. Indeed, this was a momentous election and it determined a new configuration in the political landscape.

The ruling party, the SLPP which had the state's resources at its disposal won this election. Even though the SLPP won the election it did not get an absolute majority. Of the 62 non-chieftaincy seats, the SLPP won 28, the APC which was in alliance with the SLPIM won 20 seats. The four seats in Kono went to the APC-SLPIM alliance. The independent candidates (those supposedly without party affiliations) won 14 seats. Now the SLPP was able to form the government because 12 of the independent winners decided to side with or join the SLPP that won the majority of the seats. The seats won by the SLPP were mainly in the south and parts of the East, and also in the Western Area, (8 seats out of 12). Although the SLPP still claimed to be a nationwide party, its power base peculiarity has not changed. It has run down throughout succeeding years perhaps even more so at present.

The British have been gone for over sixty years, generally the reins of government since independence have been concentrated in the hands of the protectorate leaders – Sir Milton Margai, Sir Albert Margai, Siaka Stevens, Joseph S. Momoh, Ahmed Tejan Kabbah, Ernest Bai Koroma, and at present Julius Maada Bio, yet the scenario has not changed. The majority of the Protectorate still remains relatively undeveloped – lack of good infrastructure, social amenities, and health facilities!

Given this shift in the political balance, the Prime Minister, Sir Milton succeeded to a large extent, in maintaining regional / tribal balance in the country. In a typical Milton Manoeuvre, at once both co-opting and inclusive in intention, his 1962 post-election cabinet contained seven Mendes, four Temnes, five Krios and one Sherbro.[101]

Noticeably, the conservativeness of the Sir Milton led SLPP government displayed no signs of changing after independence. The Prime Minister continued to favour the chiefs as the representation of chiefs in the District Councils was expanded in 1961 in order to nullify the threat of the progressive elements when electing Paramount chiefs to Parliament. Given its conservative nature however, the government was able to forge some amount of development taking into account, the parlous state of the country at independence. Education and health facilities were expanded, and the "raft" of new laws and state institution were established: a National Health Plan was formulated: the Development Act, and the Sierra Leone Investment Act were passed in 1961. The Bank of Sierra Leone (Central Bank) was established in 1963. The Prime Ministership of Sir Milton was very short so it would be difficult to evaluate. One does not know if he had not succumbed to death, whether the political and developmental trajectory might have been different. He might or might not have been able to ride the troubled waters that were ahead. One will never know.

Sir Milton died on the 28th April 1964, and since there was no constitutional provision for a deputy Prime Minister, a vacuum was created for the highest position in the land. This was when things began to go awry as there was a frantic jostling for this leadership position. The main contenders were Dr. John Karefa-Smart a Northerner, Mr. M. S. Mustapha, a Krio, who usually acted as Prime

---

[101]   Sierra Leone: A Political History; David Harris

Minister during the incumbent's absence, and Albert Margai, the deceased Prime Minister's brother, a Southerner. At the time there was a widespread feeling that the opportunity should be given to a Northerner to lead the country.

As the occasion demands, it is the prerogative of the Governor-General, as determined by the constitution to appoint someone who in his opinion commands the majority in parliament. This the governor-general, Sir Henry Lightfoot-Boston did, on the advice of the Attorney-general, Berthan Macauley. He went ahead and appointed Albert Margai, the younger brother of the late Sir Milton Margai as Prime Minister. So, this position became a family affair, passing the baton from the older to the younger brother. In all probability this action by the governor-general was based on the fact that Albert Margai won a leadership challenge against his older brother in 1958. All the same, this appointment did not sit well with some senior members of the SLPP who protested, to no avail. They were subsequently relieved of the cabinet positions by the newly appointed Prime Minister.

The appointment of Albert Margai as prime minister ushered in a new era in the political dispensation of Sierra Leone. He was quite a different personality from Sir Milton, radical, acquisitive, robust and an imposing personality,[102] tending towards dictatorship. These personality traits led to his downfall in later years as he ran the SLPP aground.

Albert Margai, being the radical that he was began his stewardship by mobilising young educated individuals into the party; one such individual was Salia Jusu Sheriff who later on played an important role in the country's development. It was thought that Albert Margai resented the power and influence that the traditional leaders, the chiefs had over the decision making process. He wanted to move away from the policy of conservatism to one of radicalism. In this,

---

[102]   New History of Sierra Leone. Joe A. D. Alie

he looked towards Kwame Nkrumah of Ghana, the liberator that brought independence to Ghana in 1957. The path in which Albert Margai was moving demonstrated his admiration of Osagyefo, as Nkrumah was now being called, the Redeemer, the saviour of Ghana. In the long run Ghanaians fell out of love with the Osagyefo. In Sierra Leone the Ghanaian model did not work for Albert Margai.

The trend in those early years of independence was to maintain a lean cabinet. To this end Albert Margai's cabinet which was predominantly male, totalled seventeen, that included a woman, Chief Ella Koblo Gulama, as Minister without Portfolio. In choosing the cabinet Albert Margai appeared to be sensitive to regional and tribal balance, but those were early days as his later actions did not seem to vindicate him from promoting tribalism, and the subsequent ills that plagued Sierra Leone could be traced to his tenure as prime minister. On the other hand, to give the devil his due he did make some impact on the country's development.

As Minister of Finance in Sir Milton's government, he spear headed the establishment of the Bank of Sierra Leone, the Central Bank. When he became prime minister, he established the national currency, the Leone which was tied to the pound sterling at an exchange rate of two Leones (Le2.00) to one pound sterling. And was freely convertible.

In his quest to move the country forward, he embarked on the development of large-scale plantations, and under his tenure of office, an oil refinery and a cement factory were established in the Eastend suburbs of Freetown. To promote tourism, the Cape Sierra Hotel, by Lumley Beach was constructed. He also attempted a reorganisation of his party, the SLPP in a bid to increase its membership and move away from the traditional conservative thinking of the chiefs. Under his tenure, a national party headquarters and a party press were established. He called for a clear cut policy on how candidates were to be appointed, and an organisation of the party at local level.[103] It

---

[103] A New History of Sierra Leone. Joe A. D. Alie

was early days, but one thing Albert Margai did that was absent in Sir Milton's cabinet; he appointed Madam Ella Koblo Gulama as Minister without portfolio in his cabinet. In the SLPP hierarchy he also established positions for women as "Mammy Queens" who were responsible for organising other women into small groups to garner political support for the party.[104] In all fairness, Albert Margai was not as popular with the people as his older brother Sir Milton had been. Even within his own political party, he did not command the likeability that Sir Milton had, a paradox really considering the fact that in an earlier leadership challenge, Albert defeated Sir Milton albeit with a slim majority of a single vote. Where Sir Milton would tread softly especially in sensitive and difficult situations, Albert would use the iron fist which fuelled some resentment against him.

In a bid to shore up his dwindling popularity in the country and stifle the opposition, he advanced and legislated a series of measures which to all intent and purposes backfired. In response to a challenge by the opposition APC on the composition of the Freetown City Council, the Prime Minister, Albert Margai decided to increase the number of councillors from twelve to eighteen with the aim of putting to rest this challenge by the APC through legislative means. Unfortunately, this ploy backfired as when elections of councillors were held, the opposition APC won eleven of the eighteen seats in the council, with this win, the All Peoples' Congress had a single seat majority over the Sierra Leone Peoples' Party. It is worth mentioning here that the iconic Wilberforce Memorial Hall which among other things housed the offices of the Freetown City Council burnt down in a mysterious fire during the early hours of 17th October 1964. After almost 60 years, an impressive City Hall has been built and was opened for business in 2021. One event that stuck in the author's mind was the visit of Kwame Nkrumah to Sierra Leone in 1956. We had heard so much about him and as a teenager formed our own impression about him, as a man of towering stature. What more place to conduct such

---

[104]   Sierra Leone. A Political History. David Harris

a gathering to listen to him talk but the Wilberforce Memorial Hall. The hall was jam-packed as one would expect and many of us had to crane out necks just to catch a glimpse of "towering figure". To the disappointment of many of us small boys, he was of a much smaller stature than we had imagined! And for us of those tender years our interest was on how a man of such stature can command such respect and admiration.

Albert left no stone unturned in his effort to discomfiture the APC and stifle the opposition. Four (4) APC parliamentarians were serving jail terms (12 months) on trumped up charges for riot and assault in connection with a bye-election. To curtail the number of APC parliamentarians, the prime minister introduced a motion through which any parliamentarian who without good cause, was absent for a total of thirty (30) days during and annual session of the House would lose his /her seat.[105] Of course this was part of Albert Margai's plan to eradicate the APC from the political scene. He knew that his popularity was waning and a general election which was looming might see him lose power to the All People's Congress. Although the All People's Congress opposed the motion vehemently, it was carried; subsequently, the four APC members who were serving jail sentences lost their seats.

The next measure that Albert Margai implemented to restrict the APC gaining popularity was to prevent the APC from airing any of its programmes over the Sierra Leone Broadcasting Service. The Daily Mail, a newspaper owned by the government, was also directed to restrict or stop coverage of the opposition APC's activities. These moves did not endear the Prime Minister to the populace at large, especially those in the Northern region and the intelligentsia in the Western Area.

To further compound the problem, Albert Margai, in trying to copy the Ghana model attempted to introduce the "One party system"

---

[105]   What Life Has Taught Me. Dr. Siaka Stevens

into Sierra Leone's system of governance. We all knew that if the populace had acquiesced and he had succeeded this move would have done away with the official opposition. This move by Albert Margai was met with stiff resistance. In later years this contributed to his downfall in the 1967 general elections. What is interesting however was that Siaka Stevens, as leader of the Parliamentary opposition vehemently opposed this action by Albert Margai. He himself as President brought the country into a one-party state in later years. This is politics! In the words of Siaka Stevens "I did not think that the Prime Minister's proposals were in the best interest of the people, taking into account the historical and cultural background of Sierra Leone".[106] It was this same Siaka Stevens, as president in 1977 that railroaded the country into a one-party system of governance. Also in 1965, a bill was passed which gave chiefs extraordinary powers of assembly. Albert then instructed the chiefs to make life difficult for the APC. All of these measures being put in place by Albert Margai would climax in 1967, but not in the outcome that he was working towards; an outcome which was the beginning of instability in Sierra Leone politics.

In continuing with his war against the opposition APC, the Prime Minister initiated the enactment of the Public Order Act of 1965. This was an act to consolidate and amend the law relating to public order. In a nutshell, it sets forth penalties for persons breaching the public order, and includes such offences as public insult, intimidation, throwing of missiles, idle and disorderly persons, rogues and vagabonds, drunkenness, beating of drums, riotous conduct, street noises and trespass. Prohibits carrying of offensive weapons, regulates processions and public meetings. Sets forth provisions regarding defamation and seditious libel, and public emergencies. On the face of it a reasonable law, unfortunately its use in Sierra Leone has not been in accordance with the spirit of the law. Successive governments including the APC have used it to clamp down on

---

[106]   What Life Has Taught Me. Dr. Siaka Stevens

dissent and it is usually the fourth estate, the press, that has been its victim. That section of the law is all one hears about, but nothing on riotous behaviour, unusual noise and disorder. In fact there is so much disorder and indiscipline in the country, especially in urban areas that it is a wonder that such a law exists.

Instead of focussing on activities that would win him the hearts of the electorate, Albert spent a lot of effort in "demolishing the APC". (His own words on the campaign trail for the 1967 elections). Not that he did not try, either to demolish the APC or to develop a young democracy, he failed in both. Looking at the way things were going, it would not be strange to ask how did Albert Margai get away with all of this? After all the Sierra Leone independence constitution was modelled on the West Minister system of parliamentary democracy with checks and balances being provided by the judiciary and the legislature, although in that system, the prime minister was a member of parliament. The prime minister did not have absolute power. On paper, i.e. according to the constitution, every decision of the prime minister was subject to parliamentary approval and the governor-general had to be notified in advance. As such, as far as the letter of the law pronounces, it was parliament's responsibility to hold the Prime Minister to account. Unfortunately the parliament of the day, either was not strong enough to take the Prime Minister to task or the parliamentarians were ignorant of their responsibilities. All these innocuous bills, the Absenteeism Bill, the Public Order Act etc, sailed through parliament without objection. It would be safe to say, parliament was just a rubber stamp for the whims and caprices of Albert Margai.

Indeed he was a radical, indeed he was an admirer of Kwame Nkrumah, he also pursued a foreign policy of non-alignment and was responsible for some landmark development but on the whole he almost led the country into bankruptcy.

Albert Margai, in my humble opinion was an autocratic leader tending towards dictatorship. One cannot gainsay the fact that he had a very strong personality, and he did not take opposing views lightly. The author can recall as a sixth former during the time when he was the Minister of Education, having an altercation with him over the payment of students' allowances as sixth formers. Yes, how strange it now sounds that in those days even six formers were given a term stipend of twenty-four pounds. In any case the incident occurred when receiving information that six formers of other schools had received their stipends but in our school the principal was telling us that the Ministry of Education had not yet paid in the money to that particular school. Subsequently we decided to strike by not taking the local internal exams. The long and short of it was that the principal invited us to the school on a Saturday and of course we thought our stipend would be given us. Lo and behold, on our arrival there was the Minister of Education, Albert Margai himself purportedly being there by accident. As students we did not believe him. He gave us a good tongue lashing and went on and on about our privileged positions in society and ordered us to take the exams which we did. Eventually our stipend was paid.

Tribalism and Regionalism evoke such passion in our society, unfortunately, at the expense of patriotism itself. Even when abroad, away from the home country, this trait manifests. There are those who swear by their tribe, and even a few that hold the view that tribalism is absent in our society. They probably live in another planet, or they are just blind, or again refusing to accept because they are beneficiaries to it. It may also be that they are just callous and impervious to the plight of their fellow countrymen.

This great divide or polarisation of Sierra Leone originated during the reign of Albert Margai. By favouring the South-easterners in his cabinet and elsewhere, Northerners started drifting towards APC; by the end of his reign, this process was complete. As David Harris puts it in his book "Sierra Leone. A Political History", Africanisation of the military became an exercise in promoting Mendes in the army in order to reward supporters, but also to shore up control of the security apparatus. British officers, numbering fifteen in 1964, were whittled down to just three by 1967, most being replaced by Mendes: the percentage of Mendes in the officer corps doubled, from 26 to 52 percent. The officer promoted to replace the force commander, who was British, was a Mende, Brigadier David Lansana. This "menderisation" did not stop with the army. To effect the same process in the civil service, Albert Margai enacted a very obscure and controversial law (policy). At the time when the General Orders (a set of regulations), the G.O., as it was popularly known, that governed the administration of the civil service, the retirement age for civil servants was pegged at fifty-five years. What Albert and his cohorts did, in order to get rid of the top echelons of the civil service who were mainly Krios, they made a law of voluntary retirement at forty-five years and rid themselves of the Departmental heads of those institutions and appointed their own kith and kin. In implementing this rule, the word "voluntary" was ignored; once the age of forty-five years was attained the incumbent was removed.

For good governance to obtain, the three arms of government; - the executive, the legislature, and the judiciary – must be separate and independent, and each must have the requisite power to fulfil its function. A failure to respect this separation inevitably leads to authoritarianism inevitably creating the opportunity for bad governance.[107] One cannot defend Albert Margai on the violation of this sacred principle, and given a weak legislature, he did this at will and only to satisfy his personal propensities. Take the judiciary as a case in point. The Chief Justice and all judges of the High Court had tenure of office until 62 years of age. They could only be removed in very limited circumstances, with the approval of the Judicial Service Commission. Without observing due process Albert Margai unceremoniously removed Bankole Jones from his position

---

[107] Truth and Reconciliation Report Vol 3

of Chief Justice and appointed Gershon Collier, his friend as Chief Justice. According to the laid down criteria, Gershon Collier was not qualified to serve in that capacity. This role as Chief Justice allowed Gershon Collier to sit and decide on election petition cases and manipulated such judgements in favour of Albert's ruling SLPP. Also, he appropriated the power to appoint the President of the Native Administrative Courts through the Local Court Act of 1963 and thereby completely robbed the local judiciary of its independence.[108] All this happened within a system of parliamentary democracy, a system in which the Prime Minister himself sat in Parliament and participated in all parliamentary debates. He could not rule by decree, the governance system then did not allow it, so there were no executive orders. Given the prevailing circumstances, the word of the Prime Minister was law virtually.

Fortunately, the Prime Minister was somehow sensitive to public opinion, he never tried to manipulate it to suit his propensities. Indeed, when he sensed that his proposals for a one-party state and a republican constitution were unpopular, he did abandon them, and the electorate did breathe a sigh of relief. But for how long as the succeeding government under the then leader of the opposition, Siaka Stevens, rail-roaded both the one-party and the republican constitution into law after he became Prime Minister.

With the first post-election approaching, Albert Margai continued in the same vein going all out to rig the fourth-coming elections in favour of SLPP.

In those days, before the day of elections, we would have elections campaigns during which the parties would hold meetings to discuss their strategies manifestos etc. Campaign meetings were held in the East, West and Central parts of Freetown, and also in the Provinces. In fact, the writer could remember attending some of those meetings to learn about the parties' manifestos. One thing that stayed with

---

[108] Truth and Reconciliation Report Vol 3

him was listening to the discourse of Borbor Kamara, an illiterate waxing vocal for the All People's Congress. He had a very logical mind and this was mirrored in his arguments, In fact, the writer also remembers that eminent lecturers in their respective fields used to attend these meetings just to listen to Borbor Kamara speak. Those were interesting days and many of us looked forward to attending those meetings. Those were days of civility. No violence, freedom of association and of speech. They were not days of party rallies whereby these rallies had to be time-tabled by the Electoral Commission to avoid violence, as we are seeing it at present.

Also, the press played quite an important role in the outcome of the elections. Notwithstanding the wiles of Albert Margai to limit the space of the APC, there were very powerful and articulate journalists like Ibrahim Bash Taqi, Sam Metzger who were standard bearers for the All People's Congress. Incarceration by the ruling party did not stop them from saying and writing the truth. They were able to expose the profligacy of the Albert Margai regime and largely influenced the thinking of the electorates in Freetown, the capital city and the Western Area in general.

Indeed, the day for the elections arrived, and there was a lot of euphoria in the air. The election itself was generally peaceful notwithstanding a few skirmishes in some provincial areas like Kono. It must be said that though the atmosphere on that day was tense, as it was widespread knowledge that the ruling SLPP was attempting to rig the elections any and every which way; the electorate, especially in Freetown was extra vigilant. It came out in the Dove Edwin Commission's Report which was established after the election, that Albert Margai influenced the Election Office, which according to the constitution was to be free from political influence, to return six SLPP candidates unopposed.

Albert Margai also increased the burden on the opposition candidates to contest the elections by raising the deposit paid by each candidate from two hundred Leones (Le200.00) to five hundred Leones (Le500.00). Added to this increase, the fees for petitioning any election result were revised from six hundred Leones (Le600.00) to one thousand Leones (Le1,000.00). These measures were taken to prevent the opposition All Peoples' Congress Party from mounting any meaningful challenge against the Sierra Leone People's Party in the impending general elections. Actually, the ruling party was in control of state resources so they could easily surmount these hurdles. On the day of the elections, there were reports also of ballot rigging in favour of the SLPP candidates. All of these incidents were testified to by witnesses in the Dove-Edwin Commission of Inquiry, set up by the Military Junta Government, the National Reformation Council, to probe the conduct of the 1967 general elections.

The election itself passed on peacefully. The problem began when the results were being published through the government media, the SLBS and the Daily Mail newspaper.. On the instructions of the Prime Minister, the results that were being released always put the governing SLPP in the lead, in effect refusing to announce to the public the true picture of the outcome of the elections. It was inevitable at the end to misrepresent the true outcome of the elections. But even that was manipulated. On the afternoon of the 19th March, the SLBS broadcast the results thus: SLPP 28 seats, APC 32 seats and Independent 4 seats. There was one result, the Moyamba West Constituency, that the APC won that was never broadcast. Indeed, this was not how the electorate voted. The un-manipulated results of the elections were SLPP 28 seats, APC 32 seats and Independents 4 seats giving a total of 64 seats.

The Prime Minister refused to accept the results on the basis that the results of the chiefs' elections were not yet declared, an erroneous and confusing assertion as conventionally, the chiefs were supposed to side with the government, and not determine what party would form the government. If that was the case, Albert Margai knew that the SLPP would be declared the winner of the elections as he had manipulated the chiefs' election in his favour. He did not get his way as the Governor General decided in favour of the APC and appointed Siaka Stevens as Prime Minister. The military under the command of Brigadier David Lansana, staged a coup putting the Governor General and the newly appointed Prime Minister under house arrest at the State House and declared martial law. Thus started the period of instability in the politics of Sierra Leone. Also, but for that disastrous act, Sierra Leone would have been the first country in Africa South of the Sahel to have changed government through the ballot box and not by force of arms as was the practice then. As it was Sierra Leone still made history. The country had four different Heads of State within a week! Brigadier Lansana's coup lasted for 46 hours only, when he was overthrown by some junior officers, who chose a retired lieutenant-colonel who was out of the country to head the military junta. Mid-way, between his appointment and taking office, another military officer also out of the country was selected instead to be the head. As a matter of fact, these two military men had fallen out with the then Prime Minister, Albert Margai, so they were retired from the army.

Many reasons have been advanced for Lansana's coup, and also for the Military Junta's stay in power, from a divided nation through tribal lines, to the risk of a civil war. In reality all these were selfish and personal reasons. Yes, during the elections the atmosphere was tense but the elections passed on peacefully. It is the held view that Brigadier Lansana intervened because of his allegiance to the SLPP. After all he was promoted to be the head of the army by Albert Margai. It should be mentioned that the late Sir Milton did not think Lansana was competent to head the army. In fact, some people were of the opinion that the Prime Minister, Albert Margai, invited Brigadier Lansana into State House. Whatever excuse there was for the coup, it was a sad day for Sierra Leone when the army entered into politics. As the popular saying goes, any coup is the beginning of a counter coup. Once military men tasted the reins of power it is seldom that they leave voluntarily. They were only removed through the barrel of the gun.

Talking about the barrel of the gun, the author can recall as a student of Fourah Bay College, on hindsight an interesting occurrence during Brigadier Lansana's declaration of martial law. This incident happened when the college was on vacation, but because of the impending exams in June, the college authorities allowed students to stay in residence for the payment of a small fee of ten leones (le10.00) which was five pounds sterling in those days. On the day that martial law was declared the residing students were in one of the dining halls, waiting for the Principal, Dr. Davidson Nicol, who was to give us some advice on our safety as the student body played an active role in the ousting of the SLPP regime. While waiting one of the students who had a transistorised radio he was listening to, shouted "Lansana dey kam…." All hell broke loose. Now the student who made the call was going to say "Lansana day kam broadcast." (Lansana is going to make a statement) but since the student body was on edge as it was expected that the military would attack them because of the sterling role they played in ousting the SLPP candidate for that constituency, hearing just part of what the student with the radio was going to say, which translates into "Lansana is coming…." everybody took to flight. In the pandemonium some students left their foot-wears, glasses etc. behind, fleeing for dear life. It was hilarious when in the morning of the following day, students returned to the hall to retrieve their belongings.

During the early days of the military incursion into governance, rumours were rife that Britain would intervene to restore democratic rule as Sierra Leone was part of the Commonwealth and the head of state was the British Monarch. Consequently, people's expectations were very high that military rule was only a passing fancy. When this expected intervention did not materialise the nation's enthusiasm was dampened, and all had to contend with the fact and accept this blip on our democratic development. The National Reformation Council went on to rule by decree for thirteen months before it was toppled in a counter-coup by warrant officers in April 1968.

The National Reformation Council appointed three Commissions of Inquiry: The Dove-Edwin Commission of Inquiry to look into the conduct of the 1967 general elections; the Hyde Foster Commission of Inquiry investigated government assets; the Justice Beoku-Betts Commission of Inquiry to examine the activities of the Sierra Leone Produce Marketing Board (SLPMB). Point of note: In those days when Sierra Leone's stature as the "Athens of West Africa" was unquestionable, there was no need whatsoever to look for foreign judges to lead Commissions of Inquiry. Those justices were men of high repute, they were even called upon to serve in other courts in the sub-region. Imagine, when the military took over in 1967, the head of the Junta ordered the then Chief Justice, Sir Samuel Bankole-Jones, to do his swearing-in as head of state. He did not refuse because he was under the barrel of a gun but did protest publicly that he was doing this against his conscience. Let's look at another case, when the dastardly group of AFRC rebels staged a military coup in 1997, the leader, Johnny Paul Koroma ordered the then Chief Justice, Beccles-Davies to do his swearing-in as head of state. Rather than subjecting himself to such ignominy, he refused, and absconded from his post. Those days were history in the making, and those were men of impeccable characters, who refused to be influenced by politics or coerced against their will. They held their "oath of office" in high regard.

At the beginning of their thirteen-month reign, the NRC went about their tasks with gusto. Apart from the deteriorating political situation, the economy was in a bad shape. When Albert Margai was removed from office, the balance of payments were in dire straits and the Sierra Leone Produce Marketing Board was in shambles. The economic problem leading to the balance of payment crisis was not unconnected with the mess that Albert made in the SLPMB. The Beoku Betts Commission which was examining the activities of the Marketing Board discovered that most of the profits of the Marketing Board ended up in the pockets of the party rather than with the farmer whose returns were to be cushioned by the Marketing Board when the prices of their produce were depressed in the international markets. Prices of primary agriculture products were and still are highly volatile. One of the primary objectives of the SLPMB was to sustain the farmers' income in time of depressed commodity prices and also to create buffer stocks for the farmers in time of shortages especially as primary agricultural commodities were highly susceptible to vagaries of the weather. For the first time in the history of the country, the International Monetary Fund (IMF) had to be called in to stabilise the economy. The packaged proposed included the devaluation of the national currency, the Leone, against the pound sterling.

Ministers and their deputies were ordered to return government cars and vacate government quarters. The Hyde-Foster Commission investigation into assets declared that SLPP ministers and civil servants must pay back the resources that they illegally acquired. In cases where liquid resources were not forthcoming, properties were seized and taken over by the state. The Dove-Edwin Commission inquired into the conduct of the 1967 elections. Its conclusions pointed to irregular SLPP electoral practices, the legitimacy of the APC victory and the validity of Steven's appointment. Most of the recommendations of the commissions of inquiry were implemented.

"Quo Vadis, whither goest thou Sierra Leone"? One might be tempted to ask. In 1967, after the removal of the government, commissions of inquiry were appointed to examine the misdemeanours of the politicians in the past regime. Fast forward fifty-three years later, the same actions were taken against politicians of the previous regime of the All Peoples' Congress, who were in power from 2007 to 2018. It is beyond the pale, that such actions should be instituted after such a long history of practising democracy. What progress have we made? Very little as far as the development of our democratic institutions are concerned. Unfortunately, the days of rampant corruption are still with us and with all the checks and balances in the constitution, politicians still take decisions and execute them with impunity, many a time against the wishes of the electorate. Instead of acting as checks and balances, the various arms of government collude to defraud the populace; a few individuals benefit because they have access or control over state resources at the expense of the beneficiaries of those resources. The outcome is the state of bad governance, leading to much dissatisfaction, poverty and suffering.

It could be said that the NRC regime was intimidating and repressive, but not brutal. Human rights and military rule are a mismatch, and the regime trampled on the rights of individuals. During those days, we did not have civil society as we have it today. But my oh my! Academics and students alike at Fourah Bay College and Njala University were very vocal in urging the junta regime to not curtail the freedom of expression and publication. Also the Bar Association strongly condemned the repressive actions of the NRC.

In spite of its repressive activities Juxon-Smith and his cohorts in the NRC did succeed in turning around the Sierra Leone economy. By the time they were toppled in April 1968, they had succeeded in eliminating the balance of payments current deficit. They implemented some austerity measures that were unpopular, and also instilled discipline into a society that was not as ill-disciplined and lawless as it is today. The regime operated on a reduced budget, for instance reducing government ministries from fourteen to nine. They terminated uneconomic state projects like the contractor finance projects that Albert Margai patronised and which led to a drain of the country's resources. The National Reformation Council also embarked on the retrenchment of public sector workers and imposed higher taxes on incomes and diamond dealers. These were the days before structural adjustment when our economy was in free fall after hosting the Organisation of African Unity (OAU) now African Union conference. Interestingly when the Bretton Woods Institutions came in these were the same policy prescriptions that they offered to reverse the imbalances and fortify the economy to withstand external shocks especially. A plus for the military regime was the fact that it was easier for them to introduce and implement policy reforms than a democratically elected government, especially when the reforms were a bitter pill to swallow. For the politicians always their consideration was not how it would benefit the country in the long-run, but how it would impact on their votes come the elections. Their electability.

Chapter Nine

MISSED OPPORTUNITY

On the 17th April 1968, another coup rocked the nation. This time round warrant officers, allegedly dissatisfied with their conditions of service amid the austerity measures of the National Reformation Council, staged a counter coup and removed the NRC from power, and formed the Anti- Corruption Revolutionary Movement (ACRM). A National Interim Council was formed to oversee the return to civilian rule. Indeed the "coupists" did not perpetuate their stay in power. They invited the former deputy force commander Brigadier Bangura, who was staying in Guinea, to return to Sierra Leone and govern. He in turn invited Siaka Stevens who won the general elections in 1967 to return from Guinea and take over the reins of government.

The day that Siaka Stevens and Bangura returned from Guinea was one never to be forgotten. The atmosphere in the capital city of Freetown was electric and highly charged. Crowds of people lined the major thoroughfares, waiting with bated breath to catch a glimpse of the new prime minister to be. Indeed, there was a lot of anticipation in the air, that at long last, Sierra Leone would take its place in the global stage, trajectoring to higher heights, considering what the country had been through, including the new prime minister who was at the butt of Albert Margai's venom. There were lessons to be learnt from past experiences and the general expectation was that past mistakes would not be repeated. And indeed, when Siaka Stevens took over for the second time, he commanded the popularity of the populace to lead Sierra Leone into a golden age of socio-economic development. Siaka Stevens possessed all the attributes to make his country great. He had been an experienced politician, an effective trade unionist and also had had the experience of opposing the excesses of the previous Prime Minister, Albert Margai.

When in opposition during the regime of Sir Milton Margai there was a thorny issue of the 1960/61 Audit report which was quite unfavourable at the conduct of some of the cabinet Ministers. An issue that the government of the day wanted to sweep under the carpet. In a bid to impress on members of the House not to take their responsibility lightly, Stevens quoted from a speech by Josiah Gilbert Holand the following: "God give us men! A time like this demands strong minds, great hearts, true faith and ready hands; Men whom the lust of office does not kill; Men whom the spoils of office cannot buy; Men who possess opinions who can stand before a demagogue and damn his treacherous flatteries without winking; Tall men, sun-crowned, who live above the fog. In public duty and in private thinking."[109] A good and inspiring speech, for any occasion. Did our new Prime Minister leave up to his billing? History would decide. This was the man who stood up to Albert Margai in his quest for absolute power: imposition of a one-party state and a republican constitution on the people of Sierra Leone. As a matter of fact Siaka Stevens campaigned on these two issues and the outcome of the elections vindicated him. The intended one-party state and the republican constitution that Albert Margai wanted to push forward were a political blunder. On his assumption of power, Siaka Stevens was faced with some very difficult challenges, security, a divided nation and a weak economy plagued by corruption. Late in the decade of the 1960, military coups had become fashionable in West Africa,

---

[109] Cf What This Life Taught Me Dr. Siaka Stevens

evidenced by military take overs in neighbouring Ghana, Nigeria and Dahomey (Benin) and of cause in Sierra Leone; once the military had tasted power what would prevent them from entering into the fray on the quaint excuse that the constitution was under threat and they were protecting the rights of the people. Indeed Albert Margai had polarised the nation and now there was the North-South divide the position had now moved from Colony and Protectorate. Corruption had always been a part of our society since independence as we know. A case to substantiate was the action of the Prime Minister, Albert Margai allegedly using huge sums of public funds to purchase property in Washington and London and then rented these properties to the Sierra Leone Missions in those countries.[110] There were many other acts of impropriety that were cited in the Beoku Betts' and Forster's Commissions of Inquiry.

It is the author's view that the first three years of the new dispensation given to Siaka Stevens went well for the nation as he tried to address some of these problems, but not all. He even confounded some people by his prudent fiscal policies.

It is worth noting that Sierra Leone and Singapore became independent around the same time. While Sierra Leone has a wealth of resources including minerals, Singapore is just a tiny enclave on the Malay peninsula with virtually no resources, Nonetheless Singapore had Lee Quan Yew but Sierra Leone had Siaka Stevens!

Up until 1970, it was felt that Siaka Stevens was on the right track and he wanted to make a positive change in the political landscape of his fiefdom. One thing that had stuck in the author's memory was meeting with Siaka Stevens soon after he was sworn in for the second time as Prime Minister in 1968. Fresh out of college a friend and I were relaxing after a swim in one of our famous beaches, the Lumley Beach. The Prime Minister called us and enquired about our station, and we told him that we had just graduated from college, I

---

[110]   TRC Report as cited in the We Yone Newspaper

majoring in economics and my friend in English. He then went on to tell us about his plans for developing Sierra Leone, with emphasis on manpower development. He specifically encouraged us to enter into the security forces, especially the Police as at that point in time, there was a dearth of graduates in the Police force. He added that if we were interested we should drop in at his office; he gave us his business card. Unfortunately that was not our remit, so we never tested his sincerity.

One of the Prime Minister's first tasks in governing was to appoint his cabinet. In the opinion of the author, this is a yardstick by which the intentions of the government could be measured, politically and economically. At a previous meeting in which all the contested parties were present, it was decided that the Prime Minister should form a notional government as a first step towards cementing the fracture that resulted from the actions and activities of the previous administration.

Although he was criticised that his cabinet was heavily weighted in favour of the APC, the composition of his cabinet was eight ministers from the APC, four ministers from the opposition SLPP, and two from the independents. Three Paramount Chiefs were given ministerial portfolios also. In answering to the criticism he averred that the two independents originally belonged to the SLPP. According to its size, it was of relatively reasonable size; it might have been slightly larger than that of the previous government. But again Siaka Stevens had a trite answer. The excuse being the nature of the administration, it had to accommodate all shades of opinion.

Indeed after taking up office, he undertook an admirable venture and that was to reduce the salaries of Ministers, including himself. His explanation: the difficult situation that the economy was in after the disastrous period left over by Albert Margai. He was also of the belief that it was not the time for rewarding supporters by giving them Ministerial posts, thereby having a large and an un-wielding cabinet.

In his own words "I decided we had to set an example of austerity. I reduced my own salary by Le1,000.00 (Pound Sterling 500.00), per annum, and that of the Ministers by Le500.00 (Pound Sterling 250.00) per annum, and announced that proportionate reductions would be made all along the line except for ordinary Members of Parliament, whose emoluments would remain at Le1,840.00 (Pound Sterling 920).

Take a moment and consider our present day Members of Parliament. In 2018, Members of Parliament proposed the following for themselves: vehicle allowance $13,000; facilitation fee $2,093 per quarter; rent allowance $12,000; sitting allowance$70 per month; fuel $42 per week. Citizens did not take this lightly, there was a large hue and cry, especially in the words of the president 'de gron dry (difficult economic times), and the song, daily in the ears of the citizenry that they met a battered economy! Well compared to Members of Parliament before the turn of the century, their responsibility was to make laws and ensure that the principles of democracy were upheld, acting as the checks and balances on the other arms of government, especially the executive. These days Parliamentarians have arrogated other functions to themselves. It is not uncommon to read in the newspapers, or watch television, the activities of Parliamentarians in building social infrastructure for their communities, or constituents. They are even segmented into oversight committees, of the various sectors of the economy and one sometimes hears about this or that Minister, head of MDAs, being called before parliament to give account. With all of these systems, procedures, and practices in place, do we have a country that is doing well in the political and economic fronts? One has to go to the field to observe the great disparity between what is happening on the ground and what is usually carried in the news media. In fact it is the author's view that as far as virtual reality is concerned, Sierra Leone is a paradise!

In 1968 Sierra Leone was not a paradise, but then virtual reality was not yet in existence. Considering all that had happened before, the country was not particularly stable, a situation that Siaka Stevens as the new Prime Minister used to his advantage.

Again, in the words of the then sworn-in Prime Minister, "a few weeks later, information reached me that people who could not accept the fact that they were no longer in power were trying to get some Anti-Corruption Revolutionary Leaders to join them in stirring up trouble"[111]. Sounds familiar? This was in 1968, are we not hearing similar pronouncements from the governing party these days?

With all the tampering by Albert Margai, Sierra Leone had one of the best Civil Service in Africa. When Sierra Leone gained its independence there were still some Europeans in certain critical positions in the Civil Service. Similarly, the education sub-sector still made use of teachers, especially in the sciences, from the United Kingdom' some of the principals of secondary schools were still supplied by Britain. Even and perhaps more so in the university college, there was a predominance of Caucasians, many from Britain, but some from the United States of America. Through a policy of Africanisation and also many Sierra Leoneans were returning from abroad with the requisite qualifications to take up appointment at the tertiary level. Graduates from Fourah Bay College were also moving into the Civil Service and other technical positions. At the top of the Civil Service, qualified Sierra Leoneans had already replaced their British counterparts. This replacement at the top was already taking place in the educational system. Thus by 1968, Sierra Leone boasted an excellent civil service and a sound educational system, no matter that it was still geared towards the British system and not particularly catering to the country's manpower needs. Civil society in those days was not large and diverse, but they were effective, and so was the fourth estate, the press. At present there is a plethora of newspapers and paradoxically, in a country where 70% of the population is still

---

[111]   What Life Has Taught Me. Dr. Siaka Stevens

illiterate. Those effective newspapers that existed then have all disappeared and perhaps so have the seasoned journalists.

As an example, the Daily Mail that boasted editors like Awuta-Coker, not only carried very pertinent information, but also the stories that appeared were very well researched. They even published a booklet, titled 'Sierra Leone Year Book" an annual publication in which one could find very useful and factual information. As evidence, let us take a tour of the 1968 Year Book as published by the Daily Mail. The index is detailed hereunder:

- Preface
- Say It With Flowers
- Notes on Sierra Leone
- This is Sierra Leone
- Telephone Nos. & Public Holidays
- Census Figures, 1963
- Foreign Policy
- The Government
- Permanent Secretaries, Provincial Secretaries
- District Commissioners
- Road Distances
- Judges, Barristers & Solicitors
- Mayors of Freetown
- Sierra Leone History
- Justices of The Peace
- Constitutional Story
- Books on Sierra Leone
- Heads of Departments
- Employers' Organisations
- Bus Runs (Time-Table)
- Diplomatic Missions
- Fourah Bay College
- Njala College
- Ferry Service

- o   Postal Rates
- o   Trade Union Movements
- o   Hospital Feed
- o   Railway Stations
- o   Telephone System
- o   Licensed Surveyors
- o   Schools
- o   Weights & Measures
- o   Classified Trade Directory
- o   Who's Who

The Year Book was an amazing piece of work and to think it was a publication of a newspaper and neither of the Statistics Office nor the Government Printing Press. Unfortunately all these laudable ventures have disappeared down the drain. We are now in the digital age so a hard copy publication such as the Year Book might be obsolete. Supposedly, with the click of a button all of this information should be at your fingertips but then in a country such as ours, is it?

During those days the country was not as politicised as it is these days; politics was where it should be. With all the attacks that Albert Margai carried out on the system, the establishment, and even the military, the system still functioned as it should. The civil service for example was regarded as one of the best in sub-Saharan Africa. It was with pride that we claimed our ancestry from Sierra Leone. It was still the envy of the sub-region. Public goods were effectively and efficiently delivered. There was an established intra- and inter-city road transportation. Buses used to ply routes from the central business district of the capital city to the east-end and west-end of Freetown. There were bus services to the outlying villages on a regular basis with stops at specific intervals, right on to the terminuses. Also there were inter-city runs from the capital to other cities in the Provinces. Before the scrapping of the railway, it connected towns from Freetown right on to Kailahun in the extreme east of the country and Makeni in the Northern Region. The railway not only transported goods but it also carried passengers. Health facilities and even schools were in short supply, but where they existed, they delivered good and effective services. The ratios of doctors to patients and teachers to pupils were still appalling, but drugs and learning materials were not in short supply. There were libraries, bookshops and stationery shops where consumers bought all they needed, textbook, exercise books, science equipment, pens, pencils etc. Similarly, there were drug stores, not as proliferated as they are now, but patients bought their drugs and medications from hospitals. These days, imagine a country where there is not a single bookshop! We have lost the culture of reading. In this digital age, the mobile phone is an extension of our daily life often not used for education but used for entertainment purposes. Only in times of crisis that the mobile phone is used as an educational tool, even at that, how effective is it in an environment such as ours.

Looking at what is happening now, the mind boggles to think that in the decades of the sixties and seventies, there was a higher purchase scheme operating in Sierra Leone by the big companies and firms like the UAC, Patterson Zochonis, SCOA etc. For instance, senior civil servants were entitled to participate in this scheme. All that was required was a letter from the head of department certifying the employment of the officer and a guaranty that monthly payments would be deducted at source. Similarly, it would surprise many to know that there was a housing scheme for civil servants, whereby an officer could apply for a loan of ten thousand Leones (5,000 British pound sterling) to build a house. At the time, before it was discontinued, that amount was sufficient to complete a modest abode; that was how many civil servants, whose salaries were nothing to write home about were able to build houses. It is worth noting that these assets were not acquired by corrupt means. Everything was done above board. There was also a loan scheme for the purchase of vehicles. A civil servant was entitled to a loan of one-thousand eight hundred Leones (900.00 British pound sterling), repayment within four years. Once an officer purchased a vehicle, he was entitled to a car allowance which was almost the equivalent of the amount deducted monthly to service the loan! Also, those were the days that the cost of a gallon of fuel was only seventy-five cents (Le 0.75) that was less than a dollar; but this was before all hell broke loose in 1973, when the oil producing countries decided that they should benefit from the resources they were mining, instead of the profits going to the oil distribution companies. That was the time OPEC (the organization of oil producing countries) was formed.

Interestingly, the mantra of the present government is 'free, and quality.' During colonial days, even after independence, up to the decade of the seventies, education was not entirely free, but one could talk about quality because our educational system was up there with the best. The passport to qualify for a government bursary was passing your school certificate exam after the fifth form or passing your G.C.E. 'A' levels after the sixth form. Sure enough that secured a prospective student a government bursary. There was even a reward for excellence. If a pupil attained three 'As' at the G.C.E. 'A' levels exam, that qualified you for a national scholarship, entitling the holder to study overseas.

Considering the closeness of the 1967 general elections, the majority of the ruling APC government over the SLPP opposition party was a slim one, excluding the chiefs, thirty-two seats as against 28 seats. Apparently for electoral malpractices, election petitions were filed on twenty successful SLPP candidates and three APC candidates. These elections were declared null and void by the Supreme court. Whether by chance or by design, the APC won most of the by-elections which were characterised by violence and intimidation. African politics, that's why we have not made much progress on our democratic credentials. Considering what is happening in the present, we have not made a single iota of progress! Always looking backward, and not forward.

Now a comfortable parliamentary majority, the new Prime Minister had all the tools to set Sierra Leone on a new trajectory. He had already gained experience under the colonial regime and Sir Milton Margai regime.

As usual, with regime change, expectations were high. Up to a point, the APC government did not disappoint. In the early 1970s the Sierra Leone Commercial Bank and the Sierra Leone Trading Company were established to compete with foreign Banks and businesses, while the Commercial Bank has stood the test of time the Sierra Leone Trading Company did not last long; it was poorly conceptualised and was improperly utilised by highly placed government officials, often not paying for the goods they purchased. Recognising the agricultural potential and the difficulty of farmers to access credit from the Commercial Banks, with assistance from the African Development Bank the government established the National Development Bank. This operated for a while but in the end, it was discontinued; it did not have much impact on the development of agriculture in the country.

Without either the World Bank or the International Monetary Fund breathing down our necks, proper financial and administrative procedures were followed to the letter. For instance, before the start of each budget cycle, the Budget Committee, comprising the Minister of Finance, the Governor, Bank of Sierra Leone, the Financial Secretary and the Development Secretary would meet to set budgetary ceilings for both current and development budgets, based on the available domestic resources and commitment from donor partners, usually to finance reasonable gaps between the supply and demand sides of the budget. After this meeting, resource allocations would be made to various sector ministries based on their project requests and after a period of consultations to arrive at acceptable allocations. Almost all of the current and development budgets were funded from domestic resources. Subsequently, the government and not foreigners in the guise of multi-lateral and bi-lateral donors, was in control of policy. They were neither dictated to, nor set benchmarks on which fiscal assistance depended on. This was a time before structural adjustment brought about by hostile economic forces in the decades of the eighties. It was also a time during which not much attention was given to the recurrent costs of many development projects, which resulted in failure because of lack of proper planning. Those were the days also, that almost nothing was known of monitoring and evaluation of projects. Not that there was no M and E, but whatever activity occurred was not undertaken in a systematic manner. Nevertheless, project administrators, vote controllers had some semblance of integrity. Thus, as expected, resources allocated to various projects were used for the implementation of those projects.

When Siaka Stevens and the APC took over the reins of government in April 1968, they governed the country for a generation under various forms of constitutional government before they were finally kicked out of power by a group of young soldiers in April 1992. So for almost a generation the APC and its charismatic leader had the opportunity to take Sierra Leone into a similar trajectory like Singapore, or even to rival Switzerland, but alas Siaka Stevens was not a Lee Quan Yew. The leader, Brigadier J. S. Momoh, handpicked by Siaka Stevens, to take the leadership mantle after him was not made of stern stuff although it could be said he was honest, to a certain extent. He had the honesty to publicly announce to the nation that he had failed, but not the guts or the courage to resign from the office of the President of the country. That in itself would have been a historical event, that in all likelihood had never happened before.

In one of his campaign speeches, Siaka Stevens pronounced "You see soak lepet you call am puss" (a wolf in sheep's clothing). As young students in those days being naïve and not wise in the ways of the world, we thought he was a witty fellow, and the more we became attracted to his leadership. Little did we realise that he was only speaking of his docility as a leader; that he could rise and be firm, and possibly ruthless as events would prove during his tenure, especially when he became executive president. Then he showed the people his true colour indeed he was a wolf in sheep's clothing. Once he received the baton of leadership, he apparently became a popular leader as time progressed. He would theatrically express his desire to retire, while the electorate would "clamour for his stay." In his flip-flop manner, he also declared "pass ah die" meaning he would remain president for life. As providence would have it, he was unable to keep to that promise; in the end, his deteriorating physical health overcame his will and he had to give up power to his chosen successor.

Almost twenty-five years of APC's rule! Within two years of Siaka Stevens taking over the leadership of the country, he sought to "demenderise" the army. During that period, the Mendes were reduced to just thirty-two per-cent of the total number of officers. Many of the Mende officers were pensioned off. One might aver that the justification of this action was because of loyalty, especially considering the unstable nature of the country at the time. After all, between the general election of 1967, and the assumption of power by Siaka Stevens in April 1968, there had been three coups and counter-coups; it was a counter-coup that restored constitutionality in 1968. If one should accept that argument, it would only serve to illustrate the fragility of our political system, putting the region, the tribe before the nation. Events in the present day are showing that the country has not moved much from that position, it may have retrogressed.

In March 1971, there was an attack on the home of the Prime Minister, allegedly by disgruntled soldiers. It was alleged to be an attempted coup, led by the Force Commander, Brigadier John Bangura, who returned Siaka Stevens to power in 1968. This coup proved unsuccessful as it was quickly put down by loyal soldiers led by lieutenant-colonel, Sam King. [112] As circumstances played into his hands, Siaka Stevens swiftly signed a defence pact with President Sekou Toure of Guinea resulting in Guinean troops arriving in Sierra

---

[112] The details of this coup plot make for interesting reading from different perspectives. Refer Aminatta Fornah's "The Devil that Danced on the Water "and Dr Siaka Stevens' "What Life Has Taught Me"

Leone just six days after the coup attempt and stayed until 1973. In the aftermath of the coup, the brigade commander John Bangurah and three of his follow conspirators were executed. Significantly, this attempted coup involved the future Revolutionary United Front leader, Foday Sankoh who was imprisoned for failing to inform the authorities of the coup attempt as it was alleged that he had prior knowledge of the coup. Stevens then appointed Colonel Joseph Saidu Momoh as Force Commander, who also in later years replaced Siaka Stevens as president of the Republic of Sierra Leone. The action of Siaka Stevens in all of this, demonstrated his ruthlessness and perhaps can we say an unforgiving spirit? But for John Bangura, he might never have attained the premiership of Sierra Leone. Rather, than terminating his life, he could have commuted his death sentence into a jail term.

During the coup attempt, according to Siaka Stevens, he tried to communicate with the Governor-General as Head of State and Commander of the armed forces to stop the coup but failed. In his own words, "even a Governor-General determined to oppose the coup attempt would have been powerless to frustrate it". He then concluded that "only an elected Commander-in-Chief and Head of State would be in a position to defend democracy against any future avalanche."[113] This kind of thinking was absurd, and probably being used as a pretext to execute his plans and satisfy his propensities.

Thereafter, in April 1971, Sierra Leone was declared a republic by the very man who opposed it in 1967, barely four years after his opposition to the concept of republicanism. The Bill was rushed through Parliament as the APC had a massive majority, and changed the very safeguards designed to prevent a leader from flouting the Constitution and seizing power. After the resignation of the ceremonial president, who was the Governor-General, a day after

---

[113]   What Life Has Taught Me. Dr Siaka P. Stevens

the promulgation of the republican status, Siaka Stevens took over not as a ceremonial but as an executive president, of Sierra Leone.

Indeed, these were challenging times for the new Prime Minister. Some of his younger and progressive Ministers, the likes of the Minister of Finance, Dr Mohamed Fornah, and the Minister of Information, Ibrahim Bash-Taqi broke away from the APC, and joined with Dr. Karefa-Smart, a former Minister in Sir Milton's SLPP government to form the United Democratic Party (UDP). Apparently, they were dissatisfied with the way Siaka Stevens was running the country. There was a smell of cessation infiltrating the corridors of power and government circles and they wanted no part of it. Dr. Fornah accused Stevens of wanting to impose autocratic rule. As a young man then, the writer could remember the rumours that were circulating then, such as the United Democratic Party was tribalistic. However, there was a lot of tension in the air that bordered on fear.

The cause of the UDP was not helped by the violent clashes they had with the ruling APC government. Siaka Stevens dealt with this opposition threat to his authority ruthlessly and swiftly. Within three weeks of the formation of the UDP, it was banned and its leaders, Dr. Fornah, Ibrahim Taqi were arrested and detained. Karefa-Smart evaded arrest by fleeing to Geneva. Ultimately, in a largely staged-managed trial, and despite evidence to the contrary, both Dr. Fornah and Taqi were implicated alongside Juxon-Smith, Lansana and several others, in an attempted coup in July 1974. Indeed, there had been an explosion of some sort at the house of Minister of Finance, on the night in question. They were convicted and hanged in 1975. This was a very sad day in the history of this fledgling democracy. Considering where the APC was coming from, the role that Ibrahim Taqi had played in selling the APC to the Sierra Leone electorate, what was the justification of killing Taqi and Dr. Fornah? They probably should have been treated as heroes rather than villains.

One question that has exercised some of our minds had been the response of Siaka Stevens to the fluidity of the society he inherited when he took over the reins of government. Assuming the environment was calmer and free from political turmoil, would Siaka Stevens have chosen a less violent and less autocratic part in governing the State of Sierra Leone? That is a question that would remain unanswered, but an excuse that could be made by those who revered him for his apparent excesses.

As it was, he took certain decisions which he thought would address the security situation. At the onset, he used the military to quell disturbances, and he did not hesitate to impose a state of emergency when the occasion arose, as it did following clashes during the by-elections in the South and East. Another state of emergency was imposed after clashes occurred between supporters of the governing APC and the break-away United Democratic Party (UDP).

In a move to get the army over to his side, one of Siaka Stevens first moves was to "Northernise" the army and increase military spending. Furthermore, during his tenure of office, as a placating gesture, he allocated monthly rice quotas to the army and the police. In another stroke of ingenuity, the heads of the security forces, were appointed to Parliament and became members of cabinet also. This decision was taken after the failed coup in 1971. His romance with security did not stop with the army. In the early 1970s, Siaka Stevens formed a special police unit called, the Special Security Division or SSD as it was popularly known. In common parlance, they became known as "Siaka Stevens Dogs". Even though they were absorbed into the regular police force, it took its authority from Siaka Stevens. Apparently, with these initiatives, Siaka Stevens, surely thought he had addressed part of the security problem, especially those involving the military adventurism into politics through the staging of coups and counter-coups. These were the days that military intervention in politics was quite fashionable. The trend started in English speaking West Africa in the mid-1960s in Nigeria. A Ghanian history lecturer at FBC categorically averred how such an incident would never happen in Ghana. Within a short time after the Nigerian coup, the first coup occurred in Ghana. Of course, as one would imagine the history lecturer, disappeared and countercoups were an everyday occurrence. Worryingly though, while South America seems quite settled and free from the military poking its nose into governance, West Africa seemed to take the mantle from them.

The decade of the seventies brought in a new political and developmental paradigm in the world economy. Note, at the time 'global' was not yet in common usage. That paradigm was still some years away. We all were familiar with the world economy, especially as dominated by the OECD countries of Europe and America.

Specifically in 1973, all that changed and a new era of developmental shift began. After the Arab- Israeli war in 1973 which the Arabs, who started the war, lost to the Israelis, the oil producers who were mainly Middle-East countries decided to take ownership of their raw material – crude oil – instead of leaving it in the hands of the oil refining countries, whose companies were primarily from the Western developed countries of Europe and America; the Organisation of Petroleum Exporting Countries (OPEC) was formed into a cartel. They took over the fixing of price and the quantity of oil that was going to be produced and quotas were allocated to each member country. The outcome of this was the price of oil went up significantly and this phenomenon heralded the decline of many African countries who were net importers of manufactured goods from the developed economies, Sierra Leone not excepted.

Indeed, in the opinion of the author, 1973 was a pivotal year in the history of Sierra Leone's development. Prior to the 1973 Yum Kippur war, Sierra Leone had formal diplomatic ties with Israel. More importantly, the country received a lot of aid, both technical and project related from Israel: in agriculture, engineering, health etc. The country's Parliament was even built by the Israelis; even in security one would say, because they assisted in the training of Siaka Stevens' SSD. Now after the war, the organisation of African Unity, (now the African Union) took a decision that member states should sever diplomatic ties with Israel and Sierra Leone complied. And to think that as far as the Arab States were concerned, Sierra Leone received barely any assistance from them. This writer could remember sadly enough, after the dust had settled, Siaka Stevens in his wisdom dispatched his first Vice President to explore the possibility of negotiating favourable terms of importing oil from the OPEC. Sadly enough, he returned empty handed. Of what strategic importance was Sierra Leone to the OPEC countries? Rather than helping us, the pyramiding of the oil price laid bare the weakness of African economies.

Politically too, 1973 was a watershed in the democratic credentials of Sierra Leone. It was five years after constitutionalism returned, and according to the constitution, it was time for another general election; it was time to test the popularity of the ruling APC party. In May of 1973 as one would imagine, under a state of emergency, the tension was palpable. Not only that, but there was also quite an amount of violence, even between rival candidates vying for the ticket for the same seat under the ruling APC party. For example, one of the rivals for the ticket in the Central 1 constituency as it was known then, in Freetown had the temerity to use a cane to flog women, some even old enough to be his mother, because they supported a rival female candidate. Campaigning was a bloody affair, and consequently, the opposition SLPP, fearful of the prevailing violence withdrew from participating in the general elections. Of course, this played into the hands of Siaka Stevens. The outcome was that the APC became the single party in parliament, and de facto, Sierra Leone became a one-party state.

In appointing his cabinet, Siaka Stevens tended to lean more and more to the North, demonstrating that the stronghold of the APC was in the Northern Province. The tribal composition of the cabinet was ten Temnes, two Limbas, five Krios and four from the other smaller tribes and three Mendes. To give the devil his due, the cabinet was dominated by the Temnes, but many of the other tribes including the Mendes were given participation in the governance of the country.

Indeed, the decade of the seventies was quite eventful in our country's history. There were good developments and some unsavoury. On the part of the good, in the early 1970s, the APC government embarked on national development planning, the first of its kind in our history. An attempt was made by the SLPP government in the 1960s but it did not succeed. Primarily, it was a one-man show as a renowned Sierra Leonean economist was consulted to formulate a development plan for the country. Indeed, this he accomplished sitting behind his desk at the Ministry of Development: it was neither participatory, nor consultative; it was never implemented.

In 1971, the Ministry of Development, implementing government's policy established a Central Planning Unit, charged with the responsibility of formulating a five-year national development plan. This initiative was funded partly by the Government of Sierra Leone and the United Nations Development Programme (UNDP). The Unit was staffed by technical experts in their respective fields and Sierra Leonean graduates mainly from Fourah Bay College. After extensive work in data collection, consultations with public and private sector personnel, work on the formulation of the plan was completed in 1974 by which time the technical experts were phased out and the entire implementation of the plan was undertaken by the Sierra Leonean counterpart staff.

There were other good aspects of development occurring in the country undertaken by Civil Servant personnel. Roads and bridges were constructed by the professional staff of the Ministry of Works. Those were the days that capacity constraints were not so much a feature in the Public Service. There were constraints of course but it did not require the spending of huge amount of money on workshops and seminars, which to say the least, were largely unproductive. Technical courses on various disciplines were run by the World Bank and the International Monetary Fund (IMF). Some technical courses were offered by universities in the United Kingdom and Development Institutes in the Netherlands. For administrators, there was the Royal Institute of Public Administration (RIPA) in the United Kingdom. Public Servants had access to all of these opportunities and since sponsorship by the institute or some other international organisation, primarily the United Nations and the Commonwealth Secretariat was guaranteed, government made full use of them. Selection to participate was based on 'need' and merit and not the colour of the party one belonged to. Those were the days the politicians and the public servants knew their respective roles and kept to them in governance. Promotions in the Public Service was done through the Public Service Commission based on the recommendation of the head of department and which in turn was based on the performance of the officer. In a similar vein, staff movement within the service and the diplomatic service was undertaken by the Postings Committee comprised of Civil Servants. Interference by Ministers who were the political heads was not entertained.

There were times though when political considerations took precedence over sound economic decision making. Many a time when the technical arm of the government was appraising projects sent for that purpose by cabinet, before the appraisal was completed, one would hear an announcement over the air waves that the particular project had been approved by cabinet. There were times also when government delegation was going to discuss certain technical projects with donors that the technical personnel were not included in these delegations: the composition in most cases, was the Minister as leader, the permanent secretary of the particular Ministry and some other staff; scarcely would the professional head be included in the delegation. So many good projects were not implemented because proper technical advice was either not sought or was disregarded. A typical example was the fruit canning plant that was constructed in Konsho. That was the bright idea of Siaka Stevens who on a visit to Holland witnessed a fruit caning plant in operation. There and then he had a brainstorm to establish fruit caning in Sierra Leone on the backbone of the tropical fruits that are abundant but seasonal. Without the benefit of assessing the technical viability of such a venture, a fruit caning factory was opened. The long and short of it was that after one single round of operations, there was a scarcity of fruits to feed the equipment; thus, ended that bright spark of the President.

Sierra Leone is always described as an agricultural country, It has an abundance of arable land and a climate not hostile to agriculture, the climate is tropical with an abundance of rain that precipitates for between five and six months of the year, usually between April and November. Successive governments have been trumpeting food self-sufficiency especially in rice production. Every time that is trumpeted, it turns out to be a pie in the sky, even when initiatives were taken, they turned out to be white elephants.

As far as the author remembers, there was always talk of developing the Rhombe Swamp, a vast area of swampland in the Southern Province. In those days the development resources both mobilisation and dispensation were done by the government of Sierra Leone. No matter how resource poor the government budget was, resources were always allocated to and released for the development of the Rhombe Swamp. To this day Sierra Leone is still struggling to feed itself. Definitely something is wrong. Rice is not a crop that has a long gestation period. In fact there is a popular school of thought that maintains that rice can be grown twice a year in Sierra Leone, but either because of cultural norms or something else, this idea has failed to take hold in our society. On two occasions the APC government had embarked on increasing rice production, the one spearheaded by the Minister of Development, a project which was ill-conceived and poorly implemented. It subsequently failed. At another time in the eighties, the then Minister of Agriculture came up with a green revolution project which was widely trumpeted. Like its predecessor it failed woefully and with a lot of money down the drain. As is usual in Sierra Leone, these projects did not benefit the country; in fact, their outcomes were disastrous, taking into consideration their financial outlays, but individuals may have derived some profit out of it!

In a bid to revitalise the economy, Sierra Leone received funds from the World Bank in the decade of the seventies for integrated rural development. These funds were used to implement a project that became known as "The Integrated Agricultural Development Project" (IADP). With the exception of the Western Area and the riverine areas of Bonthe, the country was divided into eight agricultural zones. The project's main thrust was to provide farmers with agricultural inputs and improved seeds at subsidised prices, and also to construct feeder roads for market and farm access. Unfortunately, it never achieved the expected outcome. Most of the supporting elements of the project were improperly managed. The result? Some farmers used the proceeds of the loans to marry more wives![114] The long and short of it was the project was not properly conceived, it was poorly managed, farmers were not properly sensitised and trained and importantly there was no proper monitoring mechanism in place.

Unfortunately, with all the natural resources she is endowed with, Sierra Leone is and has always been consumer- and not a producer- oriented country. Commodities were exported in their primary form to developed nations who in turn converted these raw materials and sold them as finished products to developing countries at much higher prices. As such countries like Sierra Leone always experienced adverse terms of trade, no matter the volume of products increasing prices of imports precipitated foreign exchange crises in many developing countries, Sierra Leone not excepted. Ghana was a worse-case scenario then when their ability to import

---

[114] A Nationalist History of Sierra Leone. C. Magbaily Fyle

goods fell catastrophically. In those hardship days travellers from Sierra Leone to Ghana had to take all their basic necessities along because those basic consumer items were scarce in Ghana. Thus was heralded the famous or notorious World Bank/IMF Structural Adjustment Programme (SAP). At the time, Sierra Leone was not in need of structural adjustment. However because of poor economic management, the country had to go through that painful process; a process which started in the 1970s.

Sierra Leone's main source of foreign exchange was the export of minerals, diamonds, iron ore, bauxite and rutile. By 1975, production of iron ore had stopped. The production of diamonds also the largest foreign exchange earner started to decline. By 1979, diamond production was only 198,000 carats. Some of this decline was blamed on smuggling, and it was believed that members of the government had gone rogue and were involved.[115]

These external shocks, coupled with the profligate spending of the Siaka Stevens led government brought economic and financial hardships upon the masses. A large number of resources was invested in the army; an amount much higher than what was allocated to health, and there was no war being fought at the time. But of course, Siaka Stevens used this as a ploy to take the minds of soldiers off governance and politics. Apart from their monthly quotas of rice, senior officers were allegedly granted loans for housing construction. It was also reported that pre-financed contracts were given to the army without adhering to due processes. Unfortunately, it was the cadre of senior officers that benefited the most. The rank-and-file soldiers did not benefit from this largesse of Siaka Stevens.

In spite of cozying to the security apparatus, certain portions of the population were becoming disgruntled at Siaka Stevens' autocratic style of governance creeping into his government. Circumstances came to a head in 1977 when students of Fourah Bay College

---

[115]   ibid

protested with placards accusing Siaka Stevens of corruption in a convocation ceremony in which as the Chancellor of the University he was conferring degrees on new graduates. How did the government respond? Despicably, the government's response was worse than the students' demonstration. Who would believe that they unleashed thugs on the students, who damaged property and beat up students. Imagine an institution of higher learning being vandalised because the students were exercising their democratic right. What value then do we place on education? Small wonder then that education has been going downhill, and to think Sierra Leone used to be called the "Athens of West Africa". But then, it was the same Siaka Stevens who said "nar sense make book, nor to book make sense" (denigrating the value of formal education). In another occasion he publicly averred that "dem say Bailoh Barrie u say Davidson Nicol." Interpretation: Davidson Nicol was an intellectual and former Principal of Fourah Bay College. Who was Bailor Barrie and how did he feature? He was an illiterate businessman but wealthy. So according to our erstwhile President, the end game was wealth. Unconsciously he might have been setting the scene for the country's fall from grace to grass; a country where at present corruption is endemic in every stratum of society and even in this twenty first century; a country that was known as the "Athens of West Africa" is still grappling with a large population of illiterates.

Siaka Stevens might have thought he had dealt with the student protest by using thuggery to intimidate the student protestors, he was in for a rude shock. They were not curbed. Instead, they called school children out into the streets, and this call was heeded. Siaka Stevens did unleash his personal security bodyguards, the internal Security Unit (ISU) and the SSDs upon the children. But they acted humanely and refused to open fire on children. Let those in governance today take note of the behaviour of these personnel. They did not open fire on innocent children. Alas! Not so today under the new direction government: any protest has to be put down by unnecessary force, even in situations where the protesters are unarmed, the first recourse of the security forces is to open fire! The upshot of all this was the spread of the protest to the Provinces which caused panic within government circles. However, the religious leaders were called in and together with the student leaders, they were able to calm the situation. As of then and now it is worth noting that notwithstanding the public order act of 1965, people were allowed to protest. In these days the public order act is used as an instrument to stifle freedom of speech and the democratic right of protest. One excuse extant these days is the failure to comply with Police order not to protest, often leading to the killing of innocent civilians: the security forces seem to be out of control and it looks like the order of command is being violated willy-nilly. Top guns in governance can order the security forces to quell demonstrations with utmost brutality, resulting in the destruction instead of the protection of lives and property.

Usually, Siaka Stevens liked to test how well he was resonating with the people especially during the latter part of his presidency. Often, he would publicly proclaim that he was retiring, or he was thinking of retiring. Then, whether spontaneous or contrived we would witness delegations upon delegations from every corner of the country coming to pledge their loyalty and requesting that he continued his tenure. And of course, being a man of the people, he would accede to their call, and there ended the issue, until another cycle when the same would be repeated. To many of us, this was a bit irksome at the time and we would wish if only he had kept his word to vacate the position honourably. This would have been another plus for Sierra Leone as in those days African leaders were not in the habit of relinquishing power peacefully.

Accordingly, with the student unrest skilfully laid to rest, Siaka Stevens thought it was time to test his popularity. Incidentally, one of the demands of the students was for a general election to be held. Indeed, by calling for a general election, Siaka Stevens gave the impression that he was acceding to their wish. But of course, the cards were stacked. The APC mobilized thugs who meted out violence in many of the constituencies in the North, thus securing un-opposed nominations for the entire Northern Province, their stronghold. Despite this naked violence, the SLPP contested the elections and succeeded in winning fifteen seats in their own stronghold.[116]

A thing Which seemed of little importance, but which the author believes changed the trajectory of Sierra Leone's Civil Service. In the mid-1970s, an astute secretary to the President, Mr G. L. V. Williams vacated that post and Siaka Stevens appointed his successor Mr. Koroma. Until then the civil service was administered strictly by the regulations prescribed in the General Orders (G.O), for administration and the Financial Orders (F.O) for the financial aspects of government, from tendering for the procurement and awarding of contracts. When the secretaryship to the government changed hands, these regulations were interpreted differently, to suit political rather than administrative, development outcomes. For instance, in the General Orders, promotion in the service can be achieved by 'merit'. "Merit" in the sense of ability or administrative acumen. When the subsequent incumbent took the office of Secretary to the President, 'merit' was given a broader definition that had nothing to do with administrative performance, but about political allegiance. This period heralded the interference of the politicians, especially the President into the civil service. "The party could not neglect elements like the army and the civil service ... The case of the civil service was a delicate one. It was an institution whose structure, and to some extent, whose personnel were inherited from the colonial regime. The British Tradition of a politically neutral civil service was strong. But as a government, - and we must remember after seven years in opposition, the party was deeply engrained with the need to take the party to where power was. If the APC was to be the vehicle in which all the talent of the country was to be mobilised politically, the civil servants had better be taken on board, as the armed intellectuals and

---

[116] A Nationalist History of Sierra Leone. C. Magbaily Fyle

chiefs had been, as the armed forces and other parties would be."[117] An innocuous statement? Not so. The SLPP of Albert Margai started it and the Siaka Stevens' APC stretched it to the extreme.

The President, Siaka Stevens started meddling in the Civil Service by sending top officials, Permanent Secretaries, Professional Heads on leave; an act itself that seemed innocuous. But did he have the authority? Even though he had become an executive president, the Constitution did not give him that right. Unfortunately, other top civil servants who could have put their foot down against such a behaviour did not raise a single voice, thinking this was not of much importance and would not become a regular occurrence. It was as if the President was testing the waters to gauge the reactions of those who would stop him. Unfortunately, their passivity encouraged the President to make more forays into the administration to a point where the General Orders and Financial Orders were constantly flouted with impunity. Indeed, when fiduciary and administrative authority were removed from the remit of the professionals, square pegs were put into round holes and the economy started spiralling into the abyss.

Up to the mid-seventies, the economy was not in a bad shape, but began spiralling downward, thereafter especially with the closure of the Marampa (iron ore) mines. As domestic revenue started to dwindle, the government resorted to reckless fiscal and monetary policies, and the pillaging of the economy. By the eighties, the situation worsened, and the government had recourse to run to the international and bilateral donors for assistance which of course came with costs.

Those days, there was no anti-corruption, not meaning that the running of the government was corruption free. Corruption is a human flaw, and where there is money, power and other material things, there will be corruption. It is present in all corners of the

---

[117]   Direct quote from "The Rising Sun. The All People's Congress Party of Sierra Leone. A History of Building for the Future.

globe: in Europe, in America; in Asia; in Australia and of course in Africa. In the developed nations, when you are found out, you will face the music and pay the price, no matter your station in life, be it president, a prime minister or a labourer or a beggar. In many African countries, this is not the case, the system is highly discriminatory; usually the big guns and those in power loot the treasury with impunity.

Thus, it came as a surprise in the late 1970s when what become known as "Vouchergate" was unearthed. This event created a lot of noise as it was generally felt that the establishment usually turned a blind eye to acts of corruption, especially when those involved either "belonged" or were "toe – the – liners". With bated breath, the populace was waiting to see what the outcome was going to be, back-burner or heads would roll. Indeed, this was corruption on a massive scale, Vote Controllers, and their co-conspirators in the Ministries, and Departments contrived a smart but simple scheme of making vouchers and requests for purchases that were less than the threshold amount that would require the approval of the Financial Secretary and the Accountant-General. Thus, these requests were internally approved and sent to the Accountant-General for payment. It was smart '419' scam, but it all went wrong because of too much greed. All the vouchers, whether it came from education or health, or social welfare or development, were requesting the same amount for purchasing the same things. Fortunately, a smart official in the Ministry of Finance noticed the similarities in all of the vouchers and queried all of them. As a matter of fact, some of the departmental accountants had the audacity to forge the signatures of the Vote controllers. An official of one of the ministries whose signature was forged, after suffering the humiliation of being incarcered in prison for a considerable length of time, escaped jail time because the forgers made a great blunder: on that date she was purported to have signed the vouchers she was out of the country attending an official seminar in the United Kingdom! What was the outcome after a protracted investigation? Only a few of the perpetrators were called to book. The majority of them continued in the service and rose in the ranks, some becoming Heads of Departments and Vote controllers themselves. Corruption is not a new phenomenon; it has been with us from the days of Jacob and Esau!

An important event that marked another turning point in the country's political development was the successful push by Siaka Stevens to turn Sierra Leone from multi-party, into a one-party state, a position he vehemently opposed when Albert Margai attempted the same in 1967. In fact part of his campaign ticket was against the move by Albert Margai to establish a one-party system in Sierra Leone. As far as Siaka Stevens was concerned 1967 was not the right time to establish a one-party state, but 1978 was appropriate; the circumstances prevailing remained the same and also the environment had not changed.

True to form, after the 1977 elections which the APC contrived to win, several calls were made by APC stalwarts, to change the multi-party Constitution into a single party constitution. Whether real or contrived, delegations from all corners of the country visited the President calling for the imposition of a one-party state. Primarily, the reasons given were to eliminate the on-going violence between the two main parties and coalesce the opinions, knowledge and skills of the various factions under a single umbrella, to enhance the political and socio-economic development of the nation. As a reminder, these were the very same reasons Sir Albert Margai advanced in 1967, that were opposed by Siaka Stevens.

In June 1978, after a referendum, Sierra Leone became a one-party state. Under the new constitution, the term of the President was changed from five years to seven years, but not so for the term of the Parliamentarians.[118] Significantly, the SLPP who had sitting parliamentarians, was outlawed! The course of least resistance was for them to switch allegiance which almost all of them did. These were

---

[118]   A New History of Sierra Leone. J. A. D. Alie

greedy, self-seeking and unprincipled individuals. They were jostling for positions, ministerial or otherwise, under the excuse that "we were all under the same banner." This swing-tendency, "chameleonic" as recorded in the Truth and Reconciliation Report (TRC) is prevalent particularly among politicians of our country. Thankfully, there was one man, a single-minded individual, now deceased, who stuck to his guns and never moved over to the government side in Parliament.

Reflecting in some of Siaka Stevens decisions and actions, it could be said he was good at networking. Indeed, it could be safely said that he continued his predecessor's policy of non-alignment, when it came to foreign policy, but he also broadened the sphere of international relationships with other countries. While the immediate post-independent era, Sierra Leone was still romancing with the western democracies, Siaka Stevens reached out to China and Russia. In fact, in the early days of the APC, the view was widely held that they leaned to the Communist East of Russia, and that the resources to establish the APC were coming from the Soviet Union as Russia was known in those days.

Nevertheless, Siaka Stevens established a very strong relationship with these countries, a relationship that became exploitative rather than beneficial to Sierra Leone. We cannot run away from the fact, that much of technical assistance in the form of training of our professionals, doctors, engineers, came from the Soviet Union, but they exploited our fisheries willy nilly. It was the popular belief in those days that even the Russian vessels had built-in factories that processed the marine resources that were harvested from our waters. It was also usual for the local labour to be ill-treated by these foreign fishing companies; their plight for whatever reason was completely ignored by the sitting government, who also turned a blind eye to the effect that the large foreign fishing companies was having on our local artisanal fishing industry.

The Chinese were more subtle. In fact, when the APC of Siaka Stevens was in power, they were responsible for most if not all of Sierra Leone's infrastructure development and also invested in agriculture. The Chinese constructed the National Stadium which was formerly named the Siaka Stevens Stadium; it was the National Provisional Ruling Council of Strasser that renamed it, the National Stadium. The Chinese also constructed some roads and bridges and built the massive Youyi Building structure that houses many of the government offices at Brookfields. The Chinese also invested in agriculture, establishing a sugar-plantation and processing plant at Magbass in the Tonkolili District, Northern Sierra Leone. Unfortunately, due to poor management the Magbass processing plant did not meet the expected output and it finally ran out of steam. It was an unproductive investment in its totality. These projects were supposedly done through the largess of the Chinese, or so it seemed at first, only for the government to realise mid-stream that there was no free lunch. To compound matters, since there were no contractual obligations before the start of the project construction, the Chinese donor could charge whatever fee they deemed fit once the project was completed. They expected all sorts of concessions from the government.

Understandably, Siaka Stevens could not be casting his net so far and wide without trying to foster good relationships with his neighbours, especially as it is held that Sierra Leone shared a common history, heritage and destiny with Guinea and Liberia. Thus, the concept of solidifying this relationship through a kind of Union surfaced in the early 1970s. For a start, some informal surveys were undertaken by the Ministry of Development and Planning in Sierra Leone to map out areas of economic cooperation. Nevertheless, it was only in October 1973, that Siaka Stevens and William Tolbert, the President of Liberia signed the Mano River Declaration. Guinea acceded to the agreement in 1980, and now the Mano River Basin has been extended to the Ivory Coast who became a member in May 2008.

The primary objective of the Mano River Union was to intensify economic cooperation and accelerate economic growth, social progress and cultural advancement among the Mano River Union, to establish a firm economic foundation for lasting peace, friendship, freedom within the Mano River Basin.[119] It's been over forty years since, in reality, it would be safe to conclude, that this lofty aim has not been achieved. To all intent and purposes, this Union seemingly has been eclipsed by the larger Union of Economic Cooperation of West African States (ECOWAS). For a moment let us speculate. When the Civil War broke out in Liberia, ECOWAS played a very important role to stabilise the chaotic situation in Liberia. Sierra Leone was used as a base by ECOMOG forces to try to stop the rebel attacks in Liberia, during which a considerable amount of Liberia's infrastructure was destroyed. The rebel leader Charles Taylor, now serving jail term for the atrocities committed by his troops in Liberia and Sierra Leone vowed that Sierra Leone would have a taste of the war, which she did, through the willing hands of Foday Sankoh who became the leader of the Revolutionary United Front (RUF).

On a larger international level, Sierra Leone was one of the foundation members of the Organisation of African Unity (OAU) founded in May 1963 with headquarters in Addis Ababa, Ethiopia. It became the African Union in 2006. The broad aims of the OAU were: to coordinate and intensify the cooperation of African States in order to achieve a better life for Africans' to defend the sovereignty, territorial integrity and independence of African States; dedicated to the eradication of all forms of colonialism and white minority rule.[120]

It was the practice that the country assuming the Presidency of the OAU for the subsequent year, would host the OAU Conference which was seen as a prestigious affair, with all the pomp and ceremonial. Imagine a small or little-known country in the global community

---

[119] A Nationalist History of Sierra Leone. C. Magbaily Fyle

[120] Wikipedia

playing host to all the heads of state of African countries' that surely would catapult a country into the international map as observers from developed countries were invited to these conferences. It was an opportunity for any country to show-case herself, but at what cost?

Stevens in his bid seemingly to put Sierra Leone on the map but perhaps more to feed his ego, by hosting the OAU Summit, almost bankrupted the country. The two hundred million Leones that was spent on the construction of the Mammy Yoko Hotel, the Bintumani Hotel Conference centre and sixty luxury villas above Hill Station and generally upgrading summit-related infrastructural facilities, was twice the original budget and added significantly to the growing debt burden. In all of this there was a dissenting voice. The Governor of the Bank of Sierra Leone, an astute economist who was knowledgeable of the deals made was highly critical; and he should be, knowing the impact such deals would have on the economy. He was an intelligent and strong character. There was astuteness and professionalism, whether true of false, who knows? The Government flagship bank, the Sierra Leone Commercial Bank was established during the tenureship of the Governor of the Central Bank, Sam Bangurah, The government proposed a salary which the Governor had to approve for the Managing Director of the newly established Commercial Bank. As it happened the proposed salary was much higher than what the Governor of the Central Bank was earning. Any normal human being would find it difficult to accept such a situation, but Sam Bangurah, being the intelligent man that he was, approved without an iota of dissatisfaction. When the salary of the Managing Director of the Commercial Bank was finally rubber-stamped by the Government, the Governor posed a conundrum: what respect would he receive as the supervisory authority of the Commercial Bank when his remuneration was lower than that of the individual he was supervising? Simple really: his remuneration had to be increased. What a wise fellow!

In any case, because of the professional and unbiased views, his advice did not go down well with the government. Without doubt, he met an untimely end as he was killed after being thrown from a high window in his official residence, shortly before the summit. There was a lot of speculation over his death, whether it was officially sanctioned or accidental. Difficult to know, however, there was no speculation whether it was suicide or murder; it was murder, pure and simple. It went on for a long time, not the trial, but bringing the perpetrator to book, who was finally convicted for the crime.

The decade of the 1980s proved difficult for the economy of Sierra Leone due to both internal and external factors. What Ghana was experiencing in the 1970s Sierra Leone started experiencing in the 1980s. In 1980, Sierra Leone hosted the OAU Conference. Consider, at that time, the country's infrastructure left much to be desired. It could not boast of any reputable and distinguished body. Siaka Stevens however was determined to be President of the OAU, a position that carried a term of one-year, and so it eventuated in 1980. It was his belief, whether real or misplaced, that the OAU summit would stimulate the economy and put Sierra Leone on the map.

It would require a massive dose of investment to revamp the country's infrastructure to bring it up to the desirable standards for such a reputable conference. The infrastructural and other amenities to be constructed included 60 modern flats to house the various heads of state, a new hotel with the requisite conference facilities, and the refurbishment of existing ones, improvements of airport facilities and the construction of jetties, erecting major streets lighting and improvement to the distribution system. Where would the resources come from to effect these changes? Definitely not from domestic resources. The country had to look for loans and donations from outside sources. All of these were achieved at break-neck speed. The speed with which these projects were completed, the procurement, and distribution of contracts, involving huge sums of money raised cries of widespread corruption; but it was only noises dissipated into the atmosphere. Nobody dared to question Siaka Stevens. Although an attempt was made to put a cost on the hosting of the OAU Summit, it is the author's belief that any figure adduced did not represent the true picture or actual cost. Honestly, there were so many leakages that benefited private individuals and impoverished the state.

Environmentally, the hosting of the OAU Summit was something of a disaster as vast acres of forests had to be cleared to construct the OAU villas. The level of deforestation was very high and completely changed the eco-system of the area. There was hue and cry to plant trees in the surrounding area but it has gone largely unheeded. Instead, the surrounding areas have been further denuded and buildings have sprung up all over the place. Hitherto the area had been a forest reserve and a water shed. Unfortunately, after the civil war, the entire forest reserve was sold off by the government to private individuals. An area that contained a reservoir to supply water to the surrounding communities, was encroached upon and subsequently the reservoir disappeared; it no longer exists. There was even a damn nearby which barely contains water because there has been a lot of land encroachment around the dam area; where there used to be trees, there are now palatial structures. Usually, where there are hills and mountains, there is a tree line, a height whereby one cannot go beyond in putting up buildings or enjoying any man-made activity whatsoever. Not so in Sierra Leone. If there is such a law, it does not operate. How else could an entire hill, be mowed down just to put up a diplomatic building!

The benefits that were anticipated from hosting the OAU Summit never materialised; if anything, it worsened a situation that was already bad. In fact, huge increases in public expenditures were incurred in hosting this conference. In effect, the fiscal policy was characterised by large budget deficits, with a shift towards recurrent rather than development expenditures. Unable to generate enough resources through taxation, domestic non-bank borrowing and external loans the government relied more and more on the banking

159

system to finance its ever-increasing budget deficit.[121] These policies as should be expected reflected adversely on the Sierra Leone economy. The rate of inflation increased and the value of the Leone to the United States Dollar fell rapidly. By 1987, the inflation rate was an incredible 180 per cent, and the exchange rate in 1986 was just under Le4,000 to $1.00 (US$).[122] Sounds ridiculous, considering what the rate is now, but just in 1980, before the delinking of the Leone from the Pound Sterling by Siaka Stevens, the exchange rate was almost at par; in fact before the delink, one pound sterling was equivalent to two Leones, while one United States Dollar was equivalent to about eighty cents (Le0.80)!

Before the delinking of the Leone, the currency was internationally recognised. In those days before the proliferation of plastic money, one could walk into a local bank and purchase travellers' cheques in pound sterling or United States Dollars. Similarly, if you travelled to the United Kingdom with your local currency, the Leone, you could walk into any Thomas Cook Travel Agency Office and exchange it for the equivalent in Sterling. Also, if one held a foreign account in any foreign bank, you could instruct your local bank to effect money transfers from your domestic account to your foreign account. Those were the days before exchange control regulations came into force. In a similar manner, overseas purchases could be made through the Post Office and / or the Parcel Post, for goods not manufactured or sold in-country. There was also the opportunity to walk into stores like the UAC and SCOA and purchase brand new British or French made vehicles, paying for them with the local currency, the Leone. This was before the era of the second-hand vehicles, the prevailing culture in our beloved country. Perhaps it is the government and a handful of businessmen that command the resources to purchase brand new vehicles.

---

[121] Structural Adjustment and Vulnerable Groups in Sierra Leone. Richard Longhurst, Samuel Kamara and Joseph Mensurah

[122] Sierra Leone's Economic Record; 1961 – 2010. Economic Policy and Research Unit, Ministry of Finance and Economic Development.

No more! By the early 1980s, Siaka Stevens' non-budgeted discretionary spending was estimated at more than sixty per cent of actual budgets. The small manufacturing sector actually managed to shrink and there was no report of exporting these products after 1980. In the sign of the times, the big European Companies such as Compagnie Francaise de l'Afrique Occidental (CFAO), Paterson Zochonis (PZ), and the United Africa Company (UAC) started winding down their operations in the country.[123] On the flip side, this was a window of opportunity for local entrepreneurship to move into that space. But alas, this did not happen; that awakening was just not there and other factors of production like capital were lacking. The access to capital was limited as the few banks that existed did not provide long-term loans for businesses of that nature. Well, local entrepreneurs did not move in but an opportunity was created for Lebanese and Indian businessmen to thrive, at whatever costs. Since then, the Sierra Leone economy has been in strangulation by these unscrupulous and unprincipled businessmen with the connivance of our political leaders unfortunately. It is no secret that they can bribe their way through any system.

Everything appeared to come to a head after successfully hosting the OAU Summit, successful in terms of organisation, not necessarily the outcome of the summit itself. The standard of living of many Sierra Leoneans began to deteriorate as the cost of living started to rise. Various factors, both internal and external were responsible for this. Apart from the fact that the spending on the hosting of the OAU placed a strain on the budget, Steven's profligacy did not help an already precarious situation. Coupled with the fact that earnings from iron ore had stopped and diamond exports were dwindling, and also the terms of trade became negative, meaning the prices of imports were higher than the prices of our exports, a balance of payments crisis was triggered. To cushion the trade and budget deficits, the government had to seek loans and grants from bi-lateral

---

[123]   Sierra Leone. A Political History. David Harris

and multi- lateral sources. This presaged our indebtedness to the international donor community and perhaps allowing these donors, especially, the World Bank and the International Monetary Fund to obliquely determine our economic and financial policies. Once the IMF and World Bank determine to augment your resources through loans and grants, this is a signal of the credibility of the borrowing country. So apart from the resources these institutions will make available to the borrowing country, they provide the credibility that the borrowing country is fit to do business with. Usually, the cost of that credibility was very high, subsequently pushing the borrowing country into more economic distress, barely understood by the Bretton Woods experts, let alone the technocrats of the borrowing countries. As a result, there were successive phases of these structural reforms programmes, each subsequent phase seeking to improve on the preceding one.

Generally, market forces were no longer efficient in regulating the foreign exchange market; administrative controls had to be imposed to regulate this market. The mantra was, your currency was over-valued, so to make your exports competitive, the currency had to be devalued. Next, to bring back fiscal sanity and discipline, subsidies had to be removed even on essential imports, like rice, the country's staple food and fuel. These measures not being enough, there should have been retrenchment and retraining of the labour force, unfortunately, this did not happen. Also, there was structural unemployment because of capacity deficiencies in the labour force. This was like a panacea to address all our economic woes, and once there policy prescriptions were followed, your economy would become buoyant once again. Right? Unfortunately, experience proved otherwise.

Generally, implementing these policies might have been economically sound, but it was politically suicidal. As expected, these policy prescriptions were implemented half-heartedly or never at all. Consequently, developing countries kept sliding into a state of economic fragility, a state that very few have been able to continue to exit because of the millstone round their necks imposed by trying to meet their debt obligations. How can they when the greater portion of their export earnings are mortgaged to debt repayment? It's been an unending cycle.

The Leone which used to be convertible up to the 1970s was no longer so by the decade of the 1980s. Did devaluation enhance the competitiveness of our exports? Unfortunately, no! The main exports were primary products like coffee and cocoa, whose demand were price inelastic. "If I am used to drinking three cups of coffee a day, the price would not affect my addiction to coffee." In any case, the market for these products was such that the farmers in the producing countries did not benefit from the sales of these commodities, The benefits accrued to the processing factories in the developed countries. Also, it perhaps escaped the framers of these prescriptions that most developing countries, in Africa particularly were competing for the same products in these markets, where the prices are not fixed by the producers but by the consumers. Therefore, who would benefit from the devaluation of our currencies? The answer is elementary.

Did the retrenchment of public sector workers with the aim of retraining them bridge the capacity gap? Again, this policy did not work as most of the retrenched labour could not be trained to adjust structural employment and the resources to achieve this outcome were unavailable. Thus, a large number of public sector workers were laid off and became unemployed. Add to this the removal of subsidies on rice and fuel, one could imagine the economic hardship this brought to an already distressed economy. Really and truly, the 1980 decade was very difficult for Sierra Leoneans in general. But of course, there was the privileged few, mostly belonging to the political class, not all of them politicians, who held the country hostage.

Amid this burdened environment, the Sierra Leone Labour Congress called a general strike in 1981 that almost brought the Stevens government down. Stevens cajoled and employed all kinds of strategies to get the leaders to call off the strike. Some of these strategies were violent, as thugs were used to attack some institutions that were sympathetic to the strike. More often than not, these thugs were given drugs by some party officials for them to carry out their dastardly acts. For instance, the Tablet newspaper's office was attacked and set ablaze; the editor had to flee the country for dear life. The army was kept under the watchful eye of Stevens' loyal Brigadier Joseph S. Momoh and was deprived of ammunition which now became the preserve of the Special Security Division, the President's special guards.[124] In spite of all this intimidation and violence, if the leaders of the strike had stayed the course Siaka Stevens' government would have fallen as the strikes had the support of the nation.

As time progressed in the 1980s, especially after the OAU summit, life for the majority of Sierra Leoneans became more and more onerous. Notwithstanding the wealth in the natural resources, Sierra Leone has always been, and is still an import-dependent country more of a consumer-oriented society. The decade of the seventies, the paradigm of economic diversification and industrial development was frequently touted by policy makers. But imagine we are in the twenty-first century, having left the last millennium behind now for twenty years, and over fifty years since this realisation surfaced in our policy making. Un-encouraging news, to us who are still alive after this policy came to the fore. Sierra Leone is still undiversified, and our production regime and consumer pattern have not changed, not even an iota; perhaps it has gotten even worse. Even our staple food which is rice is imported and the amount of money spent on rice importation alone is in the region of two hundred million dollars. Being an agrarian country with rice as the country's staple, it beats the imagination that it has never entered the minds of our policy makers that it would make more sense to spend that quantum of money in developing our agriculture, rather than waste that money

---

[124]   A Nationalist History of Sierra Leone. C. Magbaily Fyle

on the development of foreign agriculture. Perhaps, there is more to it than meets the eye. And when you look at the rubbish that are sold in the market for human consumption, 25% broken, 75% broken etc; rice perhaps fit only for animal feed. What is wrong with our leaders?

Be that as it may, given the nature of our economic structure, the country's ability to import became severely constrained. And the consequence witnessed scarcity of essential commodities, petroleum products, rice, and other consumables. In simple economic terms, when there is a shortage in supply that falls short of the demand, to clear the market, prices would rise and that was what happened in the eighties. It was a common sight to see long queues of vehicles at fuel stations waiting to purchase fuel. Also, it was sometimes not un-surprising for drivers to spend the night in their vehicles, just because they desired to make the head of the queue when the stations opened for business.

One unfortunate outcome that became detrimental was that whenever the opportunity arose, people started hoarding fuel especially for their generators. Without proper storage and care, the fuel sometimes ignited resulting in the loss of life and property. At the time, petroleum and its products were handled by the private and not the public sector, so an essential commodity such as that could not be used as a political tool. Not so rice! Dramatically during the recent shortage of fuel in the country the First lady attributed this situation as acts of the fuel dealers who belong to the opposition APC. How fantastic. Under normal circumstances that statement was inciting, but who will bell the cat?

Considering the wealth of arable land that the country has yet its main food rice became scarce just like other essential commodities because of lack of foreign exchange. As one would expect, scarcity would push up the price. However, in those days, possessing the liquid resources to buy did not provide the necessary access to those commodities. This was before trade liberalisation whereby; the government controlled the importation of rice. What operated under the regime of Siaka Stevens, was the Hajas were the sole operators in the rice market. To be able to purchase rice from them, a buyer had to secure a "chit" from the APC hierarchy which was then used to collect supplies from the Hajas.

Under Siaka Stevens' reign, the country's resources were mortgaged to a few Afro-Lebanese businessmen. Two businessmen in particular, known allies of the APC government, controlled the minerals, fisheries and import sector. One, Jamil Sahid Mohamed, had extensive contracts with Siaka Stevens. He became a shareholder in the Diamond Mining Company (DIMINCO) shipped loads of diamonds out of the country.[125] Stevens essentially ceded the diamond industry to Jamil, with official exports of diamonds reduced from slightly above half a million carats I 1980 to below 50,000 carats in 1988! As a business partner of Siaka Stevens, he had the control of the manufacturing industries, insurance, and marketing. Thus, although Jamil Sahid Mohamed was not a government official he wielded a lot of political power.[126] Imagine giving acquiescence or approval to official government appointments at both ministerial and civil service levels.[127] Going beyond the pale, imagine this businessman, Jamil, who was not a member of the Siaka Stevens cabinet, nor the Bank Governor nor any of its official for that matter, setting the price of the exchange rate? Hard to believe but that was the reality which had a considerable negative impact on the economy of the country. For a start Jamil acted like a godfather to the government. Because he was in control of most of the country's natural resources, the government's fingers were in his mouth. As a result, he violated frequently, banking, and other regulations including foreign exchange

---

[125] The Underlying Causes of Fragility and Instability in Sierra Leone. Herbert M'Cleod and Brian Ganson

[126] Ibid

[127] Ibid

market rules with impunity.[128] Imagine when the government was cash-strapped, such a businessman was the first port of call for short-term loans.[129] How demeaning! Of course, doing business legitimately or otherwise became a costly affair so much so that small businesses were crowded out of the market and only businessmen with large financial capital were able to survive. And considering the way and manner business was being undertaken someone had to bear the cost of all this, usually the consumers because of shifting of these costs to the consumers and the state, and the revenue base contracted.

To all intents and purposes, the President, or perhaps the political class connived with private business, more especially Jamil Sahid Mohamed to operate a "shadow state", or informal market, at the expense of state-run institutions. A phenomenon not new to Sierra Leone. As William Reno puts it "state decay and shadow state construction are firmly rooted in colonial rule." Indeed, elements of the shadow state first emerged with the actions of the British Colonial officials. Diamonds also shaped the context of the struggle for political space. Portable, and of high value, easily mined, smuggled and sold abroad, this resource offered unusual opportunities to local producers and created obstacles to state control over production and trade.[130]

During the colonial period especially in the early 20th century, the chiefs were strong men. They exercised control over the Protectorate's population. So, the imperial power sought their collaboration in the collection of taxes and the promotion of trade. Also, forced labour a common practice in the Protectorate, allowed the chiefs to profit from farming despite low producer prices and high haulage fees. Consequently, the chiefs benefited from new opportunities to maximise economic power while claiming as many customary

---

[128] Ibid

[129] Ibid

[130] Corruption and State Politics in Sierra Leone. William Reno

privileges as possible. They claimed greater shares of state authority which was then translated into private commercial advantage. The discovery of diamonds in the Eastern Region defined a new relationship between the chiefs and the colonial government. As chiefs claimed resources that would eventually provide the bulk of the state revenues, accommodation between Chiefs and the colonial state encountered new difficulties.[131] Fast forward to the Stevens era, to observe the connivance of the political class with businessmen to syphon state revenues into private coffers and subverting the authority of state institutions. During colonial times the imperial government could not care less, they were more concerned with the exploitation of the country's abundant resources. The loser was the nation then under colonial rule, and under Siaka Stevens' government. Understandably, during the onerous domestic situation and hostile international economy, the only way to continue stripping the country's assets was to by-pass the formal market.

The entry of Siaka Stevens to State House was marked by pomp and fanfare. On tasting the power and authority that a head of state wields, one of his favourite sayings was "pass ah die" meaning that only death would remove him from that office. Was it Plato who said, "power corrupts but absolute power corrupts absolutely." Indeed, Siaka Stevens wanted to remain as "President for life". Again, as the saying goes "man proposes, but God disposes." Perhaps it escaped our president that he was human like the rest of us, and not even a "superman". In the latter part of his reign when he began experiencing the ravages of nature, he realised that he would have to pass the baton to a successor.

As with any institution, organisation or state there are rules that prescribe it functions. Sierra Leone was no different, and the ruling party, in this case the All People's Congress had its rules. Did Siaka

---

[131] The Shadow State, Informal Markets is adequately discussed by William Reno in "Corruption and State Politics in Sierra Leone.

Stevens adhere to these rules in choosing his successor? The answer as we know it was a resounding No!

All through the years of the APC government, Siaka Stevens was ably supported by his two able lieutenants, Sorie Ibrahim Koroma, a Temne by tribe and Christian Kamara-Taylor, a Limba from the Northern Region. In fact, even before the APC's ascendancy, these two had been with him as founding members of the party. During the difficult times when the SLPP was in governance, these two suffered a similar fate, being jailed a few occasions for their apparent activities in the party – described as destabilising influences. Indeed, for their loyalty, they were aptly rewarded. Right through the APCs reign, they were always in Siaka Stevens cabinet, holding various ministerial positions until rising to the positions of Vice Presidents, Sorie Ibrahim Koroma became the Vice President 1 while Christian Kamara-Taylor was made the Vice President II. Why did a small country like Sierra Leone need two Vice Presidents? Without doubt there was no provision for this in the constitution. Stevens was above the law.

Sorie Ibrahim Koroma was very loyal to the APC and to Siaka Stevens. He mobilised and galvanised the membership of the party and one thing that could be said of him, he was not a back-seat party member, or politician-he was always at the fore front. He was attending a meeting in Germany when he was unfortunately involved in a road accident that all but left him for dead; he survived but became physically impaired, yet on his return after treatment he continued to work assiduously for the party. It got to the point, rumour had it that Siaka Stevens commented on his eagerness that "Ah kin yerri people dem day form sick but ah nor kin yerri say people dem day form well." Interpretation: do not pretend to be well when we all know you are quite ill, just because you want to be at the fore front of politics. In any case, he carried on and was the first Vice President until the retirement of Siaka Stevens.

Sorie Ibrahim Koroma, was also a strong man of the All People's Congress Party. He was seen to be in charge of the mobilisation of the youth to carry out acts of thuggery against any perceived opposition, dissent or protest. For this role that he played in the APC's violent campaigns against opposing forces, he became popularly known as "Agba Satani" (the worst of the devils). Notwithstanding this side of him, he was quite a popular figure among the rank and file of the APC, but also to some extent because of this tendency of his to resort to violence by whatever means to gain an advantage, he was also feared, not only by opposing factions but even by members of his own party. This was the persona of the man who was next to Siaka Stevens and who was expected to take over the mantle. Well Siaka Stevens had his own plans, and strong as Sorie Ibrahim Koroma was he dared not contradict the wishes of his leader.

Accordingly, Siaka Stevens engineered his succession perhaps by mere force of will and guile. Out of the blues in 1985, he selected Joseph Saidu Momoh, the force commander of the army and a sitting member of parliament as the man to take over the baton, much to the chagrin of the party members and other Sierra Leoneans alike.

Notwithstanding Siaka Stevens' manoeuvres, he had to push through Parliament, a bill to amend the constitution, so that Joseph Saidu Momoh would succeed him. This did not go down well with some of his Ministers. Prominent among these were Dr. Abdulai Conteh who was then the Minister of Finance and Dr. Abass Bundu, now of the SLPP and current speaker of the House of Parliament. Of course, having the authority to hire and fire, Stevens dealt with this dissent by removing Abdulai Conteh from the office of Minister of Finance; a similar fate was meted to Dr. Abass Bundu who was Minister of Agriculture. After acquiring Parliamentary approval for the choice of Momoh as leader of the party, and also the Secretary General, astoundingly he got no other person than Sorie Ibrahim Koroma, who had stuck his neck out throughout Stevens' rule to manipulate elections, to move the motion to appoint Joseph Saidu Momoh as head of the party.[132] How this must have rankled with this strong man and loyal soldier of Siaka Stevens. One could imagine it was quite a bitter pill to swallow; Sorie Ibrahim Koroma must have seen himself as the natural successor to Siaka Stevens.

There were a few theories why this was not to be. One school of thought was that Siaka Stevens did not trust either of his closest loyalists, S. I. Koroma and C. A. Kamara-Taylor, to secure his retirement, more so, Sorie Ibrahim Koroma. Also, it was possible that he did not view either as a strong leader; Sorie Ibrahim Koroma especially had suffered debilitating injuries in a car crash that affected his health. There was also a perception that choosing a Military man as his successor, would forestall a military coup that might have dragged Siaka Stevens before a military commission to answer for his misdeeds.

After going through the party procedures, Joseph Saidu Momoh had to be presented to the nation; he had to be elected as President by the people. As Sierra Leone was a one-party state at the time, he was the sole candidate put forward to the nation. To enhance his popularity, Siaka Stevens took him on a nationwide tour during which he was introduced to the people as his chosen successor.

Momoh made glowing speeches of great promise that energised the people, at a time when because of mismanagement and bad policies the economy was in the doldrums, and people's welfare was severely hit. Subsequently, when the referendum on his candidacy was held, he received a resounding acclamation from the populace, on November 28, 1985.

There was so much euphoria then, as people thought a saviour had come to relieve their burden after seventeen years under Siaka Stevens rule. How can this be? Well, Momoh was a military man, not only a military man, but head of the army. So, his persona was

---

[132]   A Nationalist History of Sierra Leone. C. Magbaily Fyle.

synonymous with discipline, apparently. And being a military man, he was supposed to be straight forward, and standing up for the truth and the development of the state.

During the days of Momoh's reign, communication had not yet gone digital, international communication was still by land telephone, air mail letter and telegram / cable. The author clearly remembers receiving a mail from a friend who was working in the Ministry of Foreign Affairs about the new dispensation and hope that Momoh's presidency would bring a turn around. Sounding a note of caution the author replied that Momoh was already a member of government as a sitting member of Parliament, yet he had never raised his voice against the misdeeds that were taking place then, so one could not see how he was going to change what had already been entrenched in the system. As far as being a military man was concerned, under his patch as Brigadier-general, discipline in the army had deteriorated. In the end, Momoh did not disappoint as events would prove.

When the General legitimately ascended the throne of power, the economy was in dire straits.[133] One of the recalcitrant behaviours of the previous regime, under Siaka Stevens, our financial guarantors, the IMF, The World Bank and other bi-lateral donors were reluctant to pump financial resources into a country that was flouting the rules notably, the conditionalities upon which these loans and grants were made. Despite the distressing economic situation, economically, this was a window of opportunity for Momoh to carve his name in history, as was being done in Ghana by President Jerry Rawlins and his Finance Minister Kwesi Botchway. But alas Momoh did not have the moral fibre to embark on that reformist path. Although he promised when elected as President, to instil military discipline into Sierra Leonean life and to remove those who took and did not contribute, failed woefully as president all his military discipline deserted him. Methinks, he put the clothes of a politician on and threw the military

---

[133]   Sierra Leone. A Political History. David Harris.

uniform away. Indeed, looking back at his utterances, one is apt to think he had good intentions but did not have the singularity of purpose to implement these policies. In fact, he was led astray by a small cabal who inserted themselves around him and insulated him from the realities of what was happening on the ground.

Unlike Siaka Stevens who had control over his ministers and his party, Momoh seemed to lose the plot in midstream, notwithstanding his glowing pronouncements of a new order and constructive nationalism, Momoh found it difficult to make any headway in reforming the state.[134] If anything things did not get better, but they got worse. Perhaps, because of his liberal attitude or weakness in character. Powerful interest groups emerged that arrogated power from the presidency. There was the principal cabal, known as the Akutey Friendly Society, a predominantly Limba Ethnic grouping centred on Binkolo, the town that Momoh hailed from. Another important force was the then Inspector-General of Police, Bambay Kamara, who appeared to have a strong control over the President, and consistently taking political decisions without even consulting the president.[135]

To all intents and purposes, Momoh had good intensions for his fiefdom, but alas, he lacked the know-how and the moral fibre to take Sierra Leone to another level, more especially as the prevailing economic and financial conditions were appalling and there was much suffering imposed upon the populace.

Wanting to reverse the appalling economic conditions, President Momoh promulgated a state of economic emergency which unfortunately did not succeed, for many reasons. He arrogated a lot of power to himself but was unfortunately too weak to implement the economic emergency measures. As a result those of his cabal seized

---

[134] Ibid

[135] A Nationalist History of Sierra Leone. C. Magbaily Fyle.

the opportunity to carry out their own agendas, invariably illegally seizing people's assets and properties. Mild-mannered Momoh was too timid to act against this cabal. Instead of reversing the plunge in the value of the Leone, the scarcity of foreign exchange, and the massive corruption of political and public officials, got worse; up to the point that government could no longer afford to pay for its imports of basic essentials like rice and fuel. As a result, the country was plunged into black-outs, long queues for fuel, and also for the purchase of rice. Citizens became more and more disgruntled.

President Momoh also attempted to alleviate the scarcity of rice, by designing a blueprint for the 'green revolution'! The main thrust of this green revolution, which was going to cost about three-hundred million leones (Le300.0 million) was aimed at increasing rice production. Unfortunately for the beleaguered President Momoh, his green revolution did not succeed. Foreign donors, especially, who were expected to contribute the bulk of these resources no longer had any confidence in the Momoh government, based on the tenuous relationship between the government and the Bretton Woods institutions – another pie-in-the-sky project; American aid, under the Public Law 480 programme was employed to import rice through foreign aid. An aid coordinating secretariat (National Aid Coordinating Secretariat) was established to implement this programme. Proceeds from the sale of the rice were used to give loans to farmers. Unfortunately, a farmer had to be well connected to benefit from this scheme. But alas, about forty per cent of the rice was diverted to a local company owned by the then Minister of Trade and Industry, and state Enterprises. Astoundingly, there was scant evidence to show that the money from the sale of rice, was paid into the coffers of the National Aid Coordinating Secretariat.[136]

Indeed, it was widely felt that Momoh was under the influence of Siaka Stevens who left behind a pillaged economy and a corrupted

---

[136]   A Nationalist History of Sierra Leone. C. Magbaily Fyle.

system of government. With all his good intentions it appeared he was unable to unyoke his actions from Siaka Stevens Legacy. Frankly, that was a difficult ask, recognising the fact that he was handpicked by the 'old man' himself to be his successor, else, Momoh would not have made it to State House.

When Momoh assumed power, the economy was crumbling; not being able to rein in the rampant corruption that permeated the system and the blatant smuggling of Sierra Leone's mineral wealth presided over by some influential Lebanese, the likes of Jamil Mohammed, who had the freedom to operate illegally under Siaka Stevens, the country was almost bankrupted, and this became evident in the shortages of consumer goods, food, and fuel. Under Momoh's regime, there were shortages of fuel, delayed payments of public servants' salaries and spiralling inflation. Let's consider some economic indicators: At the time of Momoh's reign inflation had spiralled to about 70%, the foreign debt totalled more than Six Hundred and fifty million dollars ($650.0 Million). Other demographic indicators showed that Sierra Leone had one of the highest infant mortality rates in the world, and only three percent of the population had access to potable water; then, the average life expectancy rate was 36 years! That Sierra Leoneans were disgruntled and angry was an understatement. Momoh promised so much and delivered so little. The economy was in free-fall, and under the strangle hold of a few Lebanese businessmen. Economically, the Lebanese played and are still playing a critical role in Sierra Leone. It was reported that a handful of Lebanese had acquired illegally, vast fortunes, provided the government with money to purchase imported rice and funded most of government's domestic debt of about $1.0 billion. In fact, it was also reported Jamil's influence and hold over the government was so great that he was referred to by foreign observers as the 'bank of last resort". Evidentially during those days, when the foreign exchange of the Bank of Sierra Leone had run low, he brokered the country's oil imports through the wealth he had acquired illegally.[137]

One can say President Momoh tried to be an honest politician; he tried to change certain aspects of the modus operandi of Siaka Stevens. All through the reign of Siaka Stevens, general elections were characterised by thuggery and violence. When Momoh took over, an election was held in 1986, that was less violent than preceding elections under Siaka Stevens. In 1991, when seeking another five year term, Momoh warned those campaigning for the party ticket that violence would not be tolerated and indeed he kept to his word. He acted swiftly and decisively against one of his own close supporters and tribesmen when he disqualified him from the race when he disobeyed his instructions, to send an unmistakable message to other party members under the one-party state of Siaka Stevens were restricted to one or two candidates, Momoh encouraged more candidates to vie for the symbol.

Coming back to Momoh not being a politician, let alone a seasoned one, he was honest to declare publicly on the airwaves that he had failed the nation: his new order and constructive nationalism remained a dream that he was unable to transform into reality. As much as he was admired for his honesty, he was vilified also that realising he did not have what it takes to rule the nation, he did not have the courage or the decency to resign. But again, if Momoh was being controlled by his small cabal of Ekutayans, they could not have sat by and allowed that to happen as the outcome might have been detrimental to them. In another radio broadcast, Momoh declared that education was a privilege. Small wonder then that Sierra Leone once known as the Athens of West Africa is languishing at the bottom of the education scale.

In October 1990, President Momoh set up a constitutional review commission to review the 1978 one-party constitution with a

---

[137]   Assessment of Momoh's Tenure by the United States Embassy.

view to broadening the existing political process, guaranteeing fundamental human rights and the rule of law, and strengthening and consolidating the democratic foundation and structure of the ration. The commission presented its report in January 1991, recommending the reestablishment of a multiparty system of government. Based on this recommendation a constitution was approved by Parliament in July 1991, ratified in September and became effective in October 1991. There was great suspicion that Momoh was not serious, however, the APC was increasingly marked by abuses of power.

Unfortunately, Momoh was not allowed to complete his term. He was forcefully removed either wittingly or unwittingly by a group of young military soldiers in April 1992. Did he bring this upon himself? He had already promulgated multi-party democracy in September 1991, but the feeling was he was not really committed to opening the democratic constitution of 1991, that is still in use today. The enigma was, was he dragging his feet on its implementation, or was his heart not really in it? That question would remain unanswered. Even if one attempted to give an answer, it would be inconclusive. So, on that fateful morning of April 22nd 1992, a group of young military personnel stormed State House. It was alleged that their reason for that course of action was to protest the non-payment of their salaries for so many months. Whatever the case, this turned into a rout as the president and his cohorts took to flight and Sierra Leoneans witnessed another military coup. It is ironic that the APC rule was ushered in by a military coup after they had supposedly won an election in 1967, and after almost a generation of holding the reins of power, was ended by a military coup, ignominiously.

Thus, came to an end, twenty-four years of APC rule, seventeen years under Siaka Stevens, and seven years under Joseph Saidu Momoh. It would not be remiss to pose the question, how did Sierra Leone fare on under a generation of the All People's Congress Party government.

Sadly, before the forced end to Momoh's reign as President, he witnessed the start of a civil war in Sierra Leone started in March 1991 when rebels from Liberia in collaboration with disgruntled Sierra Leoneans, chief being Foday Sankoh invaded the country through a town, Bomaru in the Kailahun District. Charles Taylor, the NPFL rebel leader in Liberia had earlier vowed to bring war into Sierra Leone. When Brigadier Bangura staged a coup to overthrow Stevens in 1971, Momoh was a senior officer who refused to join the insurgents thus he was seen as a traitor to their cause: Foday Sankoh at the time was a corporal who sided with the coupists and was jailed for his part in the failed coup. He harboured a grudge against Momoh, so when Momoh was selected as the country's President, Sankoh thought it was pay-back time. And so, he unleashed this Leviathan upon the innocent citizens of Sierra Leone, all because of ego and greed. Never mind his excuse to liberate Sierra Leoneans from tyranny. Indeed, in a way, he did liberate thousands of men, women and children, even unborn babies, by slaughtering them in the most gruesome manner.

While we were berating the imperialists for their sins, pointing at the moat in their eyes, we refused to remove the beam in ours. On average after so many years of independence, we are still foundering. Between thirty and forty years ago, many African countries were ahead of Singapore and some other Southeast Asian countries in terms of development. Today you cannot even compare. Singapore has overtaken African countries so many times over. To think that Singapore is a small country on the Malaysian Peninsula, virtually with no known natural resource. In Africa, from north to south, east to West, the continent has abundant natural wealth: oil, fishing, timber, gold, rutile, diamonds, etc. There is no natural resource that cannot be found in Africa, yet the majority of its people remain in abject poverty. Poverty, brought about through the greed, mismanagement, and patronage of its so-called leaders and the open-door policy of African countries towards so-called foreign investors. Unlike foreign investment in Southeast Asia, our crooked politicians only attract foreign investment of dubious origin. Oftentimes knowing the type of system, they operate in, foreign investors seem to take advantage of this to rape African countries, if not with the connivance of African leaders but with their passive approval which is usually paid for by a very fat handshake. Moreover, these are businessmen claiming to be nationals but arc of foreign extraction, mainly the Lebanese and Indians. Much as they claim citizenship, they scarcely participate in civic affairs or contribute significantly to community development. When it comes to commerce, they are to be found doing prosperous trade, whether legal or illegal, wholesale and/or retail.

Certainly, they believe they can bribe their way into and out of every situation. The law as far as they are concerned can be flouted with impunity. For them, money talks. A spineless government composed of greedy, short-sighted, and unscrupulous individuals is entirely to blame. These are no other than our corrupt politicians and officials who demean themselves, by their actions to these foreign businessmen. It is not uncommon for a politician, be it a cabinet minister, a parliamentarian, or a senior public official, to transact business, whether it is the purchase of merchandise or a service, without paying for the purchase. His or her "position" in society accords him this right. But of course, this is a cost to the businessman which is easily passed on to the innocent consumer. All those in the vanguard of politics in Africa have as their guiding principle the accumulation of personal wealth at the shortest possible time at the expense of the masses. Indeed, it is shameful that with all its wealth, Africa should depend so much on external sources, often on foreign taxpayers, to support development and training programmes. It is immoral to be receiving foreign assistance, usually earned from the savings of the donor countries, for the purpose of developing our potential, only for these resources to be diverted to or utilised for the personal aggrandisement of politicians and public officials. How else can one explain the fact that African countries are still undeveloped, given the quantum of overseas development assistance that has been received since the decade of the 1960s? The

179

figure must be astronomical, but this does not correspond to the level of development many African countries have achieved. In fact, the amount of foreign aid poured into Africa runs contrary to its local and national development. By the decade of the eighties, when many countries in Europe, Southeast Asia, and other parts of the world were turning their economies round, many African countries were still in the doldrums. As the international environment became harsher, through massive debt burden and net outflows of capital, the international donor community, began to notice the plight of underprivileged and deprived Africans. Of course, they had to advance a cause to the ills plaguing African countries. So, what did they come up with this time? African countries had suffered the ills of long periods of economic mismanagement coupled with the implementation of inappropriate policies.

Before this period of recession, when many countries in Africa were experiencing reasonable rates of economic growth, institutions like the World Bank and the International Monetary Fund (IMF) were seldom at the vanguard of the continent's development. During this crisis period, these two institutions suddenly assumed the role for policing African economies and putting them back on track. Economic policies suddenly revolved around the jargon structural adjustment, macro-economic stability, privatisation, and the enabling environment. Once this process started, it never stopped; from La Cote d'Ivoire and Ghana to Tanzania and Zimbabwe, almost all states of Africa were under adjustment. Among others, this meant debt rescheduling, currency depreciation, rising prices, distressed public expenditure, retrenchment of labour, and divestiture of public corporations' assets. To this day, there is a great divide on the success or failure of structural adjustment programmes, among academics and non-academics alike. It may not be preposterous to state that aid to Africa, originating outside Africa, has sounded the death knell of Africa's initiative, self-esteem, hard work, and inevitably, honesty; now most African governments are classed as corrupt!

After the initial or original SAPS, it was suddenly remembered by the framers and implementers that there were people at the end of these reforms, so the human dimension had to be added ex-post. But for all this, unemployment kept rising and more and more people became caught in the poverty trap. And who dared resist the SAPS? Any country having the temerity to resist found itself blacklisted, and an already harsh international economic environment became more hostile. The Bretton Woods Institutions now became more fashionable. How else could one explain the newly industrial countries of Southeast Asia going to these institutions for financial bailouts, countries that were being hailed as the "Asian Miracle" just a couple of years earlier? About structural adjustment in Africa, the emerging view was that people continued to suffer in the short run when countries were apparently following appropriate economic policies and sound economic management. That was why successive SAPS had poverty reduction programmes attached.

Impoverishment of the masses by their leaders went hand in hand with political instability and civil wars. Again, from north to south, east to west, there was internecine strife. If the cause of strife was not tribal, then it was greed and the quest for power, no matter what methods were used to acquire it. One wondered at the multitude of killings that occurred during these times. Ironically, sophisticated weaponry not manufactured in Africa was usually employed, from missiles to AK-47s. Again paradoxically, many of these countries were so poor, and still remain poor, that they could ill afford to feed their own people. Generally, people were and are still starving, children are severely malnourished, health conditions leave much to be desired, and basic service delivery is very much inadequate. Furthermore, any sane individual was left with the impression it was the same "do-gooder" donor countries that offered alms to Africa that provided the arms for such massive destruction. Notwithstanding this situation, African governments or private armies could afford to invest in weapons of mass destruction but could ill afford to feed their people. In effect, while requesting assistance from donor countries, principally from the industrialised nations, for apparently development and training, they spent millions of dollars on purchases of arms and ammunition from these same countries.

Where then is the ethics in all this? At the end of the day, the arms industry was kept running, Africans were killing each other, and they were also starving because their governments could not afford to feed them. How pathetic. So many of our African leaders were using their own hands to destroy in masse the people that put them in power while at the same time keeping the economy of the industrialised nations running, oiled by the sweat and blood of Africans.

Is it any wonder then that Africans are shown the utmost disrespect everywhere? In Europe, from the Iberian Peninsula to the Balkans; in the Americas, from Canada to Chile; and in Asia, from the Middle East to the Far East.

Chapter Ten

THE BEGINNING OF DARKER DAYS

Long before the formal / official announcement in March 1991 that rebel forces had invaded Sierra Leone, there had been frequent raids by the National Patriotic Liberation Front (NPLF) of Liberia into remote towns and villages in the Kailahun District to pillage and cart away the possessions of innocent and docile villagers. It was only after Bomaru a custom's post in Kailahun was stormed and taken by the NPFL rebel forces aided by some Sierra Leoneans under the tutelage of Corporal Foday Sankoh that the guerrilla war began. Never mind Sankoh's diatribe about liberating the people of Sierra Leone from a tyrannical regime, his aims were far from being altruistic. It was propelled more by the lust for power and greed. The rich diamondiferous region of Sierra Leone was near the border with Liberia and Guinea. Thus the target of the rebels was the diamond mines of the South East. The nature of the conflict at the onset was a testimony to that.

According to Lansana Gberie in his book "The Dirty War in West Africa", at the early stages of the war, Sankoh was filmed, dressed in combat fatigues and carrying a rifle, surrounded by dozens of mainly ragtag teenage fighters in the town of Koidu, which they had just captured. This mining town changed hands several times between the RUF and the military who themselves were engaged in mining and other unsavoury activities. It was claimed that after the rebels had hit a town or village, carting away whatever light consumer and other products that they could transport easily because of their mobility, when the soldiers usually arrived after the rebels had left, they looted the heavy stuffs that the rebels could not transport.[138]

Foday Sankoh indeed could not have succeeded in wreaking such destruction in Sierra Leone without backers who provided him with the resources to prosecute this senseless war.

During the war years, the sources of funding of the RUF were always a topical subject with different shades of opinion being shared. Predominantly, it was felt that the prosecution of the Civil War was fuelled by external agents, and this proved to be the case as evidence garnered from various sources illustrated.

Information carried in Lansana Gberie's book shows that the war was heavily funded by Libya to the tune of over half a million dollars funnelled through Charles Taylor's NPLF. "Two letters that Sankoh wrote to a Libyan official of the Libyan People's Bureau in Accra revealed that his forces had received a constant flow of cash from the Libyans for the purchase of arms and other forms of logistical support. In one of the letters, he expressed his gratitude for the half million United States Dollars which he had received from them, while in the other letter he was requesting a further one and a half million United States Dollars "for effective and smooth operation."[139]

Foday Sankoh and his sponsors claimed to be fighting a civil war, to liberate the oppressed people of Sierra Leone, from the tyrannical

---

[138] A Dirty War in West Africa. The RUF and the Destruction of Sierra Leone. Lansana Gberie.

[139] A Dirty War in West Africa. The RUF and the Destruction of Sierra Leone. Lansana Gberie

APC government of President J. S. Momoh. Funnily, the people that they were fighting for were the targets of their atrocities.

An indication of how the citizenry was despondent over Momoh's incompetent, corrupt and self-seeking regime, when news of the ousting of Momoh's Government spread across the length and breadth of the country there was much jubilation. Amid sporadic gunfire, people went out into the streets dancing. Perhaps the dancing was not so much for the young men, but for the removal of the APC from governance for a generation that had witnessed the slide of a country rich in natural wealth, to abject poverty. By the time Momoh and his train were toppled from the pinnacle of power, Sierra Leone was languishing at the bottom of the United Nations Human Development Index (HDI).

In his first address to the nation, among the issues / challenges that Strasser mentioned was the incapacitation of the army to prosecute the war, lamenting the corrupt nature of the Momoh government and promised the nation that now that the NPRC was in charge the conflict would be brought to a speedy end.

From his base in Guinea where Momoh was taking refuge, he heard the broadcast and disclaimed that the army was incapacitated. It was a fact that the personnel recruited under Momoh lacked the basic qualities of discipline and education. Many of those recruited were street boys. On the other hand, he averred that under his tenure as president, his government made available to the army, the large sum of two hundred and fifty million Leones monthly, for rations, medicines, petroleum products and spares, for the prosecution of the war. He went on further to state that this government spent huge sums of foreign exchange for the purchase of ammunition. It was the view that most of the supplies sent to the front were purloined by senior military officers. Strangely enough, the force of the young military officers who stormed state house in 1992, displayed an array of modern military equipment – heavy machine guns, anti-aircraft guns and rocket propel grenades (RPGs). Therefore, this could not be described as an ill-equipped or incapacitated army.

Strasser's speech resonated with the feelings of the citizenry, young and old alike. It brought euphoria, which has been a characteristic trait of the country's political history. This happened in 1968 when the APC under Siaka Stevens was ushered into power. It happened again in 1985 when Momoh was chosen by the out-going president, Siaka Stevens, to take over the reins of government. Putting all of this in context, illustrate the bad governance of the political class not only in Sierra Leone but in Africa in general. Hardly is a government replaced, either legally or illegally that the governed display any regret at their passing. But then, if they were doing so well nobody in his or her right mind would want them replaced. Ironically long stretches of bad governance are dispensed by the political leaders because they scarcely elect to vacate the office of president voluntarily. In consequence African leaders hold office for two-three decades at a stretch, wanting to finish in the subsequent term, what they failed to achieve in twenty or thirty years!

Indeed, when these young men took over the government, this euphoria was translated into some level of creativity among the youth that unfortunately was not sustained. Young people mobilised into groups that started community beautification in their respective communities and for a time the capital city of Freetown, and other main towns took on a different look. Gains were made in other areas in the short-term, in the end, nothing much developed as the old cronies in authority failed to harness the enthusiasm of the youth.

That a group of young and inexperienced soldiers had seized power whether it was their original intent or otherwise was now a reality. Most of them were below the rank of captain. The first ever coup staged in Sierra Leone was led by a brigadier, a countercoup, led by the junior ranks toppled the leaders of that coup who were colonels and majors. Compared to other coups in the West African sub-region

THE DECLINE AND FALL OF THE ATHENS OF WEST AFRICA

those coups were led by senior military officers, generals mostly, in Nigeria, Ghana etc. Not to mention South America that also was having their own spate of coups, primarily led by generals. So when a group of young men, all below the age of thirty years unlawfully seized power in April 1992, promising to finish the senseless war, not only did they have to contend, an almost failed state but they also had a war on their hands led by a monster no one could control. If the writer should borrow from Lansana Gberie's book 'A Dirty War in West Africa,' the coup was anti-state, wholly self-serving and carried out by people who had no conception of governance, let alone aiming at it'.)[140] This is informative indeed, regarding the trajectory that Sierra Leone was catapulted into. Many of the soldiers who staged the 1992 coup were neither versed in the dictates of scholarship, nor a wealth of experience in holding public office. It would not be remiss to state that they were prone to peer influence and easily swayed by flattery. Not surprisingly, for a long time under the APC the professionalism of the military had been compromised and it got worse under Momoh's regime. All the prerequisites for entering the army were cast out of the window: no vetting of applicants or checking their references. Instead, recruitment was effected through a patronage system. The army was seen no longer as a career path, but as a means of enrichment and perhaps flouting the law. Through this system, many recruits, some street boys, probably minor criminals, entered the army. Again, this characteristic trait determined to some extent how the rebel conflict progressed, as if (and probably there was) there was an alliance between the soldiers and the rebel forces to pillage the villagers and their villages.

Not surprisingly when the NPRC took over, there was the usual, including the violation of people's rights, looting and general disorder. There was widespread looting of the homes of prominent politicians and businessmen. The NPRC later averred that they had recovered over forty million Leones in local and foreign currencies, mostly from the ousted government ministers and some APC functionaries. It was further disclosed that the sum of one million United States dollars, and millions of Leones in suitcases were found in the house of one of the former APC ministers.[141] Unfortunately these funds were never accounted for by the NPRC.[142]

Despite the political and economic state of the country, these young men suddenly coming into possession and command of state resources were not able to resist the attractions of a flamboyant lifestyle. In fact, a culture developed among our young ladies who were attracted to, or attracted these young military apparatchiks. It appeared that their predilection was for fair complexioned girls; this demand gave rise to a culture of applying skin-whitening creams on the bodies of these young ladies, for them to pass as fair-complexioned and thereby becoming attractive to their clientele. It was during this time that the local term "Kolonkoes" found its way into the local lingua franca, as a description for those who were bleaching their skins.

Those newspapers that had the audacity to report on the excesses of the NPRC were severely dealt with. It was not surprising that in a military regime, dissent was not tolerated, would not be one of the reasons that the Constitution was suspended, and they ruled by decree that no one can question or argue about? Those who were chosen to sit in their ruling council were not representing the people. They were not the people's choice. But for that reason alone, some who were chosen either through some connections, or friendship, or because they sympathised with the coupists would never have darkened the corridors of power. Similarly, it should be mentioned that many upstanding individuals turned down their appointment to their ruling council because they realised the gravity of violently over-throwing the elected government of a country.

---

[141]   A Dirty War in West Africa. The RUF and the Destruction of Sierra Leone. Lansana Gberie

[142]   Ibid

On the assumption of power, to keep to their promise of ending the war, one of the first acts that they embarked upon was to undertake a massive recruitment drive, and what a drive it was. Unfortunately, it was history repeating itself. Following the existing practice, those recruited were not properly screened. Many of them were street boys, school dropouts, outcasts, and others, with no sense of direction, ambition, discipline or loyalty. They visualised the army as a means of enriching themselves through the barrel of the gun.

To do justice to the NPRC, they succeeded in some areas of governance that were moribund under a generation of APC misrule. Economic reform which was much needed but had been half-heartedly supported by Momoh and his cohorts, was put back on track. Some progress was made in macroeconomic stabilisation and the creation of the enabling environment for private enterprise development. For instance, the growth of real gross domestic product which had slowed during the Momoh years, displaying negative growth of about eighteen per cent in 1992, picked up in 1993 and 1994 reaching about two-to-three per cent.[143] In 1992, the inflation rate was 65.5% by 1994, it was down to 24.2%.[144] Under a war economy, the NPRC demonstrated its resolve to pursue economic reform and structural adjustment. In point of fact economic reform is usually painful, bringing much suffering to the average John Doe in the short-term. Even in the long run, one was not certain how realistic the outcome would be. Thus for a democratically elected government, it might mean political suicide, so African governments usually shy away from it. Not so for the military: policies and decisions were decreed, case closed. They did not derive their mandate from the ballot box, but by the barrel of the gun.

---

[143] Sierra Leone Economic Records, 1961 – 2010. Alimamy Bangurah, Director, EPRU, MOFED

[144] Sierra Leone: Inflation Rate from 1985 -2025. Statista, Economy and Politics - International

Under this setting the military junta did much better than their civilian counterparts. To a large extent, the junta was well on its way to achieving the set macro-economic targets of single digit inflation, financial sector reforms etc. Also, in the area of physical infrastructure development, there was commitment to develop a more desirable infrastructure. Let us take an example: The thermal generating plant at Kingtom that was in a state of disrepair, and only capable of supplying less than 20% of the capital city's energy demand was rehabilitated; indeed, there was a marked improvement in the supply of electricity to the city. One was left wondering whether the problem was only with the machines. There were also problems with the management and workers. Even in times of dire need when the country was strapped for foreign exchange it was not uncommon for workers to steal the oil for operating the machines, sometimes, from the generators themselves. Of course, under the civilian government this act of sabotage was given a blind eye, the culprits might have political connections. With a military regime in control, who would dare, especially given the brutal nature of such a regime. On the other hand, impoverished as the country was, the government then was paying an undisclosed fee in foreign currency to a foreign management firm to manage the corporation which it was then (Sierra Leone Electricity Corporation SLEC).

Apparently, it was the popular belief that they made their mark on the sanitation of the country generally, but more especially the cities, of which the capital Freetown received the most attention. It was no secret that the sanitation in the entire country was extremely poor. Using the capital as an example, the drainages were clogged with garbage as the citizens did not see the need to dispose of their domestic wastes otherwise. Main thorough fares, even in the centre of town, littered with market stalls and streets were covered in filth. Sierra Leone had become a country of hawkers. It was and is not uncommon to see young men and women, healthy and strong hawking their wares perhaps a few consumables and other items in the streets. No wonder then that cities are overpopulated while the productive areas are deserted. This state of affairs became more predominant during and after the rebel war.

To confront this unhealthy state of the country's poor sanitation, the NPRC designated the first Saturday of each month as "cleaning Saturday". For its implementation, every individual should clean his/her surroundings both indoors and outdoors; this exercise lasted from 6 A.M to 10 A.M and going out into the streets was prohibited and was a criminal offence. So the first Saturday of every month was a hive of activity when compounds, drainages, streets etc. were religiously cleaned or in the opinion of the author the filth and garbage were transferred from the drainages and dumped on the streets. In most instances garbage would occupy the roads for days on end before being cleared; there were instances even when roads were entirely blocked off to vehicular traffic. The capacity (trucks etc.) to dispose of the garbage did not exist, and many times the military would commandeer private individuals' vehicles to remove the garbage from the streets. This activity was sustained throughout the lifetime of the NPRC.

It might be the general opinion that the outcome was successful, but that is doubtful to some of us. In the first place the time value of money was not given much thought. Again, cleaning is a continuous exercise and not a once-monthly exercise. What this policy did was to reduce the culture of cleaning to a one-day exercise where the entire city was turned into a garbage dump that would take days sometimes weeks before the streets were cleared of garbage. This policy of designating a day to cleaning was reactionary instead of pro-actionary. We never asked the question 'how did the garbage get to where they were'? Some agent was responsible for that, and there are laws on littering public spaces that are not being enforced. Places like Singapore and now Rwanda are not clean by accident. Laws and the mechanisms were put in place to see that this desired outcome was achieved. But alas, not in Sierra Leone; we do not mind wallowing in filth. Even today, the Central Business District is a disgrace, not to talk about our markets. Gone are the days when the markets were cleaned by the Fire Force every week, usually on a Sunday when there was no business. These days, one cannot distinguish between a Sunday and a market day.

Now to the prosecution of the war, not forgetting the fact that at the taking over of the reins of government, the NPRC promised the citizenry that they would finish the war. When they were in the war front, they complained of poor support from the government, a claim disputed by the government. In truth, it was beyond belief when Foday Sankoh proclaimed that he would overthrow the sitting government, that he would attempt such a risky venture, especially considering the fact that Foday Sankoh was not a Che Guevara. The writer for one did not take him seriously, and it was possible that many Sierra Leoneans held similar thinking. As we say in our lingua franca, "when blen yaye man say ee go stone you, know say ee done mass the stone" (when a blind man tells a person he would stone that person, it is because he has the stone already). Little did we know that Foday Sankoh had his backers, the Ghaddafis, Charles Taylors, the Blaise Campaore. What really was their interest in such a venture? It cannot be for altruism, not to liberate the people of Sierra Leone. As a point of fact, their own regimes were more repressive, Ghaddafi's Libya was a rich and developed country but did the inhabitants enjoy their freedom, etc? Burkina Faso was governed with an iron hand; as for Liberia, it was in shambolic state. So let us not be fooled, there were other motives that propelled Sankoh's benefactors, the wealth of this tiny African nation which had been subjected to a series of bad governance since it gained its independence in 1961. This then was the context that the war was being fought, added to that was the fact that the rebels were not a regular army, but a band of blood thirsty, uneducated individuals who were in it for personal gains. Also, there were the misguided souls, with very low intelligence who revered their 'Poppay' and in their simple minds thought they were fighting for a cause to liberate the people of Sierra Leone from oppression. How misguided they were.

From the make-up of the rebel forces, this was not going to be a conventional warfare, but a guerrilla type hit and run and depending on the local dynamics, hold territories. Imagine the Sierra Leone Army was ill-disciplined, poorly trained and without the motivation to save their country from falling into the hands of ill-disciplined brutes like themselves. Consider this then should we Sierra Leoneans have expected a successful prosecution of this rebellion by our military men? Given the situation at the time, if somebody was drowning and he came across a straw, that individual would clutch at it. That was what Sierra Leoneans did, trusting our NPRC soldiers to finish the war as promised. Unfortunately, that was not to be.

In furtherance of their objective of ending the war, the NPRC imported sophisticated weapons and ammunitions, and communication equipment from Belgium and Romania, and how was this transaction conducted? They paid for it largely with diamonds.[145] So the question that immediately came to mind was, how did the NPRC junta come across these gemstones? Could they have purchased it through legal means? That could not be; the state by then was impoverished and starved of foreign exchange. The only plausible explanation was that they or their agents were involved in mining. In fact, one of the local newspapers, 'the Tablet" reproduced an article from a Swedish newspaper which purported that the chairman of the NPRC had exported a large consignment of diamonds "to some overseas territory." A claim that was vehemently denied and the editor of the local tabloid was locked up and the publication sanctioned.

On the war front it was a see-saw battle between the military and the RUF. In the early days of the conflict, the war was concentrated in the south and east and that was not by accident, that was the diamondiferous zone. As Harris put it "the blame for the war can be placed squarely on resources, in particular diamonds and those who

---

[145] A Dirty War in West Africa. The RUF and the Destruction of Sierra Leone. Lansana Gberie

wanted them".[146] This conflict has nothing to do with the so-called ideology, tribal or regional differences, nor the marginalisation of the youth. The root of the conflict was diamonds, diamonds, diamonds.[147]

It appeared as if the protagonists and the antagonists took it in turns to hold the diamondiferous areas. It exchanged hands so many times. Unlike Liberia though, the rebels were not able to hold the territory for long. They did not have the sympathy of the people, nor their support due to the way and manner they treated the people, very brutal and with bestiality.

Twice, at the end of 1993 and again in 1995, the NPRC pushed the RUF forces to the limit. Instead of finishing the war, the NPRC leadership decided to call for a ceasefire thereby halting the advances that they had made. The RUF called for a dialogue, in response the NPRC offered an amnesty to the rebels in return for an unconditional surrender a gesture that the RUF soundly refused. After a month the RUF had regrouped, and their supply replenished. Bang! The war recommenced. The question, how were the rebels able to rearm within such a short time? Stories abound of contingent of soldiers retreating from rebel attacks, leaving their entire weaponry behind. There were also stories by captured villagers, of military helicopters dropping weapons and ammunitions in rebel held territories. A term which became popular after the escalation of the conflict in 1994 was the word "SOBEL", a combination of soldier and rebel; this was how the soldiers were described by the people who were highly suspicious of the way they were prosecuting the war.

Although the RUF were not holding territories as such, save for the ping pong nature of the conflict in the Kono area especially, inter-city travel was quite hazardous as the rebels would mount ambushes on the highways. To mitigate this challenge, the authorities decided that

---

[146] Sierra Leone. A Political History. David Harris

[147] Ibid

people and goods travelling to and from the Provinces would travel in convoys on set days, accompanied by heavy military presence. Did this arrangement prove a solution? Far from it. Every time a convoy left Freetown for the provinces, it was attacked by the rebels, even though the schedule for the movement of the convoy was never disclosed. Even the passengers were not given this information; they would wait for days before being given the go ahead to move by the military. Wonders upon wonders, each time the convoy moved, they were attacked by the rebels who of course had advanced information, leaked by the very same military. This served to re-inforce people's thinking that the soldiers collaborated with the rebels and the term 'SOBELS' became a popular description of the soldiers.

As expected, these were challenging times, not only were the citizens being vandalised, maimed and killed, movement of goods, foodstuff and other essentials between the markets and producing areas posed a desperate challenge. Notwithstanding these hardships, the inhabitants rose to these challenges through various coping mechanisms, the extended family system, areas not previously known for their agricultural potential, especially in the Western Area, were put under cultivation.

The romance with the NPRC junta by now was getting frayed at the seams as their promise of ending the war was not being adhered to and they appeared to have no intention of returning the country to constitutional rule. This situation was compounded when according to Gberie, in a sordid moment of frenzy the junta summarily executed twenty-nine persons, including a pregnant woman, a palm wine tapper, some newly recruited police constables, a popular Freetown socialite and some soldiers for allegedly plotting a coup.[148] Among the executed was the former powerful Inspector General of Police, Bambay Kamara, who was already under lock and key when the NPRC seized power. When the news spread, the entire country was

---

[148]   A Dirty War in West Africa. The RUF and the Destruction of Sierra Leone. Lansana Gberie

in shock, the thinking being this was a put-up story and no trial was carried out. But the NPRC claimed these accused were tried by a military tribunal and the verdict endorsed by the Supreme Military Council. Now it appeared that the NPRC were going their own way, lacking the ideology of how to govern and also the strategy of how to prosecute a guerrilla insurgency. According to testimonies given at the Truth and Reconciliation Commission (TRC), they even turned deaf ears to the advice given by their senior officers, a rather intriguing situation that of all institutions, considering the hierarchical and command structure of the army, that was the last bastion for discipline. It was also farcical that after these executions, a civilian member of the junta claimed ignorance, as he was not a member of the inner cabinet.[149]

Unbeknown to the public, the military was plagued with indiscipline, renegade soldiers and conflicting messages between the senior officers and the junior officers of the NPRC. As reported to the TRC some of the officers were responsible to the point of deserting their assigned posts in the war front, coming down to Freetown to lobby for lucrative appointments. As one of the senior officers told the TRC, the military headquarters that was supposed to command and control the forces in the prosecution of the war was not included in the decision-making process. On a number of occasions, the NPRC Chairman advised his colleagues not to interfere with the day to day operations of the Army, but his advice was ignored, Furthermore the Chairman's intention to restructure the Army making the Force Commander, the Chief of the Defence Staff (CDS) was met with stiff resistance by the junior ranks as they were eyeing these positions themselves, forgetting the fact they were neither experienced nor competent to man those positions. Notwithstanding the anger of the Chairman who was 'powerless' to stop them, half trained lieutenants became colonels and captains became Generals.[150] So one might ask

---

[149] TRC Report, Appendix 2, Part 3: Submissions

[150] TRC Report, Appendix 2, Part 3: Submissions

rightly, how could such an undisciplined army successfully prosecute a rebel war. There was too much internal strife within the military itself. But again, their excuse for holding on to the reins of power was to finish the war.

However, the popularity that greeted the NPRC when they overthrew the APC was now turning to disdain as they were proving no better than the regime, they removed from power both in their lifestyle and oppressiveness, perhaps even worse than a civilian regime as they were backed by a gun. This unpopularity manifested itself in calls for them to hand over power to an elected civilian regime by various civil society groups. Nonetheless, the soldiers clung to the theme that there should be peace before election, and this became their mantra. On the other hand, disillusioned by the acts of the NPRC and their failure to end this strife the populace insisted that there should be elections before peace. And the role played by the women and women's groups in calling for the return to civilian rule could not be overstated. At the risk of intimidation and threats to their lives, they stuck to their guns.

In November 1993, the Chairman of the NPRC set out a detailed timetable for the restoration of constitutional rule. The timetable processes were outlined as follows: -

- Non-Partisan District Council Elections   Nov 1994
- Presidential Elections   Nov 1995
- General Elections   Nov 1995
- Swearing in of New President   Jan 1996

Concretising people's thinking, the NPRC instructed the INEC to convene a National Consultative Conference on the Electoral Process which it did. This conference took place at the Bintumani Hotel, in its Conference Centre, from the 15th to the 17th August, 1995. And indeed, what an historical event that was. With so many dissenting views on the peace before elections or elections before peace, by the end of the conference, all the delegates spoke with one voice "Elections before Peace," with the military as guarantors to a peaceful election. In recognising the role the women played in the entire process, the Report on the Conference states "it was the exceptional ability of the women's groups together with their determination to promote the democratisation process that galvanised the conference into effective action, and the women did not give up until final victory on election day."[151] Unfortunately this was not the end of the proceedings as subsequent events in the NPRC unfolded, putting the democratisation process at a severe risk.

Imagine the first set of elections was slated for December 1995, and the General Elections in February 1996, resources permitting, and the INEC was busy making preparations for this historic event. What happened? On the 16th January, the populace was greeted with the news that there had been a Palace Coup, led by the self-styled Brigadier Julius Maada Bio, toppling the then Chairman Captain Valentine Strasser. The reason given by the coupists was that the toppled Chairman was reluctant to accede to the democratisation process agreed at Bintumani I. Now, here is the thing: the new Head of State averred that in search for peace, and an end to the rebel war, the government had started fruitful deliberations with the RUF leader Foday Sankoh, and that there was a chance of real peace and returning to the country.[152] This of course raised a lot of unanswered questions in the minds of Sierra Leoneans. Why now, and why was this not done before the Bintumani I conference etc. etc.? To add fuel to the fire, the new Chairman instructed INEC to convene a second Bintumani Conference on the same theme? What was the rationale of this when the decision, a popular one for that matter, had already been taken, to go ahead with the process to return the country to civilian rule. Many people saw this move by the new chairman, to

[151] Report of the First National Consultative Conference on the Electoral Process. Bintumani Conference Centre 15 – 17 August 1995

[152] Report on the Second National Consultative Conference on the Electoral Process. Bintumani II

hang on to power and delay the return to civilian rule. Whatever the case, he was in for a rude awakening.

In view of the chairman's statement that the NPRC was in talks with the RUF in the search for a peaceful resolution to the conflict, the RUF was invited to the Conference but the invitation was not honoured. And no reason was given for their non-attendance.

The decision of the conference was based on the statements made by the delegates' representatives groups as follows: -

-	Elections on 26th February 1996	- 57
-	Peace before Elections	- 14
-	Neutral Statements	- 3

Based on these numbers, the decision taken in Bintumani I was upheld. Intriguingly, during Bintumani I the NPRC under the Chairman Valentine Strasser, the army was the guarantor to a peaceful election. During Bintumani II, when the chairman of the NPRC was the self-styled Brigadier, the army would not guarantee security for the people on elections day. How strange, the reluctant leader who wanted to hold on to power guaranteed peaceful elections, but the quiescent leader who wanted to return the country to civilian rule could not guarantee the safety and security of the people on election day!

Indeed, it would be revealing to quote from a few of the Reports that were tendered at the Bintumani II Conference.

Extracts from statements of the People's Progressive Party (PPP);

"Last August, the people of the country spoke through this Bintumani Conference. They agreed that INEC should organise Presidential and Parliamentary elections not later than February 1996. That Conference brought together under one roof all shades of opinion in the country.

Civilians, military, police and the NPRC (under former chairman Strasser), were all represented. They were all privy to the mandate. Now suddenly the NPRC (under self-styled Brigadier Julius Maada Bio) and only the NPRC is saying it is confused. Then suddenly, two nights ago, the NPRC announced its agreement with the RUF to meet for talks at Abidjan on February 28, two days after the scheduled elections on February 26. Is this a mere coincidence or a deliberate decision? No family in this country escaped bereavement from this senseless war. When the civilians called for peace, the warring men did not listen, when the women and children called for peace, again they did not listen. The only time they say they want to talk peace is when the entire nation had prepared itself to choose its leaders by democratic elections and right on the eve of these elections."

Statement by the People's Democratic Party (PDP Sorbeh)

"...The people of this country want to elect a government of their choice. They are fed up with military rule. [Sierra Leone had military rule before, but the NPRC had illegally stayed in power the longest]. The temporary occupants of State House must realise that they cannot subvert the will of the people. The antics of today begin to make Valentine Strasser look like the foremost Military Democrat, if there was ever one. if you change February 26 the war will drag on and on; the carnage, killing, deprivation and suffering will continue, the displaced and refugees will not return to their homes. There will be no elections for 5 – 10 years. Sierra Leone will be blacklisted by the International Community."

Statement by the Academic Staff Association (ASA)

"...The sincerity of the NPRC genuinely wanting to hand over power is circumspect. After spending millions if not billions of Leones, nearly all their previous undertakings have suffered from abandonment, setbacks or non-implementation, namely, constitutional Advisory Committee recommendations, consultative conference with Chief commitment for a quick end to the Rebel War. What guarantee do we have that this is not a ploy to delay the handover process?

Also, the Le60 million refurbishment of State House against the backdrop that we have never had the commitment to feed our refugees or pay adequate salaries to workers – is not a John the Baptist paving-the-way style for relinquishing power".

Finally, I juxtapose excerpts from the statement of the Military

'.....If it is the view of this conference that elections be held before peace, then the Armed Forces will request that a decree be speedily promulgated to give powers to the Chief of Defence Staff (CDS) to conscript able-bodied male and female Sierra Leoneans to complement the present strength of the Armed Forces to defend our country."

"The Armed Forces also want it to be known that in view of the on-going war, and the avowed determination of the RUF to disrupt the elections, which they have made openly and quite explicitly, it cannot within its present resources provide the necessary security during the elections and at the same time fight the rebel war."

Contrasting and comparing what this same military said in Bintumani I is quite revealing. Here are a few excerpts.

"The problem of the war is here and a section of the very electorate whose support parties want to canvass are the same ones causing the carnage. The Armed Forces are going to continue to defend this nation to the best of their ability. It is thus left to the people to decide whether they will allow the group of bandits to deny them their right to vote."

"Violence meted out in a violent situation breeds carnage. If we are sincere about the future of this nation let us support the Armed Forces' efforts to prosecute the war by closing ranks against the common enemy of peace and prosperity – Foday Sankoh. This should be done against the backdrop that we shall have elections. If you want elections, we are all going to fight to get it. Democracy is the only way out and the Armed Forces support fully the idea of handing over governance to an elected civilian regime". The case rests.

No matter what, the people were determined to have their elections. This also illustrated the fatigue under a military dictatorship, one that had become brutal and violent. The people were tired to be governed by decree that they cannot contend against. Whether it was right or wrong, good or bad, everybody had to fall in line. Well, the NPRC did not have their way, and after Bintumani II, there was no turning back. They had exhausted all the avenues to cling on to power.

The Independent National Electoral Commission (INEC) as mandated finally did conduct the Presidential and Parliamentary elections on the 26th and 27th February 1996. It stretched over two days because of some violence perpetuated allegedly by the RUF in some rural communities. It should be noted also that this election, the first multi-party adventure after almost twenty years, departed from the first-past-the-post norm" as was the usual practice. Due to financial and security constraints, it was determined at the Bintumani Conference to abandon the first-past-the-post and try the proportional representation system in which a minimum threshold of five (5%) per cent of the total votes cast for a party to have parliamentary representative. For the parliamentary elections, thirteen parties contested the sixty-eight parliamentary seats at stake. The SLPP, led by Dr. Ahmed Tejan Kabbah emerged victorious winning twenty-seven (27) seats; the United National People's Party (UNPP), led be the veteran politician Dr. John Karefa Smart, won seventeen (17) seats; the People's Democratic Party, led by another veteran politician, Thaimu Bangurah (now deceased) captured twelve (12) seats; the All People's Congress, which had been in power since 1968 until its overthrow in 1992 won only five (5) seats, not surprisingly as there was a power struggle going at the time, regarding who should lead the party.

In the Presidential election there was no outright winner in the first round so the two leading aspirants, Dr. Ahmed Tejan Kabbah of the SLPP, and Dr. John Karefa Smart of the UNPP had to contest for the second round which was conducted on March 15th 1996. The contest was won by Dr. Ahmed Tejan Kabbah of the SLPP. On the 29th March the NPRC relinquished power, handing over the baton of State to the Leader of the SLPP.

Noticeably, the elections were not without incidents, from the RUF's activities to destabilize the process. Indeed in the capital city of Freetown the military was deployed at the polling booths and it must be said the elections went on peacefully. But then getting to almost the end of voting at evening time when the ballot boxes were supposed to be carted away to the INEC offices for tallying, there was a sudden bombardment around the city, which looked and sounded like the city was under attack. Of course, people were terrified and hastened for the shelter of their homes. In fact, this sudden bombardment of the City prompted the chairman of INEC to go over the air waves to categorically state that the elections had been completed and nothing, nobody was going to derail the restoration of constitutional rule. The RUF at that time was nowhere near the city; that was for some time in the future. Who or what was responsible for this bombardment has remained a mystery. There were rumours circulating around that it was the army, and it has remained just that. One thing though, this act did not frighten the populace to abandoning their quest to restore a legitimate civilian government.

The NPRC left certain legacies behind, which could not be termed admirable. They established the driving around in vehicles without number plates. Now this has become commonplace, vehicles driving around without number plates. One cannot fail to ask the question whether these vehicles were even registered. This is a sign of disrespecting the law. This is mere speculation, nowadays this behaviour is still with us, they must be the big men/women connected to the powers that be; these vehicles ply the streets and even the police dared not pull them over. Conclusion? Some people are above the law. So, if this behaviour, the disregard and disrespect of the law is done by our so-called elite, how would the rest of the citizenry behave? As the Krio saying goes "nar before horse behen horse day fallah" (the horse's forelegs determine the direction it takes.)

Next, the NPRC soldiers used to drive in long military convoys along the streets of the capital at breakneck speed, utilising both lanes of the road. This meant no other vehicles would ply the roads not even on-coming vehicles when they were using the roads. Even pedestrians were at risk of being mown down and this was not uncommon, especially when driving in the provinces. These days, Presidents drive in long military convoys. Even the current first lady has her own military convoy; a first for Sierra Leoneans. Although both lanes are not used, yet all vehicular traffic has to come to a stand-still. This waiting for these dignitaries to pass can take sometimes up to one-hour. No joke! A fall out from this is the blatant disregard of the traffic rules by government officials especially. Driving on the wrong side of the road is not uncommon. Is this recklessness or stupidity. The writer prefers the latter for putting not only the lives of others at risk but even their own lives; it goes beyond recklessness. The general saying that no one is above the law does not hold in Sierra Leone; it permeates all facets of our society.

Many aspects of the war including the atrocities have been documented in various media, books, films etc. However, an aspect of the war that changed the face of the country was the amount of displacement of people and entire communities. Migratory patterns changed very quickly with disastrous outcomes. Suddenly, cities and urban areas are teeming with people, many of whom do not have anywhere to sleep; many use public markets as sleeping hostels. The rural-urban drift affected not only agriculture but also general employment: most of the youth that moved to the urban areas did not have the skills to survive, The result? The development of "Attire base" where many spend their time relaxing on the smoking of 'pot'. The cities bulging with a population that they can barely support; slums spring up in areas that were previously unfit for human habitation.

On the other side of the coin, many Sierra Leoneans, some highly qualified left the shores of Sierra Leone, seeking greener pastures elsewhere; some highly qualified professionals never returned, preferring to stay and work in foreign lands. In other words, the rebel war resulted in 'brain drain,' yet we cannot cope with the capacity constraints that is so evident in the country. After sixty years of independence, at one time being described as the Athens of West Africa, almost all the other countries in the region have left us behind.

So, on the 29th March 1996, when the new president was sworn in, in spite of the on-going war with the intransigent RUF. Sierra Leoneans thought they were on a new chapter, leading to democracy and eventual peace.

Chapter Eleven

SHORT – LIVED DEMOCRACY

When Ahmed Tejan Kabbah took up office as President after the elections in 1996, he had a Herculean task on his hands and a position that was unenviable. Apart from bringing the war to an end which meant negotiating with a group of blood – thirsty men and with the possibility of including them in the governance structure, there were wounds to be healed, between and among families, communities, reconstruct and rehabilitate infrastructure, schools, health centres, community centres etc., and the relocation / repatriation of internally displaced persons (IDPs), repatriation of refugees and restoration of people's livelihood; indeed, the list is endless. To think in a country that was already impoverished by unscrupulous politicians and leaders, how did one go about restoring the dignity and livelihood of men and women, many breadwinners in their own right? Sierra Leone, as typical of many African countries did not have a social security system. Indeed, the entire populace was traumatised. The international community was sympathetic to the plight of the people of Sierra Leone. But was the newly elected president up to the task?

Rumour has it that Tejan Kabbah was a compromise candidate to lead the SLPP into the elections. Notwithstanding, it is believed he came with good credentials: an international civil servant in the United Nations system, as such he should be well connected with the international community. Though it should be recalled that he was a civil servant in the Albert Margai's government, and the conclusion was he did not pass with flying colours. All that was history now as he had carved a career in the U. N. system.

There was this trite saying that was even bandied around now that 'without peace, there would be no development'. So President Kabbah had his work cut out for him. In spite of the wanton destruction to lives and property by the RUF bandits, he did reach out to Foday Sankoh to broker a semblance of peace so that the lives of a traumatised people could begin to return to normal.

Subsequently, peace talks with the RUF were started in Abidjan. The newly appointed Attorney – General and Minister of Justice, Solomon Berewa, led the Sierra Leone delegation while Foday Sankoh was the leader on the other side. After much deliberation the Abidjan Peace Accord was signed in November 1996. When the news of the signing of the Peace Accord filtered through the various news media in the country, as one would imagine, there was much jubilation; on that day, motor vehicles' horns were blaring loudly all over the city, and people were dancing, even without knowing anything about the terms of the Peace Accord. Also, it must be stated that the Attorney-General and Minister of Justice, Mr. Solomon Berewa, was seen as a hero by many Sierra Leoneans; he had achieved something that seemed impossible and doomed to failure.

In some circles of society, there was scepticism about Sankoh's sincerity, while in others, people were optimistic that peace had come to a beleaguered nation at long last. On hindsight the sceptics were holding the correct view, but even at that material point in time, Sankoh's sincerity was questionable, and this was borne out by his actions. Foday Sankoh wrote two letters to the Libyan People's Bureau, who were his sponsors, requesting funds for the purchase of arms and other forms of logistics support. The first letter was dated 26th June, 1996, before the signing of the Peace Accord. The second letter to the same recipients was written in December 1996, after the signing of the Peace Accord. In that letter, Foday Sankoh thanked his Libyan sponsors and requested further "to urgently provide ….. seven-hundred thousand United States Dollars for the purchase of more arms". Sankoh stated that he signed the accord for tactical reasons, in his words "just so as to relieve our movement of enormous pressure from the international community while I will use this opportunity to transact my business in getting our fighting materials, freely and easily."[153]

Among the clauses that the RUF insisted on including in the Abidjan Accord, was the removal of the Executive Outcomes, the unit which together with the Civil Defence Forces and the army pushed them out of Mile Thirty-Eight and also out of the mining areas. Foday Sankoh knew what his goal was, but, unfortunately, the government took him at face value. He was a power-hungry, bloodthirsty megalomaniac who was not to be satisfied with playing second fiddle. The government was slow in implementing the terms of the Accord, especially getting rid of Executive Outcomes. But then the international community would not have any of this and brought pressure to bear on the Kabbah government to implement this aspect of the Accord. Executive Outcomes were sent packing. One could imagine Sankoh's glee at this, his masterstroke.

When the constitutional government was restored in 1996, work began immediately to put Sierra Leone on its feet. The main tasks then, were, building a bridge for a lasting peace with the RUF, heal a very traumatised population, restoration of people's livelihood, resettling the displaced persons, the demobilisation and re-integration of ex-combatants, and the rebuilding of a devastated social and economic infrastructure. A Ministry tasked with the responsibility for the Reconstruction, Resettlement and Rehabilitation of the devastated economy was set up. The work of this Ministry was really cut out as

---

[153]   A Dirty War in West Africa. The RUF And The Destruction of Sierra Leone.

the terrain was difficult to work in. Although there was a ceasefire in place, many areas of the country were still experiencing banditry and attacks from the RUF. Villages were still being plundered, women raped and so on. So, there were people who needed humanitarian assistance that were beyond the reach of the government machinery.

The humanitarian crisis witnessed the proliferation of Non-governmental Organisations (NGOs) mainly international but a few local in the country. Some brought their own resources, but many of them depended on funding from their countries of origin; America would fund American NGOs, the United Kingdom will fund British NGOs, etc. etc.

The government together with those NGOs started making preparations for the Herculean task ahead. The distribution of food and non-food items were undertaken in internally displaced camps which had been established in the main urban centres. Reception centres were also being established in various parts of the country for the receiving of and demobilisation of ex-combatants. In the meantime, a National Resettlement, Rehabilitation and Reconstruction Programme termed the QUAP, Quick Action Programme, was being formulated by the MNRRR and its donor partners, to be presented at a Round Table Conference of Donors, in Geneva from 17 – 18 September 1996. Consultative workshops were held at Regional and District levels to sensitise the people about modalities and systems that would be established for the implementation of the Quick Action Programme.

The Round Table Conference yielded pledges of more than what was in the Quick Action Programme; the government was seeking just over two hundred million (US$200.00 million) United States dollars to start its rebuilding programme. However, the amount pledged at the conference was over two-hundred and thirty United States dollars, which should in itself be satisfying to the organisers of the Round Table and the government of Sierra Leone. But alas, these were pledges and not actual amount contributed or donated. Unfortunately, no proper mechanisms were established to track and monitor these pledges. And here was the rub. Although these pledges were towards a government's National Programme of Resettlement, Rehabilitation and Reconstruction, lo and behold, when the donors were confronted to make good their pledge, the government was informed that they made their contributions to their respective Non-Governmental Organisations (NGOs). Nor was the government informed by these NGOs that they had received these monies on behalf of the government for the implementation of the QUAP! Whether these monies were used for the designated purpose, nobody knew. In those days the machinery to monitor and coordinate these programmes was not yet in place and the Non-Governmental Organisations did not submit formal report of their activities to the government. There was no NGO policy.

These efforts and actions were overtaken by unfolding events when on the 25th May 1997, Sierra Leoneans woke up to the disturbing news that the Government of President Tejan Kabbah had been overthrown in another military coup, more devastating with far more reaching consequences than the NPRC coup. To many Sierra Leoneans this incident came as a shock, but then in his forthrightness the President did admit that he knew that the military was planning a coup and he brought this information for investigation to the Chief of Defence Staff. Well, all of us knew what the outcome was. If there was an investigation nothing came out of it. Intriguingly enough, in late 1996 a military captain, Johnny Paul Koroma, was arrested for allegedly plotting a coup, and incarcerated at the Central Prisons. On that fateful day, a small band of soldiers, released Johnny Paul Koroma, who became their leader, freed other convicts, and gave them arms and ammunition to assist with the taking over of State House.[154] That the coup was successful was in itself an attestation to the state of the army. The junior ranks felt hard done by. The senior officers for

---

[154] Sierra Leone. A Political History. David Harris

THE DECLINE AND FALL OF THE ATHENS OF WEST AFRICA

example were receiving over twenty-five bags of rice monthly while the junior ranks were entitled to one bag only. Some factions of the army also felt that the Kamajors (CDF) were treated more seriously by the government, than the army, whose reputations, considering their chameleon nature (soldiers during the day and rebels during the night) was in tatters, they no longer had the trust of the people they should be protecting. There was also the fact that the Kabbah government was discussing with the international community, strategies for training and restructuring of the army into a more efficient machinery; the issue of downsizing the army also featured, especially considering the way and manner the soldiers were being recruited during the war. Looking at the way many of them behaved during the conflict, there were rogue elements in the army indeed.

That less than a year after the restoration of constitutional rule, the armed forces, who for several years had been fighting against the rebels, to the dismay and disbelief of Sierra Leoneans joined forces with their arch enemy and supposedly bitter foe, to abrogate the democratic rights of all peace-loving Sierra Leoneans. Their excuse? They were bringing peace to a country devastated by several years of civil war, the result of the acts of the same AFRC – RUF junta. How ironic.

How did a situation like this arise? The so-called leader of the coup Johnny Paul Koroma invited the rebels to partner with the soldiers to govern the country. Perhaps in his misguided thinking Johnny Paul thought this would bring an end to the conflict. Or, perhaps also, he recognised the weakened position of the military in defeating the rebels. Whatever the reason, the RUF had no political ideology. Foday Sankoh made a lot of noise, just to be noticed by the international community, but none of his cohorts had an inkling what governance was about, neither did Johnny Paul for that matter. From all that had happened, the rebels were an uncontrollable and lawless group taking orders from their leader Foday Sankoh only. How on earth was Johnny Paul going to work with these criminals, in government?

As the saying goes 'first impression goes a long way', and so it was with the AFRC – RUF putsch. There was complete and utter chaos during the first week of the coup, culminating in rampant looting of public and private properties in what was termed 'operation pay yourself', the burning of parts of the Treasury Building, and the Central Bank, in their bid to 'root out corruption' from the society and the wanton killing of innocent civilians. With Sankoh in detention in Nigeria for the illegal possession of a weapon, he was nevertheless made the vice chairman of the AFRC and the vice president of Sierra Leone. It did not come as a surprise that the AFRC – RUF junta ruled Sierra Leone with terror, surrounded in violence against the citizens. While these activities were taking place, the President had been evacuated to neighbouring Guinea by the ECOMOG which was stationed at Lungi. Meanwhile, this unnecessary coup was stoutly resisted by the Sierra Leonean citizenry, but also roundly and soundly condemned by the international community: the Organisation of African Unity, now the African Union, the Economic Community of West African States (ECOWAS), the European Union (EU), the United Nations and its agencies. They had no support from any sane individual or organisation / governments. But of course, being of retarded minds, Johnny Paul and the RUF thought they could rail-road the citizens and non-citizens into accepting their reign of terror.

Those with sane minds, like the British High Commissioner then, Peter Penfold, tried reasoning with them. In the midst of their intimidatory stance a series of meetings were held to convince Johnny Paul Koroma, about the futility of his endeavour. Although Karefa-Smart did not sit with the AFRC – RUF, in one of these meetings, yet he was sympathetic to their cause. At the last set of meetings, the international community thought they had reached an agreement with the AFRC, who were represented by senior military personnel. They were promised an amnesty for their dastardly acts and so many other perks including money, cars and being flown out of the country. In fact, this so- called break-through was announced over the airwaves bringing so much relief to the beleaguered Sierra Leone population.

On consultation with the RUF side of their bilateral arrangement, the deal was scuppered by the RUF. Not only did the RUF kick against this deal, it was later learnt that the Chairman, Johnny Paul Koroma who was going to announce to the public that the junta had reached an agreement to hand over the reins of government to the elected president, was arrested and detained by the RUF arm of the junta, so he did not make this broadcast.[155] One wondered whether it dawned on Johnny Paul that he had released the genie out of the bottle, and he was no longer in control.

Of course, the international community meant well in seeking a peaceful or diplomatic solution to these breaches of democracy in African countries, especially when an entire country is held to ransom by some rogue individuals. On the other hand, most western Democracies have a policy of not negotiating with terrorists when their nationals are kidnapped or held for ransom. The situations are different? One can aver that there is a similarity, the difference is one of degree, whereby one scenario involves an entire nation, while the other scenario involves an individual or a group of individuals. In both cases there are ransom demands. In the case of Sierra Leone, the AFRC was given a large incentive package to leave the seat of power, but they did not reckon with the RUF factor whose objectives were completely different from the AFRC. For the RUF it was all and everything, power, control of the wealth of the country etc.; they would settle for nothing less. Now here was the crux of the matter. For the previous coupists in the NPRC to return the government to constitutionality, they were provided with an incentive package. Subsequently, where would this end? The AFRC of cause were following in the footsteps of the NPRC who had their piece of the pie in 1992. They also went for a piece of the action in 1997! This is the view of the author, but for the RUF, Johnny Paul and his cohorts

---

[155] Atrocities, Diamonds, and Diplomacy. The Inside Story of the Conflict in Sierra Leone. Peter Penfold.

would have accepted the initial package proposed by some members of the diplomatic corp.

It was rather unfortunate that at the time of the coup, Sierra Leone was at the point of take-off. The government (de jure) had concluded negotiations with the bi-lateral and multi-lateral donors for another phase of the structural adjustment and reconstruction and rehabilitation programmes, including a safety net programme for the youth and other vulnerable groups. The European Union had already incepted a reconstruction programme in some parts of the provinces. The World Bank had also approved twenty-seven (27) projects, costing almost one billion Leones as a pilot programme which was to start immediately. The Islamic Development Bank had also lodged two million United States Dollars with the Central Bank as contribution to the government's rehabilitation and reconstruction programme.

The AFRC – RUF junta stayed in power for nine months. Nine months during which the people of Sierra Leone went through hell, but with resolute determination the people resisted the junta, no manner of intimidation or violence could cow their spirit. In the end the junta was removed, not through diplomacy, but by the barrel of the gun.

In any case, for the nine months the AFRC – RUF junta had control of the government, they did untold harm to the nation. The smallest infraction could lead to one's death. Take for example listening to the radio, turned to a particular station, Radio Democracy, established to air government and other pertinent information, especially about the transgression of the AFRC – RUF regime. Death was usually the price paid by someone caught listening to this station. Well, the people were so resolute that this was not a deterrence to their airing the Radio Democracy station, all one needed to do was to take the necessary precaution of reducing the volume of the radio broadcast.

In his maiden radio broadcast to the nation in castigating the elected government and proffering the rationale behind the coup, one of the points Johnny Paul Koroma made was restoring the freedom of the press. Strangely the press did not escape the barbarity of the regime, especially as one of their responsibilities was to report on pertinent activities etc. affecting the welfare and well-being of the nation. Most of the press did not toe the line of the junta. As a result, journalists, editors, proprietors were assaulted, harassed, locked up in windowless containers, tortured and killed.

The students also joined in the condemnation of the unholy regime. In August 1997, they called for a massive nationwide demonstration against the junta, a call heeded to by the labour congress, the Sierra Leone Association of Journalists (SLAJ) and other Civil Society groups, including the Women's Movement for Peace. This call for the demonstration was for the 18th August 1997, but what a sad day it was. The People's Army, as the AFRC – RUF junta marriage came to be known crushed this peaceful demonstration violently and ruthlessly. Live bullets were fired upon crowds of peaceful demonstrators, machetes carried unashamedly by the people's army were used to hack off the limbs of demonstrators including beheading. Students more especially were chased everywhere and even the hospitals and college dormitories did not provide safe havens for them; some of them were chased into these buildings and killed.

As Lansana Gberie penned in his book "A Dirty War in West Africa: The RUF and the Destruction of Sierra Leone." Quoting from an editorial of the Standard Times Newspaper, "The brutal action of the AFRC in killing, wounding and maiming pro-democrats is an affront not only to the people of this country, but to the whole world. The nation, particularly the students, had nonetheless succeeded in letting their voices be heard, that they have not and will not tolerate the leadership of the Junta no matter what resistance they face."

Considering their acts of calumny, one wonders whether these so-called peace bringers had an iota of conscience. Apart from the violence meted out to those expressing their dissent, the junta did not hesitate to turn their guns on innocent civilians. Many Sierra Leoneans in the capital city of Freetown were aghast and shell-shocked on a fateful night there was much artillery fire and bombardment in the capital, which according to junta propaganda left fifty innocent civilians dead. According to this propaganda, the ECOMOG forces which by this time were stationed in parts of the country were shelling parts of the capital. However, as it turned out, it was the junta themselves who trained their guns on Freetonians, for the reason of showing the ECOMOG forces in a bad light while garnering sympathy for themselves. This ploy however backfired. The AFRC – RUF forces were seen on that fateful night firing heavy artillery from strategic points in the city, Tower Hill, Fourah Bay College and Falcon Bridge. People even witnessed them off-loading Rocket Propel Grenades (RPGs) from Pajero and Mercedes Benz vans and firing them at different points from Fourah Bay Road into some of the highly populated slum areas in the East of Freetown.

To illustrate how ruthless and callous the junta was, on the next day they had the temerity to mount a propaganda assault against the ECOMOG claiming this was the act of the forces that wanted to restore democracy in Sierra Leone. According to the junta, it was the ECOMOG forces stationed at the Lungi Airport that caused the havoc. Continuing on displaying their callousness and having no regard whatsoever even for the dignity of the dead, they went ahead to desecrate the bodies of these victims by parading with them in their coffins around the streets of Freetown, to finally lay all fifty (50) coffins at the doorsteps of the United Nations Building, the U. N. House. To complete this tragic farce, those who were supposedly the "victims" of the ECOMOG bombardment were given a mass burial service at the National Stadium, with the Chairman Johnny Paul Koroma himself leading the service. While he was awaiting trial at the Pademba Road Prisons he had become a "born-again Christian" according to his testimony.

Of course the junta had its supporters, mostly disgruntled and opportunistic politicians, the likes of Karefa-Smart, who for a time was their mouthpiece, calling for the ECOMOG forces not to deploy in Sierra Leone, and also not to mount any offensive to remove the junta from the seat of power There were also Victor Foh, at the time the Secretary General of the APC who later became the Vice President of Sierra Leone in the last years of the second-term of President Koroma's APC government. Not to talk of Dr. Abass Bundu, a former Minister in Siaka Stevens APC government, currently the SLPP speaker of the House of Parliament. There was also Joe Amara Bangali, one-time Financial Secretary, under Siaka Stevens government: he was the Financial Secretary at the time the OAU Conference was hosted by Sierra Leone.

Victor Foh even accepted employment from the junta, as chairman of the government's telecommunications agency, SIERRATEL. Pallo Bangura, the former NPRC Ambassador to the U. N., and later presidential candidate for the RUF in the 2002, took up the post of Secretary of State for Foreign Affairs. Dr. Abass Bundu went so far as advocating for the junta by sending letters to the U. N. explaining the dangers of a military intervention by the ECOMOG forces. How difficult it was to fathom the intentions of these so-called political stalwarts. Could one attribute this behaviour because of hatred for the government or the president, or because of unbounded ambition and sour grapes? It was unbelievable that they advocated for the return to military dictatorship, under the misguided belief that it would bring peace and stability. During the early days of the coup, it was difficult to ascertain the feelings of Sierra Leoneans, who had never experienced anything of this nature before. There had been uprisings, strikes, and military coups but none to compare with the AFRC-RUF putsch; this must go down in our history as the deadliest and mother-of-all coups!

Unlike previous events in Sierra Leone when only segments of society were affected, the events of 25ᵗʰ May and the subsequent days touched all and sundry alike. This time round there was no immediate escape. During the years of civil strife which started in March 1991, many Sierra Leoneans became internally displaced, while others fled to neighbouring countries. After the AFRC-RUF coup of May 25ᵗʰ, there was a mass exodus of people, not only from the Urban Centres, but even from the rural areas. By the war's end, it was reckoned that nearly 400,000 Sierra Leoneans were refuges and asylum seekers: an estimated 300,000 in Guinea, about 70,000 in Liberia, nearly 10,000 in the Gambia, about 4,000 in Nigeria and some 2,000 in Ghana and another 2,000 in La Cote d'Ivoire, 1,000 in Mali and more than 7,000 asylum seekers in Europe. Between 500,000 and 1 million Sierra Leoneans were internally displaced.[156]

These were trying times. Imagine fleeing your country without any possessions, taking your life in your hands, not even thinking of tomorrow only that moment of escape from the carnage and destruction in your country. Although the future was bleak, imagine the first days of gunshots, or bombardment, or even not living on tenterhooks because one did not know when one's doors would be broken down by the rebels, in a bid to "pay themselves" for the work they were doing. Indeed, it was a sad period in our history that witnessed from the high and mighty to the least and lowly, waiting in queues in Embassies and other charitable organisations, for hand-outs, mainly food, and in rare cases some non-food items.

What about the internally displaced? Owners of houses in their own right, some tenants in proper housing, suddenly finding themselves homeless, either through displacement by the conflict, or their homes had been razed by fire to the ground by senseless vagabonds. Now they find themselves in strange areas and in displaced camps

---

[156] USCR Country Report Sierra Leone: Statistics on Refugees and other Uprooted Peoples, Jun 2001
(USCR – US Committee on Refugees)

which proliferated in the urban areas, in conditions worse than slum conditions, and people had to endure this kind of life until the rebels laid down their arms.

Unfortunately, nobody was dealing with the AFRC-RUF junta. For the entire period that they took over the reins of government, they were ostracised. Not only by the global community, but even Sierra Leoneans treated them with disdain. To be honest, one wonders whether they took themselves seriously. Most of the time they were as high as a kite, hoping that in their drug-induced minds, some workable solution would be found that would remove them from the pit they had dug themselves into. That was not to be and, in their resoluteness, the nation suffered but there was no turning back from the path they had embarked on. This was a time that Sierra Leone had no government. Add to this mix, the UN Sanctions on the junta and the ECOMOG blockade of the Port because the junta was bringing arms in the guise of rice imports, consequently, there were shortages in the markets of even our staple food. Nevertheless, efficient coping mechanisms kicked in to help alleviate the desperate situation that was prevailing in the country. Many inhabitants embarked on backyard gardening, the growing of rice the staple food, in areas that it was never grown before, and the extended family system provided a safety net.

Oh Salone! (a lament over Sierra Leone's calamitous times). As was to be expected, during this period, the economy was going nowhere. How can it when the governance system was in absolute shambles. The country's economy was virtually at a standstill. In their determination to resist the junta rule, people stoutly refused to go to work. Even in those government departments that workers turned up, the departmental heads, junta selected, did not have a clue about governance, nor how the system worked. Imagine during the vandalising of government offices, at the initial period of the coup, computers and other office supplies were carted away, and other logistical equipment stolen. Many of them thought they had hit a rich vein on seeing the computers, thinking they were television sets. Such thinking typified the mindset of the rebels, so what should one have expected from them. Those civil servants who went to the office at the time only went to swap stories, pass on information about the current happenings and pass the time.

This period was the most devastating for the country. Mining, the backbone of the economy was in the hands of the various war factions including government troops and some ECOMOG personnel. Economic activity deteriorated significantly, aggravating unemployment and deepening the poverty situation. The economy contracted by 18 per-cent in 1997, stagnated in 1998, and contracted further by 8.1 per-cent in 1999. Domestic revenues declined to 7 per-cent of G. D. P., and the budget deficit rose to 15 per-cent of GDP.[157] Of course, this abysmal situation did not come as a shock. The AFRC-RUF junta was completely isolated; nobody was doing business with them. Thinking that they would receive some sympathy and perhaps some advice, they approached President Rawlings (now deceased) of Ghana, who had also staged successful coups in Ghana, before discarding his uniform, but he gave them a deaf ear.

Meanwhile, on the diplomatic front, in July 1997, a five-nation committee, comprising the foreign ministers of Nigeria, Ghana, Cote d'Ivoire, Liberia and Guinea was formed, tasked with the responsibility of bringing this war to an end through any means. Already, the chairman, of the junta, Johnny Paul Koroma went over the airwaves to pledge the nation of Sierra Leone to God and proclaimed that the junta would remain as the de facto government until the start of the new millennium, 2001. In spite of the widespread condemnation of this junta rule. Johnny Paul and his cohorts thought in their befuddled mind that they would get away with it. After all, a military coup had never been reversed before by might, only by negotiations with the coupists walking away with undeserved

---

[157] Sierra Leone's Economic Record 1961 – 2010 Alimamy Bangura, Director EPRU, Ministry of Finance and Economic Development

bounties. Note, the NPRC got away with it, why not the AFRC. Poor fool: he did not take into consideration the monumental blunder he made by inviting the RUF to buttress his rule, unfortunately for him he brought in a Frankenstein that he could not control.

Nevertheless, in December 1997, an agreement was reached, in the signing of the Conakry Peace Plan. Both factions, the government and the junta agreed: the restoration of the legitimate government, immediate cessation of all hostilities, the demobilisation of all combatants, the start of humanitarian assistance, the return of refugees, and the granting of immunity to the junta members etc.[158]

Should one contend that the unholy junta was just going through the motion just to give the impression that they were ready for peace just so as to prolong their stay in power? The chairman had already declared that they were in for the long haul, at worst, to hold on to the seat of power at the beginning of the new millennium. Add to this, the intransigence of the RUF faction and their own different agenda: the lust for power and greed. Thus, it did not come as a surprise that after the signing of the Conakry Peace Plan, they started bickering among themselves, trading allegations and counter allegations. Rumours of coup plots started making the rounds and some junta members were arrested. At the same time Johnny Paul arrested some AFRC members, including Tamba Gborie, the private who announced the coup, for working in the diamond mines instead of concentrating on the peace and security. Also, the junta started making all sorts of demands. They called for the reduction, and then the removal of Nigerian troops from the ECOMOG force, as well as the immediate release of Foday Sankoh who was incarcerated in Nigeria. On the part of the AFRC faction, they opposed the plans to disband the army on the grounds that it was a national institution, protected by the

---

[158]   A detailed description of the Conakry Peace Plan can be found in Lansana Gberies "A Dirty War in West Africa. The RUF and the Destruction of Sierra Leone."

constitution.[159] Once more, its diamonds again! One wonders, if there were no diamonds, would all these goings on have happened; even if there was a war, would it have been so atrocious and this prolonged with all the players it attracted within and out of the sub-region? It is an idea worth reflecting upon. In the midst of all this pussyfooting the ECOMOG decided to remove the junta from power by force, and that was exactly what they did.

At the end of January 1998, the ECOMOG forces began "operation sandstorm" to remove the junta forces from the seat of power. People were advised to stay indoors, but as should be expected it was more or less a difficult time for citizens. With all their bravado, when the push came to shove, the junta forces fled the might of the ECOMOG force, under the command of General Maxwell Khobe, with their tails between their legs. Was this the end of the conflict? Unfortunately, it was not, to the regret of Sierra Leoneans. The junta forces fled into the provinces, primarily to the Northern parts of the country. By this time about 90% of the country was under government control, save for the diamond areas.

Throughout the period of the AFRC, it was fortuitous for Sierra Leone that a government-in-exile, was supported by the international community, more so the British. They even arranged for a conference to be held in the United Kingdom, sponsoring some members of the government-in-exile in Guinea, to attend this conference which was held with the aim of developing a ninety-day programme to address the humanitarian catastrophe, once the government returned from exile. The ousted President Tejan Kabbah even attended the Commonwealth Heads of Government which at the time was being held in Scotland. And the Commonwealth Heads unequivocally condemned the coup and the bestial behaviour of the junta.

Once the junta was kicked out of government, the restoration of the ousted government commenced with the dispatch of an advance

---

[159]   ibid

taskforce, comprising of Sierra Leonean professionals, and some members of the donor community, to prepare the way for Kabba's return. On the 10th March 1998, the president returned to Sierra Leone to a tumultuous welcome, with crowds lining the streets of Freetown to welcome home their exiled president. For Sierra Leoneans, the hero of the day was General Maxwell Khobe and the Nigerian Head of State General Sani Abacha, much to the dislike of the international community, especially the United Kingdom which saw Abacha himself as a rogue and unconstitutional leader. Notwithstanding this distaste Sierra Leoneans owed a wealth of gratitude to Abacha and Nigeria for the sacrifice they made to free Sierra Leoneans from the tight yoke of junta rule. This was a time of much happiness in Sierra Leone and rightly or wrongly, having the feeling of being freed at last, especially as around this time about ninety percent of the Sierra Leone was under the control of the civilian government. Unfortunately, we were all living in a fool's paradise, as subsequent events. As the saying goes in the lingua franca, "monkey nor day lef im black an", meaning a monkey never changes his/her behaviour: a monkey will always be a monkey.

Chapter Twelve

BRIEF INTERLUDE

Yes February 12th 1998 was a day never to be forgotten when the AFRC-RUF monster was driven out of power, and forcefully removed from the capital city of Freetown by the ECOMOG forces, led by General Maxwell Khobe. The relief that Sierra Leoneans, the displaced, the oppressed and refugees felt, no matter in what country or place one was sojourning was indescribable. That indeed was a moment of ecstasy and one of joy. The feeling has to be experienced to be believed. But yes, the country was free once more and the opportunity created to rebuild not only our physical and social infrastructure, but also our traumatic state, as the entire nation was put to the sword for over nine months by the junta. It was not an easy task. Sierra Leoneans could make do with all the assistance it could garner from the international community, and the goodwill of the entire citizenry, for the problems and challenges confronting the country were not only multi-dimensional, but they were also very complex. There was the immediate humanitarian crisis of the displaced who were housed in tents, provision of food and non-food items, and also their relocation to their places of domicile; also, there was the repatriation of refugees, long-term reconstruction and rehabilitation of destroyed social and economic infrastructure together with the restoration of people's livelihoods that did not escape the wrath of rebels. Fortunately, the government in exile continued working after the junta coup, and with assistance from the donor community plans were already formulated to address some of these problems and challenges.

So, when President Kabbah returned to Sierra Leone, the SLPP government continued where it had left off. However, an unsavoury period followed just after the restoration of constitutional rule. About one hundred civilians including some prominent politicians and journalists, thirty-four soldiers were charged with various crimes, ranging from collaborating with the junta to committing treason. Chief among the offenders was the leader of the RUF Corporal Foday Sankoh who was released from jail in Nigeria and handed over to the government of Sierra Leone. Other civilians charged included Victor Foh, former president Momoh, Ibrahim Ben- Kargbo, Hilton Fyle etc. They were tried, found guilty and some sentenced to death, including Foday Sankoh. They had the right of appeal, and they appealed their sentences. Meanwhile thirty-four soldiers were tried in a military court, and twenty-four sentenced to death; they did not have the right of appeal. They were all executed by firing squad publicly; the right of appeal in a military court had been removed from the statute books during the reign of Siaka Stevens. While this action was condemned by the international community, notably the United Kingdom, the local population who bore the brunt of the junta excesses did not oppose this action taken by the government against these people. In fact, some members of the public pursued seeming collaborators and sympathisers of the junta, to bring them to book. Some of these so-called junta sympathisers were unfortunately killed by lynch mobs. This was an issue that the people of Sierra Leone was not in agreement with the international community. This period was one of uneasy calm. Yes, the AFRC_RUF junta had been routed from the capital city, but they were still in the country.

Considering the way and manner the junta was removed from the seat of power, it was a shock to many how they regrouped. In the countryside, rebel forces regrouped under Sam Bockarie, alias

Maskita (Mosquito) in the East, and the NPRC and AFRC veteran, SAJ Musa in the North. These two groups attacked Koidu, then Makeni and Waterloo, the gateway to the capital and wrenched possession from the ECOMOG forces. The attack on Koidu resulted in the capture of a large cache of arms; also, it was reported that Ukrainian and South African mercenaries had joined in the fray on the side of the rebels.[160]

Mercenaries, from Ukraine, from South Africa. What would propel somebody so far removed from the war arena to join in the fray? Theoretically the mercenary has no allegiance but follows the money. In this case the diamonds. It was also alleged that even the ECOMOG soldiers who were guarding the mining town were involved in mining, all and sundry seeking for quick wealth, at what expense? The security of the state. One could speculate that had they focussed more on their military duties, Koidu might not have been taken by the rebels. So here we have diamonds again at the heart of the conflict.

With the game of see-saw being enacted in the arena of conflict neither the government nor the people realised the true picture of the calamitous times ahead. The security situation in the country was deteriorating by the day, but then the information being put out by the government was that everything was under control. Meanwhile, the rebels were making advances which the government kept denying. One of the RUF's kingpins was constantly being interviewed by the BBC on the "Focus on Africa" programmes. In one of these interviews, he did state that the RUF would carry out an operation against the citizens, terming this as "Operation No Living Thing". As late as December 1998 the government kept denying that the rebels were close to Freetown. Apparently, it would appear that the people in the field, the ECOMOG forces were not providing the government with the true picture of what was happening in the arena of conflict.

---

[160] Sierra Leone. A Political History. David Harris

But upon all this, the RUF was quietly infiltrating the capital, not only with personnel, but also with arms and ammunition, which were hidden in cemeteries. Strangely enough while these activities were taking place, communities in and around which these infiltrators were staying would claim ignorance of these actions. They never once thought to bring it to the attention of the government or those connected to the corridors of power. Well, the population paid dearly for such lapses. Again, it might have been these infiltrators were relatives and /or friends, so community members thought nothing of it.

The military assault on the capital city, Freetown quickly evolved into one of the most concentrated spates of human rights abuses and atrocities against civilians perpetrated by any group or groups during the entire history of the conflict. In the initial breach of the ECOMOG defences in the far east of the city, they used innocent civilians as human shields to prevent the ECOMOG forces from engaging them. An entire city was subjugated under inhuman acts of brutality, culminating in the wanton destruction of both life and property. These rebels, who in reality were the disbanded soldiers of the Sierra Leone army who had been living in the jungle for some years forcefully marched onto the corridors of power, thinking that by force of arms, they could govern a nation that in the recent past was looked upon as the 'Athens of West Africa'. There had been military coups in Sierra Leone before now, but at no time was the civilian population so overtly and comprehensively betrayed by the soldiers who took an oath not only to protect our territorial integrity, but also the safety of the civilian population against all acts of aggression. Ironically the day this happened, 6th January had been declared "African Liberation Day".

From the East-end of Freetown, the rebels proceeded to central Freetown and thence to Pademba Road Prisons where they freed convicts, but unfortunately for them Foday Sankoh who was in fact awaiting the execution of his sentence prior to appeal had been transferred from the Pademba Road Prisons. Rampaging through the city, the rebels employed various means to terrorise the inhabitants: execution, rape, amputations, the burning of households and abductions.[161] For two good weeks, central and eastern Freetown was under a blight.

Hundreds of people had hands, arms, legs and other parts of the body hacked off by the rebels. Many of the perpetrators of these atrocities were children, often high on drugs, some of them barely capable of carrying their AK47 rifles. Throughout the occupation of the central and eastern Freetown the rebels perpetrated organised and widespread acts of rape against girls and women.[162]Their bestiality was not only confined to raping and looting, but even the taking of innocent lives was like a game to them. People were being burnt alive in their houses. People described scenes in which rebels were throwing children into burning houses and shooting those who tried to escape.

Even when the rebels were being driven out of the city by the ECOMOG and Civil Defence Force (Kamajohs), they did not cease their acts of brutality. "As the rebels withdrew from the capital city, they set entire city blocks and suburban streets on fire. Eighty per-cent of Calabar Town was left in ashes and sixty-five per cent of the densely populated Kissy was destroyed. Many factories were put to the torch, thus destroying thousands of jobs. Diplomatic premises, such as the Nigerian and United Nations offices, government buildings, mosques, churches and several notable historical landmarks were all damaged.[163] To crown it all, in their retreat, they abducted hundreds of boys and girls and took them to the bush. What a sad episode in Sierra Leone's history, one that would not be easily forgotten;

---

[161] These acts are expansively covered by Lansana Gberie in "A Dirty War in West Africa. The RUF and the Destruction of Sierra Leone."

[162] Atrocities, Diamonds and Diplomacy. The Inside Story of the Conflict in Sierra Leone. Peter Penfold.

[163] ibid

even after so many years since the brutal conflict ended, there is evidence all around us, people with hacked limbs, burnt-out houses, to remind us of that catastrophe / calamity. Most Sierra Leoneans were traumatised for a long time after the war. Unfortunately, successive administrations have only paid lip service to addressing the problem. Some of the time, they have used and are still using the lawless and undisciplined youth to stifle opposition and intimidate their critics. Imagine, in this day and age. Only in Africa, the world has moved along but Africa still wallows in backwardness. If we did not have the Rwandan story of a country devastated by ethnic conflict but has risen from the ashes to post spectacular growth and development, the writer would have averred about the effects of the war on the economic system. Just as one cannot compare the natural wealth of Singapore to that of Sierra Leone, in the same way one cannot make similar comparisons between Sierra Leone and Rwanda. But look at where these two countries are today. In Sierra Leone, the citizens are still wallowing in poverty and political parties locked in regionalism and tribalism. No matter what is being said or written, the two countries mentioned have been blessed with visionary leaders. Well, Sierra Leone, that is something else; the country had produced visionless and selfish leaders who in this modern day and age are still steeped in their parochial thinking.

Our sympathy must be with the beleaguered president, Tejan Kabbah. He assumed the reins of office at an inauspicious time. Less than a year when he took office as president, through the ballot box, he was removed from office by a military coup but with the help of the international community, was prevailed upon to establish a government in exile. On his return in March 1998, again less than a year, he had to flee the seat of power, but this time not to a neighbouring country but to one of the safe zones garrisoned by the ECOMOG force. On his return for the second time the carnage and challenges confronting him were worse than what he met on his return from exile in Guinea. Because the junta were not pursued to the limit of exterminating that vermin in 1998, they regrouped, and the see-saw war continued with them holding large swathes of territory in the North and East. Added to the destruction of the country during the war years, over sixty percent of the capital city was destroyed, including both public and private buildings, not only were people more traumatised more displaced, but now also families were rendered more distraught as many of their children, who were used to living in homes, were abducted to live with animals in the bush. What catastrophe!

Another Peace Conference, this time organised by the Commission for Democracy and Human Rights was convened to consult with the people, the way forward upon all this turmoil. This conference was held from the 7th – 9th April 1999, and was representative of all facets of the population, civil society groups, students, teachers, women's groups, religious leaders, trade unions to members of the army and civil defence forces, amputees, displaced persons and political parties' representatives and paramount chiefs. Even the monster Foday Sankoh was invited, he did not attend but sent a message of regret for the ills of the RUF, his trust for President Kabbah, and his commitment to peace. At the end of this conference the populace laid down their conditions for peace.

They wanted: a cessation of hostilities; RUF should recognise the de jure government; unconditional release of abductees and no power sharing with the recalcitrant / intransigent RUF; and the return of the ECOMOG forces in Sierra Leone soil.

From the Peace Conference at the Central Bank Complex in Freetown, proceedings moved to Togo, where President Eyadema, the then Chairman of ECOWAS offered the capital city of Lome for the venue for the peace talks between the Sierra Leone Government and the RUF.

Although the Sierra Leoneans had made it clear that they wanted no part of the RUF to be involved in the administration of the country - who would blame them considering the bestial nature of the RUF – the international community, primarily, the Americans, the British and the United Nations, were suing for peace at any cost. The RUF were making unreasonable demands and it would appear, the brokers were in tune with them. The Reverend Jesse Jackson who was President Clinton's envoy in African Affairs was pressuring president Kabbah to sign an innocuous peace deal with the RUF; even the British Prime Minister then, Tony Blair was partial to this deal. Not to talk of President Eyadema of Togo who was by then the current chairman of the ECOWAS, who wanted this deal to be done under his patch as his term of office was coming to an end.

Initially, President Kabbah himself was not in Lome, the Attorney General, Solomon Berewah, led the delegation. However, there was some to-ing and fro-ing between Lome and Freetown, to get the President to acquiesce to the RUF proposal. Imagine, in its initial form, the RUF was not only calling for a power-sharing agreement, but they wanted ten cabinet positions, five deputy ministers, six ambassadorships and the heads of eleven parastatals, with Foday Sankoh accorded the position of vice president.[164] Preposterous? Of course, but not in the mindset of the RUF. Since their regrouping after being kicked out of Freetown in 1998, they had attacked towns in the North, Lunsar and Makeni particularly. And with their strong propaganda machinery gave the impression to those not on the ground, the likes of the Reverend Jesse Jackson that they controlled seventy-five percent of the country.[165] It was obvious then to the uninformed that the RUF proposal was not unreasonable. Nonetheless, it was hard to imagine a rapacious group like the RUF who had meted out untold havoc to both the lives and property of the Sierra Leonean, now given lordship over them. Apart from their greed, the RUF did not even know what they wanted. No ideology or manifesto, inferior

[164] Atrocities, Diamonds and Diplomacy. The Inside Story of the Conflict in Sierra Leone. Peter Penfold

[165] ibid

personnel etc, how then could they have participated in governance? The idea of governance was abhorrent to them. Not to blame them, blame the self-esteemless Sierra Leone Government that go cap in hand for hand-outs from the international community. He who pays the piper calls the tune; that's why what they will not accept in their own country, they can easily foist on others.

Under all this pressure by the international community to conclude a peace deal with Foday Sankoh and his cohorts, Tejan Kabbah had to fly to Lome to sign this contract, could it be against his will, but then a peace deal not supported by his advisers. The Accord was duly signed. On examination, any sane thinking individual would have thought the RUF were the victors in the war: perhaps they were!

In the Lome Peace Accord, the RUF were given four ministerial, and four deputy ministerial posts, not the eight that Foday Sankoh asked for; they were also promised some ambassadorial and public service positions. What was galling to the traumatised citizens was the blanket amnesty that was given to all the combatants. The RUF should release all prisoners and abductees, and on the government side, all mercenaries were to be given their marching orders. New mandates were to be sought for both the ECOMOG and the United Nations Observer Mission, Sierra Leone (UNOMSIL), that was policing the peace. The original mandate of the UNOMSIL was to observe and not to participate in any hostile action by the RUF against the citizen of Sierra Leone. Disarmament of all combatants was to commence immediately and certain commissions for the protection of human rights were to be established. Additionally, the RUF was to be given all the necessary support to transform into a political party. To crown this ignominy, Foday Saybanah Sankoh, the RUF leader who had been depleting the population and the country's diamond wealth was elevated to the position (newly created), Chairman of the Commission for the Management of Strategic Resources,

Reconstruction and Development. This position was to have the same status as Vice President![166]

Although a peace agreement was signed in Lome, yet this sought-after peace proved elusive. As in previous times the rebels could not be trusted. They reneged in Abidjan, so also did they in Conakry. So why on earth should Foday Sankoh be trusted now? As the saying goes, "a leopard never changes its spots." After several years of civil strife, there seemed to be a fragile peace, guaranteed by the international community. However, when the peace finally arrived, it was sudden and unexpected. Like in the Trojan War, Sierra Leoneans were flabbergasted by war, and in 2002 when the pronouncement was made by the President that the war "don don" (war was over), indeed it was like the Phaeton Horses ushering in the real peace. However, between the signing of the Lome Peace Accord and the dramatic events of 2002, leading to the cessation of hostilities, there was no peace. The rebels were still in control of large parts of the Sierra Leone territory, more especially the mining areas.

So Foday Sankoh's was legitimised to the point of giving him an important position in the Government's hierarchy. Any rational being or sane-thinking individual would have embraced this opportunity to atone for past misdeeds and show some amount of contrition. But no, there was no such thing as remorse or regret. In fact, Sierra Leoneans would listen to the RUF spokesman spouting ideological nonsense about the liberation struggle with corrupt and polluted leaders and such trash. All this time though, they were lining their pockets with illegal diamonds. It was even rumoured that they were doing business with the Al-Qaeda terrorist group.

---

[166] A detailed account on the signing of the Lome Peace Accord is given by Peter Penfold in his book "Atrocities, Diamonds and Diplomacy. The Inside Story of the Conflict in Sierra Leone. There it is even mentioned that when the UN's Human Rights Commissioner visited Sierra Leone and Detailed the atrocities of the RUF in her Report the UN could only sign the Accord after making a disclaimer.

Scarcely was Sankoh installed as Vice President when he started showing his true colours: refusing to attend cabinet meetings and other official functions, sending contrary signals to his commanders in the field, selling our mineral resources to international rogues and planning to subvert the government in all possible way. Of course, Sankoh was a law unto himself but who dared to bring him to book, not even the President. The late President Kabbah did not rule with an iron fist as some of his predecessors, and his successors. One might be tempted to say his was a weak presidency. He was scarcely in control of government policy considering the prevailing circumstances. There were the peace sponsors who primarily paid the piper, there was ECOMOG, a military player that was not under his control, and of course a recalcitrant and undisciplined faction, the RUF, now brought into governance.

With an air of invincibility Sankoh and his godfather, Charles Taylor, decided to operationalize their grand plan of finally dethroning the legitimate government. Skirmishes erupted in the Northern axis, especially for control of the town that was the gateway to and from the provinces. After claims and counterclaims by both sides to the conflict, this town and its environs fell into the hands of the RUF. Also, during this period, the UNAMSIL peacekeepers stationed in the Eastern Province in Kailahun was encircled by the RUF and cut off from their supply lines. The government had to speak to their godfather, Charles Taylor for the lifting of the siege which he succeeded in doing. More seriously though, a contingent of five hundred (500) peacekeepers was seized with their weapons including, some heavy weaponry, and all, by mere boys and held hostage. How farcical it was to carry all these weapons, but they could not be used, even to deter these rag-tag rebels from seizing their weapons and holding them hostage. A more robust and realistic mandate would not have resulted in this farce. Not to blame the U.N., we were all on a learning curve, they took cognisant of this fact to strengthen the mandate of the Peace Keeping Force. The irony of it all which perhaps never dawned on the decision makers and the power brokers, was that the rebels were fighting a government of which they were part.

Foday Sankoh's grand design was to arrogate absolute power to himself. It is well documented that he signed the Peace Accord not because he wanted peace, but because he wanted to relieve international pressures, including the ECOMOG, on the RUF[167]. In the field, he ordered his men to keep fighting. His grand design was to overthrow Kabba's government on 8th May 2000. According to UNAMSIL, on the 19th May, 2000, the rebels were less than twenty miles from the capital. The U. N. spokesman, in a panic mode made that announcement, resulting in sending the entire Western area into catatonic shock. The area mentioned by the U.N. spokesman was an area in which the UNAMSIL battalions were bivouacked. By inference, that meant that the UNAMSIL positions had been breached by the rebels. Visions of May 1997, and January 1999 must have been evoked in the minds of Sierra Leoneans. Once bitten twice shy, "Freetonians" did not wait this time to run for dear lives.

The following day, the 20th May 2000, it was alleged that Sankoh was going to be proclaimed President of the Republic of Sierra Leone. Providence as always lent a hand in the affairs of Sierra Leone. That day was the day that Civil Society unknowingly decided to march against this megalomaniac. The protest was called to inform the international community that enough was enough; Sierra Leoneans were fed up with Foday Sankoh's posturing. True to their colours, Foday Sankoh and his cohorts at his residence opened fire at innocent civilians, a peaceful protest turned into a massacre of innocent civilians; over twenty lives were lost.

The crowning folly of all this was that UNAMSIL was at Sankoh's residence with tanks, apparently to guard Vice President Sankoh. In the heat of the moment, with all the tanks and UNAMSIL around, Sankoh was able to escape from his residence. At the time, the

---

[167]   Sierra Leone. A Political History. David Harris

thinking was that UNAMSIL spirited Sankoh away, for his own safety. In reality Sankoh was at large, so the Government was able to gain access to his residence, and what a find was made! Astoundingly there was incriminating evidence galore implicating even some members of parliament, foreigners as so-called investors; arms and ammunition, even though the residence was under constant surveillance by UNAMSIL. It was a great find for the government and true to form, they wasted no time in calling a press conference to reveal the treasures discovered in Sankoh's residence. Much propaganda was made about this so-called treasure trove, but alas, the disclosure as to the materials found was pretty scanty. After the announcement of the find, the government went as "silent as night."

Eventually, really not too long after his escape, Foday Sankoh was captured and locked up in prison where he belonged and there, he met his death. However, the doom of the RUF was sealed, when their Godfather, Charles Taylor, decided to take the war to neighbouring Guinea, enlisting the help of RUF. In the meantime, another rebel faction ULIMO had mounted an attack on Taylor's forces, from Sierra Leone. During these clashes, many of the RUF top guns met their death and a headless entity was much easier to deal with.

Perhaps this is a point that one can step back and take a microscopic look at the general development of the state of Sierra Leone, from colonial days.

A question one could pose is really, how stable has Sierra Leone been? During colonial days there were no coups. Of course, one would not expect the colonial government to violently turn against itself. In fact, in the early days the country did not have an army. Before 1961 there was a Royal West African Frontier Force, whose allegiance was to the British Empire. And as its name implied it was responsible for the former British West Africa Territories, Nigeria, Ghana (Gold Coast), Sierra Leone and the Gambia. Primarily it was formed to safeguard British interest against the French. Before 1961, there was no army, but there were upheavals, even a civil war, the Hut Tax War of 1898, not too long after the colony and the Protectorate were joined together. Then came the anti-Syrian Riots in 1919, to be followed by the Railway Workers' Union strike in 1926. In 1931, there was a short skirmish, the Haidara Revolt, led by a Muslim missionary Haidara Kontorfili. This revolt was quelled quite easily. Again in 1955, after an interlude of over twenty years riots broke out in Freetown and spread to other areas in the country.[168] Apart from the Haidara Revolt, the next cause of these upheavals was not political but economic.

After Independence, the context shifted and military coups reared its ugly head in the country's political space, causing a lot of instability in Sierra Leone. The crowing event was of course the Civil War that broke out in 1991. Strange as it may seem, for a small country like Sierra Leone, between 1965 and 1993, there were nine (9) military coups and attempted coups.[169] It will not be an understatement to conclude that Sierra Leone as a state was generally unstable, politically. There had been strikes and upheavals, but those incidents did not cause the instability that the coups caused. In In the final analysis, one can opine that these coups, counter coups, and attempted coups point to either military adventurism, on the part of the soldiers, or bad governance on the part of the political leaders. Whatever the case, one does not need rocket science to ascertain the parlous state of the country; bad governance and/or military adventurism cannot provide the environment for the well-being of the citizens to be improved. Hence for a long time, Sierra Leone was classed under the least developed countries and also lately, a "fragile state".

There is no way that wars can be termed as good. There are no good wars, but at the same time, we have heard the term a just war.

---

[168] A Nationalist History of Sierra Leone. C. Magbaily Fyle

[169] A Chronology of Military Coup Attempts and Coups d'état in Sierra Leone described in "Sierra Leone Digest 1993. A Handbook of Facts and Figures.

The Civil War in Sierra Leone was not only catastrophic, but also, it was not just. Assuming that the country had had successive bad governments, there was no reason or justice to wreak such untold havoc on civilians just to satisfy the lust and propensities of some individuals. Notwithstanding the catastrophic impact on the lives and property of Sierra Leoneans, this was a time for all to put our acts together and forge a new political, social and development paradigm. Rwanda is a case in point.

Chapter Thirteen

QUO VADIS?

No doubt, the destruction caused by the war, set Sierra Leone's progress in development back fifty or more years; it will take a long time to get back to where we were before the war. Imagine some three hundred (300) towns and villages, three hundred and forty thousand (340,000) houses, two hundred and eighty-seven (287) "court barays", two thousand (2,000) educational facilities, two thousand (2,000) health facilities and five thousand (5,000) water wells and other infrastructure were destroyed during the civil war. An estimated two million 92.0 million) people were internally displaced, not to talk of the economic livelihood that was destroyed, even budding manufacturing industries and tourism infrastructure did not escape the violent acts of the rebels. Police stations, law courts and other social infrastructure were damaged. There were an estimated five hundred thousand (500,000) refugees, from neighbouring countries to be repatriated. The rebels also plundered the diamond, bauxite and rutile mines, thereby depriving the government of the much-needed revenue to undertake reconstruction and development initiatives.

As there seemed to be some relative calm, after Foday Sankoh and the RUF had played their last act of calumny and failed, the government and people of Sierra Leone had the task and challenge of bringing Sierra Leone back into its pre-war footing. The Lome Peace

Accord made provision for the establishment of a peace consolidation commission which had already been set up with Johnny Paul Koroma, one of the antagonists as its head. Also, an Act of Parliament established the Truth and Reconciliation Commission, and although a blanket amnesty was given to the combatants, a special court was set up to try cases of crimes against humanity that occurred after the signing of the Peace Accord. It should be emphasized that most Sierra Leoneans were not happy with this blanket amnesty given to these sub-humans. Moreover, the Truth and Reconciliation Commission would try to heal the nation of hate and antagonism, but it would not provide justice to the traumatised people. Because of this blanket amnesty, Foday Sankoh and the RUF ware of the opinion that they had won the war, lauding it upon the people by their utterances and the way and manner they were behaving in the society. They were lawless, undisciplined, with a total disregard for the law. And if today, there is so much lawlessness and indiscipline in our society; communities, offices, schools, even the family, the roots could be traced to the integrating of the rebels into our normal day to day life.

The situation was not helped by the delay and slowing down of the Disarmament, Demobilisation and Reintegration (DDR) Programme. There were many reasons for the delay: it was felt that the tie frame was ambitious. In one of the Articles of the Accord, it was stipulated that the DDR promise should commence six weeks after signing the accord, in line with the deployment of the peace-keeping force i.e., in July 1999, and should be completed by the end of the year. Then there was the question of trust or distrust all around, between the government and the combatants, so the initial response to the whole exercise was very slow. But more importantly the resources to finance the exercise were not immediately available. The government had agreed payment of three hundred dollars ($300) to each combatant, apart from other packages of skills training etc. At a minimum, this was going to cost over twelve million dollars, just for the incentive payments to these ex-combatants. It was estimated in total that the

DDR Programme would cost just over fifty million dollars ($50 million).[170]

Considering all of these challenges, it was remarkable that by January 2002, seventy-two thousand (72,000) combatants had been registered in the DDR Programme; twenty-four thousand (24,000), were RUF and thirty –seven thousand (37,000) were CDFs. To all intent and purposes, the DDR Programme was considered a success and it became a model for the process in Burundi, Liberia and far away Haiti. Over seventy thousand (70,000) fighters were demobilised.[171] Work was also being undertaken in key sectors, especially the security sub-sector. The new Republic of Sierra Leone Armed Forces (RSLAF) was being rebuilt, and a retired British Police Officer was engaged to revamp the Police Force and bring it up to professional standards.

On the political front Tejan Kabbah had to seek a new mandate from the populace to continue as President. His term of office had constitutionally expired in 1991, but because of the military interregnum, it was extended by a year, so, Presidential and Parliamentary elections were held in 2002. These elections followed the usual trend, election violence (not at the scale of previous elections), over voting, incumbency influence, voting on regional and tribal lines etc.[172] In all, Kabbah and the SLPP performed much better than in the 1996 Presidential and Parliamentary elections. Not only did Kabbah increase his majority this time round, but there was also no second round, he polled seventy percent of the votes, while his nearest rival, the APC Ernest Bai Koroma polled twenty-two percent

---

[170] Post Conflict Governance in Sierra Leone. Abubakar Hassan Kargbo

[171] A detailed account of the DDR process including challenges at the Macro and Micro levels can be found in "Disentangling the Determinants of Successful Demobilisation and Reintegration. Macarten Humphreys and Jeremy Weinstein (August 2005)

[172] An interesting analysis of the Presidential and Parliamentary elections of 2002 can be found in David Harris' 'Sierra Leone, A Political History.

and Johnny Paul Koroma polled only three percent. The RUFP did not contest the Presidential elections, but they put up candidates for the Parliamentary and performed woefully. Unlike 1996, instead of using the proportional representation system the stakeholders opted out for a District Block system. Indeed, the SLPP made inroads into many regions of the country, perhaps making them a true national party. They won every seat in the South and East, their traditional stronghold, but made significant inroads into the North and Western Regions. The SLPP took sixty eight percent of the nationwide vote, compared to thirty-six percent in 1996, and increased its number of parliamentary seats from twenty-seven out of sixty-eight in 1996 to and overwhelming eight-three out of one hundred and twelve in 2002.[173] So this time round Kabbah and his SLPP government had a clear mandate to embark on the rehabilitation of a broken economy, and tackling the humanitarian crisis.

It should be noted that humanitarian crisis especially, brought about a proliferation of Non-Governmental Organisations (NGOs) in the implementation of aid funded programmes in Sierra Leone. Of course their working in Sierra Leone pre-dated the war. As government institutions experienced capacity constraints in project implementation, donors began to employ their NGOs to implement their aid funded projects. Before this time, when Ministries, Departments, and Agencies (MDAs), were implementing these funded projects, there were complaints about procurement – tying by these donors: goods and services provided through these funds should be procured from the donor countries, even when cheaper alternatives were available. It is the writer's opinion, that employing their own NGOs to implement their funded projects was a convenient excuse to get out of the procurement-tying allegations. More or less the outcome was the same, and worse, the recipient government scarcely had any idea what amount of aid was being provided by the donor government. These NGOs were a law to themselves as they

---

[173] Sierra Leone. A Political History. David Harris

were not under any governmental control; at the time, there was no NGO Policy. In effect we moved from a situation where aid was tied to the procurement of goods and services of the donor country to a situation where aid was given to the government through the donor countries' NGOs. This was the situation at the end of the civil war, and it has not changed much. The paradigm has changed from humanitarian to development assistance, but that the policy of implementation has been formulated and approved by all of the stakeholders, leaves much to be desired.

Indeed, the government did receive massive aid from the donor community for the reconstruction and rehabilitation of social infrastructure, schools, health centres, community centres, court barays, and feeder roads in some cases to connect farms to market; some assistance was also given for the rehabilitation of plantations especially by World Bank and the European Union. Assistance was also provided for the relocation of the internally displaced and returnees but unfortunately not for the reconstruction of their houses. Subsequently, initially, these people returned to their villages temporarily, but gravitated to the urban centres after the initial phase of the relocation exercise. It was after the war that this massive migration to the capital city of Freetown started.

Indeed, as was to be expected, a lot of effort was put on reconstruction and rehabilitation of the country's infrastructure not only by the donor community, but also by the government and people of Sierra Leone. The scale of the devastation was massive and to the ordinary Sierra Leonean, unbelievable, especially as the destruction was carried out by Sierra Leoneans. That really says a lot about us. No matter what cause or disgruntlement Foday Sankoh and his cohorts had, there could be no excuse for their wanton destruction. No, not the killing and maiming of innocent civilians, nor the burning down of their properties, some of which were inherited. The splendour of the city was completely destroyed, the scars that existed may have been removed by the construction of new gigantic structures, but that elegance that used to distinguish the face of Freetown is no longer there. Perambulating the streets of Freetown, it is hard to distinguish residential from business areas. Now is a mix that has turned the city into one big market place, littered with garbage all over the city. Streets, not only main through fares but even minor roads are no longer for the exclusive use of pedestrian and vehicular traffic; traders' kiosks are littered all over the place, even on the foot paths of these roads: the inconvenience caused to both pedestrian and vehicular traffic, degrading the façade of the city but of course the authorities are powerless to take action as these traders threaten to withhold their votes at elections. They are in the majority. It is not uncommon to hear them intone loudly wherever they are involved in some demonstration or agitating for a course that "we will not be voting for you, blaa blaa blaa." Our political decisions are influenced not by the knowledgeable, but by the "critical mass" of drop-outs and illiterate. Street trading was a phenomenon that pre-dated the war, but it became more preponderant after the war. During the Siaka Stevens and Momoh era, as the economy went into free fall, with cost of living soaring above the means of many Sierra Leoneans, coupled with the high rate of unemployment, especially among the youth, many people became engaged in petty trading as a means of economic livelihood; its profitability could not be ascertained. However, there is no value added, subsequently, these activities do not expand the gross domestic product of the nation. These traders do not even pay tax, but pay market dues to the Freetown City Council, thus legitimising erecting market stalls in public throughfares.

Some of the decisions taken by the government to address post-conflict problems had good intentions but their implementation brought about other inconveniences. Transportation has always been a challenge in Sierra Leone, more so after the decommissioning of the railway, the only means of mass evacuation in those days. With a road system that was poor and the unavailability of buses and lorries to move stock and passengers, the government of the day, on the advice of the World Bank discontinued the rail service on the grounds that it was unprofitable and a drain on government coffers. Since then, mass evacuation has always been a challenge, not only intra-city, but also inter-city. Subsequent governments have come up with grand expensive schemes to address this problem, but to no avail. Either through bad procurement of equipment, poor road conditions and mismanagement, all these schemes have ended in failure. It has never entered the imagination of the decision makers to consider alternatives and perhaps more effective means of mass evacuation like the railway which at present is gaining import on other African countries. Not only will such a venture alleviate the transportation problem, but it will solve some amount of unemployment among the youth and like the old railway create a cadre of skilled machined-workers, fabricating tools and equipment to be used to transform other sectors instead of importing these equipment from abroad.

Coming back to the case in point, the Kabbah government introduced the scheme of providing transportation through motorbikes known as Okadas. Many unemployed youths got caught up with this idea and since the regulations about bike riding were loose, and given the demand for this service, suddenly there was a proliferation of motorbikes all over the cities. Under normal circumstances one would think it was a way of easing the transportation problem. Of course not, because it is unsuitable for mass transportation. Rather than easing, it has compounded the problem.

Many people use the Okada, and also the Kekeh, a covered motorbike with three wheels. They are preferred, not for their safety and comfort, but because they get their passengers more quickly to their destination than a taxi or a poda-poda. In trying to get their passengers promptly to their destinations, the kekeh drivers and okada riders do not obey traffic rules, and they are always in a hurry. They drive on the wrong side of the road, they make sudden U-turns in the middle of traffic, they stop abruptly in the middle of the road, driving in convoys, sometimes three or four abreast. They are a law unto themselves and regrettably, the traffic authorities seem powerless in controlling them. Stories abound that a lot of these Kekehs and Okadas are owned by policemen. As one would expect, given this kind of scenario, accidents are commonplace occurrences involving Okadas and Kekehs; sometimes these accidents are fatal.

There were other schemes started after the war which were good; some productive, some others were not. The DDR programme for example was not confined to disarmament and demobilisation, only, the ex-combatants were provided with skills training such as hairdressing, motor mechanic training, gara tie-dyeing, masonry, carpentry, and those interested in agriculture were provided with seeds, implements and fertilisers. On the civilian side, various local NGOs were provided with the resources to run skills training programmes for young people interested in developing their vocational skills. Unfortunately, no mechanism or system was established to track and monitor those that went through these programmes to ascertain whether they were successful in being engaged productively.

There were also some very good policy initiatives that were developed. It was during this period that the government and the donor community spear-headed "Poverty Reduction Strategies", a primary mechanism required to access development aid from the donor community. Its first attempt culminated in the "Interim Poverty Reduction Strategy Paper" (IPRSP). The IPRSP summarised the pervasive extent of poverty in the country, intensified by the eleven-year civil war. The government indicated its commitment to poverty reduction through participatory processes, the core, of the poverty reduction strategy. In brief, the IPRSP emphasized private sector development, by promoting micro-enterprises, and limiting the role of government within public enterprises, prioritising economic sectors, namely, agriculture, mining and infrastructure. Priority was given to improving sub-sectors in education and health.[174]

---

[174] Reference: 'Interim Poverty Reduction Strategy Paper (IPRSP) GoSL

Another Poverty Reduction Strategy Paper (PRSP) was formulated for the period 2005 – 2007, the last one under the then SLPP government. The main thrust of this strategy was a programme for food security, job creation and good governance.[175] On hindsight it can be said that the main thrust of the strategy was not achieved. All that it set out to do, food security, job creation, good governance continued to be challenging if not worse, because of bad governance and corruption.

As was reported inter alia in the immediate post-war period, aid was mainly geared towards humanitarian assistance, however as the country emerged from war, there was also the need to focus on development. Approximately, 20% of aid at the time passed through the budget and balance of payment support. On the other hand, the vast majority of aid in Sierra Leone was still being channelled through project assistance and a large proportion of this through Non-Governmental Organisations.[176]

To improve the aid infrastructure, the GoSL together with its donor partners carried out a number of initiatives; the establishment of an on-line, open access and tracking system, a mechanism to foster dialogue between the GoSL and its development partners, the Development Partners' Committee (DEPAC) of which the Vice President was its chairman was established. In order to coordinate these activities a Development Assistance Coordination Office (DACO) was established in 2004. Despite these initiations it was realised that there was more room for improvement in the area of aid effectiveness. At the time, there was no consistent aid policy in Sierra Leone given the high dependency of the country on external donor assistance.

Recognising the importance of formulating a coherent aid policy framework, work began on its development in 2007, but was

---

[175]   Government of Sierra Leon: Poverty Reduction Strategy Paper 2005 - 2007

[176]   Government of Sierra Leone Aid Policy

interrupted by the impending Presidential and Parliamentary elections. However after the elections, the new administration that came in continued work on the aid policy architecture development. The key objective of the aid policy was to assert GoSL leadership in aid coordination, harmonisation and alignment in order to ensure the effective utilisation of donor assistance in the pursuit of government priorities, the strengthening of state institutions and the promotion of effective division of labour between donors.[177]

In reconstructing a battered economy, the focus was not on the physical, social and economic structure only, but also to rebuild and /or create integrity systems that were considered to be partly responsible for the eleven years civil war. A first of its kind, the President on returning to governance established a national policy advisory committee, an advisory body to the government on policy. Members to the council were directly appointed by the President. An excellent initiative that some citizens while in exile in neighbouring Ghana, were already thinking about, but as a private institution with support from friendly donor institutions. A good example of this is the Institute of Policy Research, privately funded, in Ghana. The council functioned for a time only for tensions to surface as some high ranking public officials thought it was usurping the role of the Cabinet.

The office of the Ombudsman was established in the year 2000, according to provisions in the 1991 Constitution. This was a new phenomenon that provided for private citizens to seek redress from administrative injustice. The Ombudsman's Office was given the authority to take appropriate steps to remedy, correct or reverse any act complained of, through such means that were fair, proper and effective, including the facilitation of negotiation and compromise between or among the parties concerned. Of course, being a new experience, it had and still has its challenges but to a large extent,

---

[177]   Reference: Government of Sierra Leone Aid Policy

its success and effectiveness depended on the political will and commitment of the sitting government.

Although the rehabilitation and reconstruction programme was being implemented by a government agency, the Ministry of Rehabilitation, Reconstruction and Repatriation (MNRRR) which was later transformed into a Social Fund, the government came to realise after the war, there was no infrastructure system in place to spearhead the response to disasters, not only man-made but even natural disasters. The establishment of the Office of National Security in 2002 was predicated on this initiative.

Another plus, a very big one, for the Kabbah government was the bringing back of the local government which had been in the doldrums for over thirty years. Under Presidents Siaka Stevens and Saidu Momoh, governance was highly centralised, to the point of absurdity. By the time Momoh took over the reins of government in the 1980s, "State House" was the master computer that controlled any and everything. Imagine, a public official working in the Provinces, yet to facilitate his work he had to apply to "State House" for his fuel allocation to enable the individual to perform his task. It did not make sense, and as to be expected government bureaucracy was intensified all the more, resulting in very poor service delivery. It was widely believed that the establishment of the over-centralised system of government by the corrupt APC government, with its attendant ills of bad governance, alienation of the rural population, the neglect of basic service delivery, health, education etc. contributed greatly to the outbreak of the civil war in 1991.[178]

In 2004, the Local Government Act was enacted which established Nineteen (19) local councils. The enactment of the Local Government Act envisaged three important outcomes: -

---

[178] Reconstruction National Integrity System Survey. Sierra Leone 2007 Tiri, Jabbi, Sonnia_magba Birbuakei and Salia Kpalka

- The decentralisation of key services (health, agriculture, education etc.) to local councils by 2008.
- The institutionalisation of transparency, accountability and participation through the involvement of citizens in the whole decentralisation process.
- An active civil society that inputs into policy formulation and monitors the delivery of services.[179]

The decentralisation and devolution of authority to the local district councils was a challenge, to say the least. Initially there was a reluctance on the part of the Central Government to cede control to the local authorities. There was some improvement, but local authorities still depended on the central government for the bulk of their resources to perform their functional roles. Rather the ability of local authorities to raise their own revenue is restricted, and they did not have a free hand in this matter, even where the occasion arose to raise revenue to finance their activities which would logically have relieved some of the pressures on the central government to grant subvention to these councils. A case in point was tension between the central government, the Ministry of Local Government, and the Freetown City Council. This was compounded by the fact that the opposition APC party controlled the Freetown City Council.

The new administration under the APC, decided to do a cadastral survey, which had not been done for decades, even though the city has expanded, and buildings were being erected willy-nilly. This was accomplished and based on the outcome, city rates were re-evaluated and levied accordingly. The rates for modern structures as would be expected were increased, but some others were re-valued downwards. This decision to collect these taxes by the Freetown City Council, based on the new rates was firmly resisted by the Central Government, citing all kinds of excuses, in the meantime, they were increasing some tax rates.

---

[179] Ibid

During colonial and post-colonial days, there was no social security scheme for public servants. The nearest scheme to a social security scheme was what was then called 'Widows and Orphans' a system in which a fixed sum of money, (in those days, less than fifteen (Le15.00) Leones, was deducted from the salary of every civil servant. There was no employers' contribution. At the end of service, one's pension was calculated on that sum of amount that was being deducted. As one would expect, once the public servant left service, life was a struggle. One almost lived like a pauper. Employees in the private sector were more fortunate as their employers / firms established insurance schemes that took care of their retirement benefits.

Once Kabbah's government was installed the President commissioned a study to establish a social security scheme; a principal member of the team that undertook the study was the man, Ernest Bai Koroma, who succeeded Kabbah as President, when the APC won the Presidential and General Elections in 2007. Thus, the National Social Security Scheme (NASSIT) for all workers in Sierra Leone was created. This time, the employers are obliged to contribute ten percent (10%) of the employee's salary, while the employee contributed five percent (5%). This system is much improved over what used to obtain during colonial and post-colonial days.

Indeed, the post-conflict regime led by President Kabbah, was confronted with severe challenges, but at the same time, there was tremendous international goodwill towards Sierra Leone that enhanced the subsequent peace that prevailed in the country. The donor community was charged towards removing the humanitarian burden that the country was experiencing. On that basis, the infrastructure of the country was neglected, especially after it was vandalised by the rebels. In this regard, Freetown the capital city, during the entire reign of the SLPP government continued to be plagued with darkness. Electricity was severely rationed. The bulk of the population came to depend on generators to supply their own power. Hence people came up with the popular term "Kabbah Tiger" the most popular generating plants at the time. This was a period when noise pollution in the country was extremely bad as almost every home had one of these small generating plants. Freetown was still called "the darkest city in the world".

Given that the term of office of the government was five years, elections time was coming up, both the government and the opposition were gearing up for another term of electioneering.

An interesting but perhaps strange phenomenon was the seemingly retirement from public view of President Kabbah, during the final years of his reign. Then his Vice President, Solomon Berewa, one of the architects of the Lome Peace Accord, became quite visible to the public eye. He took charge of everything, political as well as administrative. The President was seldom seen at administrative meetings, especially chaired by the Vice President. Even the DEPAC meetings where donors and cabinet ministers met to discuss on aid coordination and effectiveness was chaired by the Vice President Solomon Berewa. It was as if Berewa was being put in the limelight so that the electorate would become familiar with him and perhaps come to 'love' him, seeing him as the natural successor to President Kabbah. During those days, there was no contention for the mantle of President Kabbah, as it was clear, Berewa was the heir apparent. What was in contention was, who would be his running mate.

The SLPP were poised to continue what they had been doing, considering all they had achieved seemingly? The 2002 Presidential and General elections saw a landslide victory for the SLPP, unlike 1996. Kabbah polled about seventy percent (70%) of the vote ahead of Ernest Bai Koroma of the APC, in second place with twenty-two percent (22%) of the votes, Paul Koroma, a distant third with three percent (3%) of the votes. Ultimately, there was no need for a second round. Similarly, in the General Elections, the SLPP polled sixty-eight percent (68%) of the votes, increasing their number of seats in Parliament from twenty-seven (27) in 1996, to an overwhelming eighty-three (83), of the one hundred and twelve (112) seats, in 2002.[180]

All things being equal, the elections in 2007 should have been no contest. The main opposition or better still, the traditional opposition, the All People's Congress was just emerging from a bitter internal conflict. A situation in which nobody wanted to be a follower, everybody wanted to be a leader. By 2007, they had put this all behind them and were gearing up for the forthcoming contest. The governing party in their wildest dreams, never thought they were going to lose the elections. Not when the APC party was in governance when the war started, and then it was the SLPP that was in governance when the war ended. Should one be looking for any causality? Again one would be apt to conclude, that the SLPP who were in opposition after Sir Albert Margai lost the elections in 1967, were tired of the APC corrupt government and perhaps disillusioned to the extent that the governing APC was using all kinds of tactics to perpetuate their stay in governance, President Momoh, at the time might have been dragging his feet in re-establishing the multi-party democracy, that the electorate was yearning for.

Then came that fateful day in April 1993, when a group of young soldiers toppled the intransigent regime under the APC. When the dust settled, the Head of State was from the Western Area, but to all intent and purposes, the coup was seen as a South-Eastern led coup. What is pertinent here was the fact that Ahmed Tejan Kabbah and Solomon Berewa were important members of the Advisory Council to the NPRC. Again, when the dust finally settled, once Ahmed Tejan Kabbah, became the President, through the ballot box, however dubious and later on Solomon Berewa, became the Vice President and the SLPP flag-bearer for the 2007 Presidential and Parliamentary elections.

---

[180] Sierra Leone. A Political History. David Harris

So, with all the trappings of incumbency, how did the SLPP manage to lose the elections in 2007? One can speculate but all it would result in would be mere speculation. With all of their claims of successes, especially parroting the claim that they were responsible for the reconstruction of the country from massive donor funding, appropriated as their doing, they never inculcated a system of good governance. Corruption was still rife, in spite of the Anti-corruption Commission that was established by the very SLPP government of Kabbah; and there were sacred cows. When the commissioner then tried to bring the big guns to book, he was rail-roaded out of office by the very same government that appointed him.

Another policy that was taken by President Kabbah and his government was the privatisation of Public Enterprises that were deemed inefficient and unprofitable. Governments, the world over had come to the realisation that it had no business running business enterprises as it was not its forte. So, the divestiture of these government enterprises became very popular as far back as the 1980s. The British Prime Minister spear-headed this activity in Britain and successfully, privatising even the water supply, energy and rail transportation. All of this was accomplished to the benefit of the British government.

In Sierra Leone the National Privatisation Commission was established and tasked with the assessment of all public enterprises, making recommendations to the government for their subsequent divestiture. Indeed, a survey was undertaken, and it was discovered that there were enterprises, mainly defunct, that the government did not even know about. Similarly, there were enterprises that were unprofitable because of bad management. This was not a profitable venture for the government, but the functions of the commission had assumed another dimension in the sense that it seemed to now have authority over all MDAs resulting in tensions between the Management of the MDAs and the Privatisation Commission. This state of affairs sometimes impeded the implementation of sectoral policies as there were arguments as to who was in charge and who was the decision maker?

One interesting facet in the last years of Kabbah's presidency when the vice president, Solomon Berewa was in charge apparently, he used to criss-cross the country on government business primarily the handing over and opening ceremonies of community facilities, health centres, schools, court barries, community centres, that had been completed. At the time, considering where the country was coming from, much ceremonial was made out of this, and the ruling SLPP government made much capital out of it to enhance their standing with the electorate; it was more like a party function than government business. This assertion was bolstered by the fact that almost all of the Ministers would traipse along the Vice President to attend these functions. Not only was it unnecessary as it imposed unwanted costs on the budget (per diems, fuel, etc.) but it was also sycophantic, as if not 'showing face' would count against their political standing. As the time for the elections drew near, these official trips by the government officials, led by the Vice President became more frequent. Not that they were campaigning officially, because the time for that was not yet, but they were using their position of incumbency to flout the law.

For the elections in 2007, the District Block System of voting that was used in 2002 was abandoned for the return to the 'first past the post' system. Also, there was a redistribution of seats, to better reflect the population distribution after the war. The result of this redistribution was, the Western Area gained five (5) seats, the Eastern Region three (3) seats, while the Northern Region lost one (1) seat and the Southern Region seven (7) seats.

True to form, the elections were not without incidents, violence and drama during the campaign, during the elections and even when the results were being declared.

It cannot be over-emphasised that the nature of political campaign had taken a different turn: it was more like a show of strength, rather than explaining the parties' intended plans for running the country. Hence political parties were allotted different days to rally to avoid clashes and violence. Even at, that political rallies seldom passed without violence, and harassment. More often than not main thoroughfares of cities become no go areas for vehicular traffic as the roads are clogged with party supporters, likely to be drunk, dancing and behaving disorderly in the streets. Innocent civilians were normally harassed, and making the mistake of putting on a dress, the colour of a party that is not rallying would result in violent harassment, sometimes leading to severe beating by supporters of the 'rallying party'. The elections of 2007 were no exception, they followed the same pattern.

As in 2002, the incumbent party in government, the SLPP benefited from state and donor resources which the opposition parties did not have access to. In a radio interview of, the SLPP flag-bearer, the Vice President did not deny this advantage of the incumbent party. The voter register for a start, appeared suspiciously inflated in certain SLPP strongholds.[181] A few journalists were intimidated. Violence, mostly but not entirely associated with the SLPP occurred, particularly as tensions increased between the first and second rounds of the elections. There was violence in Pujehun and Kono Districts, and an alleged assassination attempt on the opposition Presidential Candidate, Ernest Bai Koroma, and this led to Koroma's security severely tanning the hide of an SLPP supporter. As to be expected there was confrontation between the SLPP and the APC in the main cities, the one in the capital city of Freetown had to be quelled by the police. In the SLPP strongholds of Kenema and Kailahun, the APC Presidential Candidate, and the PMDC leader,

[181]   Sierra Leone. A Political History. David Harris

were forcefully prevented from campaigning while the PMDC leader and the secretary general of the APC were harassed in Pujehun.[182]

But for a few incidents, election day was rather peaceful, and the elections went on smoothly, and the turn-out was very high at seventy-six percent. When the results were announced finally, the outcome was remarkable, if not astounding. The All People's Congress won both the Parliamentary and Presidential elections, gaining a slim majority in Parliament; the Presidential election went into a second round and the People's Movement for Democratic Change (PMDC) a breakaway party from the SLPP, threw in its hat with the opposition All People's Congress, bucking the system just as the People's Party (PDP) a breakaway party from the APC had done by throwing its hat with the SLPP in 1996.

The second round was won by the opposition candidate but not without controversy. Because of the over-voting / ballot stuffing, a decision was taken that ballot boxes containing a certain number of ballot papers more than the stipulated number of voting papers (500 ballot papers) would be disqualified. The returns from four hundred and seventy-seven (477), out of six thousand one hundred and fifty-six (6,156) polling stations, nearly eight percent (8%) of the total were discovered to contain more ballot cast than registered voters. Of these four hundred and seventy-seven, four hundred and twenty-six (426) were in the South and East, a clear attempt of vote rigging by the ruling SLPP in their strongholds. This process of manufacturing greater turnouts at particular location was obviously opaque, but one method appeared to be a conspiracy to interfere with the voting by local notables and traditional leaders, the party observers and NEC officials at the polling stations. In sharp contrast to the way over-voting was dealt with in 1996, and 2002, all four-hundred and seventy-seven (477) results were invalidated by the national Electoral Commissioner. Some people, especially SLPP sympathisers viewed

---

[182] Ibid

this action by the Electoral Commission as partial to the opposition APC candidates, although the Commissioner was appointed by the SLPP administration. Strangely, the Commissioners for the Eastern and Southern Provinces resigned after the run-off and refused to append their signatures to the results; it was obvious they were SSLPP sympathisers, and not working for the national good.

There was much grumbling from the SLPP camp and their supporters about the outcome of the Presidential election. They felt that the invalidation of so many votes in the south and east cost them the election, a belief that had no grounds. It was proved, painstakingly by the electoral Commissioner, even if these invalidated votes were included, the former Vice President, Solomon Berewa would have lost the election. Many reasons were adduced for the woeful performance of the SLPP in an election they should have won comfortably, given the resounding victory they had in 2002. Briefly, it was noted that the SLPP had become complacent and assumed with all the noise they were promoting about the reconstruction and rehabilitation programmes, they still had the support of the electorate. In reality their record, especially the second term was perceived to be pitiful. They were seen to be corrupt, and DFID their principal donor had suspended budget assistance to the government. There was also the question of a shipment of rice from Libya, to be sold and the proceeds used for improving the welfare of the people. This was unaccounted for, and it became a topical issue in many radio programmes. What is it with the SLPP and rice? In 1967 a warehouse full of rice disappeared and the explanation given then was that the rice was eaten by rats. Incredible! And there was more to come on the same topic of rice and the SLPP.

It was a momentous occasion when the final result of the second round of the election was announced, declaring the opposition candidate, Ernest Bai Koroma the winner. The atmosphere in the capital city of Freetown was electric, the sounds of victory reverberated from East to West and North to South. The atmosphere was that palpable. But before continuing this narrative, let us take a brief pause and look back on some of Sierra Leone's political and social development.

It will not be incorrect to state that Sierra Leone, but for brief periods of military rule, has been governed by two political parties namely, the Sierra Leone People's Party (SLPP) and the All People's Congress (APC). This is illustrated as follows in the matrix below.

SUCCESSIVE REGIMES SINCE THE FIRST GENERAL ELECTIONS[183]

No.	Leadership	Political Party	Year (Period)
1	Sir Milton Margai	Sierra Leone People's Party SLPP	1952 – 1964 (12 yrs)
2	Sir Albert Margai	Sierra Leone People's Party SLPP	1964 – 1967 (3 yrs)
3	Andrew Juxon-Smith	National Reformation Council (NRC) Military Regime	1967 – 1968 (1 yr)
4	Siaka Probyn Stevens	All People's Congress (APC)	1968 – 1985 (17 yrs)
5	Joseph Saidu Momoh	All People's Congress (APC)	1985 – 1992 (7 yrs)
6	Valentine Strasser	National Provisional Ruling Council Military Regime	1992 – 1995 (3 yrs)
7	Julius Maada Bio	National Provisional Ruling Council Military Regime	1995 – 1996 (1 yr)
8	Ahmed Tejan Kabbah	Sierra Leone People's Party SLPP	1996 – 1997 (1 yr)
9	Johnny Paul Koroma	Armed Forces Revolutionary Council Military and Rebel Regime	1997 – 1998 (1 yr)

---

[183] Reconstruction National Integrity System Survey. Sierra Leone 2007. Sonnia-Magba Bu-Buakai Jabbi and Salia Kpaka

10	Ahmed Tejan Kabbah	Sierra Leone People's Party SLPP	1998 – 2007 (9 yrs)
11	Ernest Bai Koroma	All People's Congress APC	2007 – 2017 (10 yrs)
12	Julius Maada Bio	Sierra Leone People's Party SLPP	2018 – to date (4+yrs)

It is interesting to note that since Party Politics began in 1952, the Sierra Leone People's Party had governed this country for twenty-eight (28) years, while the All People's Congress had ruled Sierra Leone for thirty-four (34) years. Not that there have not been other parties, but they were too small to make any dent in the results of successive general elections. In most cases, these smaller parties were break-away factions of these two main political parties, more especially from the All People's Congress. Apart from the 2007 elections when Charles Margai broke away from the SLPP to form the People's Movement for Democratic Change (PMDC), the SLPP had had a solid base from the South – Eastern Region. Many of the smaller parties have their origins from the North, which is more fragmented tribally than the South and East. In 1996, a splinter party from the APC, the People's Democratic Party (PDP) cast its lot with the SLPP led by Ahmed Tejan Kabbah. It was the thinking that this cost the United National People's Party (UNPP) led by John Karefa-Smart to lose the elections to Ahmed Tejan Kabbah in 1996. In a similar vein, when Charles Margai broke away from the SLPP to form the PMDC, he cast his lot with the APC for the second round of the Presidential election in 2007.

If for nothing else, the late President Kabbah would be remembered as a man of peace. It was under his patch the war came to an end. Uniquely, unlike other countries in Africa where wars have been waging without end, the Congo being a case in point, in Sierra Leone when the end of the war was proclaimed in 2002, indeed that was the end of the civil conflict. One cannot attribute the bringing of peace to Sierra Leone to the late President alone, there were other actors and stakeholders who played their own part, the donor community led by the British Government of Tony Blair and the Economic Community of the West Africa States (ECOWAS) led by Nigeria. But one factor that took the sting out of the RUF that was overlooked, was the mistaken belief that they could assist Charles Taylor in taking or shifting the conflict to neighbouring Guinea, which proved quite disastrous to the RUF. Their positions were pounded by Guineans with heavy artillery and many of them perished including some of their top commanders. Indeed, this weakened the RUF as a force to be reckoned with.

Before entering the political arena, Ahmed Tejan Kabbah worked in the United Nations. Perhaps his being an international Civil Servant was seen as a means to attract international donors to help rebuild the country and its economy. This may be responsible for his resounding victory in the 2002 Presidential and General elections. However, Sierra Leoneans had withstood a destructive civil war and were resolute in not supporting a tyrannical rebel government, which enhanced their standing with the donor community. In this regard during President Kabbah's second term, an abundance of aid flowed into the country through a sub-set of donors. The International Monetary Fund (IMF) supported Sierra Leone through its Emergency Post-Conflict Facility and the Poverty Reduction Growth Facilities. The World Bank also supported the government's recovery efforts through a series of Economic Rehabilitation and Recovery Grants and Credits (ERRGs), and the Reform and Growth Credits (GRGCs). The African Development Bank came in with its Economic Rehabilitation and Recovery Loans and the Economic Governance Reform Programme. The European Union (EU) gave their support through Poverty Reduction Budget Support. Arab Funding Agencies including the Islamic Development Bank (IDB), the Arab Bank for Economic Development in Africa (BADEA), OPEC and Kuwait Funds, also gave their support through loans and grants. Bi-lateral donors also supported the government's economic recovery programmes, the United States of America, Japan, China, Germany, Ireland, Nigeria etc.

A major achievement under the SLPP regime was that Sierra Leone reached the Decision Point Under the enhanced HIPC Initiative in March 2002 which resulted in the country benefitting from Interim Debt Relief which was used to augment budgetary allocations to key poverty reducing activities. Then in 2006, Sierra Leone reached the Completion Point under the HIPC Initiative and thereby benefitted for full debt relief. This substantially reduced the country's external debt.[184]

What the late President Kabbah will not be remembered for was that yes, during his second term of office, a host of donors came to aid the Sierra Leone in its recovery process, but the infrastructure was still in tatters and he was not able to garner support for development. The capital city of Freetown, after eleven years (11) years of SLPP rule was kept in darkness. After the war, internally displaced persons (IDPs) were given wet and dry rations and transport to their hometowns but alas because of the lack and paucity of amenities in the rural areas and villages they never stayed but returned to Freetown and other urban centres. Many of them could not cope as they were ill-equipped for city life so they swelled the ranks of the unemployed and although schools and health centres were rebuilt and rehabilitated in the rural areas, most of the school going children no longer resided in the rural areas. Consequently, the classrooms in the rural areas were empty while those in the urban centres were over-crowded, even with the double-shift system that was introduced after the war. This overcrowding in the cities brought with it lawlessness and indiscipline, and so many years after the war, we are still grappling with it. The authorities seem powerless to act and sometimes they used these things to carry out unholy activities against perceived opposition. Also, not surprisingly, the spate of

---

[184] Sierra Leone's Economic Record 1961 – 2010. EPRU. Ministry of Finance and Economic Development

armed robbery increased; the police usually complained of lacking the logistics to deal with it. More or less, these were the prevailing conditions when the APC led by Ernest Bai Koroma took over the reins of government in 2007.

Chapter Fourteen

CHANGING TIMES / OLD WAYS

The 17th of September, 2007, ushered in a new era in the political history of Sierra Leone with the swearing in of the new President, Ernest Bai Koroma, at State House. Or was it a return to old ways, considering the fact that the country had previously experienced almost a generation of misrule under the APC government of Siaka Stevens and Joseph Saidu Momoh? Ernest Bai Koroma worked at the State's National Insurance Company (NIC); later on, at the Reliance Insurance Trust Corporation (RITCORP), where he became Managing Director, before branching into politics. According to a Reuters interview, it came as no surprise when he averred that he would run the country "like a business concern", with a focus on agriculture and tourism rather than mining. He stated also in that interview that he was averse to corruption, a claim that resonated well with Sierra Leoneans. In another interview, with the BBC, he even emphasised that there would be no sacred cows. However, when the President made the statement about running Sierra Leone like a business concern, what he did not say, who would reap the dividends, the politicians and those within the corridors of power as is usually the case in Africa, or the people, the general electorate who gave him the mandate to govern.

Unlike previous Presidents, Ernest Bai Koroma took his time to announce his cabinet. While some saw this as a good omen, others saw it as party wrangling with strong supporters, especially financially jostling for positions in the cabinet. Notwithstanding, between the 7th and 15th October, he announced his cabinet of twenty (20) ministers, ultimately rising to forty-four (44) by the time he was done with his selections. For a small country, that was anything but bloated, job for the boys as usual? Without doubt he was popular with the people and endeared himself to the electorate when he made himself visible, very visible during the cleaning day exercise. He also visited victims when there was a disaster, very much unlike his predecessor, Ahmed Tejan Kabbah who stayed in his ivory tower.

Indeed, in keeping his word on the fight against corruption, one of his first acts was to strengthen the Anti-Corruption Commission (ACC). Previously the Commission did not have prosecutorial powers, all their cases had to be sent to the Law Officers Department for prosecution, this was a very slow process as so many intended cases were not brought before the courts. Under President Koroma, all that changed. The ACC could prosecute their own cases, therefore it had to be staffed with professionals. Lawyers were then appointed to head the ACC.

Among his pronouncements, he promised to tackle the mismanagement of the country's resources, that his government would increase the per capita gross domestic product, reduce poverty and create employment. This was nothing new but political speak, others before him made similar promises, but Sierra Leone is still languishing at the foot of the development table. For the icing on the cake he promised to light up the capital Freetown, within his first one hundred days in office, but also provide electricity to the urban areas and other parts of the country.

To ensure a smooth transition from the old to the new, President Koroma did not instruct the immediate hand over of the reins of government to the new team. The old cabinet ministers were allowed to stay in office to ensure a smooth and proper handing over of power to the new team of cabinet ministers. In the meanwhile, the President established a transitional committee to review the activities, policies etc. of the erstwhile administration, an exercise which occupied all the parties concerned for some period of time, with the old cabinet ministers still in office. The transitional committee completed its work, published a voluminous report, by which time a smooth changing of the guards was effected. To the chagrin of the public, the transitional report was not placed in the public domain: as far as John Doe was concerned the report was not accessible. What come out of the report to the ears of the public was that a commission of inquiry would be set up to probe the activities of certain MDAs. And indeed, a commission of inquiry was established with a foreign judge, from the Gambia, as chairman, to ensure transparency in its dealings.

This Commission began its proceedings with the Ministry of Education being the first entity (and the last) to appear before it. Again, to the consternation of the general public, proceedings were abandoned in the middle of the sea, with nobody from the general public being the wiser, as to the reason(s) for stopping the probe into the activities of the Ministry of Education. This act of silence did not portend well for the political development of the country, especially given the so-called findings of the Transitional Team. When all that had happened, and given the pronouncements of the President, it was a climb down from his robust stance against corruption. In spite of this initial disappointment, there was still hope it was not going to be business as usual. Why oh why!

Africa with all its renewable and non-renewable resources cannot provide sufficient energy, to run a country and gender development, Sierra Leone not excepted. But for a handful of African countries, electricity generation, and even distribution have proved to be a herculean task, so much so that essential services such as mobile communication are so very expensive just because mobile companies have to generate their own energy. They are not hooked up to the National Grid, even in the cities and urban areas. When the administration of President Koroma took over governance in 2007, Sierra Leone was referred to as the "darkest country" in the world, a nomenclature which was coined since the late 20th century, during the days of President Momoh. President Koroma in his handing-over notes to the current President, in 2018, stated that the country's electricity production was only forty-seven million kilowatt hours, and less than ten percent (10%) of the population had access to electricity. Running his campaign, Ernest Bai Koroma did promise that he would provide electricity not only to the urban areas, but to all parts of Sierra Leone.

The first hurdle was to light the darkest capital and the President did pronounce this would be accomplished by the end of the year, 2007, which was within his first one hundred days in office. He did not meet this timetable. To accomplish this task, the President established a task force under the direction of the Minister of Energy and Power. This task force was comprised of eminent electrical engineers, among others. The chairman was an urban planner, who worked with the Minister in the previous Kabbah's administration; at the time she was the Minister of Lands, Housing and Country Planning.

Ultimately, the contract for the supply of emergency power was awarded to Income Electrix, a Nigerian Firm. Surprisingly, Income Electrix was not among firms recommended by the Technical Committee, to fulfil this contract. Against the advice of the Technical Committee, the Chairman included Income Electrix in the evaluation report. According to the Final Report of the Working Group, Income Electrix Limited presented a proposal that had favourable financial implications for the government. Two reputable members of the working group (the Electrical Engineers), protested strongly against the action of the Chairman, however this was to no effect. There was also much public unease when the whooping cost of thirty-two

267

million United States Dollars ($32.0 million) to provide emergency power to the Western Area, reached the public domain.[185]

Stepping into the fray the Anti-Corruption recommended the termination of the contract but was silent on the actions of the Minister even though the Minister together with the Chairman of the Presidential Task Force was found to have been grossly negligent in the award of the contract. The question on the lips of many Sierra Leoneans, was why did not the ACC indict the Minister at the time because under the previous Anti-Corruption Act, 2002, which was in force when the contract was awarded, wilfully failing to comply with laws and procedures and guidelines relating to procurement etc, was not considered an offence.[186] As to be expected, this did not go down well with the public, especially in the light of the President's zero tolerance of corruption. As a test case, many considered this a failure on the part of the President to fight corruption.

The President did act, not by sacking the energy minister, but by transferring her to another Ministry, the Ministry of Fisheries and Marine Resources. Again, allegations of misdemeanours came up against her. This time round, the Anti-Corruption Act of 2008 had been strengthened, and she had to face the music. Although opinion was divided, she was charged, prosecuted and found guilty. She was fined a hefty sum of one hundred and fifty million Leones (Le150.00 million). She was also ordered by the judge to pay back to the consolidated fund, the three hundred million Leones (Le300.00 million) that she misappropriated. She appealed against the conviction, an appeal which she won, as the conviction was overturned. Lo and behold, the court ordered that the fines imposed be refunded, but not the amount misappropriated as there was no clarity on ownership of this three hundred million Leones, whether it was public or private

---

[185] Reference, Anti-Corruption Report on Income Electrix Contract. – Family lines in a Flawed and Costly Contract.

[186] The Follies of Addressing Corruption in the Court of Public Opinion. Centre for Accountability and Rule of Law (CARL)

funds. Corruption is a human flaw, peculiar not only to the African Countries, but the world over. The difference? In Africa, while corruption is seemingly gratified or accepted as the norm, in the Western democracies, if found out the culprit will pay the price, sometimes a price greater than the crime committed. Definitely this puts a break on the level of corruption in these countries, and once found out and brought to book, seldom would that individual receive public trust or be entrusted with a position of trust. Unfortunately, many African democracies are not there yet.

When the former Minister of Energy and Power was found wanting, in spite of public outcry, she was not sacked, but transferred to the Ministry of Fisheries and Marine Resources. Again, when found wanted in the Ministry of Fisheries and Marine Resources, she continued to be recycled in the system, as she was pitch forked into an ambassadorial position, as the Sierra Leone's High Commissioner to the Federal Republic of Nigeria. Also, there was the case of Allie Sesay, then the Commissioner-General of the National Revenue Authority (NRA). As the Commissioner-General, it was alleged that he misappropriated resources donated by the then Department for International Development (DFID), for the construction of sub regional offices. The ACC filed a case against him, but in the strange ways of the law in Sierra Leone, he was found not guilty. There was public outcry, and different schools of thought in clarifying the decision, nonetheless, he was not pushed but vacated his job for another appointment at the ECOWAS. Unfortunately, he was also found deficient there and was removed from the position he was holding.

In some other cases, some Ministers in breach of procurement rules were removed from their positions. A case in point was the Minister of Health, Tejan Koroma. The minister was indicted for reportedly mishandling a government medical supply contract, and was charged by the ACC. Also sacked was the then Minister of State in the Vice President's Office, Balogun Koroma, for unethical behaviour in the award of timber contracts. Many believed he was made to carry the buck for a crime he was not guilty of. Lending credence to this belief, he was later on appointed a cabinet minister for Transport and Civil Aviation. At this early stage of the President's reign, the general thinking was the President was not serious about tackling corruption. During his inaugural speech in 2007, President Koroma emphasised that sustained economic growth cannot be attained without positive attitude and behaviour of the population towards the consolidation of its human and natural resources, Therefore, it was no surprise when the President in his wisdom established the Attitudinal and Behavioural Change (ABC) Secretariat within the Ministry of Information and Communication. Generally, the ABC Secretariat was charged with taking the lead in influencing and cultivating positive attitudes and behaviour in the heart and mindset of every Sierra Leonean. At the time of its establishment, there were some who questioned its relevance, while there were those who were clamouring for its establishment; this, especially on the basis of the indiscipline, lawlessness and violence that were eating into the fabric of the country's youthful population.

So many years after this landmark speech together with the actualisation of President's ideas on attitudes and behaviours, indiscipline, lawlessness, violence and corruption, have not gone away: these attitudes and behaviours may have worsened. As the saying goes, you cannot give an old dog a new name; in public offices, in schools, in the universities, in communities even in the state security apparati, there are aspects of bad attitude and behaviour. One does not earn fame, plaudit or such like by hard work and merit, but by connection or graft. This is the society we are now living in. Integrity? What is integrity? It is gone out of the window. In the schools, pupils disrespect their teachers and how can't they? Sometimes one cannot distinguish between the teacher and the pupil. Besides, the parents do not gender hard work and studiousness, but harbour the belief that they can bribe the teachers and even lecturers to give their children a pass. Also, lecturers are preying on female students for sex, while spying in examination halls is now commonplace. Invigilators even assist students to cheat. The story goes on and on, not limited to educational facilities, health facilities are no different. Where medication is provided, and government has enacted policies that certain strata are exempt from fees the health officials are flouting these regulations and demanding fees. Why are they doing this? They would retort, because of poor conditions of service. One thing that can be said, self-esteem is a rare commodity in our society. Attitudinal and behavioural change, how laughable! Imagine the capital city had been dark for decades. After the hosting of the OAU (now AU) meeting in 1981, the city started experiencing power outages, and load shedding was introduced but in an orderly manner. Bu the time the Presidency changed hands it had deteriorated into disorderly load shedding. In the meanwhile, work was going on in the construction of the Bumbuna Hydro- Electric Dam. Then the war came, though the construction site was protected by a mercenary outfit, the firm's works yard where their equipment and machinery were kept, was vandalised by the rebels, and work on the dam had to be suspended.

Now then, when President Koroma assumed office, he promised to remove the stigma of Freetown being the "darkest city" on earth. After some teething problems, indeed, Bumbuna was completed, and the lights were switched on. Lo and behold, did that bring joy to all Sierra Leoneans, or to be more precise to all Freetonians? Unfortunately, no! Incredibly, there was a group of people who debunked the idea that indeed, Bumbuna had come on stream. Even when a brave or foolish thief was "fried" on attempting to steal the aluminium cables attached to the pylons, they remained in doubt. Question, did the source of the energy matter and should it have been a topical debate? Should not the effort of the President be acclaimed for bringing electricity to the capital. No wonder the President was clamouring for attitudinal and behavioural change.

Indeed in 2009, the Bumbuna hydro-electric plant started generating electricity to the Western Area, an achievement in itself but it should be pointed out the Koroma government, for one reason or another, but more likely political did not adhere strictly to the contract with the African Development Bank and the World Bank, two main backers. The Banks stipulated that the National Power Authority as it was called then, should be headed by an engineer, and also that the government should open a maintenance fund into which the African Development Bank would contribute one Million United States Dollars (US$1.0 Million). The Koroma government sidelined these clauses and blatantly appointed a general manager who was not an engineer but who claimed that he was managing such energy authority in the United Stated of America. And as to be expected, this individual was so full of himself because he supposedly had political clout. Unfortunately, instead of concentrating on doing his job, however poorly, because he was untrained, he concentrated for the most part on propaganda, especially in projecting himself, in the meanwhile Bumbuna was not being run properly. The National Power Authority was inefficient, and a loss-making concern. Many communities in the Western Area continued in darkness for weeks and months on end. In all of this, the General Manager continued to make noises about his proficiency. That's all he was good at, making noise.

Again, the Banks advised that the firm that constructed the facility, that is the Italian Firm Salini, should not be contracted to manage the plant, government should look for another reputable firm for its management. This advice was also disregarded. Strangely, sometimes, one is left wondering as to the ownership of the Bumbuna hydro-electric facility, whether it was the government and the people of Sierra Leone, or the Italian firm that owned the facility: one usually hears that the government was buying electricity from EGTC, the generating side of the energy sector, or the usual that the government is owing X amount of Leones to the EGTC. Question, where is the destination of this payment?

Recognising the parlous state of health delivery to vulnerable population the government came up with a good policy of free health care to pregnant women, lactating mothers and children under five years of age. Arguably, indeed, this was a good policy, if only it had succeeded. In the first place, the minimum standard of care was not being delivered. Disgracefully, scandals hit the news in 2011 involving the disappearance of UNICEF-Procured drugs and in 2013 the ACC indicted twenty-nine of the country's top health officials, for alleged embezzlement of over one million United States Dollars (US$1.0 Million) of vaccine funds. This high jacking of state drugs apportioned and procured for the most vulnerable population was commonplace and sometimes these drugs found their way into private pharmacies which were mushrooming all over the place. While on this one cannot but mention the volume of fake drugs sold by hawkers in the streets without any pharmaceutical background, and clients patronise them, thinking they are cheaper but forgetting that these drugs can be more harmful. So many attempts have been made on crack down, but the phenomenon would not disappear.

To continue where the previous regime left off, when President Koroma assumed the reins of government, during his first term in office, the central core of his government development paradigm was the "Agenda for Change", otherwise known as the PRSP II, the Interim Poverty Reduction Strategy (IPRSP) and the PRSP I, having been completed during the eleven-year governance of the Kabba regime.

Accordingly, the Agenda for Change prescribed that "as a government and in partnership with our people and international friends, we believe that only an economic transformation of the country over the coming years will enable us to address these challenges (of underdevelopment). Broad-based economic growth is the primary route out of poverty. Our current economic growth rate is around 6.5 percent per annum and if we maintain this growth rate, by 2018, Sierra Leone's gross domestic product (GDP) will reach $350 per capita meaning that, the majority of Sierra Leoneans will still live on less than $1 per day".[187] To transform the Sierra Leone economy through the Agenda for Change paradigm, four priority areas were postulated. Providing reliable power supply to the country, through improving the management and regulation of the energy sector, strengthening revenue collection and increasing generation capacity: from a pro-poor perspective, raising quantity and value-added productivity in agriculture and fisheries as majority of Sierra Leoneans are engaged in agriculture and fishing activities: develop national transportation network to enable the movement of goods and people and thereby facilitate increased investment and economic activity. Improving road, river and air transport will be a priority for the next few years; lastly, ensure sustainable human development through the provision of improved social services. Effective delivery of basic social services is essential for ensuring economic growth and poverty reduction.[188] The Agenda for Change was based on the principles of good governance, macroeconomic stability, financial and private sector development, and managing natural resources.[189]

During Koroma's first term as President there occurred events that were favourable and not so favourable to the successful implementation of the government's Agenda for Change. In 2008, there was a global financial crisis sparked on by toxic investment in the developed economies which resulted in the collapse of some very reputable institutions, such as some investment banks in Western economies. Yes, the crisis was global but fortunately, it did not impact adversely on the economies such as Sierra Leone directly. The impact was more or less felt due to the fact that the economy of Sierra Leone was and it is still donor driven. One of the adverse effects on donor economies was the limitation imposed on their financial resources, thereby curtailing their ability to invest in loans and / or grants in

---

[187]   The Republic of Sierra Leone. An Agenda for Change. Second Poverty Reduction Strategy (PRSP II), 2008 - 2012

[188]   Ibid

[189]   Policy. Deepening Democracy through Access to Information

developing economies. Thus Sierra Leone was spared the disastrous outcome that the collapse of the financial markets had on the more developed economies.

On the plus side, in 2009, the government of Sierra Leone together with a company by the name of African Minerals, announced the discovery of ten billion (10.0 billion) tons of iron ore deposits in the Tonkolili District of Sierra Leone. It was heralded as the largest deposits in the African Continent and the fourth largest in the world. According to the announcement, gold and nickel were part of the deposits. According to the plans of the African Minerals, the company would invest an estimated twenty-five billion dollars (US$25.0 billion) on a project that would involve the construction of a road, rail, port and power supply through hydro-electricity.

Sierra Leone has always depended on its mineral wealth since diamonds and iron ore were discovered in the 1930s. Unfortunately, because of bad governance, selfishness and greed of our political leaders, the country did not benefit much, no, not the John Doe. With this massive find in iron ore, would things be different? Indeed, before the Ebola outbreak in 2014, Sierra Leone was touted as one of the faster growing economies in the world, postulating a growth rate of over twenty percent (20%) per annum. In reality, did this translate into reducing poverty levels in the country? The answer is a resounding no. In spite f this phenomenal growth rate, it has been very difficult to see how it had trickled down to better the standard of living of the ordinary Sierra Leonean. Of course, Sierra Leoneans will not benefit from the country's wealth because the natural resources are contracted by successive governments to foreigners or foreign firms for exploitation, giving these firms tax holidays and what not. At the end of the day, they are supposed to pay tax, royalties and surface rent. It was not usual for these mining companies to claim that they were making losses so how could the government tax a company that was unprofitable. Interestingly they continue their operations for years without breaking even, yet it never occurred to the public officials that a loss-making enterprise was not sustainable. But only in Sierra Leone. It did not even occur to the government that our mineral wealth are assets and not to be treated as commodities only. As assets, it could be valued, and shares taken out by our governments for the people of Sierra Leone. A recent case in hand: The late President Mugufuli of Tanzania put a stop to this exploitation of Tanzania's resources by foreigners. He bargained for shares in the mining companies for the people of Tanzania, and even took a British Company to court and won. The net result, the revenue accrued was incomparable to the pittance that those companies were paying as taxes. He then utilised the proceeds wisely to develop not only the infrastructure of Tanzania, but even some of the social amenities. He accomplished all of this within five years. We in Sierra Leone have been struggling with our mineral wealth for decades and still waiting to see the impact on the country's development.

Indeed, President Koroma was popular with the people, a trait he had in common with the late President Siaka Stevens. Nevertheless, his government was not as repressive as that of Siaka Stevens. There were human rights violations and lapses, but nothing to be compared with Siaka Stevens era. To the author's knowledge he did not stifle the opposition Sierra Leone People's Party as they exercised their right to demonstrate freely.

Coming up to the end of President Koroma's first term in office in 2012, workers of the African Minerals staged a protest in the Bumbuna mines over low wages and unfair treatment meted out to them by their employers. The police acted unprofessionally, not for the first time really, and their highhandedness led to the death of one person and the wounding of several others. In those days Civil Society was very vocal and they trumpeted the cause of the down-trodden, but then nothing came out of this, the government remained passive over the protest, interpretation? They sided with the big guns; he who pays the piper calls the tune, yet our government make a lot of noise about how these foreign companies were creating jobs for

Sierra Leoneans. What employment when there is no value chain addition on the minerals exported. Even the earth is exported with the ores. The rest is left to our imagination.

It should be accepted that at independence in 1961, the infrastructure of Sierra Leone was in a poor condition, not that it deteriorated because of lack of maintenance, but that during the colonial period, the British had no inclination whatsoever to develop the country's infrastructure. They perceived their stay as being temporary, and only to extract what raw materials they could from the country's wealth of resources. Unfortunately, after independence, successive governments failed to improve the country's infrastructure to desirable standards. In fact, whatever infrastructure the British left behind was allowed to deteriorate further, to such a state, that in the long run, infrastructural development and maintenance became quite a challenge to the government. This deterioration applies not only to the few paved roads that existed then, but even to public buildings, and other infrastructure. It was disgraceful and it still is to see the deplorable state of the original Fourah Bay College, at Cline Town, the institution that contributed to Sierra Leone being called the "Athens of West Africa". Let us take another important landmark, the 'Bunce Island' where during the slave trade period slaves were kept before being transported too far and beyond. That important landmark was allowed to degenerate, giving the impression that our governments do not pay much attention to history and historical landmarks. All over Africa from the west to the east coast, their governments have maintained these slave castles in pristine condition; for example in Ghana and the Gambia on the west coast, to Zanzibar on the east coast.

The President Ernest Bai Koroma and his government did promise to improve the infrastructure of the country. The government did set about this task by tackling the deplorable road infrastructure in the capital, Freetown. The first on the block was the Wilkinson Road, a very important road linking the Congo Cross and Lumley. Since colonial times this road had been a two-lane road, that carried a huge volume of traffic. Usually in the morning hours when people were travelling to work the traffic used to be grid locked, especially travelling from the west to the east. In the evenings after working hours, it was also, usually grid locked travelling from east to west, people returning home from work. The government engaged a Chinese engineering firm to reconstruct this road making it into a dual carriage way of four lanes; and indeed, this facilitated the movement of vehicles tremendously, cutting travelling time on this road by less than half. Other important roads in the capital were upgraded similarly: the Spur Road, linking Wilberforce to Lumley and beyond; the Jomo Kenyatta and Kingharman Roads, were upgraded to four lanes. A piece of engineering marvel was the Hill Cut Road, a winding road with steep gradients was upgraded to a four-lane road, the beauty of it was that it was constructed by a local contractor working with local (Sierra Leone) labour force! The government also attempted to pave the main roads in all provincial capitals.

A very important road linking two Eastern Districts that had been a thorn to travellers, the Kenema – Kailahun highway, that was in a disreputable condition was taken on board by the government and the reconstruction or rebuilding of this very important road was done by the government. Before the reconstruction of this road, travelling to Kailahun was very hazardous. Especially during the wet season, it was almost impassable; even driving a four-wheel vehicle was a challenge. It was not an uncommon sight in those days to see vehicles virtually trapped in the mud. And unfortunately, if one of this long trucks got stuck on the road, it could take days sometimes before it was removed. Then, travelling to Kailahun was not child's play, and usually was fraught with tension for the simple reason that the traveller was ignorant of the road conditions.

Other road projects embarked upon and are still under construction were the Peninsular Road and the Hillside By-Pass Road, very important arterial roads. The Peninsular Road as the name implies, runs around the Freetown Peninsular and is an important artery, carrying tourist to the pristine beaches and rolling hills of the Western area. The Hillside-By-Pass-road links the Western and the Eastern parts of the capital which would greatly reduce travelling time to and fro. Both roads are designed as four lancs. Imagine the costs of these roads and what lasting benefits the country would have gained, if these projects were implemented by local civil engineers? It might be argued that most of the financing for those projects was from donor assistance, but some of the costs were from the domestic budget. As expected, this placed some strain on the domestic budget which was reflected on fiscal balances. However, the concern here is that although some local labour was employed the bulk of the wage bill accrued to foreign workers. Let us take the firm constructing the Peninsular and Hillside roads; the contract was awarded to the French firm CSE. If only Sierra Leone had its own engineering road construction firm and they had won that contract, imagine the direct and indirect benefits the country would have gained. Similarly other important road construction projects were implemented by the Chinese. In both cases, local labour was employed, but that was at the un-skilled level, and even at that level, foreign workers were imported, especially under the CSE construction projects.

Two other grand infrastructure projects that the government came up with: the Lungi Bridge and a new international airport at Mamamah, a town about thirty-eight miles to the North-East of the capital. The proposed Lungi bridge would cut down travelling time from the international airport to the capital tremendously while at the same time open-up Lungi for business. Indeed, after being in the air for over six hours, let's say coming from Europe, a passenger arriving in Lungi usually would have to endure another wait of anything upwards of three hours before arriving at his hotel or his/her home in Freetown. For a country on the look-out for foreign direct investment, this was not a promising omen. Upon undertaking feasibility studies and holding meetings, this project which was costed at around six hundred million United States Dollars (US$600 million) was shelved because, it did not prove attractive to investors. As a matter of fact, the World Bank was of the opinion the Lungi bridge project was not economically viable.

Accordingly, the Koroma government pressed ahead with the Mamamah airport project, again an initiative that would reduce travelling time to Freetown facilitate travelling to other parts of the country. Another aspect of the Mamamah airport project was to establish an industrial / business orb as a means of decongesting the capital. This project was estimated to cost about three-hundred million United States Dollars (US$300 million). Again, this project was shut down by the World Bank. Nevertheless, the government decided to proceed with its implementation. For the airport to achieve its desired outcome, the road from the capital to Mamamah, had to be upgraded. So the government came up with the grand plan, "to construct a toll-road from the city to the airport. For them it meant upgrading the existing road to carry four-lane traffic and erect toll gates of which there were three on a road length of about forty miles. One of the interesting aspects of this contract was that after the Chinese engineering firm had constructed nine (9.0) Kilometres of this road they started collecting toll, not for the nine-kilometres of the road, but for the entire road of over 50 Kilometres as three toll-gates were erected at intervals and road users started paying toll fees for the greater stretch of road that was not yet upgraded. As to be expected, there were lots of complaints and discussions about this, but nobody listened. It was also strange that a contract such as this one went before Parliament and was given the green light to proceed. It buggers the imagination!

For the airport project, feasibility studies were conducted, and scientific observations of weather patterns were mapped out. Suddenly Mamamah's importance loomed large in the eyes of Sierra Leoneans, some of whom began claiming title of portions of land in the area that the new airport was sited, looking for pecuniary compensations from the government. Implementation of this project was overtaken by circumstance. The APC government that initiated it was removed from power before full implementation commenced. And in their campaign, the opposition SLPP then, averred to terminate the toll road contract with the Chinese as they deemed it unethical and unfair for their citizens to be paying toll for a road that was not yet completed; this of course by implication could be interpreted that they were not overly keen on constructing a new airport and decongesting Freetown. In fact, rumour had it that the site which the Koroma government had delineated for the Mamamah airport had been sold to some foreigners by the present SLPP government. If this is true, logically, the question will be asked, how legitimate was the transaction; were proper procedures followed?

Taken as a whole, no matter how poorly the Koroma government performed because the opposition SLPP then and people generally raised questions on governance, it could be maintained that as far as developing the country's infrastructure, the bar had been raised and it was the expectations of Sierra Leoneans that successive governments would continue to raise the bar higher.

By the end of his first five-year, one would conclude that the President and his APC government were still popular. While in the 2007 Presidential elections, there was no clear winner in the first round, calling for a second round which Ernest Bai Koroma won, in the 2012 Presidential elections, the incumbent won by a landslide in the first round, trouncing the SLPP flag bearer, Julius Maada Bio by over fifty-eight percent to Bio's just over thirty seven percent. Similarly in the Parliamentary and local council elections, the APC were the victors, wining all the seats in the western area and the Northern Province, and making in-roads into the South and East. Although the APC victory might be attributed to the use of considerable incumbent patronage resources, it may not be far from the truth to point out that it was also due to their performance: improved roads and electricity supply particularly in the capital, and in other areas of the country[190].

During Koroma's second term Sierra Leone was touted as one of the fastest growing economies in the world, postulating a rate of growth of over twenty percent (20%) per annum. Then the Ebola struck in 2014, from Guinea and spreading to Liberia. These were the three worst affected countries in the sub-region. By the time it was contained in 2016, the economy was in free fall, contracting from a high of 20,8% before the Ebola crisis to a low of minus 21.5% by 2015. The reason attributed to this unprecedented contraction was the tumbling of the World's market price of Iron ore leading to the un-profitableness of continuing with the mining of iron ore. As such during this period the mines were not in operation and iron ore exports were nil. According to World Bank estimates, the total impact of the Ebola crisis on Guinea, Sierra Leone and Liberia was the loss of 2.8 billion United States Dollars with Sierra Leone losing the most almost two billion United States Dollars.[191]

Submitting an alternative view, the author is of the opinion that from time immemorial, Sierra Leone had not only been over-dependent on its minerals, but no processing of value-addition has been taking place and it is still not happening. The country exports only its raw materials. If the economy had been diversified, various external shocks would have been cushioned. But no! Successive governments make pronouncements on economic diversification from the days of Siaka Stevens, but alas, the country is still operating on the system of a "single basket economy", and exporting unprocessed raw materials.

The impact of the Ebola outbreak could have been minimised if the powers that be had not placed the health of the economy above the

---

[190] Reference, President Koroma's handing over notes for a detailed description of infrastructure work undertaken and completed. 2018

[191] Handing over Notes of Former President Dr. Ernest Bai Koroma to President Dr. Julius Maada Bio. 2018

health of the people. There was a lot of official denial of the outbreak for the reason of not upsetting the status quo that might drive foreign investment away. Although people were dying, they tried to keep it a secret. Also, there was community denial and given the nature of the culture of the people, there were those who attributed the Ebola Virus Disease to witchcraft. There was also a disconnect between the governors and the governed. The populace no longer trusted the government as they were perceived as not giving out the correct information. The government was slow to react and take preventive measures all in the nature of politics. So many wrong turnings were taken during the crisis; should the authorities have put the proper measures in place when the EVD struck, the country would not have lost so many souls and the economic impact would have been minimised also.

For a start, square pegs were placed in round holes; an example was the then Minister of Health, who many felt was not up to the task. Even on advice, decisions that should have been taken to minimise the impact were ignored. Although the said Minister was replaced later on, the damage had already been done. When the Ebola Virus Disease was eradicated finally from the sub-region, in Guinea, Sierra Leone and Liberia, the total number of cases (suspected, probable, confirmed) was 28,616; the number of people who died was 11,310[192]. In Sierra Leone alone, the total number of cases (suspected, probable, confirmed) was 14,124, and the number of people who succumbed to the Ebola Virus Disease was 3,956.[193] Many front-line workers including doctors and nurses perished in their quest to save the lives of others, not because of carelessness or negligence, but primarily because of the poor quality of the equipment they were using, and the inadequacy of the existing facilities. At the start of the outbreak the was only one treatment centre in Kenema, in the Eastern region;

---

[192] Ebola Virus Disease. 2014 – 2016. Ebola Outbreak in West Africa. Centre for Disease Control (CDC) and Prevention.

[193] Ibid

later on a centre was constructed with assistance from the British in Kerry Town, located on the Freetown Peninsular. The country's health system was overwhelmed, but with overseas assistance, all over both in personnel and equipment, the outbreak was brought under control and finally Sierra Leone was declared Ebola virus free in March 2016.

Other countries in the West African sub-region took prompt measures to stem the spread of the Ebola Virus Disease. In Nigeria there were only 20 cases and 8 deaths; in Mali there were 8 cases and 6 deaths; in Senegal there was only one case, nobody died. This outbreak spread as far as the United Kingdom, the United States, Spain and Italy, but the incidence of cases and deaths was quite low: one case and zero death in the United Kingdom, four cases and one death in the United States; one case and zero death in Spain, and one case and zero death in Italy.[194]

In relative terms, President Koroma's first five-year term passed off more easily than his second five-year term. The external shock of the financial crash in 2008/2009 did not impact adversely, on the economy, as the Ebola crisis did. The financial crisis of 2008/2009 affected the big investment banks and the financial market of the developed economies more than the developing countries that were scarcely involved in the bond markets. On the other hand, the Ebola crisis was regional, involving the three West African countries of Guinea, Sierra Leone and Liberia. Interestingly another country hit by the Ebola Virus Disease, Guinea also a large producer of iron ore, did not cease its mining operations, but Sierra Leone experienced a cessation of iron ore mining operations. This should be a pointer towards, the type of foreign investment that the country attracts and also the kind of contractual agreement entered into with these foreign firms.

---

[194]   Ibid

In August 2017, there occurred a catastrophic mudslide on Mount Sugar Loaf, a mountain overlooking the capital Freetown. The mudslide swept away buildings and killed over one thousand people. There has been much debate about the cause of this mudslide. While some ascribed it to the heavy rains that occurred on that fateful night, many believed it was caused by a more deliberate human activity. Sugar Loaf, which is still covered at the top by lush green vegetation, forms part of supposedly protected areas, officially termed the Western Area Forest Reserve. After the civil way which saw the devastation of most of the countryside, there was massive migration of people into the capital Freetown and its environs. Because of bad politics and bad governance, even though this was supposed to be a Forest Reserve, the lush vegetation was denuded to be replaced by massive structures on the slopes and on the foot of the mountain. Concomitantly, communities sprang up along the foot of the mountains. Thus, this once exclusive area now became home to the rich and poor alike; a mesh of shacks occupied by the poor, alongside fabulous mansions and unfinished brick houses. The majority of these mansions were owned by politicians and people connected to the corridors of power, otherwise those structures would not have been constructed because there were laws that prohibit land use of these areas. This was one of the sites described as fragile, among other areas, in the Western Area. As usual, the law was enacted not to be respected, but to be flouted especially by those who thought they were untouchable because of political connections.

The government's response to this catastrophe brought into stack focus its unpreparedness to deal with these kinds of catastrophes. In countries where their governments are prepared, some lives are saved usually after the occurrence of the disaster. Unfortunately, not in Sierra Leone. The capacity does not exist, neither in the form of trained manpower, nor in the form of the necessary tools and equipment to undertake rescue work. The government had to enlist the assistance of construction companies that possessed heavy earth-moving equipment for the clearing job, and this could not be a rescue job. The sad part of the exercise, when the survivors were being processed for humanitarian assistance, suddenly people who were not even living around the vicinity of Mount Sugar Loaf, presented themselves as victims. Of course, this caused some confusion in the registration process, so some methods of verification had to be devised to get proper victims registered. In the spirit of the true Sierra Leonean, not only were landslide victims expected to be relocated, but they were also looking to the government to build homes for them.

There were scandals during the second term of President Koroma's tenure in office, but this is not a peculiar occurrence. Scandals happen everywhere, in other African countries, also in the developed economies. The peculiarity in Africa, Sierra Leone not excepted is the fact that in developed economies, public officials found wanting would pay the price for their misdemeanours. Only in Sierra Leone, the popular term in the local parlance to describe the outcome of such cases, is "nar buff case", meaning nothing will come out of it. And there were a few of these unpalatable and distasteful incidents that did not augur well for the victims and the wider populace. In 2017, Muslims wanting to participate in the Haj Pilgrimage complained that they were duped, over-charged and misled by the Haj committee. Some of them went so far as complaining that they paid the stipulated fees for the Haj, but when the final list was released, their names were absent, it was even alleged that Muslims from Gambia had their names included. As it transpired, it was not the Haj Committee members alone who were involved in this scam; it went right up into the corridors of the ruling APC hierarchy, a former vice president and some ministers were mentioned as being complicit in the whole affair. One of the accused alleged that his boss, also implicated removed forty-five million Leones and eighty thousand US Dollars, which he would give to this former vice president. But he alleged that he was not present if and when this transection took place. Many questions come to mind but let's leave them to our imagination.

All the time the APC government was in power, it remained a "buff case". It was only when the new SLPP assumed the reins of government, that the Anti-Corruption Commission mounted up the prosecution of these alleged culprits. Did anything result from this initiative, and was restitution to the aggrieved victims made? Nobody knows. Although this former vice president was in the ruling APC government, he had very strong links with the ruling SLPP, as he is a south easterner. Not surprisingly, when the verdict was handed down by the courts, this former vice president was found not guilty. By then, he had switched allegiance to his natural roots, the SLPP.

The bumpy road continued, when the then vice-president was removed from office, using a clause in the constitution that says holders of such positions must belong to a political party. All the party authorities did was to summon a NAC meeting and excommunicated the vice president from the party. As to the reason for this decision, there were many conspiracy theories, from not seeing eye to eye with the President to engaging in un-party activities. Whatever the case may be, there was a lot of fallout from this action which the APC came to rue later on. The SLPP who was then in opposition, made a lot of noise, but there was also a public hue and cry about this action which engaged legal and un-legal minds alike. An action was brought against the APC in the local courts which the aggrieved party lost. This again, raised some eyebrows in the society with labels of a corrupt judiciary, playing the tune of the government. The case was also taken to the ECOWAS Court but for whatever reason, the Attorney-General decided not to contest the action and the decision of the court found for the plaintiff. He was not reappointed however, but the court instructed the government should pay damages to the aggrieved individual; to date, the decision of the ECOWAS court has not been heeded. When government changed in 2018, even the SLPP, who were so vociferous during this action refused to accede to the decision of the ECOWAS Court. Presently the aggrieved party, the former vice president, has petitioned the ECOWAS court to place some sanctions on the sitting SLPP-led government.

The conundrum was the clause in the 1991 Constitution that the APC used to remove the Vice President from office. Since the drafting of that Constitution there had been so many constitutional reviews from the days of Peter Tucker. All of these reviews remained on the shelf gathering dust. The government of President Koroma, in their wisdom set up a Constitutional Review Committee, headed by a former Chief Justice and speaker of the House of Parliament. The Committee went about their task in a consultative and participatory manner, engaging civil society groups, professional bodies and even the general public. In due time, they completed their task and submitted their recommendations to the government. A task considered generally to be well done. For whatever reason, the government sat on it but then they came out with a white paper, the usual practice, that scarcely reflected the recommendations of the Constitutional Review Committee. The public did not take kindly to this, and it made its position known. Outcome? After spending so much on the exercise, both in time and money, the recommendations were not implemented. And even though the erstwhile APC government came under a lot of flak from the then SLPP opposition, to date, over three years of their ascent to the seat of power, their pre-occupation has been the "New Direction" which may not include constitutional review. Lately they came up with a so-called white paper which has also not done justice to the recommendations of the Constitutional Review Committee. The general public is also uncomfortable with the clauses included in this white paper.

As if that was not enough, another scandal hit the beleaguered APC government. This time involving a very senior member in the APC hierarchy, a one-time cabinet minister, who at the time was a senior adviser to the government, who had been removed from his ministerial position because of some misdemeanour. The general public came to know about this when a letter on an official government letter head began circulating on social media about a contract between the government of Lebanon and the government of Sierra Leone to import Lebanese waste, sewage into Sierra Leone.

Demeaningly, Lebanon did not explore the possibility of exporting their sewage to neighbouring Middle East countries as that would have been anathema, but only to far away Sierra Leone whose leaders are susceptible to bribery, even at the expense of the nation's health, but also to a country that they had been exploiting and are still exploiting. The government was quiet even disclaiming the letter, but this did not quiet public opinion. Finally, the President came out with a strongly-worded statement that investigations would be undertaken and whomsoever was found wanting would be severely dealt with. Whether this investigation was carried out or not, it finally transpired that the entrepreneur to this deal was this former minister and a senior party member of the APC. In any other country but Sierra Leone, the parties to this deal would have been charged for criminal activities against the state that put the health of the nation at risk. Fancy Sierra Leone could not deal with its own waste effectively and efficiently, but these people because of greed did not hesitate to enter into such a deal. How could they stoop so low? Well as per the usual, the case was a buff case. The principal to that deal is now a member of Parliament, only in Sierra Leone!

Because our politicians from time immemorial have been paying lip service to economic diversification, when the Ebola Virus Disease struck, our economy degenerated into a situation where, the government had to introduce a series of austerity measures, to stabilise the then current (dire economic) situation. These measures included: -

- Thirty percent reduction in recurrent expenditure across the board;
- Suspension of all domestic finance capital projects and suppliers' contracts (until further notice);
- No new procurement of government vehicles (until further notice);
- Fifty percent cut in fuel allocations to all MDAs;
- Fifty percent cut of monthly imprest;

- Seventy percent of all payments to suppliers/contractors with foreign component to be paid in Leones;
- Fifty percent cut in DSA for local travels;
- Elimination of overtime payments;
- Restrictions on overseas travels and rationalisation of delegation sizes;
- No top-up allowance for sponsored international travels
- Fifty percent cut across the board in vehicle maintenance;
- All seminars, retreats and workshops should be held in office facilities;
- Eliminate double payments of pensions and salaries across board.

Did these measures succeed in stabilizing the economy? To a large extent they did not, most likely because they were the wrong policy prescriptions. For instance, the Leone continued to depreciate, with attendant increase in domestic prices. Also, a school of thought blamed the country's economic woes on a bloated public service, following the establishment of many commissions and agencies, involving the recruitment of additional staff in Ministries and new staff to man these commissions. Also, the IMF thought that government subsidisation policies were responsible partly for the economic downturn, creating an artificial pricing system that did not allow market forces to determine price.

In a seminal article, a private legal practitioner (now the ACC boss), Francis Ben Kaifala wrote: "Looming Bankruptcy of Sierra Leone: Perspective of a Doomsayer" that in a panic mode, the government has introduced subtle austerity measures (a good move if applied properly), like the unilateral cut on workers benefits to their disadvantage (a clearly illegal move, considering that there was no legal basis for it), increased taxes on income (as high as thirty-five percent (35%), and various other planned actions to salvage the embarrassing state of the economy." He added, "it confirms the belief that those we have elected to look after our affairs are not as in charge of doing so as we would expect them to be, or perhaps they do not fully understand what it would take to save the economy. His solution, "We need to export more to other countries as we import goods from them so as to reverse the trade deficit that is weakening our currency".[195] He offered alternatives like import substitution.

For the All People's Congress government and the people of Sierra Leone, there was one more surprise to come. During the campaign for the 2012 Presidential and Parliamentary elections, the incumbent President Ernest Bai Koroma was described as the World's best by his supporters. Apparently, he took this World best along with him so that some months before the 2017 Presidential and Parliamentary election, rumour started making the rounds that President Koroma should run for a third term; this went against the constitution that clearly states that no president should run for more than two consecutive terms, by which clause President Koroma, no matter how well he had performed was ineligible for another term. This went beyond rumour when some supporters went on the airwaves to defend his standing for a third term. Of course, there was an opposing school of thought, and this became a topical debate between rivals. Also, there was a third school of followers, those who were propagating that President Koroma had never intimated that he wanted to run for a third term, thereby violating the constitution. This debate raged on without any let up. This time though, the principal himself was around, and he could have put an end to this debate, by simply making his intentions known publicly. But that was not forth coming, and the debate continued. The long and short of it was public opinion was resolutely against a third term and this finally put a stop to both the rumours and the intention or un-intention.

One would not be right to view the second term of President Koroma's reign as a failure, but there were many challenges than he encountered during his first term. By the second term, the honeymoon was over.

---

[195]   President Koroma Sanctions Austerity Measures. Concord Times Newspaper' article. October 4, 2016

The government's expectations at the start of their term in office were not realised. The blame? They cast blame on the Ebola crisis and the depressed iron ore international prices, never on the mismanagement of the economy.

Never mind how good an intention they had, with an outcome contrary to their expectations, they could always blame the un-realisation of such plans on external shocks, in this case, the Ebola Virus Disease outbreak in 2014. Indeed, in its Agenda for prosperity, the government was seeking to attain middle income status by 2035 but the country still carried it post-conflict attributes of high youth unemployment, corruption and weak governance, the country continued to face the daunting challenge of enhancing transparency in managing its natural resources and creating the fiscal space for development. Although the government delivered in some areas of infrastructure development, yet much still remained to be done. Also, widespread urban and rural impoverishment persists, despite some remarkable strides and reforms.[196]

Under President Koroma's tenure of office, especially after the disastrous hit of the Ebola Virus Disease, the impact on the population was cushioned by the maintenance of a subsidy regime that was not favoured by our donor partners, especially the International Monetary Fund and the World Bank. Subsidies were maintained on rice, fuel, electricity. Although schools were suspended during the crisis period, the government continued with the payment of teachers' salaries. When the schools reopened, the government subsidized school fees so as to cushion the burden of poverty on parents. At the time, according to President Koroma, Sierra Leone was the only country in West Africa paying seventy (70%) percent of university tuition fees for all students, and also provided full tuition coverage (100%) for

---

[196]   World Bank Report

various other categories of students eg. Female (girl child) accepted to read science, students from very poor families.[197]

It did not stop there, that is the upside of his tenure of office. The late President Ahmed Tejan Kabbah contributed a lot into bringing peace into war-torn Sierra Leone. That is an undisputable fact. However, his successor, President Ernest Bai Koroma also contributed a lot into maintaining this peace, so much so that by the time he left office, Sierra Leone was billed as one of the most peaceful countries in Africa, quite an achievement. Apart from maintaining the peace, notwithstanding the Public Order Act which was still in force, civil liberties and democratic freedoms, were rarely infringed upon; of course, there were times the public felt the government curtailed on these liberties, especially when the government refused the right to protest. Throughout the tenure of Ernest Bai Koroma, there were no political prisoners, even though the death penalty was still in force, no prisoner was executed. Perhaps one could proffer that Ernest Bai Koroma, as an individual is a peaceful person. A case in point, during the campaign period for the 2012 Presidential and Parliamentary elections, President Koroma's convoy was obstructed deliberately by the Sierra Leone People's Party flag-bearer. Rather than having the obstructionist arrested or having an altercation, the President used his common sense to diffuse what could have been an ugly situation. He reasoned with his own security not to use force to clear the obstruction. Still on the campaign trail, in another instance, during a public debate on television a highly placed SLPP member stated that they were prepared to go to war, if the elections were overly delayed. He was neither detained nor harassed; today this individual holds a deputy ministerial position in the current Bio-led government.

Other gains Included making the auditor-general's report accessible to the public at large. Before his time Parliament had the first call on the auditor-general's report, and that was the end of the story. Fancy,

---

[197] Handing Over Notes of Former President Dr. Ernest Bai Koroma to President Dr. Julius Maada Bio

before this time, the auditor-general's report was not to be given to the President until after it had been laid before Parliament, and remained a secret document, not disseminated to the public. President Koroma's government changed all that. Under his dispensation, the legal steps were taken so that as soon as the auditor-general's report was laid before Parliament, it was made available to the public; this was the upside. The downside, almost all MDAs were found wanting primarily on procurement matters, recommendations were made, but these recommendations were seldom implemented. Subsequent reports have followed the same pattern.

All the world knows about the indiscipline and lawlessness in Sierra Leone, a feature that has been with us for a long time but became more pronounced after the war. It is not a question of not fearing the law, but one of not respecting the law, as the law enforcement agencies themselves are found wanting, often pandering to the government in office, and to those of seemingly high standing in the society, usually those with so-called connections. Notwithstanding, Sierra Leone society became almost anarchic after the war, with seemingly powerless law enforcement agencies. Cultism emerged among the youth, and sometimes altercations between various cultish groups resulted in death. Sporting activities had to be banned as rival gangs (of school going kids) would vandalise properties of homeowners, shopkeepers, vehicles etc. after these activities. On the roads, keke riders, okada riders (motor bikes, three-wheeled vehicles), even taxi drivers were a law unto themselves, often disregarding the instructions of the traffic police and traffic wardens, because they themselves are not disciplined and straightforward. Oftentimes, these drivers complain of police harassment and the taking of bribes even when they had not committed any traffic offence. This was the situation that prevailed after the war, or manifested after the war years, and was never addressed by the government of (now late) President Ahmed Tejan Kabba.

During the final term of President Koroma, in his valedictory speech to Parliament, he emphasised the curbing of the indiscipline and lawlessness that was destroying the fabric of the society. Many level-headed Sierra Leoneans breathed a sigh of relief that alas, this cankerworm was going to be eradicated from our society. To the disappointment of Sicrra Leoneans this pronouncement by President Koroma, was never implemented. When he left office, the character of the society had not changed: if anything it had gotten worse.

It could be said that Ernest Bai Koroma was one of the most popular leaders Sierra Leone has had, as popular as the late President Siaka Stevens, if not more. In that vein, given the resources the country is blessed with, notwithstanding the Ebola crisis, his government could have done much more for the nation. Like his predecessors, he failed to deliver the basic needs of the people. His statement on the crackdown on corruption was very strong on taking office when he was interviewed by a BBC journalist on the Focus of Africa Programme, about no sacred cows etc. Unfortunately, his actions were not matched by his statements. Let's take a case in point. Early on in President Koroma's first term an incident involving his Minister of Transport and Civil Aviation occurred at the Freetown International Airport (Lungi), which became known as the "cocaine burst". What was on the lips of many a Sierra Leonean, was it a burst, mistiming or the hand of providence?

Sometime in July 2008, an Antonov plane landed at Lungi Airport with 700 kilograms of cocaine, coming from a country in South America, and Sierra Leone was to be used as the orb for distribution to Europe. It was alleged that the landing was approved by the Minister, an allegation he denied, and according to him in a later statement, his guilt was not proven after investigations were concluded. Nineteen people including foreigners from South America were arrested and charged, A principal individual who was allegedly involved, a cousin to the Minister of Transport and Aviation escaped and he has never been found. Perhaps, considering his connections to the ruling APC government, there was an unwillingness to look for him. It was alleged that this individual contributed to financing the APC. He was supposed to have been rewarded for his financial backing of the 2007 elections, as manager of the national football team. The point to be made here, when the Sierra Leone Police requested the arrest of the Minister, the President did not grant them that request. He was interrogated, and released later on, the President relieved him of his Ministerial duties. However, the President's stance on the arrest of the Transport and Aviation minister contradicted previously reported information that the President intended to see any guilty party brought to justice, regardless of their personal or professional connections. This was an unwelcome development that did not augur well for the President's integrity.[198]

The party die herds would exalt the achievements of the ten years of the APC governance, just as some of these die herds are still extolling APC's reign under Siaka Stevens. Unfortunately, with all these exultations, Sierra Leone remains undeveloped, given the resources she is blessed with. Upon all these achievements, the country is still largely import-dependent, and donor driven. Our leaders still go cap in hand lobbying and begging for funds from the international donor community. Even our staple food, which is rice, the government spends over two hundred million dollars on rice importation and yet continues to boast of our agricultural potential in vast arable land etc. etc. Instead of subsidising foreign farmers, that money could have been spent on developing the food crop sector, beginning with production right up to food processing. But no successive governments came up with dubious agricultural schemes that look brilliant on paper but proved massive failures on implementation, all because of corrupt practices by public officials. Sierra Leone has the resources to become a middle-income country but unfortunately lacks the leaders with the vision to achieve such

---

[198] United States Embassy Cables: Sierra Leone Minister Sacked after Cocaine burst, as reported by the Guardian Newspaper. August 6, 2008

heights, they usually put politics above economics, and regional and tribe above the national good. Not from Sir Milton Margai to Ernest Bai Koroma has Sierra Leone been blessed with a leader in the mould of Kagami of Rwanda, or the late Magufuli of Tanzania. What a travesty?

Chapter Fifteen

BATON CHANGE

During the penultimate year of President Koroma's term of office, certain preparations / changes were made for the 2017 general elections. Parliament increased the number of parliamentary constituencies from 112 to 137. The National Electoral Commission's (NEC's) initial boundary declaration exercise was widely seen as transparent, participatory and professional. However further down the line in 2017, Parliament decided to increase the number of districts from 14, to 16 Districts, by de-amalgamating some chiefdoms. This action resulted in the resuscitation of Karene and Falaba. Of course, a section of the electorate saw this as a political ploy by the ruling party to increase their seats in Parliament. In 2017, the first ever nationwide civil registration was compiled from which the NEC extracted a voter register of three million one hundred and seventy-eight thousand citizens.[199]

President Ernest Bai Koroma's second term in office ended in 2017 and Parliament was prorogued in December 2017, but elections were not held until March, 2018. However, once Parliament was dissolved there was plenty of time for campaigning once NEC declared the date for the political campaign to begin, and indeed campaigning by

---

[199] Presidential and Parliamentary Elections in Sierra Leone. March 2018. Final Report, The Carter Centre.

the various parties, especially the APC and the SLPP, was a sight to behold. It was no longer about ideologies or intentions, but a show of numerical strength. In Sierra Leone, there is a popular slogan that in democracy "nar numbers" (show of party- political strength). The political landscape, this time round appeared to have changed even if slightly. There were the usual smaller fringe parties, and it seemed a credible third force had emerged in the nature of a new party, formed and led by former SLPP member, who as a matter of fact held a ministerial position in the former Kabbah-led SLPP government. Dr. Kandeh Yumkella, worked for the United Nations and on leaving the U. N., returned home to form a new party, the National Grand Coalition (NGC) that many Sierra Leoneans thought would be a third force and perhaps would inject a great shock into a system that had been dominated by the APC and SLPP.

In the meanwhile, the unsavoury action that the APC and President took to remove the vice president Sam Sumana, an APC stalwart from office resulted in his quitting the APC to form his own party, the Coalition for Change (C4C). Another disgruntled former APC potential aspirant Kamaraimba Mansaray, a young man also expressed his dissatisfaction with the APC hierarchy by breaking away to form the Alliance Democratic Party (ADP).

Was the political landscape becoming more interesting, or more complicated? Added to that mix, while all the parties had settled on their presidential aspirant, the APC was still grappling with selecting their flagbearer. Imagine twenty-seven party stalwarts were aspiring to lead the APC to the election! That was indeed a contest, and a mirror image of what was happening on the national or wider arena. Instead of coming out with tangible reasons why they should be considered as leadership material, they were out parading on the streets, usually obstructing pedestrian, and vehicular traffic, to demonstrate their popularity, by show of numerical strength.

While candidates were being readied for the forthcoming elections, someone opened Pandora's Box and out popped, a clause in the 1991 constitution that stated that Sierra Leoneans holding dual citizenship should not become members of Parliament. One school of thought believed that this issue was brought up by the APC to discredit and disqualify the leader of the Nation Grand Coalition who they saw as a "thorn in their flesh", he would make a worthy opposition whatever the case, Kandeh Yumkella had renounced his American citizenship, so he was not caught in the trap, but others were. If one believed on poetic justice, a few of the prospective APC candidates had dual citizenship, that resulted in their disqualification from contesting the elections; many of them were aggrieved and disgruntled. Add to this mix the choice out of twenty-seven (27) aspirants for the APC flagbearer. The mantle fell on the outgoing Foreign Minister, who was the Minister of Finance during the days of the NPRC. This choice left twenty-six disgruntled candidates, and this was the prevailing scenario as the country headed to the 2018 Presidential and Parliamentary elections.

During campaigning a televised programme, assembled all the potential presidential candidates together, to get them elaborate on their plans to take over the reins of government. At the end of the discussions, the clear winner was the leader of the National Grand Coalition. The APC and SLPP aspirants trailed behind him. It must be stated that for eloquence, none of the other candidates came close, he was very articulate, something that cannot be said of the APC and SLPP candidates. Unfortunately, eloquence and clear policies were not enough to win elections in Sierra Leone.

General elections were held on the 7th March 2018, to elect the President, Members of Parliament, and local councils. In the first round of voting, none of the presidential candidates received fifty-five percent of the votes required to win outright, so a second round was conducted on the 31st March. In the first round, the two main candidates were separated by less than fifteen thousand (15,000) votes. During the second round, the SLPP candidate, Julius Maada Bio won by a slim margin taking 51.8% of the total valid votes cast. During campaigning for the second round, the People's Movement for Democratic Change, a break away party from the SLPP, declared for the SLPP. The APC tried to woo the leader of the Coalition for Change the ousted vice president of the APC to declare for them, but their attempt failed.

For the Parliamentary elections, there were seven hundred and ninety-five (795) candidates vying for one hundred and thirty-two (132) seats, out of these seven hundred and ninety-five, one hundred were women. The results were quite intriguing, considering the unsophisticated behaviour of the Sierra Leone electorate. The All Peoples Congress Party polled 989,431 votes, giving them sixty nine (69) seats in Parliament. The Sierra Leone Peoples Party that won the Presidential election polled 964,659 votes, giving them forty-nine (49) seats. This phenomenon was very difficult to explain, although the head of the Institute of Governance Reform Secretarial (IGR), in an interview proffered an explanation attributing this pattern of results to the de-amalgamation of some districts. This might not have been the case.

After the elections there were many conspiracy theories doing the rounds, especially the SLPP winning the Presidential and losing the Parliamentary, from there being a schism in the APC camp because of the manner in which the presidential candidate was selected, to some presidential hopefuls being so very much aggrieved, that they threw in the towel and did not campaign for the party, a possible reason worth considering, in the dynamics of the political landscape in the country. Without argument the SLPP is a South-East based party, and the South-east block is to a very large extent, homogeneous. On the other hand, that cannot be said of the APC. On cannot gainsay the fact that it is northern-based. But again, the North is not as homogeneous as the South-East, dominated by the Temnes, but there are other smaller tribes like the Limbas, the Lokos etc. Add to this mix the fact that many of the smaller parties are northern-based, or breakaway factions of the APC. The only party formed out of the SLPP was the PMDC. But then by 2018 its influence had waned; in the 2018 elections it did not win a single seat. Also, the leader of the NGC who broke away from the SLPP hails from the North, and he managed to win four (4) seats in the Kambia District which is in the North. One also should not discount the Sam Sumana factor. The former vice president broke away from the APC to form his own C4C party and won eight seats in the Kono District in the East, where he hails from. In the South East Julius Maada Bio polled 887,384 votes, while Samura Kamara polled, 132,982 votes, representing 87% and 13% respectively. In the North, Samura Kamara polled 646,992 votes, while Julius Maada Bio polled 141,806 votes, representing 82.0% and 18.0% respectively.

Again, it would be apt to state, Sierra Leone had done it again, changing government through the ballot box, one of the foundation stones of democratic process. After ten years in the opposition, the Sierra Leone People's Party, now forming the new government would have the opportunity to implement these "good things" in their thinking, that the former regime of the All People's Congress failed to do to improve the welfare of the people.

Chapter Sixteen

THE NEW DIRECTION

During the campaign, or even before the campaign, Bio and his cohorts christened themselves, "PAOPA". PAOPA in the local parlance means by will or woe, one does what one wants to do and damn the consequences. For them, the end in their own thinking justifies the means. The PAOPA came up with the catch phrase, "the New Direction Government", so since the SLPP assumed the reins of power in March 2018, Sierra Leone has been under a new direction, a deviation from the traditional or orthodox?

Quoting from the Sierra Leone Telegraph, of 22nd July 2018, in his forward to the Sierra Leone People's Party Manifesto 2018, Julius Maada Bio their presidential candidate stated that "Our New Direction therefore offers the people of Sierra Leone a stark choice between the current 'business as usual status quo of the APC that had converted Sierra Leone into a land of poverty, rampant corruption, gross indiscipline and underdevelopment, and the SLPP's New Direction's promise of efficient and effective management of the State that will make Sierra Leone a significantly better country through inclusive politics, inclusive economic growth, inclusive development, and inclusive governance."

He went on to expound on the economic burden inherited from the APC regime: "external debt amounting to US$1.6 billion, domestic debt amounting to Le4.99 trillion, an exploded payroll of Le 2.0 trillion, Government arrears to local contractors and vendors amounting to US$ 1.4 billion (Le10.7 trillion), the suspension of the Extended Credit Facility by the IMF, the suspension of the operations of Shandong Steel a major exporter of iron ore." A Herculean task indeed, to restore the country to an even economic keel. Indeed, did the New Direction envisage this task as impossible, to the point of prompting the Minister of Finance, before he was shifted upstairs to proclaim that even with three successive presidents, the economy of Sierra Leone would never be stable? Admitting failure before even attempting to put things right? Reminiscent of the days of former President Momoh, broadcasting over the airwaves that he had failed the nation!

Indeed, the New Direction came with a bang, and perhaps a departure from the way and manner things were done, giving Sierra Leoneans a breath of fresh air and hope or a feeling of despair and despondency?

Historically and traditionally, the elected head of state was sworn in at State House, or the State Lodge. Yes, the Constitution of 1991 stipulates that the President should be sworn in on the same day the results were declared. In the case of the New Direction Head of State the swearing-in ceremony was held at a hotel, the Mammy Yoko Radisson Bleu Hotel, and not the State House or the State Lodge. Unconventional it was. Did staging the ceremony in a hotel not owned by the government impact on the budget? These were early days. The inauguration of the President at the National Stadium was a family affair that was organised by President Bio's wife, or should we say the First Lady? A rather unusual arrangement: this was a state and not a family affair.

According to the election results, the opposition APC held the largest number of parliamentary seats. If the status quo had remained the

SLPP would have been a minority government. Realising the difficult position, the executive will be in, in a minority government, the first test of the new regime presented itself for the election of the speaker. The election of the speaker raised serious constitutional interpretation which largely exposed the executive arm of the government influencing the judiciary by slamming an unconstitutional interim injunction on 10 APC elected members of parliament. If the results were allowed to stand, this would spell disaster for the governing SLPP. If the 68 APC Members of Parliament were allowed to participate in the election of the Speaker, any candidate nominated by the APC would win by virtue of their majority. If that was allowed, taken to the extreme, it meant that should any calamity befall the Executive, the APC was in line to have the Presidency, coupled with their Parliamentary majority, they would become the ruling party. The outcome of all of this was that the judiciary ruled in favour of the SLPP, and 10 APC members of Parliament were removed and 10 SLPP members, not elected by the people nor representing their constituencies, took these seats according to the misinterpreting of the electoral law that states, there should be a by-election. When confronted the SLPP response was that they were only following the precedent, set by the previous APC regime. New Direction, really!

Of course, the APC did not succumb without a fight. They objected vehemently to this injustice and executive manipulation. After a lot of commotion in the Well of Parliament, the security forces were called in by the Clerk of Parliament to evict those APC Members of Parliament, forcefully. Definitely new direction!

Now, let us focus our attention on the reality of governance. Indeed, the President wasted no time in getting on with the job through a series of Executive Orders. Among his campaign pledges, were the fight against corruption and providing free quality education. In keeping with his campaign promises, led by his Chief Minister, the administration compiled an investigative report, accusing the former president, Ernest Bai Koroma and his government of widespread financial malpractices. These allegations included stealing millions of dollars from government revenue, selling of state properties, selling significant amount of state mining company, stealing funds meant for the country's Ebola victims and the mudslide victims; and stealing funds meant to help some poor members to go on the Haj to Mecca. As a matter of fact, the Chief Minister in one of his televised interviews called Koroma and his Ministers "ayampees", in the local parlance. The nearest English translation would be "Alibaba and his forty thieves". The Attorney General's office set up commissions of Inquiry (COI), to probe into the financial conduct of the Koroma government's tenure in office.

This of course was not without controversy. The APC and their supporters cried foul and considered this move a political witch hunt, considering they singled out individuals instead of probing institutions. They also advocated for the establishment of rules of evidence by the Attorney-General's office which they never got; it was never produced. As such, they refused to attend the inquiries, but instead sent their legal representatives; the defendants were referred to as Persons of Interest (POI).

Three Commissions of Inquiry were established, two under the direction of foreign justices from the sub-region, and one a Sierra Leonean justice, domiciled in the United States of America. The Commission of Inquiry No.1 was headed by Justice Sir Beobele Georgewill of Nigeria. The terms of reference was to investigate widespread allegations of corruption against the immediate past government from November 2007 to April 2018. The Commission was charged with undertaking thorough, independent, fair and impartial investigations into the allegations of corruption and abuse of public office, and submit its findings and appropriate recommendations to the government.[200] The Commission of Inquiry No. 2 was headed by Justice Bankole Thompson with the terms of reference, to investigate

---

[200] Government of Sierra Leone - Commission of Inquiry (COI) No 64

the assets and other related matters in respect of all Persons who were Presidents, Vice Presidents, Ministers, Ministers of State, Deputy Ministers, Heads and Chairmen of Boards of Parastatals, Departments and Agencies, from November 2007 to April 2018.[201] The third Commission of Inquiry was chaired by a Ghanaian Justice, charged to examine the assets and other related matters in respect of persons who were Presidents, Vice Presidents, Ministers, Ministers of State, Deputy Ministers, Heads and Chairmen of Boards of Parastatals, Departments and Agencies, from November 2007 to April 2018.[202]

The Commissions of Inquiry went on for some time as to be expected, but it finally ended during the second year of the New Direction Government of President Bio, when the three Commissioners submitted their reports, as already referenced. The proceedings were quite interesting as the various misdemeanours of the past government were revealed to the public, sometimes these proceeding bordered on the hilarious. This was what transpired in the Justice Bankole Thompson's Commission of Inquiry when the government's valuation officer was being cross-examined on his valuation of the former president Koroma's property in Makeni. It came out that he did not even know the property, neither internally or externally, but mounted a sub-urban utility vehicle (SUV) that was parked by the roadside and based his valuations which ran into millions of US dollars, from what he beheld at that vantage point! Who would take such a valuation seriously?

In any case, just as the setting up of these Commissions of Inquiry was controversial, so also were the findings and recommendations, although provisions were made for the Persons of Interest to seek redress from the High Court if they felt aggrieved at the

[201]   Government of Sierra Leone - Commission of Inquiry (COI) No 65

[202]   Government of Sierra Leone - Commission of Inquiry (COI) No 67.
        Reference detailed Terms of Reference, Findings and Recommendations

recommendations, within a specific time period. In their zeal to tackle this cancer of corruption that had invaded the fabric of our society, the Anti-Corruption Commission went after some of these Persons of Interest without giving them the time to seek redress as specified in the various Commissions of Inquiry Reports.

Well, the New Direction came with a bang, it was like an avalanche, sweeping everything along its path. It was no secret that punctuality and absenteeism were not virtues imbibed by Public Servants. To rid the Service of this cankerworm the President Julius Maada Bio took upon himself to visit unannounced government offices, very early in the morning, by the opening of business. Indeed, many senior public officials were found wanting and strongly admonished to desist from such unproductive behaviour. Was this procedure by the President sustainable? It is doubtful. In actual fact, rather than this knee jerk solution, all the President should have done was to see that an effective electronic 'clocking system' was established in all public offices, to be monitored by the Human Resource Department. This is a more effective and sustainable system.

Continuing on its way, the avalanche under the New Direction Government swept away personnel in the Public Service. Through an Executive Order, President Bio sacked almost if not all the top personnel in the Public Service, all executive Boards of Parastatals were dissolved and ambassadors recalled from their posts, obviously to be replaced. It was even rumoured that some minor, lower cadre staff like drivers were even sacked. Was this action as a result of their incompetence or negligence? Indeed, as is usually maintained, the president has the right to hire and fire, and even if this authority comes from the Constitution, there are procedures to be followed, which were not followed in this mass sacking of public servants. In fact, the excuse given by the President when asked was that he wanted staff that were loyal, competence and experience were not part of the equation. The institutional capacity that had been established over time was suddenly wiped out overnight, why, because of the apparent disloyalty of the existing staff. This was pay-back time for party supporters and almost all of them, pitch-forked into these positions turned out to be square pegs in round holes. If that was not enough, the Human Resource Department was instructed that all promotions in the Public Service must go through State House. This was a first in the country's history.

Looking at President Bio's first one-hundred days in office, depending on what side of the fence one was standing, one would paint a rosy picture of his tenure in office. According to State House tremendous progress was made in resuscitating a bankrupt economy bequeathed by the former APC-led government.[203] The Bio-led government's achievements in its first 100 days can be seen in four key policy areas: transforming the economy; human development; improving governance and improving infrastructure.[204] Through a series of Executive Orders, certain policy and operational measures were effected which yielded an increase in domestic revenue collection between April and June 2018, of Le1.07 trillion, an average of Le356.7 billion per month, exceeding by far the monthly average of the Le271 billion collected for the same period in 2017 (under the APC-led government). Indeed, the former APC government started the process of the Single Treasury Account, but it was never implemented. Part of the so-called increase in revenue collection might be because all revenues collected now were paid into one basket.

According to the State House Report, this revenue mobilisation drive resulted in the creation of fiscal space, for the government to be able to pay salaries of Civil Servants and staff of sub-vented agencies without resorting to domestic bank borrowing, a claim made against the past government. Also, the government instituted a cleaning of payroll policy that was expected to yield a savings of

---

[203] Reference: Office of the Press Secretary. Report on President Bio's First 100 days in Office

[204] Ibid

Le5.0 billion monthly. In terms of human casualty, 2,118 employees lost their jobs. Was this politically motivated? Further, restricting the overseas travelling of MDAs, the government was able to make savings of Le11.0 billion, with Le760 million on foreign travel alone. Much progress was made on several fronts, the implementation of the Single Treasury Account, the setting up of a committee to examine duty waivers, taking a decision that government contracts would from henceforth be paid in local currency, and many others.[205] These policy decisions resonated well with Sierra Leoneans, and presented the hope that at long last, here was a leader to take the country forward.

It would be an act of remission, not to mention the President's flagship programme, the 'Free Quality Education' that most likely won him victory over the APC-led government. During the launching of this programme, the President averred that the government was ready to cover the expenses of tuition fees for students, providing textbooks, exercise books, pens and pencils, sports equipment, rehabilitation of schools, provision of furniture, and the commencement of school feeding programmes in government and government assisted schools. Indeed, policy wise, this was a good initiative, assuming that the government had the resources to undertake such a programme, proper implementation is paramount to its success.

Before the launching of the free quality education programme, education in Sierra Leone was a challenge. The number of classrooms was inadequate, resulting in almost all schools being run on two-shifts, the morning shift, and the afternoon shift. Subsequently, length of time students spent in the classroom was and is severely constrained. Even the running of dual shifts did not solve the problem as classes were inordinately large, with as many as a hundred children or more in a class. Add to this the fact that the IMF had imposed a curb on the employment of new teachers. Imagine the effect this

---

[205]   Ibid

has had on the education system resulting in accentuating the poor teacher/pupil ratio. Not planning for the proper implementation of this programme would not alleviate the parlous state of the education system is in. Nevertheless, the concept is a good one and hopefully will benefit the nation in the long run.

A sensible and listening government would try to take stock of the pitfalls of the initial implementation and make proper use of the lessons learnt and try to improve the programme. Complaints have been made by parents, the school authorities, and the public at large. This should not be seen by the SLPP-led government as the opposition impeding the development of the nation, but the opportunity to do a proper review and make the necessary improvements for the programme to achieve its desired outcome, more importantly, the quality aspect.

Another platform that the SLPP campaigned on for the 2018 elections was tackling corruption that had eaten into the very core of the Sierra Leone society. Hence the transitional report that called former actors in the APC-led government, 'ayampees' (barefaced and shameless thieves) the report itself, based its findings on subsequent reports of the Auditor-General's office since the APC assumed power. Since their coming into governance, the Bio-led government has never stopped proclaiming to the nation how they met a broken-down economy, failing to realise that if it had been otherwise, the SLPP would not have succeeded in toppling the APC. For over two years, this was the mantra of the SLPP government, "we met a broken economy", prompting one to think they themselves did not have the capacity or the ability to fix it, hence the excuse! What really the new direction government should have done was to proclaim that they would fix the broken economy, instead of lamenting all the time how broken the economy was.

So when the ACC Commissioner took up the fight against corruption, he had the approval of the electorate especially if it was pursued robustly and impartially. And in those early days in governance, the public was informed that they were after miscreants and had already recovered over Le8.0 billion of stolen resources which they had paid to the government. For his own part, President Bio did state that such recovered resources would be used to develop the health delivery system in the country, which is very fragile to say the least. However, the public was not too comfortable with this strategy, thinking that there should also be some custodial sentence for their misdeeds. Nevertheless, the ACC continued their work on the same modus operandi. Probably, so much the better. Any of the culprits caught in the ACC net, were 'alagbas' (important personalities) of the former APC regime. This prompted people to raise the question, whether the ACC was only interested in pursuing past corrupt officials as if public officials in the current SLPP-led administration were unsullied and of impeccable character.

Not too long after their coming into power, a journalist uncovered a transaction involving the then Chief Minister that he thought bordered on corruption. He discovered that the sum of US$1.5 million was paid into the Chief Minister's account at the Ecobank. All attempts that the journalist made to throw some light on this transaction, in contacting the Chief Minister failed, so the information found its way into some social media platforms and newspapers. Next thing we knew, this journalist was harassed, arrested, mafia style and locked up at the Criminal Investigation Department (CID). After some public hue and cry, the ACC came out with a statement that they were investigating the matter, which in the usual tenor, became a buff case. It was not that they went silent, it was only that they conducted their investigations and the Chief Minister's hands were clean. The ACC never explained to the public the origin, the payer and payee and the destination of this said US$1.5 million. Case closed. The saga did not end there, and it still continues. Not too long after the Chief Minister brouhaha, another ugly incident reared its head, that really taxed the sincerity and credibility of the ACC Commissioner, and perhaps reinforced the thinking that the ACC was only interested in pursuing miscreants of the past government, but not interested in rooting out corruption from the Sierra Leone society.

By way of assisting the government with its school feeding programme, the Chinese government donated 50,000 (fifty thousand) bags of rice to the Bio-led government. Note, not a thousand bags of rice, not five thousand bags, not twenty thousand bags but fifty thousand bags! As it turned out, all but 1,000 (one thousand) bags disappeared into thin air. Again, after a huge public hue and cry, the ACC as usual must investigate, and decided to investigate, in the meanwhile, the Minister of Basic Education, his deputy, the Permanent Secretary and the nutritionist in charge of school feeding were suspended from office: well and good. Investigate they did but came out with a surprising and intriguing report. All the alleged culprits were charged to court, but the court discharged all of them, note not acquitted, so according to the officials they still had a case hanging over their heads. The reason for their discharge as given by the then Attorney-General: the office of the Attorney-General wanted the accused to be tried by judge alone but did not succeed in this, and the trial was done according to the jury system. As a result, the accused were discharged until such time that the trial would be by judge alone. Could you beat that? Is the Sierra Leone public so stupid or is it the other way round, an inane and callous government? Who is fooling who? Not long after the Minister was appointed as Minister of Labour and all the other accused persons were returned to their former positions; how is that for good governance under a "new direction"? More insultingly the ACC has never come up with any information on what happened to the 49,000 (forty-nine thousand) bags of rice. According to the usual rumour mill, most of the rice found its way into the SLPP 'alagbas' (top guns) This again was another 'buff case'.

The New Direction government began work in 2018 and by end of the year, they had already been in office for about nine months. Thus, at the end of the year marching on to the new, many Sierra Leoneans were waiting with bated breath to see whether the New Direction had placed their mouths where the money was; pointing fingers at APC's corruption, the expectation was that they were without blemish, especially as at this time. It was habitual in their propaganda, to trumpet the bare-faced thievery of the APC government. Usually, the Annual Report of the Auditor-General's Office does not lie, and it is a document that speaks to the operations of MDAs. It is not a report that includes the plans of MDAs, but examines the past operations of these MDAs, especially looking at compliance of procedures and processes, to determine whether budgeted and other resources were expended for their specified purpose or utilised otherwise.

Once the report was tabled in Parliament and became accessible to the public at large, one commentator remarked that it was replete with massive evidence of rampant corruption, maladministration, and brazen theft of public funds under the watch of the new government. What became apparent was that the report for 2018 read worse than previous reports,[206] and painted an abysmal picture of the New Direction government's fight against corruption, lending credence to the belief that in reality, its focus was on bringing the APC politicians to book. Interestingly or intriguingly the report discovered that one hundred and forty-one billion Leones went missing, but lo and behold, the supporters of the Bio-led government blamed this loss on the previous Koroma government. Considering President Bio's pronouncements and his Executive Orders to plug the leakages in the system, one would wonder at their effectiveness.

This was just the beginning. After casting blame for the country's ills on the previous government, the new administration under the new direction manifesto now had the opportunity to put Sierra Leone on an even keel, steering the country out of troubled waters. Perhaps realising that they were not doing enough, towards the end of 2019 the President convened a retreat of all his ministers to review what

---

[206] The Auditor-General's Report can be accessed on the website for the details.

was achieved so far. At the end of the retreat, what came out was, they had not delivered, so, the year 2020, was declared to be their year of delivery. Alas, that was not to be. By the beginning of 2020, the global community was beginning to learn about the corona virus disease and by February, the WHO declared COVID-19 to be a global pandemic. By then many countries in the West, suffered untold devastation of lives. Lives were lost, infections spread rapidly, and many health facilities the world over were swamped and unable to cope. At the time research on the strain of Covid-19 was very scanty, so not much was known about it. The entire world was petrified with fear. Indeed, the experience with the Ebola Virus Disease, stood Sierra Leone in good stead to deal with COVID-19. As soon as COVID-19 was declared a global pandemic, President Bio and his government initiated measures, if not to deal with the pandemic, but to minimise its effect on a fragile health system and an unknowledgeable population. There were glitches, complaints and what you will, but the first wave was not as devastating as it was in other countries. A state of health emergency lasting twelve months was declared and ratified by Parliament. Even there, there were complaints as the government failed to design the instruments to be ratified by Parliament for the administration of the health emergency, as was done during the Ebola Virus Disease. Nonetheless, the state of health emergency was implemented. There were lockdowns, there were also curfews. In a fragile and poor society, the lockdowns and curfews had a devastating effect on the ordinary man in the streets who eked out his daily living from hand to mouth. Sometimes they were caught breaking these rules, but the security forces were unsympathetic to their plight and dealt severely with them. There were many complaints about the brutality of the security forces on curfew breakers. A case in point was the collection of water which was inaccessible to many Sierra Leoneans. At night when the standpipes were opened, many rushed out to collect water.

Thankfully, Sierra Leone was not hit as hard as other countries. There was an upside and downside in the effects of the pandemic. There was an economic slowdown globally which affected all countries, there were scarcities which pushed up prices. The hospitality industry was hit very hard, and owners of restaurants, bars and hotels and their workers bore the brunt of it. On the other hand, restricted movement of people, slowing down of industry etc., resulted in a glut in the supply of oil bringing down oil prices. In Sierra Leone the effect of this was very slight and it was only temporary. Just like when the country was hit by the Ebola Virus Disease, the international community gave a lot of assistance, not only in financial terms, but in-kind donations, expert personnel, equipment, supplies etc. Unlike the transparent and accountable manner in which the Ebola funds were administered to the point of carrying out an audit which disclosed so much mismanagement and malpractices, the administrators, spear-headed by the Attorney-General of the Bio-led government, prevented the Auditor-General from auditing the funds, citing that the country was under a state of emergency as the excuse. The Attorney-General perhaps had a short memory – during the Ebola crisis a state of emergency was also declared, not only that, but there was also a letter written to the former president Ernest Bai Koroma by the current president Julius Maada Bio (when SLPP was in opposition) commending the Auditor-General for a work well done and lambasting the former President for their profligacy! On his own patch which is the new direction, transparency and accountability are out of the window. The President is 'lord of all he surveys.'

As far as the Bio-led government was concerned, they extricated themselves from the indictment of the 2018 Audit Report by shifting the blame onto the former APC-led government who left power in March 2018. What they forgot was that this was not a one-off exercise but according to law, the Auditor-General is mandated to undertake this exercise annually. Should they be squeaky clean, of course they had nothing to worry about. On the other hand, if their hands were in the till, no magic wand would remove this from public view.

Indeed, when the 2019 Audit report was released, this time covering the operations and activities of the Bio-led New Direction government, to all intents and purposes, it was the same old story. A leopard cannot change its spots never mind the noises that ACC Commissioner was making about fighting corruption. The infarctions discovered by the 2019 Audit were worse than previous audits!

The 2019 Audit Report indicted the office of the First Lady for receiving and misusing monies from the Consolidated Revenue Fund. The investigative journalist Africanist Press, based in the United States published detailed information of transactions between the Ministry of Finance and the office of the First Lady. The office of the First Lady which does not submit requests for funds under the budget (usually provisions for initiatives or projects in this office are budgeted for under the respective implementing MDAs; no direct allocations are made to this office of the First Lady), received billions of Leones, directly from the Ministry of Finance; for emphasis, these funds were unbudgeted as already explained. What was most disturbing, the allocations made to the Office of the First Lady were more than the amount allocated to some of the MDAs, who had projects to implement. It is doubtful whether the Office of the First Lady has the technical administrative capacity to implement projects.

Believe it or not, it was this very First Lady in one of her video messages on social media, who claimed that she did not receive a cent from the government; she claimed to have money and generated her own resources for her projects. All this noise or propaganda was made before these revelations by the Africanist Press, came to light. Now the powers that be, including the Anti-Corruption Commissioner, instead of refuting the evidence, tried to justify the first Lady's misdemeanours. In a BBC Focus on Africa Programme, during an interview, this First Lady who denied receiving money from the government explained this slip by claiming that her office was under the President's office and unashamedly justified the allocations. To put the icing on the cake, how did the ACC boss respond to all this? Well according to him, this was uncharted waters, so, instead of investigating these claims against the current First Lady, he would have to go back in time and investigate, the previous First Lady Madam Sia Koroma, wife of ex-President Koroma. Note, not all the other previous First Ladies to test his theory only the immediate previous First Lady! How porous can you be? The ACC boss forgot that the previous Audit Reports never indicted the then First lady; also, the Commissions of Inquiry established by the Bio-led government did not find that office wanting. Who is fooling who? After over four years of investigations, the ACC Commissioner had not come up with his findings; the public is left in limbo.

The corruption battle is never ending. The Bio-led government used the audit reports to bring the government of ex-President Koroma to book as evidenced by the Commissions of Inquiry report and findings. When it was the turn of the APC-led government, the Auditor-General performed laudably in detailing the deficiencies of the former government in financial management. Now, the ball game has changed. No longer is the performance of the revered Auditor-General, locally as well as internationally acclaimed. When it became their turn, the Bio-led government and their supporters started vilifying the very same Auditor-General, whom they praised when they were in opposition.

Since President Bio took office in 2018, both audit reports for 2018 and 2019 found corrupt practices in his administration; even State House and the office of the First Lady were not exempted. And for a champion in the fight against corruption this state of affairs cannot be allowed to prevail. As far as Sierra Leoneans were concerned, this was shameful especially when the ACC boss, the leader against this fight came up with all kinds of excuses to vindicate the Bio-led administration. Oh yes, he made a lot of noise about the officials who had been indicted, investigated, found guilty and had paid back the pilfered money. To this day the populace is left wondering who these guilty officials are: their identity is clouded in secrecy. More importantly, as far as the ACC Commissioner was concerned, it was the former APC government that was corrupt, and not the Bio-led government. Conclusion? The ACC was fighting corruption of the past and ignoring present day corrupt practices in the Bio-led government.

Revelations by the Africanist Press about the profligate spending in 2020 by President Bio and his cohorts raised the expectations of the populace for the publication of the 2020 Auditor-General's report. But alas, that was not to be. A few weeks before the release of the 2020 Auditor-General's report, President Bio in his wisdom, decided to suspend indefinitely this revered Auditor-General for professional misconduct, and instituted a tribunal to investigate and make recommendations about her guilt or innocence. As one would expect this sparked a lot of debate, especially the manner in which she was suspended. There are those who maintain, the President has the right to hire and fire. There are those also, who think the President violated the Constitution. According to the provisions of the Constitution, the President should have appointed a tribunal to look into the complaint and acted based on the tribunal's recommendations. In this instance, the President put the cart before the horse.

More worryingly, the President appointed a new Auditor-General, without again following the proper procedure. And abracadabra, within a few weeks of the Auditor-General's appointment, the 2020 Audit report was laid before Parliament. In the meanwhile, the substantive suspended Auditor-General is in limbo. Since her suspension and the appointment of the members of this tribunal, which was some time ago, the tribunal has met a few times only for the sittings to be adjourned because on the government's side, the lawyers were not prepared and also the tribunal was not properly equipped.

Now, the 2020 Audit report is before Parliament, an issue that is taxing the minds of Sierra Leoneans, is the authenticity of the report laid before Parliament. Considering the circumstances leading to its release, many Sierra Leoneans are of the opinion that the tabled report has been compromised by the new Auditor-General; that the original report done by the suspended Auditor-General was altered to not depict a government so noisy about the fight against corruption, in a bad light. The findings of the 2020 report were worse than any previous reports: cash losses were greater, almost all of the MDAs were guilty of corrupt practices, either of the flouting of procurement rules or the profligate spending of public resources. This display of nonchalance prompted the suspended Auditor-General to comment that "very little had been done to ensuring that MDAs act on our audit recommendations. We still continue to observe the same recurring issues."

Subsequent governments, but more especially the current regime, have a wrong perception of audits. In Sierra Leone the Audit Service Sierra Leone is seen by the Bio-led regime as being anti-government, to the extent of holding the view that the Auditor-General has her own agenda. How unfortunate. Audits should aid and improve the governance system. When deficiencies are pointed out with attendant recommendations, should government adhere to these findings, the outcome will benefit the government by improving service delivery and save the country such unnecessary losses. But no, these findings and recommendations are ignored.

Fancy, after all the recommendations made in previous reports, and given the stand that the current regime has taken against corruption, to the chagrin of Sierra Leoneans, the "doctored audit report" revealed that the office of the President was involved in the forgery of hotel receipts, during the President's travels. Unpaid hotels bills by the President, in his travels were also revealed. How disgraceful! And in all of this, during one of his travels, President Bio was asked why he was travelling so much, his response? The government of ex-President Koroma had tarnished the image of the country, so his travels were to redeem the image of Sierra Leone. This was before the release of the Audit report. How hilarious. To restore a country's image is it necessary for a President to spend millions of dollars travelling just for that? What is the economic sense in that especially when there are diplomatic missions in so many countries? Would not these missions have done a better job at a lower cost? Are Sierra Leoncans sure that this is not a form of leakage of the country's resources that President Bio promised he was going to plug during his campaign for the Presidency? Indeed, what a new direction; or is it a mis-direction as is now the common parlance in social media.

True to form, the ACC boss made the usual noises and proclaimed that the ACC would arrest the public officials found wanting, and they would spend Christmas behind bars. According to reports, that was just his usual posturing and propaganda for the consumption of the internal community and the public at large.

Taking all of this into consideration, the SLPP government has failed in the fight against corruption. Their success is based more on propaganda than what is happening on the ground. The government makes a lot of noise on scoring very high on corruption, rated around 70% for the MCC score card, and qualifying the country for the Millennium Corporation Compact (MCC). This score was based on surveys undertaken by Sierra Leoneans. Strangely, the Mo Ibrahim index on corruption scored Sierra Leone a mere forty-three percent, for the same period a variance of almost thirty percent. What the ACC is presenting to the world at large is a façade; behind this façade there is a lot of rottenness.

Let us move on to the second movement of the symphony. The first movement is complete. As a matter of fact, the impression left with the audience by the orchestra, was one of failure. Not that they did not have the instruments, in spite of all the noise that the Bio-led government made about inheriting a broken economy, they had all the proper instruments. What they did not have was the experience, the skill, and more importantly, they refused to learn on the job;

instead of focusing on the job at hand they went after the former APC-led government and their sympathisers on social media. For over two years after taking office, all that the populace heard from the government was that they met a broken economy, as if they were talking to an ignorant people. Of course, the electorate were knowledgeable of the misdeeds of the past government, hence they voted for a change.

As in most democracies, Sierra Leoneans would like to experience and enjoy all the constitutional freedoms, equity and the rule of law. Has this been happening to Sierra Leoneans under this current regime?

Portions of the draconian criminal libel law, enacted under the tenure of Sir Albert Margai in 1965 have been repealed, a plus for Maada Bio and his government. The former APC government promised its repeal, but for the ten years they were in power, it remained a promise. Also, the government has just removed the death penalty from the law books, this after a long and protracted debate. Sierra Leone can now state proudly that it is now among that group of countries that does not put condemned prisoners to death. To give the devil its due, during the ten years of Ernest Bai Koroma's reign, no condemned prisoner was hanged. If one uses these pointers to conclude that Sierra Leone was a country that human rights were respected, that conclusion would be far from the truth, especially during the tenure of the Bio-led government. Yes, this government has repealed the criminal libel law, the death penalty no longer exists in Sierra Leone, but there have been instances of violence against the citizens that portray the un-seriousness of this government in observing the rule of law.

Some high-profile APC stalwarts, the likes of Paulo Conteh, were incarcerated at the Pademba Road Correctional Centre. On the morning of 29th April 2021, Freetown woke up to the sounds of heavy firing at the correctional centre, which brought back memories of the days of junta rule and the civil war. Very early in the morning the Minister of Information went to one of the TV stations to inform the public that there was an attempted prison break out which had been quelled by the military in an operation that resulted in one or two fatalities. Soon after, the social media was flooded with information proffering various theories, primarily homing in on a plan by the ruling government, to use this alleged attempted prisoner break out to pass off the high-profile APC incarcerates. The numbers also given for the death toll was very confusing rising to as many as sixty inmates slaughtered by the authorities. As the day wore on, the real picture started coming to light. By night fall it was the moment for the President to castigate the opposition. Blaming them for the incident and labelling them as terrorists, a very hard term and uncompromising, maintaining that there would be an investigation and that the culprits would face the full force of the law.

The international gateway, the Lungi Airport, is not connected to the national grid, for quite a while its electricity was and still is provided by standby generators. As it happened the generator packed up, and the Bio-led government, strangely either did not have the resources to purchase a set of new generators, or they were unwilling to capacitize the airport. Thus, the decision they took was to remove one of the generators, serving the town of Makeni and replace the defective machine at Lungi with it. The people of Makeni did not take kindly to this, they protested on the streets. This resulted in the unleashing of the might of the security forces on the people. Many innocent people were killed. Why, because they protested against the SLPP government. To this day nobody had been held accountable for those killings, neither the Inspector-General of Police, nor the force commander. Who ordered the security forces to fire live bullets on demonstrators who were unarmed? Similar incidents in Lunsar and Tombo were met with the same responses, innocent and unarmed protesters being mowed down by the security forces. Consider, was it just happenstance that these protesters were mowed down, or was it because all these areas are strongholds of the opposition All People's

Congress? Compare with protests in the South-East, a stronghold of the ruling SLPP. These protesters were given free reign, even when they neither requested nor received Police clearance. There were no police presence and of course no killings. In the Western area several attempts were initiated to protest against the government's intimidation, violence against the people and the incompetence of the government. These attempts were nipped in the bud by the Inspector-General of police by refusing them permission to protest. These would-be protestors were considered a threat to the security of the state.

There were also instances in which this current SLPP government trampled upon the rights and freedom of individuals deemed not to be pro-government. Take the case of a policeman, who was relieved of his duties, and what was his crime? He unwittingly took a photograph with a member of the opposition APC. Another incident happened in Kenema, an SLPP stronghold. An APC supporter made a recording highlighting the development that took place under the former APC government. For that he was charged to court and sentenced for possession of illegal drugs. This very same individual, after serving his sentence and released from jail was harassed by SLPP members who it was alleged tried to murder him; he had to be rescued and removed to a safer location. There was also a case early on, involving the deputy internal affairs minister. That time, a young man was shot near his residence on the allegation that he was going to attack the deputy minister. How he was going to carry out the attack was unclear because he had no weapon. What was worrying then was, the victim who was shot allegedly by the minister's security guards was incarcerated at the Pademba Road Correctional Centre instead of being taken to the hospital for medical treatment.

The new direction, Sierra Leoneans, especially those who think rationally are confused, unlike those with blinkers in their eyes. What has changed? In all expectations, a new direction should be progressive, and liberal, not retrogressive and autocratic. But alas, the new direction has brought a great divide between the South-East and the North-West. There is much talk about inclusiveness and reconciliation, these are not seen on the ground, all this noise is just for propaganda, but are Sierra Leoneans that stupid to not differentiate between an illusion and reality? This is doubtful. More troubling, is the fact that all this is make-believe. No more criticism of the new direction even the Public Broadcaster parrot to the tunes of the new direction, the other radio stations are no better. The fourth estate has gone dumb. Perhaps their perception of the new direction differs from that of the majority of Sierra Leoneans. But what about civil society who were so visible and vociferous during the Koroma regime? It would appear they are now dead, or they are on the point of death. What is happening in and to our society?

Let us take the case of one of our young and prominent opposition politicians, the leader of the Alliance Democratic Party (ADP) who has been languishing in jail for close to two years now for an alleged crime of sexual penetration. The case has been called up on several occasions, but nothing seems to be happening. He was refused bail at first, on what grounds, only the court knew. Finally, a few months ago he was granted bail. Lo and behold, to the consternation of sane thinking Sierra Leoneans, the ADP leader is still languishing in jail on the pretext that his bail conditions have not been met. This assertion has been hotly contested by members of his party. Just imagine all this has been going on, and not a word of condemnation has been heard from civil society. More indignantly, the bar association has been completely silent.

Glancing at some newspaper headlines recently, there was a caption that read that President Bio had increased the subvention paid to the Sierra Leone Association of Journalist to five hundred million Leones. Whoa! How ethical, is it now fair for the government to be giving subventions to journalists? Does not that tantamount to corruption? The wasting of taxpayers' money on institution that are privately owned. Then one should not be surprised that all these newspapers toe the government line, it will not be far-fetched to conclude that they have been bought. In a cash strapped economy like Sierra Leone, and also one in which the readership is small, these journalists do not have the spunk to refuse the payment. They should know what they were letting themselves into. If this is happening to the journalists, would it also be far-fetched to conclude that similar payments have been made to civil society groups? It is too unreal to see these groups that were so vocal when things were better, suddenly go quiet and silent considering the state of bad governance in the country.

In the case of the former defence minister in the ousted APC government, if it was not a man's life that was at risk, it could have been very funny: a comedy of errors. Here was a man because of his experience, invited by the Bio-led government to assist the NACOVERC team established to control the Covid-19. Allegedly, this individual, for whatever reason carried a weapon with him; whether he is entitled to is an opaque situation. However, he claimed to have an official licence for his weapon. Unwittingly or stupidly, attending a meeting at state House at which the President was present, he took his weapon along with him. There were conflicting stories about his disclosing to security that he had a gun with him, the truth will never be known. However, he was arrested and charged with treason, not attempted murder or assassination but treason! The question on the minds of many right- thinking Sierra Leoneans, can a single individual commit treason? After a long trial he was acquitted on the charge of treason (not surprisingly) but found guilty of illegal possession of a weapon and sentenced to two years. The alternative punishment for this crime is a fine. Again, for a first offender the public was left perplexed when a fine was not imposed instead of a jail sentence. Many people were of the opinion that had it not been for a forthright jury, he would have been found guilty of the crime of treason which carried the death penalty (recently removed from our law books). As it was he had to be criminalised so he was sentenced for a lesser crime. Here is the rob. His lawyers appealed the sentence, and while he was waiting for his appeal to be heard, Bang! The President in his wisdom gave him a presidential pardon. Indeed, the individual had been sentenced, but his case was on appeal, one that he might have won. So, could not the President have waited for the appeal to be heard? As it is now would not this conviction prevent this individual from holding public office?

Here is the joke, the Attorney-General at the time was relieved of her duties. However, the lawyer who led the prosecution was promoted to be a judge. Definitely, something did not sound right. Of course, one would ask the government or the President, why was the Attorney-General sacked and the lawyer promoted? Strange things happen in Sierra Leone. Presently, there is internal strife within the opposition APC, and this has resulted in a never-ending series of court cases. Lo and behold, all these cases are tried and being tried by the prosecuting lawyer who lost the treason case, and now sits as a judge. Does one smell a conspiracy in this saga? Is there no code of ethics in our judiciary, or it is the usual "orders from above"?

Another chapter in the Bio-led government saga is the spending of money without going through the due process. When the SLPP was in opposition, they criticised the APC sitting government quite intensely. Looking back, they were really opposing all what was being done by the sitting government. From the infrastructure development which they billed as cosmetic and too expensive, public financial management that they termed reckless, operating on a bloated wage bill, to even the size of foreign delegations when the president travelled officially, as being too large. In fact, it would be accurate to state that the opposition SLPP, was not a government in waiting but a party in opposition. There was no shadow cabinet that was exploring alternative policies, or individuals charged with coming up with expert views on the sitting government policies. It was the usual spokesperson that would respond to issues, on the economy, human rights issues, and such like.

Turning our attention to foreign travels, President Bio quite easily takes the lead as the most travelled president. At one point the official explanation for his travels, was to solicit private foreign investment for the country. Lately, coming from the horse's mouth, it is to redeem the tarnished image of the country, by the previous government. Had it not been for the Africanist Press' investigative journalism, the Sierra Leone public would have been ignorant of the Shenanigans of President Bio and the First Lady Fatima Bio. It is alleged that since taking office, President Bio has travelled out of the country more than two hundred (200) times! Really unbelievable.

To put things in their proper perspective let us return to President Bio's speech to Parliament on taking office in 2018. He said, "my government will develop and introduce a standardised overseas travel policy for the Public Service and covering all categories of workers, including government ministers as part of additional expenditure control measures". Also, an internal memo from the office of the President to all heads of MDAs, announced a temporary freeze on overseas travel by public officials. However, despite these public pronouncements and promises, President Bio and his wife spent much of their time in office making frequent trips to Europe and Asia.

On the 27th August 2020, State House issued a press release stating that His Excellency President Maada Bio was travelling to Lebanon on that same day, on a private visit, and will be accompanied by the First Lady. The press release also stated that the President would use this visit to strengthen the ties between the two countries. To say that this information came as a shock to the majority of Sierra Leoneans would be an understatement. Picture the spread of the corona virus, the havoc it was wreaking globally and governments, the world over trying to cope with saving lives as not only the infection rate but also the death toll was high. There was no news about any president or prime minister traveling during that period because of the concern for their people. Not our President Julius Maada Bio, that was the time to pay a private visit to Lebanon, On the investigation of the Africanist Press, when the dust had settled, the information gathered by this press was that between August 26th and September 30th 2020 (the president and first lady departed the shores of Sierra Leone on 27th August 2020), President Bio withdrew a cumulative total of Le10.118 billion from the local and overseas travel account for this Lebanon trip! This amount was comprised of Le7.586 billion of fees paid to a private air charter, alleged payment for the Presidents medical bill (this was a lapse in the press release as it was excluded), daily subsistence allowance for the first lady and other members of the delegation etc. Being ignorant in the current operations of the Public Service, one would like to know whether the First Lady is a public servant, to receive per diem from the Consolidated Revenue Fund, even though she was only accompanying her husband, the president who was already receiving per diem for the trip. Is this not unethical and tantamount to corruption? But as usual the ACC is powerless to act, its fight against corruption is against the former APC-led government. One cannot be convinced otherwise despite the noise and propaganda coming out of the ACC!

In retrospect, by what was revealed in the 'doctored' 2020 Audit Report, one now sees a connecting thread between the indefinite suspension of the Auditor-General a few weeks before the report was to be released, and the involvement of State House and the entire government, in financial malpractices. Since the Auditor-General was suspended and the establishment of a tribunal to probe the activities of the Auditor-General over two-three months now, that is it possibility that the authorities, realising their folly, are dragging their feet? What they wanted to be kept secret, might be exposed in the tribunal? The new direction government should look before they leap.

According to the Africanist Press, President Bio and the First Lady, collectively withdrew a total of Le30 billion (more than US$3 million) from the Bank of Sierra Leone, for alleged travel expenses. Imagine, this happened in 2020, when State House travel expenses had to go through proper approval process. Towards the end of 2019, the Minister of Finance proposed a new legislation seeking to grant the President unregulated access to travel expenditure. In amending the 2016 Public Financial Management Act, the proposed legislation was seeking Parliamentary approval for non-accountable use of travel budgets by the President, the Vice President and the Speaker of Parliament, for international travels. This non-accountable travel imprest excluded the purchase of tickets, so virtually one was looking at daily subsistence allowance.[207] To the consternation of the public, Parliament initially approved the proposed amendment, lending to a huge public outcry and disaffection with the way the Parliament conducted some of its business. Thankfully, in December 2020, Parliamentarians voted again and revoked the proposed legislation. Even when the Presidents' travel budget was under scrutiny, the First couple unscrupulously spent over Le30.0 billion for travelling alone? Not surprisingly, the 2020 Audit report concluded that State House was involved in money laundering, double dipping (some public officials were paid twice for their per diem), and falsification of hotel receipts. The President's office of all places, and a president who travels this much to redeem the country's image? Somebody must be living in Cuckoo Land!

Can anything good come out of Nazareth? That's a question to be asked of the New Direction government. Their propagandists and blinkered supporters will give a positive answer, but for the majority of Sierra Leoneans, the answer will be a resounding No! The 'Yes-sayers' would cite the repeal of the innocuous libel laws of 1965, the removal of the death penalty from the law books, the implementation of the Single Treasury Account, Lighting Bo an Kenema through the West African Power Pool. The 'Nay-sayers' will disagree certainly. The libel laws are proscribed but the fourth estate had been gagged

---

[207] Referenced in "Sierra Leone: President and First Lady withdrawal over Le30 Billion on Travel Expenditures in 2020" Africanist Press. Progressive African Journalism

by the new direction government. With all these human rights abuses, their silence is too pronounced. The death penalty has been abolished but the security forces are killing innocent civilians summarily. There are cases in Makeni, Lunsar, and Tombo where the security forces killed protesters. There was the glaring case of the massacre of prisoners at the Pademba Road Correctional Centre. On the whole, Sierra Leone is under an autocratic and not a democratic regime. The most recent misstep occurred when the President granted a presidential pardon to a murderer, based on the advice of a committee chaired by the Vice President. As one would expect this action raised a public hue and cry against the President. And to pacify the public, what action did the new direction government take? The Presidential pardon was revoked, and a warrant of arrest issued by the Police, for the pardoned criminal. It would be of interest to note that the said criminal who was pardoned had already left the country after he was issued with a diplomatic passport. Quite interesting, only the head of the Attorney-General, a member of that committee, rolled. He was probably the scapegoat. And to think this was not the first time he has been sacked. He suffered the same fate when he was Minister of Local Government, quite fascinating.

Our attention is now focussed on the Justice Cowan Constitutional Review Report and the government has published a White Paper. The government is recommending among others that instead of the 55.1% margin for declaring the winner of the Presidential election, this percentage should be reduced to 50% +1. This should save the country resources that would have been spent on the second round. Also on representation, they want to move away from the 'first past the post system' to proportional representation. Perhaps, just perhaps, something good might come out of Nazareth, after all, but with the PAOPA government, there is always a sting in the tail.

There is also the issue of the new direction mid-term census. From the time that the last census was conducted in 2015, after which additional Districts were delineated in the North, the SLPP who were in opposition then, decried vociferously the inaccuracy of that census. Thus, it was not surprising that when they assumed office, they wanted to conduct another census, which for legitimacy, they termed 'a mid-term' census, first in the history of Sierra Leone, 'to correct the inaccuracies in the 2015 census'. There was a general resistance and opposition to this mid-term census, on the premise that the SLPP government wanted to use the results for political ends. However, what was interesting was the fact that the World Bank, one of the sponsors pulled out of the exercise on the grounds that certain procedures that Statistics Sierra Leone should have piloted before the actual mid-term census exercise, were not done. In the World Bank's view, this would render the results of the mid-term census "inaccurate". But as usual, the government gave a deaf ear and proceeded with the exercise. Interestingly the majority of Sierra Leoneans were not in favour, so one cannot say the census exercise was a success. The provisional results have just been published (refer to appendix B}. Apart from die-hard SLPPians, who would have thought that the population of the Western Area would decrease from 1.5 million in 2015 to just over 600,000 in 2021; also, that the number of people that voted in the Western Area during the 2018 Presidential and Parliamentary elections is higher than the total number of people in 2021. Presently, according to the provisional census figures Kenema in the East has more people than the Western area where the capital is located. Is it through demographic trends, or by manipulation that the population in the South-East has increased while that of the North and West has decreased? Again, who is fooling who? President Bio and his PAOPA must take Sierra Leoneans as fools. Fancy quite recently, the Ministry of Basic and Senior Secondary Education put out a press release, targeting 800,000 school children in the Western Area in the Ministry's school feeding programme. This must be a mistake as according to the Mid-term census, the population of the Western Area is just over 600,000.

The SLPP Bio-led government, when in opposition won the hearts of the electorate when campaigning, intimating that they would tackle the 'bread and butter issues' within six months of taking power. These bread-and-butter issues could be interpreted as the basic needs of the people, especially food; not the luxurious food items like bacon, ham, cheese etc., that are beyond the means of many Sierra Leoneans. After four years of the new direction government, have these bread-and-butter issues been tackled? According to a recent survey, conducted by one of the political parties, the National Grand Coalition (NGC), the table in Appendix A, clearly illustrates where Sierra Leone is with these bread-and-butter issues. Assuming that this table is a true representation of the bread-and-butter issues, the conclusion would be that the welfare of the people is worse than before. Cost of living has gone up, while wages have remained sticky.

Just recently, the pump price of fuel was increased from Le10,000.00 (ten thousand Leones) per litre, to Le18,000.00 (eighteen thousand Leones) per litre. Consider, when fuel price during the former APC regime of President Koroma hit Le6,000.00 (six thousand Leones) per litre, the opposition SLPP mounted a demonstration all dressed in black; interestingly, this was led by the current ACC boss. When the ACC boss and his cohorts took over the reins of government, the fuel price was Le6,000.00 (six thousand Leones) per litre. Within four years, the price of fuel had almost trebled. The reason? the invasion of Ukraine by Russia. The invasion was less than a week old, and abracadabra, it is already affecting the pump price in Sierra Leone. Who is going to protest? The Bio-led administration has violently and stifled all protests. When it was rumoured that the price of fuel was going to be increased from Le10,000.00 (ten thousand Leones) per litre, one very vocal civil society organisation intimated that it will call out people to the streets to protest. All noises, when the increase did come about, there was silence. Now the price has gone up further and there is dead silence. What is happening or who are these groups deceiving? Only themselves, the populace knows the colour of flag they are flying; even the journalists, a principal arm of public opinion are quiescent. Do they have a choice? Let us not forget that they now receive a subvention from the Bio-led administration. One cannot bite the hand that feeds him (her).

The Bio-led government would attribute all of this to external factors (circumstances beyond their control.) But also let us not forget that a large quantum of resources was received from international donors to cushion these external shocks. At the same time the government implemented a set of bad policies, like suspending mining operations in the iron ore sub-sector, because of a disagreement with some of the mining companies. In a period when the Covid-19 pandemic caused a slowdown in global economic activity Sierra Leone's public debt has increased tremendously under the PAOPA Bio-led government.

Rounding up, when Julius Maada Bio took up the Presidency in April 2018, this was what he told Sierra Leoneans (culled from the T&NTV Media Empire), "I inherited a battered and broken economy" and the expectations of Sierra Leoneans was that he was going to fix it; issues like the bread & butter, the basics for survival would be done in six months. Care must be taken when addressing such issues, as one was apt to make absolute comparisons that do not mean much or might give wrong or one-sided picture, briefly, the scenario in 2007 when Ernest Bai Koroma took over the Presidency, from the SLPP President Kabbah. In 2007, Sierra Leone's GDP was US$1.7 billion and in 2017, it rose to US$4.1 billion; in 2007, the per capita GDP was US$240.00 and in 2017, it attained a level of US$790.00 million after reaching a high of US$2.0 billion in 2013, before the Ebola crisis. Revenue generated was US$170 million, but in 2017 it was US$550 million, again after reaching a high of US$700 billion in 2013. Government expenditure on direct development was US$60.00 million in 2007 and US$274.0 million in 2017. Overall international reserves were US$200.0 million in 2007 but rose to US$509.0 million in 2018. Lastly, the monetary value of foreign direct investment was US$96.6 million in 2007, rising to US$570.0 million in 2017.

Looking at these statistics, if an economy was battered, it was what was inherited from President Kabbah, by Ernest Bai Koroma. After all Sierra Leone was just coming out of a devastating war, the goal then was not growth, but rehabilitation and reconstruction of the battered economy which set the country perhaps fifty or more years backwards. If President Bio proclaimed a battered economy, perhaps the constructs of economic growth, however little are lost on him. After four years in office, if we referenced the table in Appendix A, one would be apt to conclude, the bread-and-butter issues promised to be addressed in six months have not been addressed; the plight of Sierra Leoneans is worse off now than what it was in 2017/18. The standard of living had deteriorated. Oh! Salone lamentable.

According to the NGC survey, in March 2018, rice, the staple food was Le235,000 per 50kg bag, in January 2022, the price had risen to Le350,000 per bag, over 49% increase. A gallon of vegetable oil was Le170,000, in January 2022 the price was Le365,000, an increase of 115%. Palm oil another important ingredient in the diet of Sierra Leone rose from Le120,000 per gallon in 2018 to Le 225,000 in January 2022. The US Dollar exchange rate was Le7,650.00 to US$1.00 in 2018, but in January 2022, the exchange rate was Le11,700 to US$1.00. The list goes on and on. Refer to appendix A

During the reign of President Siaka Stevens, he created the Shadow State that controlled the resources of the country etc. This time round, President Bio has created "State Capture", a system in which all the organs and institutions of state, parliament, the MDAs, the judiciary, the security apparatus, the electoral commission are either under his control or their decision making is largely influenced by the executive. What the President has succeeded in doing is to undermine the checks and balances as provided in the Constitution, and he has gotten away with it because of a weak parliament. It is also possible that parliament is complicit in the whole affair, according to the information released by the Africanist Press. There is complete silence on the bastardisation of the constitution, not a word from

Parliament, civil society or the fourth estate. But for the tireless effort of the Africanist Press, many of us would have been ignorant of Bio's financial malpractices and his abuse of human rights. Looking at the withdrawals President Bio made from the Central Bank, to finance his trips abroad not only public but even private, one would be apt to conclude that the Central Bank was his private bank. On all of these trips he is accompanied by the First Lady who also receives per diem although she is not a public servant. The only institution that would have revealed Bio's reckless spending is the Audit Service Commission, but alas the uncompromising Auditor General was relieved of her duties.

General elections have been declared for June 2024 and the registration process started in September to end in October. In line with their crookedness and dishonesty the sitting government has put all kinds of obstacles in areas of the opposition strongholds, ranging from defective computers late opening of registration centres, lack of electricity, refusing to register first time voters, handing money to electoral commission staff and prospective voters, even meting violence to those who have gone to register, they are using all tactics to scare away those who have gone to register. In SLPP stronghold, voter registration is proceeding smoothly. This is the prevailing situation in the so-called Athens of West Africa, a nomenclature that is seldom used these days. As was mentioned earlier Sierra Leone is not a democratic State.

Chapter Seventeen

THE DECLINE AND FALL

Oh Sa Lone, Sa Lone, Sa Lone! A lament indeed. After over sixty years of self-government, apparently no longer under the yoke of colonisation, where are we heading; what have we to show for it, what have we done to hold our heads high as we did once, when Sierra Leone was known, as the Athens of West Africa, when it was the envy of other West African nations, even the so-called Western democracies viewed Sierra Leone with respect. Sixty-one years have gone by, are Sierra Leoneans holding their heads high, or bowing down not in humility, but with shame because the country that was once a gem in Africa no longer glitters but is now so dull to the point of being a non-entity.

Ours is a country blessed with natural resources, a beautiful landscape with unrivalled beaches, fertile agricultural lands and a tropical rainfall. What have we utilised these resources for? The benefit of the nation? The exploitation by foreigners some with dubious provenance, or just a few individuals mainly the political class and their cabal who auction the resources of the country for pittance, to gratify their selfish ends at the expense of the national good?

What excuse can we put forward for the parlous state of an entire nation? Poverty is endemic, basic necessities and amenities are beyond the reach of the bulk of the population. A country once known as the Athens of West Africa lags so very much behind the literacy rate of the other countries in the sub-region. Before independence the country was under the colonial yoke. Sixty-one years after the country is still under the yoke of economic dependence on Western nations – economic imperialism. Constitutionally, we have gained our independence, yet in the technical aspect, we are still tethered to the West. Can the Sierra Leonean honestly proclaim that he is in charge of the economy? Where are the Sierra Leonean businesses. Walk along the streets of the urban centres, Freetown not excepted, who owns the large businesses, the super-markets, the building material stores, the electrical and electronic shops, who are the proprietors? The Sierra Leoneans or should we say pseudo or quasi-Sierra Leoneans? Whose capital and profits do not reside in Sierra Leone. Even in the lucrative diamond trade, who are the buyers? Not the indigenous Sierra Leonean. They struggle to mine these gems and are paid pittance by the diamond buyers who are mostly Lebanese. It is so annoying that even with our labour laws, these enterprises import their foreign nationals, to work as unskilled labour? Does this happen in Nigeria, in Ghana, in Senegal etc.? Hardly, but in Sierra Leone they are the barons, they are behind what has been called the shadow state. Effectively they determine policy because our politicians have sold out to them and, though they would not accept, their fingers are in their mouths.

Probably it would suffice to make some comparisons here, cross-country comparisons. Singapore comes to mind. A tiny country with scanty natural resources. Singapore gained its independence in 1965, from the British government, four years after Sierra Leone gained hers. Where can we locate Singapore now after gaining independence in 1965? It is a country that has been considerably rated as the least-corrupt country in Asia, and among the top ten cleanest in the World by Transparency International. The World Bank's governance, indicators have also rated Singapore highly on the rule of law, control of corruption and government effectiveness.

Not all aspects of Singapore's politics make for pleasant reading, but generally speaking, it is a country that has made tremendous progress, both in governance and development since it was expelled from the Malaysia Federation in 1963.

So, Singapore is far-fetched and provides an unfair competition to Sierra Leone? What about Rwanda then, it went through a civil war and is also an African country just like Sierra Leone. But that is where the similarity ends. During the Rwanda genocide, between half a million and a million Rwandans were slaughtered and the war had a devastating effect on their economy. Inspite of these challenges for them the war created a window of opportunity to develop the country, and not make excuses attributing every facet or setback to the war. Currently, Rwanda is one of the most developed countries in Africa. Their literacy rate is over 70%. Unfortunately, Sierra Leone has never had a Lee Kwan Yui, or a Paul Kagami, who can be viewed as visionary leaders.

In truth Sierra Leoneans cannot boast of having visionary or even good leaders. Sir Milton Margai (late) of the SLPP, took the country to independence, but unfortunately three years into his Prime Ministership, he received his home-call and his younger brother Sir Albert Margai (also late) took over the mantle of leadership. The late Sir Milton Margai was considered to be conservative, and it was felt that he leaned too much to the colonial government, not putting a strong case for Sierra Leone to get all the benefits it deserved from the colonial government. Because of the short term of his premiership, it would be difficult to judge him. He probably seemed benevolent and prone to compromise, but he also displayed some dictatorial tendencies. He tried to muzzle the opposition and even had the chiefs, the traditional leaders to prevent the opposition from campaigning in the SLPP heartland. After Sir Milton's death there was a leadership tussle between Sir Albert Margai a Southerner and Dr. John Karefa-Smart, a Northerner, who lost the leadership contest. One might be tempted to ask had John Karefa-Smart won and taken over the mantle to lead Sierra Leone, would the country's political and development trajectory have been better, more accommodating and progressive? These are imponderables.

Sir Albert Margai was a different mode to his older brother. He was seen as a radical, a view bolstered by his admiration for Kwame Nkrumah, the 'Osagyefo' of Ghana. However, his reign was short-lived, as he was removed from power, technically, through the ballot box, and not by the military. He did manifest dictatorial tendencies during his Prime Ministership and wanted to foist a one-party system upon the Sierra Leone electorate, and bring in a republican constitution which the electorate did not favour. In the end he abandoned these plans but by then it was too late, to save his political career.

Indeed, it was during Sir Albert Margai's leadership that Sierra Leone started its downward spiral. Apart from his dictatorial tendencies, he was also avaricious leading to corruption and the plundering of state coffers. Because of his bad policies he brought about a balance of payments' crisis during his tenure. This led to bringing in the International Monetary Fund to shore up the country's dwindling reserves. It is also a widely held view that the military coup of 1967 was triggered by Sir Albert Margai because he was reluctant to hand over the baton of government to his one-time colleague, now his opponent. Imagine, had the military not been invited into governance, would the country's political direction have been different? There is also the challenge of tribalism. The held view is that it started rearing its ugly head during the reign of Sir Albert Margai. Under colonial rule, the divide was between the colony and the Protectorate, after independence the division now became one of regionalism and tribalism. Again, imagine if Sierra Leone's trajectory had been different, a context in which the unitary state as it was to become after 1896 had followed a national development / political paradigm instead of looking up to the tribe for support and progress. Even to the point of putting square pegs in round holes? All our political leaders had the opportunity to steer the state away from regionalism, tribalism and nepotism, but towards nationalism and patriotism but none had the courage to embark on that path, as Nyerere did in Tanzania. For them the tribal card was an advantage, especially at elections.

Then came the turn of Siaka Stevens, he it was without any semblance of doubt that took Sierra Leone into the Abyss. The usual mantra is corruption of the political class, but this goes beyond corruption; perhaps what was happening and is still happening is the erosion of institutions' effectiveness in many ways. Implementing or twisting the regulations and rules that govern these institutions for their own personal gains, actions that are reckless as they have disastrous or catastrophic effects, not only on the development of strong institutions, but even on the development of the country. There is a lot of noise casting blame on the constitution as if Sierra Leone is the only country operating on a constitution where there are ambiguous clauses. No, most countries have ambiguous clauses in their respective constitutions, and they have acceptable and legitimate (legal ways) to deal with them. But in Sierra Leone these days, it is anybody's guess as the judiciary is highly influenced by the executive.

When Siaka Stevens took over, the bastardisation of the state institutions and even the subverting of state authority began in earnest. Through thuggery and the "APC's ninety-nine ways" of being victorious, they succeeded in getting their representatives into parliament; even before the one-party state's introduction, parliamentary seats were not contested and almost all the APC's candidates were returned unopposed. In a subtle way President Stevens became a dictator, those who held offices did so at his pleasure. All arms of government, from the legislature to the judiciary jumped when he wanted them to jump. It was not that the President had the constitutional right, but he arrogated those rights to himself, and parliament did not have the will to stop him. Who would stand against him? Not the lawyers, neither the judges, nor the Parliamentarians, they were his cronies. By interfering with the important state institutions, the President, slowly but surely was undermining their authority, bringing them under his control, but unfortunately eroding the trust that the people had in them.

The other thing that occurred under Stevens leadership was the promotion of a shadow state where important decisions were made not by state players, but by non-state individuals.[208] There was the case of the business man Jamil Sahid Mohamed who not only sat in cabinet meetings, but even appropriated one of the main functions of the Central Bank by fixing US dollar exchange rate because between the President and himself, they controlled the country's foreign reserves through the looting of the diamond proceeds. Indeed, Siaka Stevens temporarily nationalised the diamond company, DIMINCO, but what did the country benefit, absolutely nothing; all the proceeds went into private bank accounts. Siaka Stevens was a dictator who did not tolerate dissent. Sierra Leone was his personal fiefdom, and he went where his fancy took him, unfortunately not towards progress, but towards backwardness. Siaka Stevens ascended power with a lot of promise. He commanded the essentials, in human and natural resources to have promoted Sierra Leone into the group of middle-income countries. Unfortunately, with the help of a pliant parliament, he ruled Sierra Leone like an autocrat while impoverishing the nation with his lust for personal wealth.[209]

True to form, Siaka Stevens did not allow the natural succession to his leadership. No, he had to impose his will on the APC by foistering on them somebody who was a political novice, no other than the former Brigadier and head of the Sierra Leone army. Imagine, S. I. Koroma, the former First Vice President and Shaki's lapdog, was passed over, and not one voice in the APC was raised against this humiliation, as in the party's convention to select Steven's successor, he forced S. I.

---

[208] Detailed discussion of the shadow state is described in "Corruption and State Politics in Sierra Leone." William Reno.

[209] Sierra Leone Digest 1993. A Handbook of Fact and Figures. Edited by Sorie Musa. A Sierra Leone Institute for Policy Studies Publication.

Koroma to nominate Joseph Saidu Momoh! An excuse perhaps was the fact that S. I. Koroma was not the strong man, the "Agba Satani" he used to be, following a near fatal accident. The question, imagine the succession had gone according to the hierarchy of the APC, and S. I. Koroma had been chosen to lead, would the trajectory of the country have been different, another imponderable?

Cometh the new leader, apparently a disciplinarian, to bring some sanity into our politics and discipline into our society. Alas, that was not to be. The less said, the better. President Momoh was not in control. The Presidency or his authority was highjacked by a group of selfish and ruthless individuals, promoting themselves as Ekutay. Momoh's tenure was a failure, he himself admitted. President Momoh abdicated his responsibility for the sake of hedonism; rather than concerning himself with the affairs of state, those were relegated to the Ekutay group, while he concentrated on earthly things. He was fondly known as Joseph Lagoonda, a top night club that he frequented. President Momoh's patch came to an end not through the ballot box, but through the barrel of the gun; not only was it the end of his tenure of office, but it was also the end of an era, almost a generation of one-party rule, under the All People's Congress. An era that witnessed dictatorship, incompetence, corruption, a failed state and at the end, the incursion of rebels into Sierra Leone.

It cannot be gainsaid that, Sierra Leone is a small country, with a landmass of 27,000 sq. miles and a population of less than 8.0 million. Its history may seem uncomplicated, but its politics is more complex and difficult to understand. During the final days of one-party rule, a multi-party constitution had already been written and accepted by the people and the Parliamentarians. All that remained was its implementation. Speculation was rife that President Momoh was dragging his feet at its implementation. In the meantime, a rebel war had been launched by Foday Sankoh, a Northerner, against the APC government. Intriguingly, Foday Sankoh, did not start recruitment of his rebels from the North, neither did he launch from the North.

Domiciled in Kailahun in the East, that was where he made his base for his horrendous campaign, and even his recruitment. Was this a coincidence or a well-planned strategy? Fancy, a northerner using the East as a base to start a rebel war against a party that takes its strength from the North. It may not be mere speculation to postulate that the South-East was a fertile ground to recruit fighters to topple a Northern-based government that had suppressed opposition from the SLPP, a South-Eastern based party that had been in the political wilderness for almost a generation!

Where Foday Sankoh failed, the military who were supposed to be prosecuting the rebel war, succeeded. In April 1992, a group of young soldiers took over State House and easily ran Momoh out of office. The citizens jubilated, perhaps not because of the military rule, but for the end of the APC misrule.

The soldiers were young but as junta rule went, it was no different. They governed by decree by abolishing the constitution, which really and truly, made their action treasonable. Perhaps they did some good, but like all military rule, they were given to excesses, execution of civilians, violating human rights and intolerant of dissent. Being young men, they were not experienced to evaluate some of the advice given them by their peers, many of whom were projecting their individual personalities, and under normal circumstances would not have attained the position and responsibilities conferred upon them. These young soldiers appointed a council of advisers that included Ahmed Tejan-Kabbah, and Solomon Berewa. An U.N. Under-Secretary-General, James Jonah, a Sierra Leonean was trying to negotiate a peaceful restoration of constitutional rule, but to no avail. Instead, the military junta stayed in power for three years before the tide of public opinion, including some strong female activists, turned against them and forced them to return to constitutional rule. Even the rebel war that they promised to end, they failed to do. Under their patch, the violence got worse, many people were internally displaced, and many others fled the country. Maada Bio, who staged a palace coup on the pretext that Valentine Strasser was reluctant to return to civilian rule proclaimed himself to be the father of democracy. How hilarious! He conveniently forgot that he was a principal of the group that overthrew a constitutional government that was already moving towards multi-party democracy. Unfortunately, some gullible Sierra Leoneans believe in the lie. His insincerity showed up when he tried to reverse the decision taken by the people that there should be elections before actively pursuing rapprochement with the rebels. He failed to perpetuate his stay in power. The Brigadier did succumb to the will of the people and election was called. Interestingly, the party that won the election included in its membership were some of Bio's advisers, Solomon Berewa and Ahmed Tejan-Kabbah who was the compromise leader of the Sierra Leone People's Party at the time. It was the held view that the SLPP only won the elections through the manipulation of some excess voting in the Kailahun District, a stronghold of the SLPP. Again, interestingly enough, when President Kabbah chose his first cabinet, James Jonah, who was the Electoral Commissioner was appointed Foreign Affairs Minister, while Solomon Berewah became the Attorney-General and Minister of Justice.

Kabbah's government in reality was more preoccupied with ending the war and stabilising the country than anything else. Really and truly, the Kabbah led government inherited not only a broken economy, but a devastated country. Peace and security were paramount, and with the help from the internal donor community, this was achieved and in 2002, the civil war was consigned to the history books. After such a devastating experience one would have thought a window of opportunity was created for Sierra Leone to chart a new development paradigm as was done in Rwanda. But no, that did not happen and has never happened. Sierra Leoneans still wallow in their old ways, institutionalised corruption, regionalism, tribalism, nepotism and sycophancy. Some lip service was paid to ridding the country of some of these ills, but there was neither the sincerity nor the commitment to do away with these age-old monuments. Yes indeed, President

345

Kabbah did establish an Anti-Corruption Commission to deal with the cankerworm of corruption, but did it succeed? When push came to shove when the Commissioner at the time went after the big guns with party connections, he was rail-roaded out of office, and it was then and only then it was realised that the Commissioner did not have a legal background. Since then, the Anti-Corruption Commissioner has always been a legal practitioner, as if that was a panacea to the problem.

Apart from talking peace with rebels, in his own way, Tejan Kabbah tried to promote an equitable society. One of his legacies is the social security that he introduced, to ensure that after public servants had served state and country, they would have a better package to live on after retirement, not that paltry obsolete British system, Widows and Orphans, a paltry sum that was deducted from civil servants' salary, at a fixed rate, at the end of which, a retired civil servants benefit was a mere pittance. In itself the Social Security is a good scheme as indeed in recognition of the employee's service, the employer also contributes a percentage into this fund together with the employee. Here's the rub, even though there are laws and systems regulating the operations of this scheme, some employers do not hesitate to flout them. There have been, and there are cases where indeed, the employees' contributions are deducted regularly by some of the employers but are never paid into the Social Security Fund. The burning issue is, they go scot-free because of 'connectocracy'; they are untouchable; going for redress and restitution to the courts is a waste of time. That is how our democracy works. Even the management of the 'NASSIT' funds have come under scrutiny as some of the recent Auditor-General's reports have found some measures of malfeasance.

After two-terms in office, President Kabbah handed the baton to his Vice President, Solomon Berewa to continue the fight. With great expectations, he led the SLPP to the 2007 Presidential and Parliamentary elections. To the consternation of many, the SLPP was unable to repeat their 'wuteteh' victory of 2002; they lost both the

Presidential and Parliamentary elections to the opposition APC, led by Ernest Bai Koroma. Before Siaka Stevens and up to the ascension to power of Ernest Bai Koroma in 2007, no other president, not Sir Albert Margai, nor Joseph Saidu Momoh, not even President Kabbah was as popular as Ernest Bai Koroma. Indeed, he attained a feat that was unthinkable. In 2002, he was like nobody who led the APC but faired quite disastrously in the polls. Within five years, he was able to topple an apparent popular regime. He had the approval and following of the people to project Sierra Leone to higher heights. Like Siaka Stevens, he failed. It is no exaggeration to state that Ernest Bai Koroma was idolised by the people. To all intent and purposes, this went down well with him, and it may not be far-fetched to state that he felt like a demi-god. Here is the thing, as soon as our politicians are elected to parliament and or are appointed Ministers, instead of serving the people, they become their overlords. Now their bags have to be carried by their jack factotums, they no longer respect the ordinary laws, and they order all kinds of treatment to ordinary citizens, abusing what little power they have and completely missing their functional role in society. But as the popular saying goes, 'a country deserves the leaders it gets'. Because of small largesse, given to their minions from time to time, not even adequate to sustain their livelihoods they become praise singers, idolising ruthless incumbent and corrupt politicians. In a way, the people are responsible for the behaviour of these politicians.

If not for anything, Koroma's tenure was a time that many believed Sierra Leone was relatively peaceful. As far as we knew, there were no political prisoners, no condemned prisoner was hanged even though the death penalty was not yet abolished, and journalists were not unduly harassed. He could be portrayed as being tolerant and was not averse to dissent. During his reign, the opposition SLPP was quite vocal both in the traditional media and the social media, but he did not clamp down on them. Civil society groups were quite vocal in their criticisms of the Koroma government. He neither clamped down on them nor did he attempt to buy them over, so that they could either keep quiet or toe the line of the government, whether good or bad. Generally speaking, his human rights record was possibly above board. One stain that remained after his term was the Criminal Libel Law Act of 1965 which they promised to repeal. Strangely, one of the renowned journalists, Ibrahim Ben Kargbo who virtually walked into the position of Minister of Information and Broadcasting never lifted a finger to remove this inimical law from the law books. When he was a practicing journalist, he advocated for the repeal of this law.

Former President Koroma's government was rooted in corruption; he had the following, but he was not able to change the narrative. This conclusion is based, on the series of the Auditor-General reports published during his tenure. It is an opinion not based on the political gimmicks and grandstanding of the currently Bio-led government, whose first chief Minister branded the members of the former government as 'ayampees'. Indeed, it was Koroma that made the Audit Reports accessible to the public, when laid before Parliament. Previously it was a confidential document that the general public knew nothing about. Nonetheless, all the reports found breaching of procurements laws and huge cash losses by MDAs. Every year recommendations were made by the Audit Service to plug these loopholes, but it fell on deaf years as these recommendations were largely unheeded.

With all these misdemeanours perpetuated by the APC-led government in 2018, when the elections were held, the President was given the boot. Intriguingly, not so the Parliamentarians. According to the election results, the All People's Congress won the Parliamentary elections. But guess what? After a few executive orders, and chaos in the opening of parliament, the APC did not command the majority as ten of their elected MPs were virtually kicked out of Parliament. Question, will such incident happen in a true democracy? If democracy is "by the people and for the people", definitely this is not democracy: depriving some members of the electorate of their elected representatives, and imposing on those electorates, members they did not vote for. The excuse of the ruling government for taking this action. The former APC government did this to one of their parliamentary candidates. APC did it for one parliamentary seat, they did it for ten! And they promised Sierra Leoneans a new direction.

At risk of incurring the wrath of experts, non-experts, and the public at large, the author is of the opinion that Sierra Leone has never been a democratic state. Yes, indeed the country has been conducting Presidential and Parliamentary elections i.e. changing of governments through the ballot box and not through the barrel of the gun, though Sierra Leone has had its share of military coups and counter coups. Holding elections is necessary, but democracy goes much further than that, and this is where the country has failed. The institutions that would enhance the building of a strong democracy have not been allowed to perform their institutional functions without let or hindrance. As early as the days of Sir Albert Margai, the independence of the judiciary, the Civil Service and even Parliament was interfered with; and when the governance regime changed in 1968, all be it after a military coup that installed Siaka Stevens and the APC in governance, the situation became worse. President Siaka Stevens interfered with the judiciary, the Civil Service and all the other institutions of government. Instead of functioning according to established procedures, they functioned in an environment of "orders from above". With "orders from above", it is not the national good that is paramount, but the selfish and individualistic political capital of the leader, in this case the President and / or the political party in governance.

As former President Obama once intoned on a visit to some African States, "Democracy depends on strong institutions and it is about minority rights, and checks and balances and freedom of speech and freedom of expression and a free press and a right to protest and petition the government and an independent judiciary and everybody having to follow the law. So, we have to stop pretending that countries that hold elections where the winner sometimes magically gets 90% of the votes because all the opposition is locked up or can't get on TV, are democracies."

Africans do not have that luxury. There are strong men who have forestalled the development of strong democratic institutions. Inevitably, strong democratic institutions would severely constrain the power of the President. The recent Presidential election in the United States of America in 2020 is a case in point. It is usual especially in Africa for the opposition to cry foul when they lose the elections. In the US election, it was not the opposition that cried foul, but the incumbent president. On observing that he was losing the election, he said the election had been stolen from him by fraudulent means. He mounted legal challenges in various states, but no fraud was proved. Even in states where his party was in control of the legislature, he failed to have the results overturned. Finally, the State of Texas, a republican controlled state took the matter to the highest court in the land, the Supreme Court and lost. Fancy, three of the sitting judges of the Supreme Court were appointed by the President Donald Trump, and he had high hopes that they would rule in his favour, but they resolutely ruled against him. He thought this was a betrayal on the part of these judges.[210] Consider, if this was in Africa, and in Sierra Leone particularly, President Trump would have gotten away with it. But no, the American people had built up strong democratic institutions and although the President appoints the judges, he does not have the power to fire them, so they did not bend to his will! In Sierra Leone, the President hires and fires, not only judges and whomsoever he will, but even his running mate!

Compared to what is happening in the country's current dispensation, the ten years of Koroma's APC-led government may be viewed as paradise. The country's fledgling democracy is being battered left, right and centre, especially by the executive and organs of state

---

[210] Landslide – The Final Days of the Trump Presidency. Michael Wolff

security, the police, whose allegiance as told by the current inspector-General of police, is to the ruling SLPP government, and no to the people of Sierra Leone.

So, how is Sierra Leone's democracy faring on under the new direction government? Sometimes one wonders whether the regime is democratic or autocratic. In a system in which the President issues so many "executive orders" to bulldoze his way through Parliament, questions must be raised. Of course, the U. S. Presidents use executive orders, but not excessively. In a proper democracy, Parliament or Congress will raise questions. Not in Sierra Leone. Although it's the President's prerogative, it can be abused, especially to implement unpopular and illegal edicts. Take for example the President's executive order to remove tenured staff in the Public Service. The action was certainly illegal especially when many of them were not paid their terminal benefits. Not a single protest was raised, neither by the Parliamentarians, nor civil societies. It is as if a spell has been cast over the nation. And what was the President's explanation for this sweeping action? He wanted to appoint people who were loyal to him. What the President or his advisers failed to realise was the fact that they were depleting the institutional capacity that had been built up over long years. Did he appoint competent replacements? That is totally topical, but seeing the way the economy is being managed, it is doubtful. Imagine a few years ago, somebody who was an administrative assistant in one of the MDAs during the APC regime, being catapulted into position of deputy secretary in the Ministry of Finance. All things being equal, it is not rocket science that the economy is being run aground.

The popular parlance one would hear is, 'our democracy just like the economy is fragile'. How long will it take Sierra Leoneans to ditch these nomenclatures? One dares not make comparisons with strong democracies, as the trite answer one would get; they have been at it for hundreds of years while Sierra Leone is just starting; after all Sierra Leone gained its independence only sixty-one years ago. As much as that might be a fair answer, it should not be used to explain our backwardness, Now, we have examples to learn from, which the older democracies did not have. We do not have to make the same mistakes that they made. The writer can hear the doubters averring that democracy is alien, not suitable for Africa. We had a viable communal system then that was working. Well and good; will it work today? Almost, if not all the strong democracies that now exist were all practicing some form of feudalism, even countries in Asia such as Japan, were under a feudal system but in order to tap resources for development and economic expansion, that system of governance was discarded as it was a large obstacle to development. We tend to associate democracy with the West. True but democracy came from the Greeks. The term democracy appeared in the 5th century BC to denote the political systems then existing in Greek city states like Athens. Democracy contrasts with other terms of government, where power is held by an individual as in an autocratic system like absolute monarchy, or where power is held by a small number of individuals as in an oligarchy. In contrast to dictatorship or tyranny, democracy gives the people the opportunity to control their leaders and to remove them without the need for a revolution. It was adopted by the West because it was viewed as a superior form of government, everybody having equal opportunity even to be the leader, not restricted to a privileged few only; minority views are considered, and more importantly, everybody was equal before the law; nobody was above the law, not even the President or Prime Minister.

Back to the Athens of West Africa or what used to be called the Athens of West Africa. All are not considered equal. Up till now we are talking about the grassroots, especially when it comes to politics. There is also the privileged class, usually those with political connections, or close to the corridors of power. In this, Sierra Leone is not peculiar. However, when it comes to the accessing of basic services, justice, basic amenities etc, this is where there is a division. There is a lot of discrimination, the trampling of citizen's rights, and even the harassment and prosecution of those not in the PAOPA camp. The SLPP, with their so-called Parliamentary majority bulldozed their way through everything.

The Western Area has never been a fertile ground for the SLPP. The Freetown City Council had always been won by the APC, whether in governance or in the opposition. When Kabbah assumed the seat of power in 1996 and 2002, the Freetown City Council was in the hands of the APC who were in opposition then. There were tensions but both systems although under opposing leadership. Co-existed peacefully, although resources allocation to the Freetown City Council was scanty. Under Bio's regime, from the onset, there was physical animosity between the SLPP government and the mayor. During the early days of taking office, she was physically assaulted by SLPP thugs, and nothing came out of it; the culprit disappeared into thin air. It did not stop there, the mayor was humiliated in public, by the Minister of Local Government, who knows very little about the City's protocols because she was firm, in following procurement procedures concerning the payment of truck drivers who were contracted to cart garbage to the dump site during the monthly cleaning exercise. Continuing this saga, for the first time in the political history of Sierra Leone a Minister for the Western Region was appointed by President Maada Bio. Apparently to curtail the functions of the City Council, but this did not work as the mayor together with the other councillors continued implementation of their "Transform Freetown", a plan that received wide acclaim nationally and internationally. Will Freetown be transformed? Despite the Council's efforts, the city is still dirty, in the main through fares of yesteryears, such as the Wilberforce Street, Howe Street, Garrison Street, Siaka Stevens Street etc. Focus should be on implementing the by-laws and changing people's attitudes towards personal and public hygiene. Up the stakes against the Mayor of Freetown City Council. Previous action having failed to deter the mayor in her quest to perform her duties, the Bio-led government took the fight against the mayor to a higher level, that is to Parliament and the courts. Subsequently the Mayor was invited to Parliament to face Parliamentary Public Accounts Committee for questioning as part of the Parliament's review of the Auditor General's Report of 2019 financial year.[211] This action did not succeed as the mayor painstakingly explained that all the activities the Council undertook were above board. This move also failed, so the fight against the mayor was taken up again by the ACC. This time round, she has been indicted on charges of breaching procurement procedures. The Freetown City Council legal team has challenged the indictment and are prepared to go to court to clear the Mayor of any wrong doing and maintain her integrity.

The 2019 Audit Report implicated State House and the office of the First Lady spending public funds freely without recourse to the dictated financial regulations, and nobody was summoned before the ACC, or by Parliament. The Africanist Press postings on social media, gave a detailed account of the profligate spending by State House and the office of the First Lady, to the extent of the First Lady having bank accounts in the Central Bank where huge sums of money were paid from the Consolidate Revenue Fund, first in the history of Sierra Leone. These payments in total exceeded what was paid to most MDAs who are supposed to carry out service delivery to the nation. Was anybody summoned before Parliament? No! When queried, the ACC Commissioner intimated that he would have to investigate the office of the former First Lady before passing judgment on the case. Sierra Leoneans are still waiting for the report. As usual, "the case nar buff".

Moving forward, the 'doctored Audit Report', indicted the State House big time: accused of forgery of hotel receipts, 'double dipping' and money laundering. Has anybody been called to book, as at this time no, the ACC boss makes his usual noises and again as usual, "the case nar buff". What is troubling the minds of many rational Sierra Leoneans, is the quiescence of our legislature and Civil Society.

---

[211] Refer, the Auditor General's Report, 2019 for more details.

The amount of money at stake runs to millions of dollars, nobody is brought to account. Also, when did the rule change? Usually, the First Lady accompanies the President on his overseas trips, for which the President receives a per diem. Now consider, the First Lady is not a public servant, but as revealed by the Africanist Press, she also receives per diem for the same trip, is this ethical? With all these goings on, not a word of caution or criticism from the body Parliament charged with oversight responsibilities. Let the status quo prevail. Sometimes, one wonders whether the Parliamentarians have been gagged or paid for. Many people are calling for impeachment of the President for the crimes State House has been accused of, but these cries have fallen on deaf ears. Yet compare, the hounding of the Mayor of Freetown for an expenditure of one hundred million Leones, which she spent legitimately, following the due processes and yielding benefits of four million US Dollars. Where is the equity and the principle of equality before the law? Is this democracy or selective justice?

Yes, those holding public offices never tire to play the sycophancy or praise singing of the President. Seldom does a minister make a public address, whether it is in a press conference or addressing the nation on some topical or controversial issue, even when informing the public of the work of his/her ministry he/she does not preface his/her address with praise for the President. They have not realised that the mantle had been given them to do their respective work, but no, if they do not perform, the buck stops with them and not the President. Sierra Leone is a country where sycophancy is part and parcel of political life. Sierra Leoneans may not accept or agree with this notion, but this is the attribute that is holding back development of our democratic institutions. Even when a leader falls fowl, his minions will continue to sing his praises!

What kind of democracy is this, wherein everything starts with and revolves around the President? It is as if one did not sing his praises, even when performing excellently, one would be sacked. Look at what is happening in the British Parliament. The Prime Minister flouted some COVID rules, and the public and members of his own party are calling for his resignation. That is real democracy. This will not happen in Sierra Leone as has been proved by a recent incident in Parliament.

The Institute for Government Reform (IGR) carried a perception survey on corruption, the report showed that the Police, the Judiciary and the Parliament were the most corrupt institutions. This did not go down well with the Parliamentarians, and they took IGR to task. Even when a member of the ruling party owned that indeed people's perception of Parliament was accurate, his party instructed him to retract his statement or face disciplinary action. The poor fellow was embarrassed and not being of a strong mettle, retracted his statement, making all kinds of excuses, but the damage had been done. In light of this kind of behaviour, how can our institutions grow? Would it not have been better for Parliament to take a closer look at this perception of the people to ascertain whether it was justified and take the necessary actions? This is one way the institutions are strengthened! In the face of all this, what moral grounds does Parliament have to bring other corrupt public officials to book? This would be hypocrisy and injustice to the people of Sierra Leone.

This current government is probably the worst we have experienced since independence. The Constitution has been abused repeatedly, the legislature rubber stamps even undemocratic decisions, giving the impression that the legislature is in cahoots with the Executive. Separation of powers? That is what the Constitution demands, but it is not happening in Sierra Leone.

Indeed, it is usually said that the constitution gives the President too much power. Yes indeed, but neither Tejan Kabbah nor Ernest Bai Koroma abused this authority as Maada Bio is now doing. There is also the saying, that there is the letter of the law but more importantly there is also the spirit of the law. The present SLPP government under the leadership of President Bio has no regard for constitutional practice and discipline. Probably they succeed in their contempt for the constitution because of either, a weak Parliament or selfish Parliamentarians. Let's take the case of treaties, agreements, contracts with private firms and such like. With utter disregard, President Bio enters into contracts with foreign entities without consultation or the approval of Parliament. A case in point, the President leases the country's ferry terminals to Turkey for 25 years without Parliamentary approval. "Investment agreements and correspondence between the government and Sierra Leone and a Turkish company reveal how the Sierra Leone President, Julius Maada Bio, singlehandedly leased the country's ferry terminals to a Turkish company for a 25 year period without full disclosure, nor parliamentary approval as required by the Sierra Leone law.... Sierra Leone law requires that all agreements and treaties entered by the President or any of his designates must receive approval from Parliament. The agreement grants the "foreign investment group" exclusive rights over all infrastructure and assets of all their ports terminals in Lungi and Freetown for a period of 25 years." Section 40 (4) of the 1991 Constitution provides that "any treaty, agreement or convention executed by or under the authority of the President which relates to any other matter within the legislative competence of Parliament, or which in any way alters the laws of Sierra Leone shall be subject to ratification by an enactment of parliament or by a resolution supported by the votes of not less than one-half of the Members of Parliament." Parliamentarians contacted by the Africanist Press appeared to be ignorant of this agreement. According to them, the agreement was never tabled in Parliament. Furthermore, this project did not go through the proper procurement processes[212] - a tendency that now has become routine for the Bio government - and this is a government that shouts over the hills and valleys about transparency and accountability.

---

[212] Culled from the Africanist Press Investigative Journalism.

Social media thrive in Sierra Leone, and a probable reason for this is the curtailment of the democratic space. Freedom of speech is not allowed, and the traditional media is now part of the establishment. Unfortunately, the information garnered from the traditional media, television, radio and the print media is usually biased towards the government, full of propaganda and really not reporting on the prevailing reality. Minority views are not reported especially views that contradict government propaganda. As such, social media have occupied the space vacated by the traditional media. There is a plethora of social media groups, some in support of the government, and many others reporting on information that one would not get from the traditional media. As such social media are awash with all kinds of information, some genuine, others fake; also, some with very strong messages that can be inciting. In any case one distinction between the current Bio-led government and the former government led by Ernest Koroma, while the Koroma government took this in its strides, the Bio-led government has sought to stifle the social media. As a result, a cybercrime law has been enacted, which has so many inimical clauses against the social media. This Act sets out to provide for the effective, unified and comprehensive legal, regulatory and institutional framework for the prohibition, prevention, detection, prosecution and punishment of cybercrimes; prevention of the abusive use of computer systems, to provide for the establishment of structures to promote cyber security and capacity building; to provide for the timely and effective collection of electronic evidence for the purpose of investigation and prosecution of cybercrime.[213] Sometime in April 2022, one of the former ministers in the APC government, purportedly made an audio in which he castigated the President for his profligate spending and looting of public coffers. For this act, in exercising his democratic right, he was invited to the Police Station and detained, now he had been charged to court.

---

[213]   Sierra Leone News Agency (SLENA)

Question – in truth what type of democracy is being practised in Sierra Leone? As has been said, minority views are not tolerated and usually sitting governments are intolerant and unaccommodating. Take the case of this current PAOPA, new direction government. When some individuals criticised the government for their profligacy and misdirection, no less a person than the First Lady posted on social media, that those who opposed the Bio-led government should be dealt with by mob justice. Is this then a democratic state where the rule of law prevails? Perhaps not, because being the First Lady, she was not taken to task; to all intent and purposes, she is above the law! It did not stop there even. She went as far as to proclaim that the only true Sierra Leoneans were those who belonged to the SLPP. Compare, although an opposition supporter domiciled in the heartland of the SLPP attempted to describe the development project that the former government undertook in the region, what happened? He was arrested and jailed on trumped up charges; it did not end there. On his release from jail, he was subjected to harassment and threats of violence against his person, in the end, he had to be rescued and resettled in a safe area. Sierra Leone is far from being a democratic state.

Soon, another Presidential and Parliamentary elections will be upon us; the Bio regime has barely twelve months to correct the ills in the society, ills created by themselves. What they did not do in four years, can they achieve in one year? Before the Presidential and Parliamentary elections, the Local Councils elections were to be held in 2022, but a new date had been set for 2023. The ruling SLPP government had determined that Local elections will no longer be conducted on party lines; after hiring a consultant to canvass citizens and opposition parties for their views, what emerged was that opposition parties were not consulted and even the populace was ignorant of this exercise. Given this scenario, the opposition parties are strongly opposed to this. Everything seems to be in limbo. The PAOPA Bio-led government in their usual pattern are prepared to railroad any opposition to get their own way, whether the electorate likes it or not. They did the same thing for the mid-term census.

Although unpopular and unsupported by one of their major sponsors, they had to undertake it by will or woe. Perhaps there is an ulterior motive behind this move. There is a school of thought that offers the proposition that the Bio-led government want to use this mid-term census to create more constituencies in their stronghold, the South-East. So, where is this democracy so being loudly talked about when the government ignores the will of the people and try to impose theirs on the populace?

Holding of elections is not the only yardstick for a state to be democratic. Yes, Sierra Leone has been holding general elections. Truth to tell, it was the first African Country in sub-Saharan Africa to change government through the ballot box. Since then, many African countries have upheld this principle of changing government through the ballot box and not through the barrel of a gun (although recently there has been a spate of military coups in West Africa). A peculiarity of general elections in sub-Saharan Africa is the undue advantage the incumbent regime has over its opposition, usually using these state resources to destabilise the opposition. Sometimes opposition leaders are harassed by the security forces, even having the opposition leader locked up on trumped up charges. On the other hand, opposition parties seldom accept the result of the general elections, crying foul even before the complete results were declared. Sierra Leone is no exception to this peculiarity. The next set of elections are upon us and already some members of the public hold the opinion that the incumbent regime are putting modalities in place to rig the elections in their favour. Research undertaken by the Africanist Press revealed that the independence and the integrity of the National Election Commission have been compromised. It showed that the NEC has been staffed with mainly sympathisers of the SLPP, or even card-carriers of the SLPP. These staff have been deployed in the opposition stronghold to facilitate the rigging of the elections in the Northern and Western regions, where the SLPP fare badly in elections. Not only that, to make them more compliant or accommodating to the new direction government, they have been given better incentive packages, huge salaries, controversial incentive packages as revealed by the Africanist Press.[214]

The recent bye-elections in Kabala, in the Koinadugu District, illustrated how desperate the SLPP are to win seats in the APC strongholds. The outcome of the election also revealed how far the Electoral Commission Sierra Leone (ECSL) has been compromised. The Regional ECSL officials, blatantly changed the results to favour the incumbent government in the presence of the opposition APC polling agents. This they resisted a drew the attention of the ECSL regional officer; they decided to correct the falsified result and replace the ECSL official who falsified the results. Lo and behold, when the results were sent to the ECSL headquarters for collation, these falsified results emerged with the falsified figures that made the SLPP candidate the winner. When the opposition APC complained to ECSL, instead of reversing the decision to reflect the true outcome of the vote, they were advised to go to the courts, and they did. To date so many months after their complaint was lodged, the case has not been called for hearing. Given this scenario, many Sierra Leoneans are dissatisfied with the performance of ECSL, and for good reason. There is no trust between the electorate and ECSL.

Generally, the plight of African countries including Sierra Leone is pathetic. After so many years of independence, elections have to be rigged to deny the will of the people; public officials, communities have to be bribed or given outrageous promises for them to elect their favoured candidate. In this day and age, it has not dawned on our leaders that once in power, use that opportunity to work for the state, and to serve the nation assiduously. No, that simple principle remains in the back burner. All they are interested in is enriching themselves and their close relatives through the pilfering of state resources. Being greedy and selfish, even when they have enriched themselves, the pillaging of state resources continues. In the end instead of being

---

[214]   Africanist Press Release

admired for their good work, they are demonised because of their corrupt practices. In fact, before these politicians are elected to the state, local legislature or appointed as Ministers, chairpersons and such like, they present themselves as humble and prepared to serve the people and their respective communities. Once they acquire these state positions, they no longer serve the people as promised, but become their overlords, very pompous and authoritative in their behaviour, arrogating powers to themselves that the constitution does not allow. Some of these so-called 'power from above' are executed by these minor state officials, and not the CEO, because they are connected to the corridors of power; there are many instances in which these minor officials act outside the law. Why? Because they are Ministers, Chairmen, etc. Small wonder we live in a society that is lawless and undisciplined. "Nar before foot behen foot day falla" - Those who make the law subvert the law.

The usual history tells about the rise and fall. Two of these that can be cited are: "The Rise and Fall of the Roman Empire" and "The rise and Fall of the British Empire". Here we have the uncommon title "The Decline and Fall of the Athens of West Africa" and not "The Rise and Fall of the Athens of West Africa". The logical question one would ask, - Did Sierra Leone rise; was there a golden age one could look towards indicating that Sierra Leone was at its peak? One might be tempted to look at the country's colonial past and cite that period as one of development and progress during which time Sierra Leone was at its peak. That might not necessarily be the case.

It is doubtful whether the British would have stayed in Sierra Leone, had it not been for her natural resources. It was the age of mercantilism and Britain was looking for sources of raw materials to fuel the growth of their industries. The views of the author are centred around the fact that the colonial government was more interested in exploiting the country's natural resources – gold, diamond, iron ore, agricultural commodities - rather than the development of the country's physical and social infrastructure.

Decision making was not in the hands of the Sierra Leoneans, as an executive council, staffed by Europeans, headed by the appointed Governor General decided how the country was governed. The views of the local inhabitants were not even canvassed for a reaction to these decisions. When there were conflicts of interest, it was the Secretary of State in the UK who made the final decision. One would be apt to conclude that the colonial and immediate post-colonial period, witnessed the administration of an orderly and peaceful society, although there were tensions between the different stake holders – the Colonialists, Colony Representatives and he Protectorate representatives – Before independence, the tensions were between the Colony and the Protectorate. Then the various Protectorate factions banded together to push for the development of the Protectorate, as opposed to the development of the Colony at the expense of the Protectorate. It is possible that there was an underlying tribal / regional leaning to these tensions as the Colony inhabitants were mainly Krios, and the Protectorate, comprising the other tribes.

Whether through selfishness or their prejudices, it never dawned on the Colony and Protectorate to rally behind a cause, to oppose or get the best out of the Colonialists. Instead of coming together as protagonists to mount credible challenges against the Colonialists who were the interlopers, they saw themselves as enemies and the colonial government capitalised on that, the "divide and rule" strategy which they undertook quite well. How history repeats itself. Note what is happening now in the opposition APC. Members fighting against each other, to the point of going to court. Instead of coming together to fight the PAOPA led-government's bad governance, which is a greater menace to the country's democracy, the APC members are jostling for power among themselves.

During Sierra Leone's bid for independence from the colonial yoke, the then Prime Minister, Sir Milton Margai was so trusting of the colonial government they went without constitutional experts. Fancy going for such an important negotiation that would chart the

363

development of a nation, the Sierra Leone delegation did not include lawyers who would have advised on the Constitutional provisions offered by the British. On the other hand, the Colonial Government had a battery of lawyers on their side. According to reports, there was not much to negotiate as Sir Milton Margai accepted all that was proffered by the British. The only dissenting voice was that of Siaka Stevens. After so many years of exploitation of the country's natural wealth, the Sierra Leone government were given a paltry sum of 7.5 million British Pounds. How ridiculous! Nobody in the delegation thought of taking the Colonialists to task, to pay for the damage done to the country's environment and people. All they were interested in was the shedding of the colonial yoke, no matter at what costs. It's going to sixty-two years now after independence, but our navel strings are still attached to international donors. The truth of the matter is, we have our independence, but we are not free. Ironical! That was an opportunity missed.

The real story of Sierra Leone's democracy started during the tenure of Sir Albert Margai. He was deemed to be autocratic and intolerant. His tenure also was not long because he became unpopular, and his policies were not right for the country. Due to his profligacy and autocratic behaviour, he ran the Sierra Leone economy aground. All this contributed to his losing the 1967 General elections, and that was when the instability of the country started. The first military coup heralded the interference of the military in the politics of Sierra Leone. Since then, there had been a series of coups and counter coups right on to the beginning of the rebel war in 1991. In 1992 there was another military coup that toppled the Momoh government at a time that multi-party was being introduced to replace the one-party rule. In 1996, Constitutional rule was restored but then in the twinkle of an eye, there was another military coup in May 1997. With this short narrative it can be inferred that in general, Sierra Leone was not stable politically. There was also political thuggery since 1973 when the Siaka Stevens government used thugs to restrict the opposition from contesting general elections. From 1973 onwards no elections were free and fair.

The changing of the political system from a multi-party democracy to a one-party state stifled the democratisation of public Institutions. In Sierra Leone decision, making became highly centralised and power was concentrated in the hands of the President Siaka Stevens, who did not encourage opposition or plurality of government. The rights and liberty of the people were trampled upon. As stated by Abraham Lincoln, "Democracy is the government of the people, by the people and for the people." It is implied that government is participatory, and the people have the opportunity to make choices – choose their leaders, their representatives etc. In the one-party state of Sierra Leone, this was not the case, Siaka Stevens and the APC made these choices. Local government was proscribed so governance was concentrated more or less at State House. In the Sierra Leone experience, the one-party system was more susceptible to corruption. Political powers were concentrated in the hand of a cabal and / or the President. Virtually, there were no checks and balances.

Constitutional rule was re-established in 1996 but again it did not last. Another coup toppled the government in May 1997; this time the rebels were invited to participate in governance. The AFRC-RUF junta rule saw one of the darkest periods in Sierra Leone's history. There is the tendency to focus on the brutal nature of the conflict, but more harm was done to the societal norms. Our values were turned upside down by the RUF leaders. It was not a crime to resort to armed robbery to pay the foot soldiers. This was termed "operation pay yourself". Innocent civilians were evicted from their houses which were then occupied by rebels. Children, both boys and girls were abducted and used as child soldiers. They were treated in-humanely by their commanders, who drugged them and used them as killing machines. Sometimes they were ordered to slaughter their own family members. Many who survived are grown-ups in society today. Some counselling was given, but even at that, considering what they experienced, will they ever live normal lives? How will they relate to others in the society? Sadly, a whole generation was deprived of their future. If the Sierra Leone society has gone violent, a society in which cultism and lawlessness, even in the schools are commonplace, should not come as a shock. So far, these ills are the outcome of the eleven years rebel war. The country's social and economic infrastructure can be rebuilt, but can one repair the mind? These are the often-forgotten damage of the rebel war.

After the declaration of the peace in 2002, Sierra Leone has not experienced any more military coups. On the other hand, for the past twenty years the country was stable, but did it experience any golden age like happened in Rwanda after the ethnic cleansing that the raged there? Unfortunately, the answer is no. Sierra Leone has not been blessed with visionary leaders. Our leaders are power-hungry, selfish and corrupt, using the authority vested in them by the people to amass wealth and oppress the people who voted them into governance.

The SLPP government led by President Kabbah's main preoccupation was the rebuilding and reconstruction of a war-ravaged economy, and the re-integration and resettlement of returnees and displaced persons (IDPs). As such the democratic space for opposing views was not imposed upon. However, at the latter end of Kabbah's reign, the government became more intolerant and there was covert intimidation – newspapers not with and for the government were frowned upon. As a matter of fact, a journalist who was not for the government was murdered by SLPP supporters, but nothing came out of it despite the clamour that was raised by the people when it happened.

Baton change and the APC under President Koroma took over governance in 2007 and stayed in that position for ten years. Was the democratic space restricted? To a large extent, the democratic space was not restricted. There were instances of orders from above, some protests were allowed especially those for the government, while those against the Koroma government, more often than not were not allowed. However, one thing to be emphasised the SLPP who were in opposition then mounted street protests walked out of Parliament and they were not muzzled. The Fourth estate and civil society were very vocal in their criticisms of the government and none of them darkened the doors of Clarkson House.

Not so with the current dispensation under the new direction PAOPA Bio-led government. The rules of the game have changed. It will be fair to say this current government of President Bio does not allow any democratic space to opponents. Criticism of the government is not tolerated, and critics are labelled as being against the government, no matter how legitimate the criticism. The police who should maintain law and order are the ones that broke the law. It is common practice for them to beat up those who have transgressed the law. The Inspector-General does not hesitate to invite political opponents and lock them up for criticizing the Government. This has become common place now.

This is a government that has repealed the 1965 criminal libel law and revoked the death penalty. This is well and good. One would like to know whether they are adhering to the law. Quite recently, the spokesman for the opposition APC was interviewed in one of our radio stations. Lamenting the state of the country since SLPP took over the reins of government, he did say that they would now implement level three, to mobilise the people and remove the PAOPA government from power, through lawful means, assumedly through the ballot box and not through the barrel of the gun. The interview was scarcely over, when he was invited to the CID to answer for charges of incitement. Streets protests against the government are not allowed. Whenever people take to the streets to vent their displeasure against bad governance, rising costs of living, they are brutalised by the police, even when the demonstrations is peaceful, they do not hesitate to fire tear gas on the crowd.

To say the PAOPA government is deceitful and dishonest will not be far from the truth. They thrive on propaganda and lies. Why should a government spend thousands of dollars on boosting their image with the international community, if indeed they were leading by examples? The President is labelled "Talk and Do" President by their fans. How far from the truth the situation is on the ground. During an interview in one of his frequent sojourns abroad, the President claimed that families were saving five hundred dollars, through the free quality education programme. How preposterous, perhaps the President did not realise that five hundred dollars translated into Leones is more than five million Leones. This in a country where the wage levels are quite low, the minimum wage is six hundred thousand Leones, less than one hundred dollars! Take another instance, when he travelled for the climate change conference, When asked what Sierra Leone's response to climate change, all President Bio could say was that "we are clearing the gutters." How embarrassing. Note when the Mayor of Freetown was interviewed, she gave the proper response, "planting of trees". Was President Bio ignorant of this project? Well, it is not being implemented by his government but by the Freetown City Council that is in the hands of the opposition APC. A diversion? No, even the President cannot acknowledge that the planting of trees would mitigate the effects of climate change.

Not too long ago, the European Union came out with a press release in which they pointed out some flaws in the electoral system, the integrity of the judiciary, the police and the National Electoral Commission (NEC). Did the PAOPA government take this in good faith? Being their "PAOPANISTIC" self they refuted these claims and attacked the European Union on various fora. Even the President refuted this claim and asked for the evidence, to substantiate such claims. It never dawned on our revered president to say, 'my government has perused your press release, and we will look into these claims and take the necessary action.' No, he had to make a fool of himself even though the evidence was so glaring.

The Africanist Press again. In their research, they unearthed a scam in the Sierra Leone Embassy in New York. Apparently, the

Africanist Press unearthed the payment by the Chinese into the account of Sierra Leone, the amount of four million dollars in 2018, for the renovation of the Embassy. However, the money was not in the account and the renovation work had not been done. The money disappeared in 2019 when all the Ministers, Ambassadors, High Commissioners of the Bio-led government had taken their positions in government. Enter the ACC boss to the consternation of many Sierra Leoneans, roping into the mix, the APC presidential candidate in the 2018 presidential and general elections. Before losing to President Bio, he was the Minister of Foreign Affairs and International Co-operation. Presently, he is one of the presidential hopefuls for the 2023 elections, and it would appear that his popularity is rising. So, to rein him in and dent his image, he has been charged to court, not for stealing the said funds, because his tenure had ended by then, but for negligence that resulted in the loss of two-and-a-half million dollars. How preposterous. Now that he has been charged, the ACC has resorted to playing delaying tactics. They have been to court on several occasions, but the prosecution is still preparing its case; and the judge would not dare to throw the case out of court which is the proper thing to do, he is paid by the piper. There are many corruption cases or alleged corruption by SLPP officials, but the ACC has been silent and indifferent to the thieving of current public officials who invariably are SLPP card carriers.

This behaviour of the ACC prompted a leading barrister, a former President of the Bar Association to post "Whether it is true or not, for most people the continuous failure of the ACC to investigate countless allegations of corruption and abuse of power against members of the current regime, in contrast to its enthusiasm to investigate and prosecute political opponents has unfortunately created the impression that the machinery of the ACC is being used as a shield for members of the sitting government and as a sword (how very apt), against the opposition with the aim to eliminate political opponents and keep then in check. This impression has been heightened due to the on-going investigation of the Mayor..... Firstly the impact of such impressions questions the very legitimacy of the ACC and the sincerity of the government to fight corruption…..." It would be ideal for the ACC and the government to change course and take on the fight against corruption impartially and avoid appearing to use their authority as a weapon to suppress their opponents.

This short passage says it all, and what is puzzling, the Bio-led government seems to be scoring points in the international arena. Let us take the American Millennium Cooperation Compact (MCC) where developing countries are rewarded for good governance, fighting corruption, observing the rule of law and human rights. With all this happening in Sierra Leone, in its corruption index, MCC rates Sierra Leone over 70%, human rights another 70%? And now Sierra Leone has qualified for the full compact? This must be a joke or a travesty of justice. Sometimes the actions of these international bodies make many of us think that they are complicit in all that is happening in Sierra Leone. Do not the MCC officials examine other reports like the audit reports, surveys carried out by specialised groups, as a means of verifying the reports done by their consultants. The report done by Random House, the consultants for MCC does not reflect the true picture of what is happening on the ground. On its part Random House sub-contracted the project to Sierra Leoneans who are seemingly SLPP sympathisers or card carriers, meaning, the information fed to the MCC was not a true reflection of reality.

How embarrassing! Sierra Leoneans live in a country that is donor driven. To conduct general elections, we run to the donors for funds, to undertake a population census, the same applies. To implement development projects like the construction of roads, providing electricity and water we run to the Chinese; the list goes on and on. Yet with all our resource potential, government in, government out, the talk has been creating the enabling environment to attract foreign direct investment. And off to donor conferences. If one was to be candid, if the investment climate was friendly, investors would be attracted automatically. When this is not the case and investment conferences are convened, our leaders give all kinds of incentives to the prospective investor, to the disadvantage of the Country. It never enters their minds that we should buy into these companies by taking up an equity, using the raw materials, usually minerals as government's contribution. In the end, when investors come, they are the shady ones whose companies are not listed in any of the stock markets. Also, they do not publish annual reports, so that the government or the public cannot check or verify the volume and value of their exports. Government relies on what they are told by these companies. It is so sad thinking that Sierra Leone is scenically beautiful, blessed with abundant natural resources, yet the majority of the population struggle to eke out a living. Greed, and selfishness of our political leaders, but also because of the mentality of the citizens, the country finds itself in this pitiful situation. Enterprise is not rooted in our culture, but going begging, cap in hand seems to be the norm, especially among the younger generation.

With all of this behind us, the author cannot visualise the rise of the Athens of West Africa. But opinions vary. The older generation would tend to view the colonial period as a golden age, when there was order, and respect of the law. Also, the civil service as it was known then functioned efficiently. In fact, there was a period during which other colonised territories, the Gambia, Ghana (then Gold Coast), and Nigeria were administered from Sierra Leone. Sierra Leonean professionals, teachers, doctors, Pastors, Merchants those adventurous enough, took their skills to these territories and established good practices there. On the other hand, the younger generation, especially the more radical would tend to blame all the country's subsequent ills on the colonial government. Their rule was exploitative and also not giving the respect due to trained and qualified Sierra Leoneans. After over a hundred and fifty years of colonialism, what did they leave behind? Not a unified country but one divided and is still divided. A country which was at the forefront of education is now languishing at the bottom. The schools and universities are nothing to be proud of these days. In former years,

Sierra Leoneans living and or staying abroad were viewed with awe and respect. Why? because of its education. Nowadays it is viewed with utter disregard, and why not? With all these plaudits, in these modern times, all of these West African countries have overtaken the so-called 'Athens of West Africa'. Even our literacy rate is still hovering at the thirty percent mark, while a country like Ghana is measuring over seventy percent. Where did it all go wrong? That is the million-dollar question. The way and manner the country is now being governed, unless there is a radical change that would usher in a completely new political and economic paradigm, one sees no end to this un-progressive and harmful cycle.

APPENDIX

APPENDIX A: National Grand Coalition (NGC) Commodity Prices Survey

ITEM/ UNIT	PRICES IN LEONES (Le)							
Bread & Butter Issue	March 2018	August 2019	August 2020	March 2021	August 2021	October 2021	January 2022	Percenta Increase (%)
Rice /Bag	235,000	280,000	330,000	330,000	330,000	350,000	350,000	49
Rice / Cup	1,200	1,700	2,500	2,000	2,000	2,000	2,000	67
Garri /Cup	500	1,000	1,250	1,000	1,000	1,000	1,000	100
Oil / Gal	170,000	210,000	230,000	300,000	310,000	340,000	365,000	115
Oil / Pint	3,500	4,000	4,500	6,000	6,000	7,000	7,000	100
Palmoil / Gal	120,000	170,000	180,000	270,000	270,000	220,000	225,000	88
Palmoil / Pint	2,500	3,500	4,000	4,000	4,000	4,000	5,000	100
Fish Dry Bonga	500	1,000	1,000	2,000	3,000	6,000	6,000	1,100
Plassas / Tie	500	1,000	1,000	3,000	3,000	2,000	2,000	300
Onions / Bag	120,000	350,000	250,000	210,000	210,000	270,000	300,000	150
Charcoal /bag	30,000	35,000	37,000	40,000	45,000	45,000	60,000	100
Bulgur (per cup)	2,500	4,000	5,000	5,000	5,000	5,000	5,000	150
Pepper / cup	700	1,000	7,000	4,000	10,000	4,000	7,000	900
Chicken Feet / Carton	125,000	170,000	170,000	190,000	190,000	190,000	240,000	92

APPENDIX B: SSL Provisional Mid-Term Census 2021 Results

	2015	2021	Variance	Percentage Change
Kenema	609,891	772,472	162,581	26.657
Kono	506,100	620,703	114,603	22.644
Kailahun	526,379	545,947	19,568	3.717
Bo	575,478	756,975	181,497	31.538
Bonthe	200,781	297,561	96,780	48.202
Moyamba	318,699	346,771	28,072	8.808
Pujehun	346,461	429,574	83,113	23.989
Bombali	606,544	387,236	-219,308	-36.157
Koinadugu	409,372	206,133	-203,239	-49.647
Tonkolili	531,435	557,257	25,822	4.859
Falaba	0	166,205	166,205	
Kambia	345,474	367,699	22,225	6.433
Port Loko	615,376	528,038	-87,338	-14.193
Karene	0	290,313	290,313	
Western Area Urban	1,055,964	606,701	-449,263	-42.545
Western Area Rural	444,272	662,056	217,784	49.02

INDEX

Chief of the Defence Staff (CDS), 196, 201, 379
child soldiers, 365, 379
China, 154, 262, 379
Chinese, 60–61, 66, 155, 278–81, 369–70, 379
Christian Kamara-Taylor, 169, 380
Church Mission Schools (CMS), 12, 380
CID (Criminal Investigation Department), 312, 367, 381
citizenry, 129, 185–86, 192, 204, 224, 380
City Council, 24, 55, 353, 380
Civil Defence Force, 208, 228, 230, 380
civil servants, 24, 115, 122, 133, 143–44, 150–51, 207, 220, 251, 309, 346, 380
civil service, 17, 19, 53, 99, 115, 130, 132, 150, 349, 371, 380
civil society, 42, 123, 130, 215, 235, 276, 325, 336, 351, 354, 367, 380
civil society groups, 197, 230, 288, 326, 347, 380
civil war in Sierra Leone, 178, 238, 380
CMS Grammar School, 12, 380
Coast, Ivory, 10, 20, 155
cocoa, 75, 163, 380
coffee, 52, 65, 68, 75, 163, 380
colleges in Sierra Leone, 13
Colonel Hart, 18, 380
colonial administration, 18–19, 43–44, 47, 55–56, 61, 66, 380
local, 64
colonial era, 62, 68, 380

colonial government, 11, 16, 38–40, 42–43, 45, 48, 50, 52–54, 61, 63–67, 69–72, 75, 79, 82–86, 89, 93, 95, 97, 102, 168, 236, 339, 362–64, 371, 380
colonialism, 20, 78, 80, 87, 99–100, 156, 371, 380
Colonialists, xii, 22, 31, 37, 46, 52, 60, 67, 76, 363–64, 380
colonial masters, 3, 32, 44, 46, 77, 380
Colonial Office, 25–26, 380
colonial past, 64, 77, 380
country's, 362
colonial powers, 9–10, 20, 43, 49–51, 56, 66, 379
colonial rulers, 32, 40, 380
colonial system, 17, 62, 380
colony of Freetown, xiv, 5–6, 20, 24, 26–27, 31, 380
Commercial Bank, 135, 157, 380
Commission of Inquiry (COI), 55, 118, 121, 266, 306–7, 380–81
Committee of Educated Africans. See CEA
communities, global, 156, 219, 315
Conakry, 233, 380
Conakry Peace Plan, 221, 380
Conflict in Sierra Leone, 213, 228, 231, 233, 380
Congo, 260, 380
Congo Cross, 277, 380
constitution
multiparty, 153
multi-party, 343
new, 53, 61, 83, 85, 88, 153
one-party, 176
republican, 116, 126, 340

IMF (International Monetary Fund), 61, 66, 105, 122, 144, 162, 172, 180, 261, 290, 292, 304, 310, 340, 384

imperialists, 21–22, 32–33, 36–37, 58, 178, 384

imports, country's oil, 176

incumbent government, 46, 361, 384

Independent National Electoral Commission. See INEC

India, 17, 21, 77, 81, 384

INEC (Independent National Electoral Commission), 197–99, 202–3, 384

infrastructure
country's, 158, 243, 277, 281
public, 29

infrastructure country, 384

infrastructure of Sierra Leone, 277, 384

inhabitants, country's, 38

instability in Sierra Leone, 112, 237

Institute for Government Reform. See IGR

Integrated Agricultural Development Project, 146

Integrated Agricultural Development Project" (IADP), 146, 384

international community, 105, 200, 206–8, 211–13, 222–25, 229, 231–33, 235, 316, 368, 384

IPRSP (Interim Poverty Reduction Strategy), 246, 273, 384

iron ore, 66–68, 72, 147, 151, 161, 275, 282, 284, 304, 362, 385

Islamic Development Bank (IDB), 214, 261, 385

Islamic Schools, 101, 385

Israel, 141–42

Italy, 11, 284, 385

J

James Africanus Horton, 15, 385

Jamil Sahid Mohamed, 166–67, 342, 385

Jimmy, King, 2, 5–6

John Karefa Smart, 202–3, 385

Johnny Paul Koroma, 121, 210, 212–13, 215, 220, 240, 242, 385

Johnson, Wallace, 55–56, 98–99

Jomo Kenyatta, 278, 385

Jonah, James, 344–45

Joseph Saidu Momoh, 170–71, 177, 264, 343, 347, 385

Josiah Gilbert Holand, 126, 385

Journal of Sierra Leone Society, 27, 385

Julius Maada Bio, 259–60, 281–82, 293, 301–3, 334, 357, 385

junta, 121, 190, 195–96, 213–17, 219–22, 224–25, 229, 385

junta coup, 225, 385

junta propaganda, 216, 385

junta regime, 123, 385

K

Kabala, 361

Kabbah government, 208, 211, 245, 249, 385

Kabbah's government, 251, 345, 385

Kailahun, 132, 183, 234, 256, 278, 344, 375, 385

Karefa-Smart, John, 65, 107, 260, 339

Kekehs, 245–46

Momoh's Government, 185, 387
Momoh's presidency, 172, 387
Momoh's regime, 175, 187, 387
Mount Sugar Loaf, 7, 285–86, 387
Moyamba, 13, 61, 375, 387
Mozambique, 99, 387
mudslide, catastrophic, 7, 285
multi-party democracy, 253, 345, 365, 387
MV Aureol, 78

N

National Aid Coordinating Secretariat, 174, 387
National Congress of West Africa (NCWA), 47, 387
National Consultative Conference, 197
National Council of Sierra Leone, 86, 387
National Development Bank, 135, 387
National Election Commission, 360, 387
National Electoral Commission. *See* NEC
National Grand Coalition. *See* NGC
National Health Plan, 107
National Insurance Company (NIC), 264, 387
National Interim Council, 125, 387
Nationalist History of Sierra Leone, 2, 146, 150, 156, 164, 171, 173–74, 237
National Patriotic Liberation Front (NPLF), 183, 387
National Power Authority, 272, 387

National Privatisation Commission, 254
National Product, 87, 387
National Programme, 210, 387
National Provisional Ruling Council, 155, 387
National Reformation Council, 118, 120–21, 123, 125, 387
National Revenue Authority (NRA), 269, 387
National Stadium, 155, 216, 304, 387
nation of Sierra Leone, 32–33, 220
NCSL, 86, 88–91, 94–95, 388
NCWA (National Congress of West Africa), 47, 387
new direction government, 148, 307–8, 311, 329, 331, 333, 351, 359–60
New History of Sierra Leone, 5, 13, 53–54, 61, 88, 100, 108–9, 153, 388
NGC (National Grand Coalition), 299–300, 302, 333, 374, 387–88
NGOs (Nongovernmental Organisations), 209–10, 242–43
NIC (National Insurance Company), 264, 387
Nigeria, 9, 11–12, 14–15, 20, 22–23, 32, 75–76, 127, 140, 187, 212, 218, 220–21, 223, 225, 236, 261–62, 269, 284, 306, 338, 371, 388
Nongovernmental Organisations. *See* NGOs
Non-Governmental Organisations, 210, 242, 247, 388

West African Youth League (WAYL), 55, 393
Western Africa, 76
Western Area, 31, 35, 45, 60, 70, 74, 106, 111, 117, 146, 195, 235, 253, 255, 268, 271–72, 279, 281, 285, 324, 332, 353, 393
West Indies, 2–3, 21, 37, 100, 393
Wilberforce Memorial Hall, 111, 393
workers, public sector, 123, 163

World Bank, 61, 66, 105, 135, 144, 146, 162, 172, 180, 214, 243–44, 261, 272, 280, 292, 332, 338, 394
world economy, 141, 394
World War, second, 56, 75, 78, 80, 92

Z

Zimbabwe, 99, 180, 394